BALANCE AND CHOICE

by

Karen Hamp

Contents

INTRODUCING FAMILY

This is an introduction to my family as I knew them. If you knew them, you may have known them differently.

My Mother's Parents :

Katherine Rosetta MacLean Watrous – 1889-1964
Leland Hankerson Watrous – 1889-somwhere around 1968 or 70.

These grandparents lived in Caro, Michigan all the time I knew them. They had 3 children; two living daughters, my mother, Maryan Ann Watrous Bradley, and Jane Elizabeth Watrous Sturmon. A son who died shortly after birth was named Jack. They themselves had the nicknames which everyone called them, Tip and Dutch. I have no idea where those names came from.

I have memories of visits and a short time of living in Caro with them. You will read about that in the main part of the book

Grandpa Dutch, an active and fun loving man, ran the Watrous Hardware in Caro. He bought the store from his dad when he was about age 26. At various times, his wife and daughters worked there with him. As kids, my brother A.H. and I hung out at the hardware store, and I have many memories of the rolling ladders, the smell of the putty in the barrel, playing with paint chips from the sample cards, and running my hands carefully through the nails in the rotating nail bin. There are more vague memories of Grandpa sharpening ice skates, or showing people guns or ammunition for hunting. A very vague memory of a man named Fats Vandercar (or something like that) who worked for Grandpa for many years. There were wood floors both on the main floor and the storeroom upstairs. Grandpa Dutch let us have free run of the store whenever we were there.

Grandpa smoked cigars, usually in the basement at home, thanks to Grandma's ultimatums. The only exception to the basement smoke was when he exercised his love of baseball, listening to the Detroit Tiger games on the radio. He had played semi-pro baseball himself in Detroit for a team called the Good Luckers. .When the Tigers were playing, Grandpa sat in his chair, cigar smoke curling out around his comments about Al Kaline, Tommy Bridges, Dizzy Trout, and any other of his favorites of the day. It was the one time he could not be disturbed. He drew us into the excitement as we sat there with him, listening to his comments. He listened and then watched, until the year he died. The voices of

Harry Heilman, Van Patrick and Ernie Harwell announcing those games were part of Grandpa's lifetime memories.

Grandpa Dutch was always busy, doing necessary, useful, or interesting things. He never minded a grandchild tagging along to watch or help. He made homemade ice cream, taught us to sharpen our jack knives with a sharpening stone, and taught us to shoot the bow and arrow. It was because of him that both his daughters and his granddaughters were raised with equal rights to tools, sports, and equipment. He gave us those knives, bows, bicycles, and other equipment, and showed us how to use and care for them. . He never differed in his interaction with boys vs. girls. My mother told of bathing suits that she could actually swim in, in spite of the fashion of her day. He taught his daughters finances and business skills and in their lives, they both kept a firm hand on their investments.

He brought together the generations by telling me stories of taking my mother for a ride on the same "rockabye" road that we were riding on. He showed us the sugar beet plant, and the stand pipc, and told us their functions and uses. He introduced us to ice cream sodas and hunting. He hunted pheasant, deer and at least once shot a bear. His hunting dog, Jack, was his pride and joy. (Although as I grew older, I puzzled over the fact that he named the dog the same name they had given their deceased son)

. He built a beautifully detailed playhouse in the back yard when Jane was young, holding a full miniature kitchen, with stove, refrigerator and dishes; and a baby buggy and dolls in the other room. Of course it had its own tool chest.

Grandpa was a man of participation, and at times was Village President, Chair of the Chamber of Commerce, a member of the Fair Board, and a 32nd Degree Mason. Throughout his life he sang weekly in the church choir.

.During the depression, Grandpa was on the board of the bank. The board used their own money to help pay depositors and Grandpa paid up and started over again on his financial fortune. He died a relatively wealthy man He was the only one in his family who did not attend college. It was his choice, buying his father's hardware store instead. He died successful by all counts and respected and loved by most who knew him.

My Grandma Tip was a steady presence in the background. She made the meals, made us fudge every Christmas, and bought the jar of wheat germ for our stockings each year (Which we treasured, by the way). She could be counted on to say "If you spill your milk on the tablecloth, I will kick you over the moon". We knew it was an empty threat, and smiled. . It felt like love.

When younger, she worked in the store alongside Grandpa. I suspect that in some ways, she held the home and family together. I have heard that her parents objected to the marriage, thinking Grandpa was beneath her. She obviously didn't agree.. I have few memories of Grandma Tip that are specific or adventurous, but lots of knowing that she was there and cared. She decorated the house with taste and formality. The knick knacks were in the same place every time we came, and we could count on the stability of the place. The books were always where we thought they would be. Her clothes were stylish and well taken care of. I had the feeling that behind her somewhat rigid and starched image, there was a person of caring and nourishing, especially with lovely meals. Her father, Hector Alexander MacLean, was supposedly alcoholic, and my mother's hero. He was a handsome white haired Scotsman.

Grandma and Grandpa balanced each other well, with grandpa being the person of adventure and action, and grandma quietly providing a stable background. One memory of my interaction with Grandma: She was proud of the new wallpaper in the bedroom. I was put to bed for my nap, saw a piece of paper slightly loose at a seam, and absent mindedly picked at it. By the time they got me up from the nap, there was a spot several square inches where the paper was peeled off and in pieces, leaving a big bare spot. I was probably between 18 months and 2 years old. There was a quiet sense of dismay, but no punishment other than an admonition to not do that again.

The adventures with Grandpa always ended with Grandma's meals and ice cream at their house. What more could a grandchild want?

My Father's Parents

AH Bradley – 1879 – 1963
Johanna Philomina Haley Bradley – 1878-1919
Step mother – Mary Pulliam Bradley -1877-1962

My father was the 4th of 6 children: John, William, Lucille, Edward Wendel (Deke – my dad), Mary Elizabeth, and Dorothy Ann.

My father's mother died of tuberculosis when he was 9. I know little about her except for snippets of character and actions from my dad and his brothers and sisters. From those past glimpses, she has become one of my role models. .

She was from an Irish Catholic family, brought up in Midland MI, and described as fun loving and loving toward her children. I imagine her as quite animated and demonstrative. Her children, my father and his siblings, told the story of how she called all the children together and said goodbye to them before she died. She was in bed on the porch of her sister, Ms. William Ryan who we knew as Aunt Honey. She and my grandpa had been married 17 years. Their youngest child was less than two when her mother died. She died of tuberculosis, common in those days. I believe at least three of the children had it also.

She seemed, from descriptions to be genuine, loving, and joyful. I may be making that up, but if I am, that made up Grandma I never met is still a good role model.

My grandfather had the name AH and later took on the name Albert. He grew up in Midland, apprenticing himself to a man named Horatio Foster to learn the funeral business. Horatio owned a livery and funeral business. Grandpa had passed the exam for the funeral business in 1907, thanks to Horatio's teaching. He then bought into a business in Gladwin which was combination furniture and funeral business, a common combination back then. Those who made the furniture also made the caskets. The business was called Hanna – Bradley, and when Mr. Hanna sold his business, Grandpa formed a partnership with a Mr. Black, and continued in business. Grandpa moved to Midland, bought another furniture store, and when Mr. Black passed away, Grandpa had the business to himself. He then purchased the site of the building that we knew as the Bradley Funeral Home. . Grandpa lost his wife in 1919, he remarried in 1922. Mr. Black died in 1926 and Grandpa then owned his own business. It must have been a fast changing world for Grandpa and his children.

When my father's mother died, the children were sent to live with relatives and friends so Grandpa could continue supporting them. My father went with the Mode Family. I don't believe they were related, but rather Bob Mode was my dad's good friend. Also, the Mode's lived very near Aunt Honey and also their grandmother, (Called Ma Haley) who outlived her daughter

Grandpa was active in the Kiwanis club, and was coroner of Midland County for over 40 years. He was a staunch Republican. And he and the sheriff were fast friends, playing cards together at the pool hall as well as partnering in attending to business when people died in Midland County.

For a long time, I had the wooden folding apparatus that my grandfather took to people's homes to lay the deceased on for embalming. In those days, people were embalmed and laid out in their homes.

My step grandmother, the former Mary Pulliam, was from Cave City Kentucky. She was a genteel southern lady, and brave enough to step into a family of 6 children and be their step-mom, even with some resentment of her, and no parenting experience. Maybe she was a typical social worker who wanted to help the world. I don't know that story, but she was the only grandma I knew. She had been around for 14 years by the time I came along.

I heard that the older children had a great deal of trouble adjusting to their new "mother" .Some stayed with the relatives, others came back home. Their Mom had been a second generation

Irish Catholic, joyful, and loving with her children. Step mom was a Southern Belle, raised Baptist, and a social worker, who had lots of theory on how to raise children, but no experience. A very different home life. She told us her family was very poor when she grew up.

Fortunately, our family was not given to telling difficult stories down through the generations, so I never heard anything but hints of that difficult adjustment. By the time that I was born, and the other grandchildren who followed me, Mary Pulliam Bradley was a story book grandma.

She taught me bible stories, as well as Canasta and Gin Rummy, sometimes with Grandpa joining in. She taught me how to use a treadle sewing machine, and helped me make a log cabin quilt. She baked the yummiest sugar cookies of anyone I knew – great big ones. She was a hoarder of canned goods, like so many people who had gone through the depression. She taught me how to make soap from lye and grease. We made soap, baked, made jam, played cards, and carried on conversations about subjects in her book set, The Book of Knowledge.

My mom made all the pies in the family, and my grandma all the cakes. So Grandma Bradley made each of our birthday cakes by special request. Mine was a chocolate angel food cake, with chocolate fudge icing, and 7 minute or boiled frosting over the top of that, and then dribbled with bitter sweet chocolate over that. Yum!! NO cake mixes in those days.

In later years, when I wanted to run away from home, it was to her house I ran. She was never judgmental of my mother, but always welcoming and comforting to me. I felt accepted and important there.

It was at her buffet we gathered for Christmas Eve, all the cousins and their parents. Grandma made boiled custard (sort of like egg nog, her special sugar cookies, many kinds of Christmas cookies, and a yummy fruit salad, along with deviled eggs and some sort of meat. We then opened our gifts and the cousins went to midnight mass. I am not sure how that worked when fasting was required before mass. It could be that my memory is faulty.)

(Step) Grandma Bradley had a long list of accomplishments. She was a graduate of the New York School of Social Work, and devoted over 50 years of her life to that profession. One interesting fact: she worked in Salt Lake City for a while, and my brother Charlie has a Book of Mormon which was at her house, and signed by George Albert Smith who was a longtime leader of the LDS church and became head of the church in 1945.

Grandpa Bradley was often slightly grumpy, or cynical about the world. Grandma seemed to take on her job to love him, and make him happy, and called him "Presh" which was short for Precious. I never heard them fight, although I heard Grandpa grump about her when they were getting older. I believe that my step-grandma came to that marriage with money, and I suspect that, for instance, she paid for the cottage at Higgins Lake which they had built. I can imagine Grandpa thought that foolish, as he probably did the trips they took to Florida later on. However, in spite of all his complaining, I suspect that they were relatively content together, and that they both enjoyed good companionship.

I was lucky to grow up with them so involved in my life. That I had 4 loving and involved grandparents was a true gift.

My Father

Edward Wendel (Deac or Deke) Bradley - May 4, 1910 – April 14, 1968.

That he lost his mother at 9 years old must have been a deep sorrow for my dad and his siblings. It always seemed a permanent hole in their hearts, whenever the subject came up.

Dad grew up in Midland, living with the Robert Mode's when his mother died, and finding arrow heads along the Tittabawassee River, among other childhood pursuits. I never heard much about his youth. It was also not uncommon for my father to be quiet about his life, and especially traumatic events in life. In later years, he never talked about his war years, or at least the difficult parts. . He seldom talked about his troubles in marriage. He also never talked about how difficult it must have been to be the funeral director who embalmed and buried his good friends, and their wives and children. He died of a heart attack (broken heart?) at age 57.

Before dad went in the army, he spent a year or two working at Dow Chemical and a year working on the local paper. He also had attended school at the University of Michigan and the University of Minnesota, where he had to go at the time to get his embalmers training. He was a licensed embalmer, the only one in the family except his dad. .

My dad was called to active duty in the army, the Field Artillery, with the Michigan National Guard Unit. You will read about the places he was stationed, and my adventures in those places, but he was eventually sent overseas to the European theater. He was in the Battle of the Bulge, and St. Lo. He came home with the Silver Star, the Bronze Star, the Air Medal and the Croix de Guerre. He was unable to talk about that time, other than funny stories, the people he met, and the incidents which were not violent. He also came home with "Battle Fatigue" and to a marriage that had suffered in his absence.

My siblings might say differently, but to me he was a fun loving and "look on the bright side" Dad. He told me of his work, and taught me about the world until he went overseas. He came back different. As he got older, he was more sarcastic or grumpy about disagreements, but by then, we paid little attention to him. Occasionally he would wield a big stick for a small offense. I don't mean a literal stick, but he made a big deal out of a small thing. (My brother and I remember arguing with him, and then making fun of him because he did not want us to use the word "shove", but preferred "push". We insolently said that then shovels should be called pushels. And he got very angry about it.

Dad often made up songs in any situation, and I find myself doing the same, as do some of my sibs. It is a wonderful way to buy time and defuse a situation, or just go at it lightheartedly.

He, taught us, in addition to backing up my mother's "don't lie, cheat, or steal" rules, about ethics. For instance, although we lived in the funeral home, he did not allow me in the prep (embalming) room because it was disrespectful to the families of the deceased. That was also the reason we could not and would not play in the caskets in the showroom. It was also the reason that my parents could talk about business matters, and people, and we, as children, knew that we were not to say anything outside of our home. As I read something my grandfather wrote, I noticed he too used the word "ethics" in connection with his profession. So I am at least the third generation to have that teaching passed to me.

Dad was incredibly conscientious about being available to people. I suppose now, one might say he was co-dependent, but both my parents put community service high on their priority list. When he died, hundreds of people came to the funeral home and told us of deeds of kindness and going beyond the ordinary connected with my dad. He took folks home from the hospital on Christmas Day, and then brought them back that night so they could spend Christmas with their families. He made time and telephone calls to check up on people. My somewhat disappointed feeling was that he had taken wonderful care of the whole town, but not so much of his family. He was often gone on holidays and weekends, helping others. I was often lonely for that person I knew existed.

He was quite ready for adventure, especially when A.H. and I were young, and used to take us adventuring and exploring, riding on dirt roads and trails, He liked to try new things, and I remember when he bought his power saw, and hardly used it. He was a gadget guy.. If he were alive today, I suspect he would be fascinated with, and own all the latest electronics, finding uses for them in his life and business.

At one point he, (on paper), invented an ambulance cot which would fold in order to bring people down stairs and around corners. It folded to look almost like a chair, but had the advantage of the hand holds to carry it with. He told a salesman about his idea and a year or so later, that company came out with his idea under their name. He was disappointed not to be recognized.

Dad was well known for his artistry in the funeral business. He made people look natural, and as if they were sleeping, using as little wax and makeup as he could. That was a great comfort to families, and he had a state wide reputation in the business for that. He was active in the Funeral Directors Association, and in Rotary Club, and was a president of the local Rotary for a term or two. He was in Toastmasters Club. He enjoyed acting in Theatre Guild for a few seasons. He participated in leadership at Beverly Farm, where my brother lived.

Life centered around the business and the Country Club for my Dad, and there was a flavor of the boy who had grown up poor, and was enjoying a wealthier life. He loved steak, and nothing but T-bones would do. He seemed pleased at being a willing and much asked golf partner to doctors, lawyers, and wealthy people in Midland. And of course it did help our funeral business be successful, as those friends called or referred when needed. It gave Dad a perfect excuse to play golf anytime. . Much of our business rested on my dad's socializing and personality. When he died, the business fell off precipitously. My uncle, the other owner, added his own talents and friends to the business. He also was well liked, but differently than my father.

Dad approached most things with an attitude of expectant curiousity. For instance, I remember him attempting to make fried donuts, and pancakes, enjoying the adventure. There were some less practical things he taught me too. I could bend my thumbs backwards for years, putting the tip of them on the back of my hand, and also hook my hands behind my back and turn my arms inside out because dad showed me how. He taught me to pick up marbles with my toes at a very young age. He also dared me to walk around the block barefoot in the snow, telling us that their doctor when he was young had told them to do that to keep them healthy. Of course I tried it. I still occasionally go out to the car barefoot in snow because I can, and because it is convenient. I have never forgotten the phrase he taught me at about two years old. I could recite it on demand "Anterior, superior, spinus process on the os innominata at the crest of the ileum"

My dad enjoyed people and was quite an extrovert. In another town on business, he would find a homeless person, take them to lunch, listen to their story, and maybe give them some cash. He might even bring someone home for dinner that he had just met, or who was passing through Midland and had car trouble, or got ill.

Dad also suggested and planned our trip to California for a month, when I was in high school .His workaholic nature came along, and he called the funeral home every night. To prepare for that trip, he used his old army skills for camping, and put garbage pails on the roof of the car to carry water. He fixed an old army supply box to carry our "kitchen ", which opened up on the tailgate

.We slept on army cots and had bedrolls. He excelled at supplies, and we even had some C-rations with us in case. Finally his war experience became useful and not just bad memories.

As many men of that generation, whenever he was tenderhearted, he covered it with anger, sarcasm, or silence. Looking back, I suspect life was somewhat disillusioning to him. No mother, no successful marriage, and a stressful life. Good at his work, but burying his friends, and even their children. He and his brother later embalmed their father-an act of profound love, but probably one of grief just as profound. .

My father, as my mother did, turned to drinking as he aged. Social drinking turned to escapism and relief from physical pain. He would not see a doctor. The last years, I sometimes saw him lean against a door frame, blue in the face, and in terrible pain, refusing the doctor or hospital. He played golf with all the doctors in town, but never trusted them medically. He had probably seen lots of medical errors in his career. When he had his heart attack in 1968, he scoffed at his roommate who complained about pain. My dad was not supposed to get out of bed at that point, but got out to use the bathroom any time no one was around. The day after they moved him from intensive care, he died, I presume of another massive heart attack. His youngest son Charlie was 14.

I suppose he lived as he had learned from his Irish Catholic background and his losses early in life. ....just keep going, have fun, do your duty, love people, help those you can, celebrate the joys, ignore the pain, damn the doctors, and go. Life is hell, and you might as well have fun and love others.

I was finally getting to know my dad better when he died, and I have regrets that he did not live longer. I always knew he loved me. It was difficult for him to show that love in later years, but you will read that I got a great deal from him. In those later years, he did not take time for his family or his marriage, putting his effort into his business and its friendships, where he probably found the greatest reward. He did a lot for many during his life, including me. I often still miss him.

My Mother

Maryan Ann Watrous Bradley -September 3, 1911 – October 17, 1995

My mother grew up in Caro. I know little about her childhood, and not much more about her teen years. She did tell me she was very smart and very popular, being valedictorian of her class, and Phi Beta Kappa in college. She was more athletic than many girls in those days, partly because of her father's urging and permission.

14

She played girls basketball, and was on the debate team in high school. .She attended Rockford College in Illinois for 2 years, and then transferred to the University of Michigan, [probably because of the depression, and change in finances at home.) I heard her say several things about her college major. I heard her mention French, Sociology, and Social Work. I do know she worked in Social Work after she got out of college.

She always said her father raised both she and her sister just like he would have a son. He took them hunting, taught them to work in the hardware store, and bought them sports equipment.

Another of her stories was of swimming in the neighbor's pool, doing a jackknife dive and not being able to straighten out. She was taken to the hospital with appendicitis. An immediate appendectomy was in order.

One of the secrets she kept for many years was her first marriage. Reports differ on when she told my father, but it was not before they were married. She married a fellow student at University of Michigan. He was a model and Arthur Murray dance instructor. He was also abusive. They married in secret, and a year later, her cousin Dolores, living nearby, called her parents, and said that Maryan was tying bed sheets together and trying to leave her apartment. The cousin also told them that Maryan had been physically abused. My grandfather went to Ann Arbor and brought her home against her wishes. He somehow, either convinced her to file for divorce or annulment, or he filed against her wishes. I heard that she was too ashamed to go to court, so her dad made it possible to finalize the action without that. I asked her, when she was quite old, about her first husband, but she would not talk about him. There were no children from that marriage.

My mom met my father in Midland. They were married in 1934, when she would have been 23 years old. I was born about 2 years later.

Five years after that, she became a traveling army wife, moving with my dad to various assignments. She was pregnant again in 1943, and you will read about her near death experience in the main part of the book. My father left for overseas 3 days later.

Six weeks later, my mother did a most courageous thing – driving, with my grandma Bradley, the 2500 miles from California to Michigan with three children.

Being apart during the war produced a lot of schism in my parent's marriage. Mom was insecure about Dad, and her fears produced accusative letters. Whether he was unfaithful or not, is any one's guess, although I doubt that.

After the war, my father bought part of his father's funeral business, and life changed again for my mother. She had to learn how to balance her own activities with those of the business and home making.

In 1949, and again in 1953, she had two more sons. Deke, the one who was born in 1949 was born healthy, became ill and was left with special needs. She seemed unable to forgive herself for not being able to fix him. She also, at the time, blamed my father and his proximity too ill people for the illness. It is a difficult situation in any family to have a special needs child.

Mom spent many years as a community leader, helping start an organization for "retarded " children, as it was called then, and being President of the local AAUW fellowship. She was respected and well known. She had a fellowship named after her in AAUW. She also served on the board of the institution that my brother was in. Part of my mother's character was to "Be a leader, or don't do it at all. And that is how she lived her life.

My father died in 1968, and her father died soon after. She attempted to keep going, but was obviously tossed on waves beyond her control, and turned to alcohol for help. She was offered a job starting the Community Voluntary Action Center, and successfully did that stopping work when she was about 65.

My mom had struggled with clinical depression, starting around the age of menopause, and eventually had shock treatment. It was only then that I learned of her earlier marriage. I am still not sure when my father learned. After my father's death, my grandfather's death, and my younger brother's marriage, her drinking continued to increase as her functioning decreased. She would not accept help or suggestion from either friends or children, and continued to deteriorate.

Mom's story is one of polarity. She had great accomplishments, great skills and talents, was intelligent, and had a lonely decline into her death. She was a great woman, forgotten by most at the time of her death, forgiven by her children, but leaving behind a messy heritage. All of us, I believe, have used her example as a warning to ourselves to continue moving toward positive directions as we grow older.

I suspect that if my mom had lived during a different time in the culture, when medical and mental health resources and advances were more available, she might have been able to do better.

I gained strength, self-reliance, and a sense of organizational structure, and common sense from my mom. She fed my mind and body well, and gave me the drive to feed myself, body, mind and soul/spirit. You will read of her influence in my writing.

My Siblings:

Alan Haley Bradley May 6, 1939
Rebecca Ann Bradley Wardell January 24, 1944
Deke Watrous Bradley , Jan 10 1949 – July 28, 2012
Charles MacLean Bradley , Jan 3, 1953

My Children and Grandchildren

Pamela Jo Hamp Wetzel October 28, 1958 married toDoug Wetzel
> Emily Karoline Wetzel September 19, 1990

James Clark Hamp, October 26, 1959, Married Kelly Sutton (now divorced)
> Jennifer Nicole Hamp Feb. 10, 1987
> Christopher James Sutton, (Kelly's son before marriage) April 2, 1982?

Robert Warren Hamp, February 25, 1962, Married to Jackee Omdahl
> Ian Bradley Hamp July 1, 1985
> Jillian Yvonne Hamp July 22, 1988
> Jenna Beth Hamp January 25, 1990
> Atticus Samuel Hamp May 23, 1991

INTRODUCTION

I decided, in 2013 to review my entire past. While doing so, I discovered my need to be known and remembered, and so conceived the idea of a book. That became two books, as one held the story, and another was needed for the products of my life. This is the first. I had no idea when I started this project that it would take so long. It was not difficult to recall my life, but it was very difficult to put a lot of memories into a consistent, flowing, coherent body of work, and find a voice which would express myself with integrity and keep others interested.

I may have succeeded, but am quite sure that, except for short bursts; it lacks a more scintillating tone and exceptional writing that more rewriting and editing sessions might have produced.

That is a fair metaphor for my life, which also has been scintillating only for short periods of time, and has been written fairly well, but not exceptionally on the pages of time. As for rewrites, life does not provide those.

Stories of those we know, or of family, become part of our history. Several parts of my life were lived geographically distant from my family; thus there were periods that they did not hear my stories nor I theirs. Would I change that if there were a way? Yes, I suspect I would, but that law of no rewrites is at work.

I want you to know what I accomplished, how I changed, and what or who intertwined with my life to enrich it. I want you to know my strengths, weaknesses, successes, failures, joys and sorrows through my own eyes. I want to leave a record behind of who I have been and who I have become.

This writing contains the history of my body, mind, emotions and heart. It contains an approximate chronological view of how I spent my time, money and energy. Chapters are divided according to major transitions, leading to new phases of my life. The title is a recurring phrase from my teaching and speaking through the years. Balance and Choice are also words considered as I live my life..

Finally, as you read this book, a caveat: If you remember things differently than they are written here, please refer to the several places in the book where I talk about how tricky, unreliable and unstable memories are. Then cut us both some slack. I have attempted to use pictures and old writings, as well as consulting various others to validate what I remember. It has felt especially risky to write about events where others were involved. Please just accept that our memories may be different. I have tried very hard not to step on toes, or hurt anyone here. I apologize in advance if there is inadvertent pain or error.

EARLY LIFE AND ARMY YEARS

Setting the Context

June 21, 1936 – The 74th Congress had ended its session, Franklin D. Roosevelt was President of the USA, and the first stirrings in Europe (later blooming into WW II) were felt and reported on. It was Father's Day, the first day of summer and the longest day of the year. The setting was Midland Michigan, home of Dow Chemical Company (providing on the one hand, polluting Dow ash raining down on the town, and on the other, resources, privileges and money for its children and citizens). The family was happy and stable. That day, in that town, to that family, I was born.

My parents had eloped two years before to Angola Indiana, a common destination for furtive marriages. Mom was 25, and Dad 26. As we grew up, we children knew they eloped, but never heard reason or details. We probably never asked. We didn't ask personal questions much in our family. I might take a guess at it having something to do with my dad being raised Roman Catholic and my mother not, or maybe, although my dad didn't know it at the time, it had to do with my mother having been married before.

I was their first child, and the first grandchild on either side of the family. You can imagine the excitement! Both branches of our family were stable, financially and otherwise. They had enough love and intelligence to nourish a grandchild as they had their children. One grandma was a step-grandma, but had been in the family for many years. I never had to experience out of control parents, abuse or abandonment. I grew up with lots of trust, hope, creativity and more. One set of grandparents lived right next door. My company was in demand. I was often told how smart and clever I was by both my mother and grandmother. It was not a perfect family, but certainly good enough. I am, in many ways, who I am now because of my family and young life. In other ways, I have evolved into someone else. Because I was first, I may have gotten the best of the multi faceted resources which nourish a child.

Midland was where my father grew up, and where my mother had been working. My father's stepmother was my mother's supervisor. It was a town of 15,000 back then. Most people worked at Dow. Our family owned a funeral home.

The building I was born in, maybe a hospital, or maybe only a birthing home, later became the home of one of my high school friends,(Gayle Porath), and we used to joke about my coming home when I went to see her. I know nothing of the time of day or night I was born, or what it was like for my mother. I remember being told that my dad considered me a wonderful Father's Day present, and I cherished that idea as I grew up.

Early Memories

Sometimes early memories are the beginning of adult patterns. I am not sure that is true of me, except for one, but I wanted you to know what I first remembered.

I am about 5 months old, and am lying on the floor on a blanket on my stomach. My head is up and I am straining my neck and back muscles in eagerness and waiting. I want people to come. I want to be picked up. I feel eager, expectant, trusting, happy, and slightly frustrated, wanting, and waiting for contact. (In fact, that feeling of eager waiting for contact and connection from others has recurred often in my life, becoming a pattern......... frustrating at times..

Another memory at about 1 ½ or two years old: sitting in my sandbox in the back yard watching the clouds. No one else is around. I am just curious, exploring, watching, relaxed and content.

One more memory, helping form my earliest theology: I am sitting on Grandma Bradley's lap and she is reading me stories and showing me pictures of Jesus from Egermaiers Bible Story Book. I like being with her, and I like the stories and pictures. (Bob and Jackee now have that book). I take on Jesus as my comforter when scared, my super hero, and my role model. I get the idea of striving to be like Jesus.

There are multiple memories of three years old at nursery school: Having to eat the gingerbread I didn't like and throwing it up. (Much later in life, I was tested for food sensitivities, and was sensitive to ginger.) I still don't like the taste or smell.

Still at nursery school, I wiggle around on the nap-time cot and am told to lie still. I wiggle some more, and someone sits on my feet, pinning them down, forcing lack of movement. I feel scared, almost desperate, and furious, but don't dare strike out. I don't think I have a choice. To this day, I have claustrophobic feet. If my feet are held down, I get anxious and angry. I have wondered about a connection with present day foot trouble, but have not found any.

Not all nursery school memories are bad. I am playing with friends. One little girl has a striped pinafore on. I think it is Linda Poffenberger who later died of polio. One of the teachers is Lucille Antonison. A few months after writing this, I got an email from one of my high school classmates talking about Nursery School and one of the children who went there. He sent me the list of children who were enrolled. Linda P. was not on it - Another instance of deceptive memories.

My belief about such memories is this: The way something is remembered, affects the person as if it were true, whether or not it is. This means it shapes the person who remembers it as if it were true. If it is later found false, reshaping is in order.

Here is a classic case of such from our family. We have made a joke out of it rather than an argument. I had a dog in high school. My sister would have been about 7 or 8. My memory is that I lifted her up, held her partly up off the dog (he would not have been big enough to support her weight), and we pretended she was dog-back riding. Her memory is that she actually rode the dog around the block. She is very clear that this is true. I am just as clear that it is not. The dog, of course, isn't around any more to settle it.

Home

My Grandpa's and Grandma's funeral home, the Bradley Funeral Home, was next door to our house. The business was downstairs, they lived upstairs. That building, built in 1911 was torn down in 2011, and I cried. It had been a constant for family events for my entire life. It was where we went for birthdays, Christmas and family funerals. It was also, as you will see, where we lived for a long season of my growing up. It became the place to bring family and community together. And then in 2011 it became a pile of rubble, and a vacant lot.

The address was 402 Rodd Street, the phone number 67. (Our home phone number was 1570.) Funny how those numbers got indelibly etched into my brain, to last a lifetime there. As a young child, I was equally at home in both our home and my grandparents. If I was not in our yard, it was likely I was next door. Later in life, when I wanted to run away, it was to this grandma's home that I ran, although by then, she lived in a different place

Incidentally, but as an important place in my/our history, on Memorial Day, the parade came by the funeral home, and the entire neighborhood gathered on the porch and steps, overflowing into the yard and the street curb to watch. My dad was commander of the National Guard, later called to active duty. When the American Legion Drill team marched by, they turned toward our porch and honored my father with a salute. This happened yearly, and the year after my dad died, they continued the tradition to honor his memory. Our tears flowed freely, and the memory brings them back.

My first few birthday parties were in the back yard between our house and the funeral home. Those attending were from the neighborhood, or children of my parent's friends. The moms came too. Back then, mothers seldom worked. Today, they are seldom available for daytime parties. That change in our culture began with World War II, when women went to work to fill the positions in the factories left vacant by the men overseas. There was a song called "Rosie The Riveter", sung by Dorothy Shay, who called herself "The Park Avenue Hillbilly". The song honored and recognized America's working women of World War II.

In 1939, just before I was 3, my brother, Alan Haley Bradley was born. (May 6, 1939) I don't seem to remember any of my siblings as babies, nor do I remember any of my mother's pregnancies. I suppose that is not unusual for a three year old. I never heard how I felt about his entry into the family. And I have no conscious memories of him until we were about 2 1/2 and 5 ½.

AH, as he was called, was named after Grandpa Bradley, except that Grandpa had only initials, rather than a name. Later, grandpa adopted the name Albert for legal reasons. Apparently one must have a legal name for some things. My brother was always called AH until later in life when he decided he preferred his given name, Al. He is still AH to his siblings, but most people know him as Al.

That back yard, where the birthday parties were held, also holds other memories. It is where my sandbox sat, wooden sides with boards nailed across for seats. I spent many daydreaming, cloud watching and sculpting hours there. There were mud pies to make, lakes to play in, and friends who joined in the play.

The neighbor's, owners of Irish's Barber Shop, had a back yard backing up to the funeral home garage. There they had a chicken pen, and I was fascinated. My early education about chickens came from peering through the fence, watching the hens eat, scratch, cluck and just be chickens. I loved to watch, standing there on the fence, in order to see over the boards that blocked my sight.

The flowers in our yard left me with memories of names, colors and smells. They were the "old fashioned" flowers growing around the border of the yard - hollyhocks, narcissus, iris or "flags", lilies of the valley, a spirea bush, and lilacs. Someone showed me at a very young age how to put lilies of the valley in water with food coloring. . Within a day, the flowers had stripes on the petals of whatever color used. I also made Hollyhock dolls, and later taught my own children both about the colored blossoms and the dolls. The backyard was my first remembered exploration of nature. Dad taught me to blow on a piece of grass between my thumbs and make it squeal.

Frisky, my dog, born the same day I was, hung out in the back yard with me. I barely remember him when I was little, except for photos. The memories get more vivid at maybe 6 years old. I was told that he was protective of me, and that no one touched me unless my parents were there. He stood between me and strangers. He was just a mixed breed dog, as most were then. Later in life, my brother and I thought his best quality was that he would eat the Brussels sprouts that we didn't like as we sneaked them to him under the table.

Life Turns

By the time I was old enough to have started kindergarten, our life took a drastic turn. My father was called to active duty along with his National Guard Unit. I was 5, the year was 1941, and the United States went to war with Japan. I remember nothing about the beginning of the war or Pearl Harbor. But my dad was to go to Fort Sill, Oklahoma. He left on a train, and soon after that, my mother, my brother and I moved to Caro, Michigan where my other

22

grandparents, my mother's parents, lived. They were Grandpa Dutch and Grandma Tip. (Leland Watrous, and Katherine MacLean Watrous.)

I remember the move, but if I was told the reason, I do not remember. I don't know whether it was my mother's original intention to stay in Caro, or whether she planned to stay a few weeks and then join my father. I have a vague memory of hearing that her father (Grandpa Dutch) told her she belonged with her husband, so she may have been conflicted about whether to stay or go.

I suspect it must have been frightening for a young woman to take two small children across the country to an unknown life. This might be especially so after the experience of abuse and betrayal in her first marriage. We did go join my father, but first there was the time in Caro.

We stayed with my grandparents in their very small three bedroom house. My mother's sister, my Aunt Jane, was still at home in High School. She would have been about 17. With 6 of us living there, it must have been crowded, but I doubt there was resentment. I suspect my grandparents viewed it as a temporary necessity.

Caro was my very first school attendance. I never attended kindergarten, but started there in first grade. My most vivid and almost only memory of that school was the huge tube from the second floor to the ground. One day there was a loud bell, and I was told to enter this pitch black hole at the end of the tube into which my classmates were disappearing. They called it a "fire drill". I had no idea what was happening. Once I came out at the bottom, the fear was gone, and I wanted to go to the top and do it again. Since then, I have seen pictures of that old school (long gone).and looked to see if I could see the fire escape. I have little idea of how long we remained in Caro. I know I got a report card, so we must have been there a matter of at least a few weeks. From my father's old letters, I think we went to Oklahoma in June. Maybe we waited until school was out.

Caro was a smaller town than Midland, and I walked to and from the school. On the way home, I would stop in my Grandpa's hardware store. The Watrous Hardware was on Main Street, and there I would "work" at the store until Grandpa went home for dinner. I was dismayed one day, selling a paintbrush, being handed a dime, and having my grandfather take the money and put it in the cash register. I thought it was mine. Thus I learned the hard way how a business was run, and didn't like it much. I guess at that age of 5 or 6 I was already a budding entrepreneur, wanting to move toward financial solvency.

Sometimes, grandpa would take me to the Hotel Montague restaurant for a treat. He was so good at giving children life experiences. The first time we went, he thought he was doing something special and ordered me a soda. (ice cream and seltzer water ?) I learned I didn't like sodas, and so after that, it was ice cream or malted milks. Grandpa always made me feel competent, grown up, and important. Once, when I was about 8 or 9, he took me deer hunting. It was important that I wear some red clothing to be seen in the woods, and they ended up putting a pair of red underwear on my head. Boy did I feel grown up going with Grandpa, but it's probably just as well there were no pictures.

There was a famous family story about my grandpa shooting a bear. Some versions say the bear surprised him, and others say he was out bear hunting, but there are pictures of him with the bear. I have a vague memory of going to someone's home in Caro, and being told that the bear rug on their floor was the one my grandpa shot. I think it might have been someone with the last name of Reed.

There are other memories of Caro which have remained with me. I remember the grocery store, with its cookie bins. Choose which cookies, reach in, and put them in a bag to take home after paying. I have several memories of business people in town and of one young girl about my age, walking with me to school. It was a small enough town so that everyone knew grandma and grandpa, and I suppose they must have known who I was by the time we left. I know I felt a sense of being among people who knew me. By the time we left, it felt like home and I felt like I belonged.

I first experienced death in Caro, and learned something about where my food came from. Grandpa's next door neighbors kept chickens. They were to kill and clean some of their chickens and I asked if I could watch. They told me they would be chopping the heads off, and that it wouldn't hurt the chickens. I watched as the neighbor held the chicken's neck stretched out on a stump. He raised his hatchet and brought it down on the chicken's neck. The head went one way, and the chicken the other, and then, to my astonishment, the chicken took off running around the yard without a head. The head lay on the stump where it had fallen!

.It made no sense to me! How could they run without a brain, or even a head? I was scared, fascinated, and it touched my sensibilities. I felt sad about the chickens being hurt, and killed. I also felt shivers of horror, and unbounded curiosity about the process. I think it is an accurate memory, as other people have told me of similar experiences. Our culture is left with the saying, "running around like a chicken with their head cut off," to vouch for those collective memories.

We're In the Army Now

After whatever period of time we lived in Caro, we left grandma's and grandpa's house, and got on a train for Oklahoma. I was excited about the train trip, and seeing my dad again. One of the family stories that got retold about that trip was about my mother having to go into the "colored" waiting room in a train station, to get my brother, who had wandered in there. After that, I remember seeing him with a harness and leash on. It is sobering to think that our country was so firmly segregated such a short time ago, and is still learning to accept those of different color and culture, albeit in more subtle ways. I have more recently learned, we are not such an all-accepting, non-prejudicial country even now, with the present targets being surreptitiously black, and openly immigrant, gay, and Muslim. I am not proud of that. It speaks to unnecessary separation and superiority, none of which follow Jesus life, or that of most spiritual leaders. Little of it seems necessary or moral.

On that trip, AH got very ill somewhere near Joplin Missouri and we were told he had paratyphoid fever. I have no idea whether it delayed our trip, although I do not remember staying in a hotel or being delayed. I also don't remember going to the doctor, but of necessity would have had to go with them. Maybe doctors made train calls as well as house calls back then. Anyway, recovery was quick and complete.

I also remember a very narrow sort of bunk bed in the train. I guess that was the sleeping compartment. I remember seeing the ground going by and hearing the click-clack of the train wheels as we opened a door and went between train cars. Maybe to the dining car, or to our sleeping car? For me, the trip was one new experience after another. I was most fortunate to be instilled with the idea that life was an adventure, and the train trip a part of that.

Beginning Army Life

During the next couple years, we moved often. Over the first and second grade period, I attended 6 different schools in 4 different states. We went to Oklahoma near the end of 1941, or the beginning of 1942, and came back to Michigan in March of 1944. In between were all those schools, many adventures, and many new places to live. This next part is about some of that.

There have been studies done on "army brats". (Those children of families who follow its Service Member from base to base.) The studies concluded that if the parents think it is an interesting and enjoyable life, the children will also. I think my parents attempted, and pretty well succeeded in making it a learning and fun time for us. AH remembers little, since he was only 3 or at the most 4 during those years. My own memories are many, and have clearly persisted.

Much later, in developmental psychology, I realized that the years from about age 6-9 had to do with developing a sense of belonging, and going on to learn a sense of accomplishment, and success in doing things. Thus I look back at this time from that framework also. I seldom felt a sense of "not belonging" no matter where we went. You will see that in my young years, I was also seldom involved in social interactions with my peers, or with adults, other than my parents. Even when with others, I was quietly focused on place or surroundings rather than on interaction between me and others. I suspect I felt a "belonging" to place and family, rather than to the human race.

I attempt to arrange my experiences from these years in geographic groups. A few memories are of uncertain geography, but of certain impact on me, so they are included because of importance, but without knowing where they happened. Let's go to Oklahoma first.

Oklahoma

We found our first home in Chickasha Oklahoma in a red brick, two story apartment building. Dad was stationed at Fort Sill, near Lawton. We lived in an upstairs apartment.

. In the front yard, one of the first things we discovered was a large pile of sand with big red ants crawling in it. We soon found out that their bites stung a lot!! My mother then heard that we could not go barefoot because of hookworms. And there must have been chiggers in Oklahoma, as there still are. Clearly the rules for outdoor play were different from Michigan. One particular time, those changes interfered with my curiosity and scared my mother:

I woke up one morning and looked over the side of my bed. In my shoe was a huge hairy spider, maybe two inches across. I was a little scared and a lot fascinated, and called my mom. She killed the spider, disappointing me, who wanted to make it a pet. She then talked to the neighbors, learning that it was a "banana spider" and that they always came in pairs. She frantically spent the rest of the day tearing the apartment apart looking for its mate.

I know now that it was a tarantula, and they do not always come in pairs. Some people actually do make pets of them. Their looks are scary because of size and hairiness, but they are rather harmless. They occasionally bite when disturbed, but are not poison. When I lived in Oklahoma later in life, I learned more about these fascinating creatures. Did you know they sometimes migrate in groups? Back then, my mother managed to impress on me that I should be cautious if I ever saw another, and I was emphatically "not to touch it".

A.H, now about 3, was naturally impressionable. He somehow learned the word "chicken-shit", and used it one day. My mother told him that if he used it again, she would wash his mouth out with soap. He did, and she did, and he was then sent to his room. A while later, he came out and in a defiant tone of voice, with hands on hips said "Well, it's OK to say just plain "chicken" isn't it?" You have to know AH to know how typical of him that was. Even at that age, he was creative, stubborn and determined to live life on his terms. He always attempted to find a creative way to do what he wanted to do. AH is still a stubbornly determined man, and puts it to use to accomplish good things in life in creative ways. I am grateful that I was his sister and not his mom. This incident became another often told family story.

My mother attempted to take advantage of local culture wherever we were. We were constantly learning and experiencing new places and things. My mother and I took horseback lessons while living in Chickasha. Our family, either with or without my dad, went to a rodeo one day, and I came home with handfuls and pocketfuls of beads and feathers from the American Indian costumes. I was so intrigued with my treasures, that I do not remember either the rodeo acts or the Indians. I would assume they must have had people in full native costume for dancing or performances. I have a vague memory of a 'bucking bronco" as it broke out of the chute. I remember the wild eyes and a sense of the power - impressive to a 5 year old, but no more impressive than the beads and feathers.

My mom searched for an occasional baby sitter for us. She carefully looked for a young woman who could use money for college, eventually hiring a "colored" girl (as the term was then), Ada Lois Sipuel. Many years later, Mother learned that Ada Lois was the first black woman in Oklahoma to force the state to let her attend law school. It was a difficult struggle for Lois, as I would read later. The state offered to provide a separate college for her, but that was refused. She was forcing integration, and wanted an equal education, along with the white students. Ada Lois Sipuel Fisher went on to graduate from Law School as the first black woman lawyer in Oklahoma.

I attempted to find her, when I lived again in Oklahoma as an adult, but she had died 5 years previously. I had photos of her with my brother and I. I located her son who had helped her write a book about her life, "A Matter of Black And White". I gave him the photos for a museum display about her. I have the book, and copies of the photos.

We went to visit Fort Sill one day where I was fascinated by the prison cell and grave of Chief Geronimo, an Apache Indian Chief. When we saw the cell, the person showing us, pointed out the grooves in the cement floor, where Geronimo had paced back and forth. That scene and my imagination, seeing a man walking back and forth enough to wear down a cement floor, deeply touched me. I was moved, in whatever way a 6 year old can be moved, and remember a sense of sad wonder, and many further unanswered questions.

The internet says the cell is still preserved. When I lived in Oklahoma as an adult, I did not go see it again, but writing this has stirred a wish to do so. Geronimo is still buried at the Apache Prisoner of War Cemetery at Fort Sill, and there are fights to return his remains to Apache land for a final resting place. As a prisoner, he was allowed to participate in various events, even one of the

World Fairs. He was still a prisoner when he died. I suspect he must have been a strong man to maintain his dignity and mental health under such conditions. He lived in the middle of a foreign culture which both imprisoned him and used him for its own purposes, keeping him apart from his people, culture, foods, freedom, and land.

I have a drinking glass, taken from my mother's house which says "Field Artillery School, Fort Sill Oklahoma". I assume my father attended there as he was in the Field Artillery. I insert a little history of Fort Sill and his unit here, just for the sake of family history. According to Wikipedia, the internet encyclopedia, the Field Artillery School was established in 1911 and still exists today. My dad was in the 119th Field Artillery, a division of the Michigan National Guard. Their motto was *viam praeparatum*—"we prepare the way." Their unit had a song by that name which Dad taught us. I could not find the song on the internet, and remembering the words, I put them here so they will be preserved somewhere. My brother and I sang this "army song" along with others as our family traveled between forts, or assignments. Our family often passed time by singing as we rode. Here is the song:

We Prepare The Way

"We prepare the way, the 119th Field Artillery
Ready night and day, the 119th Field Artillery
And as we bivouac under the stars we dream of Michigan skies
For the days that victory's ours,
That's where our happiness lies
Oh we prepare the way
With light and liberty
That's where we want to be
The 119th Field artillery. "

Another Oklahoma town that we lived in was Cement.(We moved back and forth between Oklahoma and Missouri, and I do not know in what order we lived in what town.)

In Cement, I have vague and questionable memories of our living quarters but believe we rented part of a home from a family who also lived there and ran an antique shop in the front of the home. There was a real ice-box in the kitchen. I certainly remember the ice man coming and cutting off ice to fit the ice compartment. I remember the tongs, and chips flying as he cut the ice. We were offered chips to suck on.

Behind our house was a large hill, which AH and I called "the mountain". Our big adventure was exploring that mountain. We came across a crevice in the rocks. It was maybe 3 x 5 feet, and 5 feet deep. It was wide enough to see the bottom, but too deep to contemplate going in. On the bottom were several, maybe half a dozen, womens purses. We invented a story, not too implausible, that someone was stealing purses and putting them there. I think we told our mother, but remember nothing more. When I went back to Cement many years later, I found the hill and looked for the crevice, but didn't find it. Although Cement only had around 500 people in the 2000 census, I was able to bring my brother back a souvenir-shirt saying "Where The Hell is Cement Oklahoma?. It was the only souvenir T shirt available in town.

Dad's Work – On and Around the Fort

My dad consistently tried to share his work and his world with us when we were younger. During these army years, there were visits to Fort Sill, and Fort Leonard Wood with Dad, and there were the stories about his work. He was gone much of the time, staying at the fort, but came home when he could, and at those times, we often went somewhere or did something special as a family.

I remember my dad taking us to the Artillery Range to see the 55mm. howitzer guns; (Was that their designation?) Google says that they were declared obsolete in 1945, so it is possible). Whatever they were, we had to wear ear muffs for protection. The men and the guns were on some kind of trailer or wheeled vehicle. Were those called caissons? The historical meaning of the word is a wagon or box that held ammunition, so it is probable that they were. Most people have heard the Field Artillery Song "The Caissons Go Rolling Along". (We sang that one while traveling too.) My mostly visual memory of that day was us standing back wearing ear protection and watching and listening to artillery practice.

Dad took my brother and I out to shoot his pistol one day. He held the gun, assisting us, and we shot at a tree, and at an old tin can. I suppose he helped us hold the gun because the kickback must have been pretty strong for little kids to handle. I liked doing it, but didn't want to do it again. It felt somewhat scary to see the destruction. Dad made sure to show us those bullet effects, and also tell us how dangerous guns could be. I was probably 6 or 7 at the time. I am still not much of a gun person, and don't own one.

One day I went to the fort with Dad, and my eyes lighted up watching a small plane, flying very low to the ground, and then hopping up in the air, only to come back down low again. He was low enough to have to dodge trees. My dad explained that he was "grass-hopper-ing". He explained that by staying low, the plane could not be seen and shot by the enemy, and that the pilot had to go up occasionally to keep track of where he was and to see what might be nearby. I remember hoping for a ride. However, I was not in a plane until many years later when my father was taking flying lessons. I may have been in Junior High then.

Another story dad told us was about a man who was badly hurt, perhaps in combat, perhaps not. He was now in the army hospital

29

on the fort. It seems the medics had received a supply of powder, a new discovery, with no directions, other than being told it was for infection. I now think it was a primitive form of one of the first antibiotics, maybe streptomycin, penicillin, or sulfa. The man was dying of an abdominal wound, and they cut him open and packed the powder inside. He lived, and it was considered a miracle.

Another of our repeated family stories was born at the fort. Dad was at the airport on the fort. He had to get back to the main fort quickly, and picked up an airport phone to ask if someone could come pick him up. He prefaced it with "This is Bradley". Whoever was at the other end thought it was General Omar Bradley, a well-known and highly positioned general at the time. They sent a car and driver, and an escort car for him with American Flag flying. I have no idea if my dad guessed that they would mistake his identity, or whether it was inadvertent. But it was good for repeated telling, and lots of chuckles.

Incidentally, as far as we could determine, General Bradley was not a relative of ours, but we often referred to Uncle Omar, and I still occasionally use the term or hear one of my sibs use it. We didn't use it to impress others. It just became a family phrase when we were comparing him with my dad, or talking about Gen. Bradley's accomplishments.

Then there was our introduction to the Officer's Club at Fort Leonard Wood. We were introduced to lots of soldiers who seemed to enjoy talking to us, probably missing their own children. There was one man throwing dice against the wall. I was curious, and my dad explained that this man won lots of money every pay day "shooting craps". Dad also introduced us to Gibby. Gibby's reputation preceded the introduction, so we were properly impressed. First of all, Gibby could walk on his hands the length of the barracks. Second, Gibby could figure trajectory and distance of shots from the big guns without slide rules or paper. He was celebrated as a mathematical genius. We were properly impressed. but warned ahead of time not to ask him to walk on his hands there.

Missouri and Fort Leonard Wood

Dad was stationed at Fort Leonard Wood, Missouri twice during our army time. All of these assignments were preparing him to go overseas where World War II was happening full force. Fort Leonard Wood was a brand new fort at the time, originally intended to train infantry, and switched to train Engineers and replacement Engineers for overseas.

One of the houses we lived in, we called the "D'Sousa House". I suppose that might have been the name of the owners. It was a lovely house with an exterior of sandstone blocks. The yard was the setting of my memories. At the back of the yard, was an open ditch, one end deeper and partially filled with water. Above the water line, was a ledge. It was another 4 feet from the ledge to the level of the lawn. Picture a deep pit with a ledge halfway down and water below the ledge. It may have been a septic system, or a cistern. One day, I decided to jump down there, knowing I could land on the narrow ledge. I landed on the ledge, but contrary to my usual process, I obviously didn't consider the consequences, as there was no way to climb out. The walls were sheer, and had no handholds or footholds. I was stuck there until rescue.

I remember thinking that my mom was going to be upset, and that I was in trouble. Somebody told her, and a ladder was put down so I could get out. I could tell my mother was scared. She told me I had done a very risky and dangerous thing. This was the same house where my brother climbed up a tree and could not get down. Remember, he was only 3. The ladder was used to rescue him too. The way I remember it, my mother went up the ladder and helped him to back down the tree limb and then the steps of the ladder. Ah the adventures of explorative kids, and the stamina of mostly-alone moms.

My first and only childhood sexual experimentation happened at that same house. There were two little boys who lived next door. They were about our age, and as a matter of fact, I think I remember them being around in the adventure with the water pit. One day, one of them said to me "I'll touch yours if you'll touch mine" I didn't know what he meant, but when he explained, I agreed.

That is how it happened that later that day we sat down facing each other, out behind the house and I touched his, and he touched mine. I felt curious about why he wanted to do that, because from what I saw, my brother had one of those, too. It was not a big deal. In fact, my memory is entirely visual, rather than kinesthetic or emotional. I had a vague idea that my mother would not approve, but I do not remember feeling aroused, pleasurable, or even guilty, just curious. That incident or similar ones were never again requested or repeated.

This next story is related to those years in Missouri, but actually culminated when I was over 50. It is a wonderful example of how our body /being can hold memories that are otherwise forgotten. One of the towns we lived in was Lebanon, Missouri. One day, when my dad was home, we went to a park somewhere for a picnic and a day's fun. While we were there, my dog, Frisky, jumped in the river. He was attempting to swim back to us, but against the current and could not make any headway. He was getting tired, and apparently dad could see that he was in trouble. Dad jumped in the river, and brought Frisky back, from what might have been fatal. The river was not deep, but too deep for a dog to touch bottom.

Fast forward 45 or 50 years: I was on one of those lone road trips across the country, visiting places we had lived, and I stopped to camp at a park near Lebanon – Bennett Springs Park. I went for a walk after my tent was up. I was walking along the stream, and my body suddenly totally remembered having been there before. I was on the bank of the river in the place where Frisky was swimming for his life 50 years ago I had no idea this was the same park, and had not thought of the incident in years.

At this time, my mother was still living, and when I got home, I checked out the name of the park and she remembered it. It was indeed the same place. As a counselor, I had often taught people that we em-body our life - that our body holds our life story in it. I have no better proof than that incident. I wholly recognized that spot in a way very different from a vague deja vous, or my mind remembering. The whole incident played out in front of my eyes like a movie, and I momentarily felt 7 years old, even as the adult me was full of wonder at what was happening. I knew exactly where we were sitting for our picnic, and exactly where Frisky had been in the river.

Incidentally, I revisited another place while on that same trip. We had, with my dad and mom, gone to see a large stone castle on the shore of Lake of the Ozarks. The castle was named "Ha Ha Tonka." It later burned, and when I went back there, I was able to find the ruins. I now have a friend who has a house on that lake, and knows the site and the story of the old castle.

We lived in several other places in Missouri. I can remember Rolla, Lebanon, Waynesville, and Officers Housing on the fort. I think Waynesville was only where I went to school when we lived on the fort. My mom must have had a difficult time caring for 2 small children, not having her husband around much of the time, and trying to find friends and some sort of social life apart from my brother and I, especially when moving so much.

I was vaguely aware that she felt she had to follow the unwritten rules of army rank, for instance who socializes with whom. She was college educated, a bridge player, and interested in a lot of things, and I am guessing she would have wanted people who shared some of her interests. Speaking of ranks in the army, we were taught them mostly by a song, naming them in order. Later in life, as I worked on a military base, I was confused by the E1, E2, etc. ranking system.

One day, when we lived in the Officers housing area, A.H, and I were out playing, and started talking to some men who were taking care of the lawn and bushes. We soon realized that they did not speak English. They pointed to things, and we began to tell them the words. For instance, they started petting Frisky and we taught them "dog". We later found that they were Italian prisoners of war. It was a rich experience for us to teach grownups, and receive their warm responses. I am grateful to have lived in an era, and a family that allowed me the experience rather than using fear to keep us separate.

In all that travel, and all the schools I must have attended in Oklahoma and Missouri, I have memories of only two schools and classrooms. One was in Waynesville. We rode the bus from the fort to the school each day. The school was on a hill, and one winter day, with ice or snow around, the bus got partway up and started sliding backward. I was pretty scared, and remember looking out the back window of the bus and seeing that it looked awfully steep. Soon the bus stopped sliding and we proceeded up the hill without incident, but obviously I was impressed enough to remember it all my life. 60 years later, I went back to visit Waynesville, and tried to find where the school had been located. Few people were around who had been there back then, and I could not get an accurate idea of where it was. Waynesville has grown up from the "hillbilly" town that it was back then (That is the word my mother used to describe it)

In the first grade classroom of that school, I noticed many children were barefoot and some showed up only occasionally. I didn't know what to make of that. (And of course, following my natural reticent style, I didn't ask) One day the teacher yelled at a child, "Ain't you got no learnin'?" I later learned that during World War II, there were people teaching who had not gone to college, but rather may have finished high school and wanted to teach, especially the lower grades. There was no formal teaching in that room that I remember. I spent my entire time in the back corner of the room by the book shelves, reading.

Speaking of reading, I do not remember being taught to read. I don't know where or how I learned. It was a good thing that I had a natural propensity for it, and that our family played alphabet games at home and when traveling. I may have sort have learned without formally learning.

Those barefooted occasional attendees in Waynesville? I assume they were from back in the mountains (again my mom referred to them as hillbillies, and I suspect that was a common term then.) And they probably were forced to occasionally go to school by their parents, or maybe a truant officer.

My mom took me out of that school to "build me up" for a tonsillectomy. She probably had visited the classroom and knew that I was not learning much. My mother visited classrooms often while we were traveling, probably to keep track of the quality of my education.

When I got properly "built up", I went to the Army hospital for my tonsillectomy. I was promised ice cream, and told I would have a sore throat. Having tonsils out was an ordinary thing to do in those days, believing that a child would get less runny noses, or coughs. The tonsils were thought to get infected, and keep children sick. Lots of us my age remember the smell and the whirling feeling of the ether taking effect, with promises of ice cream afterward. I didn't even want the ice cream. I was too sick, and my throat was too sore.

These were also the years when war stamps and bonds were sold at school. Once a week, a table was set up, and we brought our money, and pasted our stamps in our book. That was a way people felt they could help the government finance the war. There were posters with propaganda behind the table—winning the war, beating Tojo, helping Uncle Sam, etc. The stamps were 10 cents or 25 cents. When the book was full, which was when it held 18 dollars and 75 cents worth of stamps, one bought a war bond. The bonds matured in 10 years and were then cashed in for $25. I firmly believed that one put the bond in an envelope in a drawer, and 10 years later, opened the envelope, tore the bond open, and took a $25 dollar bill out. Fortunately, I was much older when it came time to redeem the bonds, and knew better than to tear them open.

Sometime during our travels, I added another chicken incident to my life. This one, less traumatic (at least for me, and more humorous. One place we lived required us to take care of the chickens as part of the rent. We had to feed and water them and gather the eggs. Always the little scientist, I went to the chicken house one day to gather eggs, and noticed that one hen was in the nest, in the process of laying.

As I stood and watched, she worked hard, and when the egg slid out, I reached under her and took it. She stood up, turned around and began to proudly cackle to announce her feat. As she started her noise, she looked where the egg should have been, broke off mid cackle, and started loudly squawking. I laughed out loud. I didn't laugh because I tricked her, but because it looked and sounded so funny. I felt sorry about what I had done. I could see she was upset. I put the egg back down, gathered the rest of the eggs, and walked out.

And then there was the day that I set the neighbor's garage on fire. I don't remember where that happened, but I must have been 6, as every kid I have ever known who played with matches was about that age. I had the matches in the garage, and when I got finished, I carefully put the fire out with the pile of sawdust that was there from the power saw. The next thing I knew, someone was putting out a fire in the garage. There was damage both inside and out, although the garage was not destroyed. I assume that either someone saw me, or that I admitted being there. My mother spanked me with a belt. That was the only spanking I ever got in my life that was with more than a hand. I felt horrible, both because I really thought I put out the fire when I was done, and because I had caused the garage to catch fire. Lesson well learned!!

I suspect I better add a P.S. to that story, as spanking is presently often considered abusive, extreme and unnecessary by many young parents. In those times, it was nearly universal, and neither parents nor children considered it unusual. There were, of course, still abusive families, but spanking in itself was not abusive.

34

In our family, there were few rules, and the consequences of breaking them were laid out ahead. One of the consequences was spanking. Speaking of family rules, probably the best remembered one were "You do not lie, cheat, or steal".

I knew I was being sneaky with those matches. I just didn't think I would get caught, and definitely thought I was being safe. And I doubt that I lied about what I had done. I knew it was a serious thing, and the consequences of lying would have been worse than those of sneakily playing with matches.

On the Road – Traveling Time

Our traveling between living places was as memorable as the homes themselves. We spent long hours and many miles in cars when dad got reassigned. They were times of togetherness, new experiences and learning. I believe the speed limit on the main roads was 35 miles an hour, and there was rationing on gas and tires. Neither cars nor roads were what they are now. I can remember that when we started out in the morning, we turned the headlights on to charge the battery. Was that really valid? I don't know.

We sang a lot in the car. I know songs from the early 1900's because of that. People about my age may remember the "Golden Song Book". There were songs in there such as Grandfather's Clock, The Old Grey Mare, Wait Till the Sun Shines Nellie, Bicycle Built For Two, or Down In The Valley. We sang those songs as well as songs that had been popular when my parents were first married, such as Just a Song At Twilight, or Let The Rest Of The World Go By. Then there were the songs my mother learned at camp, such as Tell Me Why. My mother's father sang in the church choir, so she was steeped in hymns, and we sang some of those: The Old Rugged Cross, or I Come To The Garden. There were of course, the army songs. Caissons, The Infantry Song, We Prepare the Way, or I've Got Sixpence. And then there were the Irish songs of my father's family: My Wild Irish Rose, or Who Threw The Overalls In Mrs. Murphy's Chowder. We also sang songs that were popular then: Clang Clang Clang goes the Trolley, or When The Lights Go On Again, All Over The World.

We read signs and played alphabet games. Best of all were the Burma Shave Signs, immortalized in the book "The Verse By The Side Of The Road". by Rowsome. Burma Shave was a shaving cream, and the verses were on 5 serially spaced signs. The first 4 each had a line of the verse, and the last said "Burma Shave" I loved the rhythm of reading them aloud as we rode by them;

"A man – A car,
A miss – A curve.
He kissed the miss,
And missed the curve
Burma Shave

The words "Googy Car" rang out, as my brother and I played our invented game. Whenever we saw an older car ahead of or behind us, we would yell "Googy Car" and duck down, trying not to come up again until it was out of sight. Of course it sounds silly to me now, but we amused ourselves and thought it hilarious.

My childhood form of meditation was watching the telephone wires. Did anyone else ever get fascinated by the illusion of those wires going up and down as the car passed by? I was mesmerized, and could easily put myself into a mindless or meditative state, or drift to sleep watching the bouncing wires as they went up to meet the crossbars of the poles and drop down again. My whole body felt like it was riding those waves.

Of course we traveled Route 66, the main road across the country back then. As an adult, I have often hunted out, and traveled pieces of the old road, marked by the falling telephone poles with the blue glass insulators, and wires hanging loose, no longer able to move in waves. Parts of the old route have been restored, and there is a cult and culture around "The Mother Road". As I have ridden or driven past broken down, or occasionally restored "tourist cabins", I think of staying there, and wonder if any of those are the ones I slept in at 7 or 8 years old.

Crossing the Mississippi River on the Chain of Rocks Bridge was an event to be anticipated and remembered. I was thrilled to see first the bridge ahead of us, and then the great river as we looked down. Kin to that was crossing the desert on the way to and from California. Every time I, as an adult, cross the desert to California, or the Mississippi River, I am once again 6 or 7 years old for an instant.

As we moved to California, we stopped at the Petrified Forest and the Painted Desert, picking up souvenirs. I had a piece of petrified wood for years. Remember the little glass globes that had colored sand from the Painted Desert arranged like mountains and sky? That was one of my favorite possessions, and when I once again visited the Painted Desert years later, I stopped and bought myself another one. My mother was in trouble with her aging years by then, and on impulse I bought her one too, hoping it would bring back memories of better days, and memories of when I was little and she was younger. It didn't, but I enjoyed mine for many more years.

As we crossed that desert back then, on the way to California, I saw the "water" on the pavement ahead, and my dad taught me about mirages. I loved the word, and I quickly pointed out more mirages as I saw them. We saw cars with cloth bags on the front, full of water, and Dad told me about the evaporation of the water and how it would help cool the car radiator and motor. So many learning experiences at such a young age.

On one of those road trips of mine, I again crossed that desert, waiting until morning, and carefully preparing with extra water for me and for the car. This was before the GPS, and I must have gone by my memories rather than the scale of miles on the map. Imagine my surprise when I was back in civilization by noon or early afternoon. My memory had tricked me into thinking it was at least an all day trip. Then too, there is a little more civilization and a few more towns now, than in the 1940's.

Our travel was not always fun, adventurous and interesting. Like all kids, we got bored and occasionally misbehaved. One day, we were pushing each other and fighting about something, and my father threatened to let us out of the car to walk if we did not stop fighting. At a point, he actually stopped the car and made us get out. I was scared, and I suppose AH was too. Of course he let us back in soon, and we, much more quietly and well behaved, went on our way.

California

We were going to California for "desert maneuvers" whatever those were. I suspect it was to train the troops in adverse conditions before they went overseas. As a way of preparing us, my mom told us there was no snow, and that we could trim the Christmas tree with roses. More fun and adventure, coming up.

As usual, dad wasn't home most of the time, and I soon heard place names like Indio and Palm Springs. We settled in a town named Banning, on West Ramsey Street. I didn't know it, but my mom was pregnant again. Our kitchen window faced the San Bernardino Mountains, and to this day they look familiar to me when I go through Banning. It is as if my mind took a picture, and I am seeing a page out of the album.(Interesting that the picture was of the mountains, and not the town or people.)

There are a couple other pictures in that California memory album of mine. One is of the bamboo patch in our back yard. It must have been from 5-10 feet across, as there were paths through it, and a place to sit inside. A.H. and I used to play there. We found some small bottles in there full of colored liquid. I would guess now that they were food coloring bottles, or flavoring. They were about that size. We sometimes decided they were medicine bottles, and used them to play hospital, other times they were flavorings to play at cooking with.

California brought new foods. There were olive trees, and of course, I picked an olive, expecting to get what came from the jar. Not so, they tasted awful! Next door to our house, there was a pomegranate tree. Now that was a delight. Our neighbors were generous, and we loved the pomegranates. They are now one of the stars of the "super food" world, and can be bought in stores anywhere, but there was much of my life when I realized I knew about a food that most people didn't know about. Date palms grew there. My grandmother bought boxes of candied dates for all the relatives for Christmas. In later years, she ordered them, from Banning I think.

My mother paid close attention to our nutrition, and had a book called, "You Are What You Eat". She always encouraged new foods, and new ways to eat healthy foods. Whenever we had a garden, she encouraged us to eat leaf lettuce straight from the garden, and showed us how to put a little sugar on it. At that time, fruit and vegetables came either fresh, or canned. There was no frozen food.

We took Cod Liver Oil, and I used to sneak extra, considering it a treat. I bet that was unusual! I can remember mom fixing healthy salads for us, such as "candle salad", a ring of pineapple on a bed of lettuce, half a banana upright in the pineapple hole, and a maraschino cherry on top of the banana for the flame. Another favorite was canned spinach, hard boiled eggs, and bacon with tomato slices. She also taught us to make eggnog for ourselves after school. This was long before the worry about salmonella in raw eggs.

That school in Banning was my only other school memory from the Army years. This time it was the school work I remembered, and enjoyed. They used "progressive education". This meant, in my second grade class, when we came in the morning, we said the Pledge of Allegiance. We were then free to go to the row of mimeographed sheets on the side table (From the Gestetner machine, forerunner of Ricoh products)) and start our work. There was a sheet for coloring and drawing, one for spelling practice, one for English, Arithmetic, and Penmanship. I think that there were also sheets once a week or so for geography, history and music.

There were reading classes going on at the front of the room, although the teacher could be interrupted if the rest of us had questions. When not in reading class, we could take the sheets in any order, complete them, hand them in, and take another. The teacher helped those who needed it, and oversaw the works in progress. I loved to do things in the order I wanted, and set my own pace and schedule. At the end of the day, we put away our equipment and tidied up the room for the next day. There was recess once or twice a day.

Progressive Math, as taught there, meant that we were expected to put the answers to the problems on the worksheets. We may have been taught how to get the answers, but if so, that was not needed on the papers. Many of us counted on fingers, or did the work in our head, and just put down the answers. I am sure we had instruction and I am sure some students needed more help than others, but the point was that we were individualized, both by the worksheets and by the teacher. When I did the problems, I mostly worked in my head. For instance, 5 x 112 meant multiplying 5 x 100, and then 5 x 10 and then 5 x 2, and adding up the answers.

That bit of learning and practice got me in trouble a few months later when we moved back to Michigan. (More about that soon.)

It was at that school that I made the only friend I remember in all the traveling days. His name was Paul, and we used to walk home holding hands. I suppose he was in my class in school, and that we lived the same direction. My mother soon questioned me about him, and told me that holding hands was not appropriate. Although I felt disappointed, I stopped. I assume it was one of those decisions that a parent has to make based on circumstances and the age of a child. I suppose that in second grade, it was indeed getting "iffy" to hold hands with a boy every day, especially when I had no other friends. I just remember feeling good walking with him. Obviously her perception of my world and my perception were quite different.

One time when Dad was home, we drove to Hollywood, and as we drove down the street, we kept thinking we were seeing movie stars such as Bette Davis, or Greta Garbo, or maybe little Elizabeth Taylor. Although it is probable that we did not, it was an exciting and glamorous trip. We also saw the ocean that day for the first time. It may have been a first for my parents also. I did not see an ocean again until high school, when my family again went to California on a family camping trip—that time to Pismo Beach.

There were two "family changing" events in California. The first was that we lost Frisky. Frisky was out exploring, as he often did, and apparently ate a "gopher capsule". In those days, people killed gophers by wrapping cyanide capsules in meat, or in something that the animals would eat. Frisky came running toward the house, got halfway up the porch steps, and fell down dead. My mother started crying, picked him up and took him to a veterinarian, but it was of no help. Cyanide is nearly an instant killer.

I was watching as he ran and fell, but have no recollection of emotions. It was my first experience with death other than seeing the chickens killed in Caro. I suspect that the action and my mother's emotions were catalysts for me to stop feeling my own emotions, but don't know. Frisky had been with us 8 years, and in all those places we lived. For my mom, I would guess he had helped her feel safer when she was alone without my dad. We did not have another dog, until I got a dog in Junior High School.

The other "family changing" event was the birth of my sister, Rebecca Anne Bradley, January 24, 1944. My father was due to ship out overseas, and the baby had not been born yet. The doctors decided to induce labor, probably not done much in those days. This would allow my father to be there. Something went wrong, and my mother's heart stopped on the delivery table. I have no idea whether it was before or after the baby was born. Apparently the doctors shot adrenalin into her heart. She later told us that she remembered hearing them say that was what they were going to do. It worked. Her heart started beating and she came back to life. She and the baby were all right. My dad shipped out for overseas three days later.

Many years later, maybe when I was in my 60's, mom told us of her near-death experience on the delivery table. That was before near-death experiences were commonly told or known about. She was in a beautiful meadow, going toward an uncommonly beautiful light. She walked toward the light, when she heard AH and I calling for her. She had to decide whether to keep going, or come back and find us, and take care of us. The light was tempting for her, but she turned, and decided to come back to us. I often weep, or feel grateful when I hear that story. It validates her love and investment in us. I wonder if it changed her life as it does for so many? The hospital was Loma Linda Hospital in Riverside or Redlands. It is a renowned Seventh Day Adventist Hospital. I assume it was then also.

With my father overseas, there was no reason to stay in California and plenty of reason to go back to Michigan where there was family. The plan was to sell the car, and ride the train back. However, as the time neared, my mother changed the plan. She was concerned that she could not buy a car, since there was shortage of materials in the country because of the war. So she decided to keep the car, and asked my grandmother Bradley to come to California and ride back to Michigan with us.

Only six weeks after Becky was born, we started out. AH and I were in the back seat, and the baby basket fit at our feet on the floor. My grandmother and mother rode in front. Here was my mother, only 6 weeks after dying and being brought back to life, responsible for a newborn and two relatively small children. She had the courage and tenacity to drive 2500 miles across the country. That would not be such a feat in these days of modern cars, and navigation systems, but in 1942 or 43, the country was at war, cars often broke or had flat tires, and it was still winter. And two women alone drove across the country.

When my mother was older, I told her how much I admired her courage in life, and cited that trip. I remember little of the trip other than the baby basket being on the floor of the back seat with my sister in it. I suppose we must have been on the road a good 10 days or more. Maybe there were many women who took those kinds of trips across the country in that time of absent husbands fighting overseas. I don't know that. But I do know my admiration for my mom and this trip.

Summary of Our Army Years

Although my father was still overseas, this finished up our Army days, and we were on our way back to Michigan, to our hometown with friends and grandparents waiting. .

As I stated before, Army kids develop along two quite different paths. They either become gregarious and make friends easily, or they turn inward and become self-reliant. I was one of the latter. I spent most of my time alone, or with my brother. Those years were enjoyable, as you have heard. But the habit of going inward too easily, and not thinking to reach out, has followed me my entire life. I have found some balance in that area as time has gone on. However, I have continued to move geographically as an adult So, while I have good friends, not many of them are around me at any given time. As I get older, (writing this at 77), it gets more difficult to find the energy to reach out and make new friends. This concerns me at times, and I remind myself to go against my grain and reach out. It is my intention to live the last part of my life with faith and friends, compassion and kindness, time alone and time with others, living a balanced life.

. Self-reliance is a strength, and my growing spiritual life and faith adds to that strength. That strength seems to make it less necessary to have others around to manifest one's life or to lean on. However, when I disappear inside myself, my needs and feelings are not easily seen by others. My life energy folds inside, and I appear flat and lifeless, or extraordinarily competent and self-reliant, which is not often true. That process does not attract connection, companionship, or spontaneous offers of help from others. Thus, self-reliance sometimes turns to loneliness.

Several years ago, when I was writing about those early years of mine as an army kid, I said this:

"And what did I learn from those years? I learned that strangers were OK and close friends unattainable. I learned to rely on myself, I learned that the constants in life were nature and change, and I enjoyed both. I learned that home was where my parents were, and that besides that, I felt at home anywhere I felt comfortable, which was mostly in the natural world."

I said, at the beginning of the army times, that the tasks of a 6-9 year old were to learn belonging and accomplishment. I say again here that I was oblivious to most people around me, and found my belonging at home or in nature. Connecting to others was not pertinent to me when it should have been. I certainly had a sense of accomplishment in becoming self-reliant, and also through being smart. All those experiences and learning lots of new things constantly gave me a sense of knowing about things that other kids didn't. So much moving and change gave me a sense of confidence in what I would now call my resilience, although I find that resilience seems to be lessening with increasing age.

Later in life, I would have to unlearn, relearn, or refine some of my basic life beliefs, but like anyone else, what I learned in childhood allowed me to adjust to my circumstances. Both change and stability have their lessons and advantages, and I count myself lucky to have made friends with both during these years.

Now let's go back to Michigan.

My mother and father somewhere around college age

My father's family plus my mother and me (1ˢᵗ grandchild)
Back row: Grandpa (AH), Bill, John, Deke, Maryan
Front Row: Lucile, Mary Lib, Dorothy, Grandma, and me

Playing in the sandbox

Mom and I

Trying on Dad's Army hat

Mom and Dad, Fort Sill OK

Capt Deke (E.W.) Bradley

Karen and A.H. Fort Leonard Wood

Back in Michigan, Grandpa, Me, AH, Becky

Becky – pictures for Dad overseas

BACK IN MICHIGAN

AGES 7-15

On our return to Midland, we temporarily moved in with Grandma and Grandpa until our own house next door was ready. I soon discovered that Grandma had a "hired girl", Marie Macomb, to help with the housework. Marie welcomed my "help" and talked to me while we worked, helping me feel grown up, and making the time quite enjoyable. There were other perks too. I learned a little about ironing (and finished up my education on my other grandma's "mangle" iron up in Caro.) And I got to go out on the small back porch of the funeral home, which overlooked the neighborhood from the second story, and shake the rugs. I could see the whole world from there, or at least the whole neighborhood.

Grandma was from down South, and came from a family with some dignity, and some money. Her maiden name had been Pulliam, and my information about her background is more an impression than factual. She always kept a gracious Southern air about her, enjoying nice things, and entertaining graciously. Although the hired help was natural to her, it was unusual in Michigan. There is a cedar chest in the family (Bob and Jackee) that belonged to Grandma's family. She told us there was one made for her family and one for the Duncan Hines family out of the same tree.

In contrast to (but never verbally contrasted) to Grandma Bradley's genteel manner, Grandpa spent his spare time at the pool hall downtown. There he played rummy, winning bubble gum and other prizes for his grandkids. He brought us real Dubble Bubble Gum, with comics inside or sometimes those little wax miniature pop bottles with sugar water inside. After we drank the sugar water, we chewed the wax like gum. He often gave us pennies, and an occasional nickel. The gum was "black market", not being available during the war.

A few years later, we rode our bikes downtown, hoping to see the inside of that pool hall. We parked our bikes and went down the side stairs to the door, but never got the nerve to go in. It was sort of dark, and we could see people playing pool and cards. It may have been called Shorty's?

One More New School

My new Michigan school was to be Second Ward School, the building where my father had attended school. It was walking distance, maybe a quarter or half a mile away from home. I would be walking four times a day, to and from school and to and from home at lunch time. Between that and recess, there was no lack of exercise in those days. The principal was Miss Maude Thompson, and later the school was named Thompson School after her. My teacher was to be Miss Elizabeth Kline.

I entered school in March, and later heard that Miss Kline was unhappy getting a new student that late in the school year. Within a week or two, she accused me of cheating on my arithmetic. She thought I was copying answers from other students. My papers showed the right answers, but none of the work of finding them. I was continuing what I had learned in California.

Michigan was not California, and although I saw nothing wrong with what I was doing, it took my mother going to school to straighten it out. Not only did Miss Kline need to understand what I was doing, but I needed to understand what she wanted, and why she thought I was cheating. Thank goodness my mother understood it all.

As a result, I began to learn Arithmetic all over again. This time I had to figure out how I got the answers, and put the process on paper. She needed to see my thinking and figuring processes in order to check them, and know I was doing it myself, instead of copying. I had never thought about how I got the answers; let alone how to write all that down. I remember concluding that although I had to do it the "Michigan way", it was much slower and more frustrating. I wanted to get it done and move on to something else more fun or challenging.

Social Awareness

At one of my earlier schools, I had become curious when I went to the bathroom and there were never any boys there. It would have been unusual for me to even ask where the bathrooms were, let alone why no boys. And at home, we all used the same bathroom. I think I asked my mom, and she explained, or maybe I just figured it out.

There were probably many subtle things in the social world that I didn't know. Lack of social contact and activities, plus being shy about asking questions certainly hindered my knowledge of the larger world of people. I had a pervasive feeling through my young life that I was on the outside looking in.

I was also one of those kids who were chosen last for almost any team. I can remember wishing it were different and feeling sort of sad, but I suppose I became resigned to it. In hindsight: 1) I was a newcomer to the school, 2) I was so shy I did not make friends or speak up in class, so no one knew me well. 3) I was one of the shorter kids in class. 4) I had never played team sports or any games with a group before. I had never batted a softball, nor thrown a basketball. 5) My hand eye coordination was poor, (I didn't know yet that I was nearsighted.) 6) I had never competed before in any way that I remember. Why would I not be one of the last? Hindsight about childhood is often so much clearer and in this case kinder.

Miss Ritchie -- 3rd Grade

In third grade, my teacher was Evelyn Ritchie. The best of my grade school teachers, going above and beyond the required class work, and really liking children. I remember her as a thin, plain, even severe woman, with dresses that almost touched the floor, and grey braids twisted up on her head like a coronet. It appears, from what I could find on the internet that she was born about 1900, so would have been in her 40's when she taught me.

After school, she offered knitting and crocheting classes for any girl who wanted to learn. I loved taking advantage of her offer, and joined several others. I have used those skills during several seasons of my life, and been grateful for her teaching. She even overcame the challenge of teaching me, a left handed student, these skills, and knew how to do it without calling attention to me or making a problem of it.

She also introduced her students to classical music. Last thing in the afternoon, she announced music hour, and introduced us to such music as the Lone Ranger Theme, music from Hansel and Gretel, or the Nutcracker Suite. Sometimes it was a composition which had been made into a popular song. We learned about the composers, and some of the instruments in the orchestra. I learned enough to make me curious about other classical music and to know what I liked – rhythm instead of tune, and tune instead of words. When I now hear the pieces I first heard back then, it brings back the gratitude of her teachings, along with those long ago memories.

We students naturally thought we were getting away with something on those music afternoons. We viewed it as "Oh boy, no more school work" Instead, it was she who was getting away with something, teaching us, and at the same time helping us through the end of the school day when we might have been fidgety, or bored. It energized us, or calmed us down accordingly. We caught her interest and excitement, and left school with more knowledge, often less fatigued, and more energy.

This bit of teaching filled a hole in my family life also. Although my mother had played piano when younger, music was not much a part of our family life. My parents were well educated and intelligent, but lacked interest and sharing of the arts and humanities.

Speaking of this reminds me of a memory of my 40's, when one of my friends, a Mensa member (Mensa is an organization for high IQ people), confessed to me that she had thought I was not very smart because I knew nothing about the humanities and little about the classics. Luckily, she was around long enough to learn more about my type of intelligence, but had first judged my IQ on that limited basis.

We had many and varied books around our house. There were fiction, old college text books, biographies, and books on communication, science or politics. I had many children's books, one of my favorites being "A Child's Garden Of Verses". Another was a set of books called Book House. This was a series to cover all ages. The volumes ranged from Nursery Rhymes in the first one, to some Shakespeare and classics in the last, appealing to all ages. By the time I was grown; the first 8 volumes were well used and even tattered. After that, I discovered social life, and didn't read for pleasure as much.

My childhood memories of being read to and reading are many and happy. My mother fed our character with stories like "The Little Engine Who Could". She lulled me to sleep with "Wynkyn, Blinken and Nod, We had the Munro Leaf books on Manners. She later listened to me read as I discovered books on my own. I am still an avid reader, with many interests, shifting toward more fiction in the past 10 years.

My other brush with classical music was the Wednesday night outdoor band concerts. The band master, Ted Nicholson, had been a bandleader for Ringling Brothers, Barnum and Bailey Circus Band, and so our programs contained classic marches, and songs heard under the big top. Before we left Midland, even when I was under 3 years old, I used to sit on the ground right behind Mr. Nicholson, and keep time to the music. When back in Midland, I attended those concerts right up through high school. As of this writing, they are still being held on Wednesday nights.

As I hinted at earlier, I am moved by rhythm more than words and simplicity more than complexity in music. That was true when I was little, and is true now. I love folk music, and especially Hawaiian music. I like drums, and all things percussive. I have often enjoyed moving my body to music, feeling the rhythm move me. I seldom know the words, but I know how it makes me feel.

The Rest of Elementary School

My fourth grade teacher was Mrs. Lloyd, and fifth was Miss House. I remember little about these years or teachers, other than their names. By then, my life was taking place on the playground or at home. You will read more about the playground shortly.

Mrs. Schwartz was my 6th Grade teacher, and is a family legend. She was a precise, rigid person with bright red lipstick. We had a student in our class named Rob Goodall, who sat in the front row with his entire Encyclopedia set and dictionary on the bench in front of him. One day, Mrs., Schwartz was talking about "tuberclosis", leaving out the extra "u". Rob promptly corrected her and immediately grabbed the T volume of his encyclopedia. They consistently butted heads over such things, with the class holding its collective breath. Who would back down first?.

Eight years later, my sister says that she had the same teacher. I am not sure she did, maybe simply hearing my stories about her, because Becky also tells about "tuberclosis" happening in her class. And she went to a different school. If it is true, I wonder if Mrs. Schwartz was simply not open to change, or purposely baited her classes to see if people would correct her.

It was some time in elementary school that I proudly gave myself a tattoo. Learning penmanship we dipped a straight pen with a removable point into an inkwell. Ball point pens came along a few years later. I clearly had too much time on my hands and one day stuck my pen in the inkwell and under my skin by my knee. The result was a very small V shaped tattoo. I went home bragging. It is still visible, although the V shape is distorted by age and changing knee shape. It still makes me smile, thinking of that little girl, the tattoo, and feeling secretive, mischievous, and proud.

By sixth grade, I was making friends in school and in the neighborhood. We walked together to and from school. This was time to prepare for the day, to get unfinished business with each other out of the way, to let go of the tension of school, to observe nature and each other, and to interact with each other without supervision. I suspect, however, that there were watchful eyes behind the curtains. It was, after all, a small town.

We practiced our social skills and worked out relationships. We had temporary boyfriends or girlfriends, or some child got "shunned" for a while, or ganged up on and teased. Indeed, there was bullying even then, and it turned physical occasionally when tempers got heated. A bloody nose was probably the epitome of it back then. (Nothing compared to now, and no Facebook to escalate the conversations and broaden the scope.)

We drew on the sidewalk with "chalkstones". Occasional hopscotch grids appeared. We swung from tree limbs, or tried skipping hopping, or walking backward. There was jump rope, or "Don't step on a crack, you'll break your mother's back".(As I recall, while the Second World War was on, it was Hitler's back that would be broken.) We occasionally found a lost baby bird, and carefully took it home to be raised, or more likely to soon die from our good intentions, but lack of knowledge. And if there was rain, snow, or extreme cold, a parent might come along and pick up a carload of kids to take home.

We experienced the seasons by kicking the leaves, rolling in the snow and throwing snowballs, or seeing the toadstools appear in the spring. We found bugs and threw them at each other, or "smoked" a horse chestnut pipe. We were carefree and involved in each other and nature. We were cooperative, competitive, and at war or in love with one another, depending on which minute or second it was. School ended with the final bell.

Health and Body Awareness

We used our bodies naturally to walk, jump, skip, wrestle, run, climb and explore our world. It was quite unheard of to play organized sports until high school. We played on the playground, or in the gym at school I was well coordinated, and seldom fell or hurt myself. I do not remember anyone in our neighborhood or in my classes who might have been seen as fat. Occasionally someone would be teased and called "fatty fatty two by four", but those children were, at the most, what we might call pudgy. Childhood obesity was unknown in our country at that time.

We all had gotten smallpox vaccinations when little; boys on their arms and girls on the leg where the scar wouldn't show. I can remember not being able to take a bath until the scab came off. (The disease is now wiped out in the world, other than stored cultures, kept because of interest in and fear of biological warfare.)

I went to the dentist twice a year. My parents were conscientious about that. On the occasions when I had to have a filling, I got a shot of "Novocain" as was customary. Afterwards, my cheek swelled up and itched for several days and I thought that normal. I later found I was allergic to topical anesthetics. As an adult, after breaking out from sunscreen, I found that there is a relationship between an allergy to the topical anesthetics and an allergy to PABA, which was used in those sunscreens.

On Being Left Handed

I was left handed, and thought little of it until I got older. Unless parents make a big deal of it, (mine didn't), lefties generally first realize that they are different when learning penmanship. Miss Ritchie and I also had to overcome that when she taught me knitting or crocheting. I remember her telling me to sit opposite her, so I could use her as a mirror. That works well for lefties in learning hand skills. I was fortunate that no one ever tried to force me to switch hands.

I struggled with poor grades in penmanship, and smeared papers in grade school. As an older adult, I suddenly saw the solution. Children learning penmanship used to learn first to slant their paper - top to the left, and bottom to the right. In that case, the leftie finds their hand smearing what they have just written. They "write upside down" The simple answer is to slant the paper the opposite way putting the hand automatically in the correct position to write without smearing or twisting.

Those of us who learned the old way will probably always write upside down. But it is my hope that young lefties are learning differently. It will help their self-esteem, and their grades. Of course as I write this, the talk is to drop cursive writing from the curriculum. Even little ones learn to keyboard now.

Getting Glasses

At some point in mid elementary school, I was caught being nearsighted. I say caught, because I had memorized the charts every year when it came time to be tested, knowing I couldn't read them. I think I thought it shameful, and so as usual, I found a self-reliant way to preserve my self-esteem. I do not remember how I was found out. Probably I couldn't see the blackboard from the back of the room. I was then taken to the eye doctor to be fitted for glasses. Back then, kids with glasses were teased and called "four eyes" or sissy. My parents anticipated that and talked to me about being proud that I could see so well. I do not remember being teased or self conscious.

When I put on my glasses that first day, I was astounded by the separate leaves on the trees, the writing on the board, and (that night) by seeing stars in the skies. It is no wonder my hand/eye coordination was poor.

Later in life (about age 32), I read some books on improving vision, and was able to reverse my nearsightedness and get rid of my glasses. I had worn glasses and later contacts for all those years. For the first time, my driver's license had no restrictions. I am now 78, and it is only the past year or so that I have needed glasses for reading. That may be because of the strength and flexibility of my eye muscles from that earlier training. Whatever it is from, I am profoundly grateful for having had good sight most of my life. Oh, and I just passed another test for a driver's license without glasses.

The Playground /Neighborhood

I may have been the last one chosen for teams at school, but at home on our neighborhood playground, it was a different story. The playground was across from our house. There were swings, bars, monkey bars and an old shed, later torn down. There was a large open space for softball, although our ball occasionally broke a window in the nearest house, whereby we chipped in our money to pay for a new one. Behind the playing area was a huge box elder tree, serving many purposes. Sometimes I climbed it for solitude and reading, other times we climbed in groups, racing each other, and daring each other higher. From the branches we looked down into the back yard of the convent for the nuns from St. Brigid's Church and School.

I was always curious about the nuns, not being Roman Catholic myself. They hung out their clothes to dry but there was never underwear. They conversed in their yard as I watched. The full habits they wore lent an air of mystery. My cousins were Catholic, and my dad had been reared Catholic. I was quite clueless and curious, but respectful.

51

One day, I was sitting in the tree feeling that curiosity, and wondering what it would be like to speak to them. I knew they were often addressed as Sister Mary, but I had no idea they had other names attached. I turned my courage up a notch and from the tree, yelled "Hi Sister Mary" Someone looked up and waved and I felt triumphant about my successful courageous act.

Our playground gang in those days was Jack Barber, Franklin Kanary Haden MacRae, David Eisenman, Larry Potts, Chuck Reid, Roger Perry, Jackie Pappas, Jerry Barber, (Jack's older brother), Martha Gregg, Pat and Terry Dean, Paula and Margo Hooker, Forest Minger, and occasionally Jackie Siler. The Hooker girls were always dressed in dresses, and didn't play with us much. Forest and the Siler's lived several blocks away, and only joined us occasionally, and Martha Gregg was quite a bit younger. The rest of us were regulars.

Observe that the regulars were all boys except for me, so out of necessity; I became "one of the guys". Interestingly, I never dated any of those boys in high school. But I certainly became a "tomboy", and proud of it. Fortunately, my mother too had been raised with many activities and skills that were mostly done by boys, so did not object until it was time for heels, lipstick, and dresses for me. Even then, I rebelled.

On the playground, I finally was past being shy, left out, or isolated. I could hold my own enough so that my self-esteem and social position stayed intact. When we went to the pool in summer, I was a good swimmer, and could hold my breath underwater longer than anyone except my brother A.H, who held the city record. (He passed out underwater setting that record.) I could bail out of a swing from higher than most. Thanks to my Grandpa Dutch, I owned a jackknife at a young age, and got good at mumblety peg. I became one of the marble champs of the neighborhood. - And still have all my marbles. (pun intended). Seriously, I do still have my marble collection, some of which were in my mother's marble collection, making them over 100 years old. I consider looking for a collector to sell to.

The playground gang, often some of the same ones I walked to and from school with had lots to keep busy. There were hours of bike riding or roller skating around the circle formed by sidewalks and the funeral home driveway. Of course our skates clamped onto shoes, and adjusted with a key, worn around the neck on a string. .

In winter, we went sledding on the golf course, skating at Emerson Park, or on someone's home rink. One day we were sledding down back of the courthouse, when my sled and my head hit a tree. I was wearing a thick fur hat that my dad had brought me from overseas. I suspect I was lucky. The hat may have protected me against a more serious injury. In following years, the bloodstain on the lining of the hat kept me cautious and reminded of that injury.

. There was plenty to do, and plenty of friends for me to do it with.

Best Friends and Entrepreneurs-Jack Barber

When not on the playground, I could often be found with Jack Barber, my next door neighbor. He was not only my next door neighbor, but my best and closest friend. He had an older brother, Jerry, and there was my younger brother, AH. But their ages were just far enough from ours that they were not interested in our activities. Jack and I provided great companionship for each other, and collaborated in making money, and playing together for many years. We never dated later, nor seemed to feel like "boyfriend/girlfriend". He was simply a best friend. Our friendship deserves this separate section. I believe it importantly gave me companionship for at least 2 to 3 years when I was still shy and did not make friends easily.

We were consistent entrepreneurs, making money in all seasons and having a good time in the process. We raked leaves, mowed lawns, shoveled snow, or collected newspapers, as the season invited. Fortunately, in those days, neighbors were willing to indulge us and pay us for our work. I suspect we did a good job, but I know we were working hard and having fun.

Our families were friends, and worked out ways that we could be in and out of each other's house, and still have boundaries, or not get in the way. Sometimes I sat at their house and read during their dinner, other times I ate with them by invitation, or got sent home while they ate. The same thing was true for Jackie at my house.

We did chemistry experiments in the basement, or dripped hot solder onto newspapers on the cement basement floor, watching the shapes and making up stories, or telling fortunes. We had our own Bunsen burner, allowing us lots of latitude in our experiments. Both homes had a lot of books, and we spent time sitting in one living room or another reading. At his house, I read the Buddy Series by Garis, Nancy Drew Mysteries, Dave Darrin at Annapolis series, and others. At my house, I read Girl of the Limberlost, and all the Gene Stratton Porter books. I fancied myself as Elnora, whose mother was non-responsive, while Elnora herself was a nature lover, and collected and sold moths as a serious hobby. The parallels to my own life were unmistakable, at least in my mind.

Our entrepreneurship ran into one stumbling block of dishonesty, although we perceived it as our good fortune. When we collected newspapers, we bundled them up and sold them by the pound to the junkyard. (Abe Surath's) For a while, we decided that if we put stones or bricks in the bundles, we would get more money. We did, and we did. We were not found out, but it is not something I would now brag about...call me embarrassed.

53

We also dug deep tunnels in the back yard, covered them with boards and dirt and called them forts. We ate mulberries from the backyard tree. We pretended to smoke those horse chestnut pipes, made with a stick for a stem. We had glorious bonfires and marshmallow roasts in fall, after jumping and diving into the huge piles of leaves for days. Oftentimes the bonfires and marshmallow roasts became a neighborhood affair. We went to the Saturday Matinee with others at the Frolic Theater for just a dime. The popcorn was a nickel extra. There, we watched Gene Autry, Roy Rogers, Zorro, and other heroes, as well as the previews and the world news—even the World War II propaganda,. Life was full and enjoyable, both in the neighborhood, and with Jack as my buddy. I have tried to locate him, and if I do, I will share this, so he will know how much he meant to my life.

Keeping Busy-Staying Active

Unlike elementary students of today, we structured our own time and activities in the moment. We probably had more time to hone relationships than children do now. There was the "to and from school time", and working out the activities, with no innate structure. We certainly had more physical activity, walking to and from school, gym classes, recess, and our after school play. Looking back, it seems that children were not thought to be in danger from as many sources as now. One did not hear about kidnappings, sexual predators, or fear of strangers. And of course, there were no electronics to sabotage face to face communication, and plenty of time to practice it.

Our Community Center, downtown next to the Carnegie Library had Saturday afternoon roller skating. I also went there for my tap dancing and ballet lessons. It had a large center lobby where lots of people came and went, or just hung out after school, or especially on Saturday. Next door in the library were endless fascinating books, and an equally fascinating card catalog to explore, (using the Dewey Decimal System. I now think of it as a primitive form of Google). One of the Ordiway girls, either Kathleen or Harriet worked at the library. They were neighbors, with their yard abutting ours, but several years older than I. I went to the library frequently, often reading 5 or 6 books a week.

Summer time brought our annual city Day Camp at Central Park For two weeks, we swam, played games, sang songs, had nature study learned to build fires, and earned badges to be drawn on the brim of our sailor caps. It was a time of fun and achievement. The band shell served as meeting place and rain shelter, and the pool was where we swam and took our lessons. On the last day, our graduation ceremony included drinking Witches Brew. There were sticks and grass floating on the surface, and we were told and convinced that there were bugs and worms in there, and that it was made with water from the pool. I rather suspect it was Kool Aid with well washed grass and sticks. We bravely drank it down, passing the test of a real camper graduate.

Miss Jane Hatton, (my tap dance teacher) and Ted Dagwell were the main Day Camp teachers. I probably attended for 3 or 4 years, as did my siblings after me. My favorite activities were swimming, and building campfires, learning both the teepee method and the log cabin method. Fortunately we never had to rub two sticks together to get our fire building badge.

Tap dancing was a highlight and a mainstay of those years for me. As mentioned, Jane Hatton was the teacher, and Fern Bender was the pianist. I excelled and enjoyed it. I took ballet for a year, at my mother's pushing, and felt silly in the tutu's (with a tiny, hopefully invisible bit of pride underneath – after all, it was not proper for a tomboy.) I did not excel or enjoy it. I think it was the lack of rhythm in the music and dance that dulled my enthusiasm.

When I was 13, Miss Hatton consulted my mother and decided that I should get louder taps allowing the rhythm of my feet to help lead the other students. Unfortunately, that year was also when my body decided to grow several inches, rendering it gangly and more awkward for that season. I was not as coordinated, and became embarrassed after so many years of competence and enjoyment. My self-esteem suffered and I stopped taking lessons at the end of that year. I would guess that my sudden changes were puzzling to my mom and Miss Hatton. I know they were puzzling to me.

As I write, I have again taken tap. A senior center nearby offers it, and it was fun and enjoyable, good for my aging body. Doing something that is an old habit often helps new problems and it has been helpful to my problem feet and legs. I am no longer embarrassed by being awkward, and by no means the oldest person tapping. I hope to yet go back to it, after dropping out to deal with some medical problems.

I had a great deal of freedom to pursue activities. Bike riding, with no particular destination, often to the woods, was a favorite Saturday activity. There I might study wildflowers, collect butterflies, or play in the ponds, streams and grasses. I told our parents I was going, but no one asked when I would be back, or where I would be. It was understood I would be back for dinner. It was a small town, and the culture was not alert for troubles, as there seemed few of them. I spent many a Saturday following my own whims, connecting with nature, and enjoying the sunny days.

Downtown was a favorite destination a few blocks from home. For a while, AH and I would head straight to Heismans Shoe Store, with its magic fluoroscope machine. Used for fitting shoes, we put our feet under it over and over again, to see the bones of our feet. Certainly my feet must have been exposed to way more radiation than most people's at a young age.

There was another creative adventure that took place downtown too. Same culprits, AH and I. Our parents dropped us off on Sunday mornings at the Presbyterian Sunday School., a few blocks from both our house and downtown. They were not attending church. One day, we were bored with Sunday School and wandered out the door to head downtown. To our amazement, there was someone opening the parking meters and collecting the money. What a fascinating thing to watch! Each week after that, we went in one door of the church and out the other, heading downtown. We came home when we heard the church bell ring, signaling the end of church. Luckily we could hear it on Main Street.

One day, we went to church early. I suppose my mother wondered why we were so eager to go. As usual, we soon headed downtown, and when the bell rang, we went home, only to find out that Sunday school was just starting, and we were busted. We had mistaken the starting bell for the ending bell. I don't remember what the consequences were, but if I had been my parents, I would have had a hard time keeping from smiling at the ingenuity. I suppose we missed out on some good solid Presbyterian theology. On the other hand, we certainly became familiar with the sound of clinking coins, one ear tuned to distant bells. That may have fostered a different theology.

Obviously, learning theology was not a big priority either for me or for our family, although there was an underlying sense of reverence and spirituality.

A stronger pull for me during that stage of life was that entrepreneurial bent, whether with Jack Barber, or by myself. Out biking one day, I rode by Place's Plastic Company. Ever explorative, I found their trash pile out back, and saw a large box of twisted plastic cords in multiple colors. These were made to wrap around telephone cords to keep them from tangling. The ones I saw were likely rejects from their manufacturing. They may have been rejects, but to me they looked like more income. I took them home and sold them door to door. - 50 cents apiece, or a dollar installed (since to install them was to wind the coils around and around the cord until the full length was wound). My pediatrician had me install one in each of his offices. Altogether, I earned over $100 on those discarded cords, and if Place's Plastic ever knew about it, nothing was ever said.

A few months later, I got the money making bug again, and gathered up all the combs in our house, carefully washing them before I set out to sell them. One lady told me these looked used, and I staunchly faced her and told her they were not. Now I was a budding sociopath. Anything to make a sale at that age. Fortunately that bud wilted on the branch, and I have turned out to be a more honest adult.

When I was about 6, I got fascinated with picture post cards. My first ones came from our travels across the country. My grandparents then began sending cards from their trips to Florida. Eventually, the word spread that I was collecting and many people gave me cards. My dad sent cards when he was overseas. I was given an old family postcard album by an elderly cousin, holding addresses and signatures of many family members from years before.

Later, in Junior High, I wrote the governors of all 48 states and asked for a postcard of their capital building with their signature on it. I probably got half of those back, and when I sold my collection, for one thousand dollars in 1984, it contained autographs of Thomas Dewey, Adlai Stevenson, and other notable people who had replied to my request. There were over 7,000 cards, a few as many as 100 years old. I have often wondered what they might have been worth if I had sorted through them and researched more, or what they would be worth now. I got a lot of pleasure out of that collection, and saved the cards my father sent, and a few others.

My creative mind went into high gear as I discovered limericks in late grade school. The rhythm played in my head, my mind filled in the words, and the results sometimes got on paper, or just repeated themselves inside me. Unfortunately none of those results are around today. My father, who was known to write poetry himself, sometimes joined in. While I was writing this paragraph, this popped into my head, echoing the old process of back then.

Limericks for this and for that.
I wrote at the drop of a hat
The writing prolific
The feeling terrific
From many, my back got a pat.

This period of limerick writing may have been my first written or spoken self-expression that consistently generated recognition and strong positive responses from others. I felt secretly powerful, and somewhat mischievous at being able to comment humorously, or change the mood in a room. I don't remember doing this to get attention, but I surely remember enjoying it. This was my first experience of being able to influence the people around me by my own skills. .

In about 5th or 6th grade, my favorite uncle (Uncle Perry) gave me a microscope for Christmas. It was by far my most remembered childhood gift. He was a dentist, and an introvert, and understood my interest in and love of science and nature. I was totally involved and occupied with the microscope for several days afterward, and used it for years. My hours of interest and absorption portended my career as a medical technologist years later. Between the microscope, Jackie's chemistry set, and the outdoor nature times, I spent many hours exploring and dissecting the natural world, forming bonds far stronger those with people. The microscope from Uncle Perry solidified my interests, and gave me a special feeling toward him.

In Erickson's developmental stages of a child growing up, as interpreted by Josephine Kelsey, (see page 135) the ages from 9-12 are for developing a sense of success in doing and accomplishing things. It is easy to see that I accomplished and had success at many things during this time. This gave me the fuel to trust myself, increase my self-esteem, and enjoy my world. I was most fortunate that my elementary years had so many opportunities and activities that I took advantage of, and that my parents were permissive enough to let me find my way. Although I remained quite shy, I learned the beginnings of social skills, and also retained the skill of being alone and filling the time with enjoyable pursuits and learning. I was seldom lonely.

Going to Camp

Going away to camp is a "coming of age" activity – grown up enough to leave home and parents and be on one's own among peers. When I was probably 11, my mom suggested camp. Strange places didn't bother me, but different people, and no family around seemed a little scary.

I went to Camp Maqua that first year, the Bay City YWCA camp near Hale, MI which my mother had attended years before. It was a large camp, and I got lost in the crowd. I still didn't ask questions readily, so I got left out and left behind. I can remember standing outside the dining hall on Sunday morning, listening to others in "church", and wondering why I didn't know it was going to happen, or what I had missed in order to be there. I was too shy to walk in late, and after standing there, I went for a walk by myself. I declined going back there the next year. According to the internet, Camp Maqua is now a group of private residences.

That next year, we found a smaller camp between Mio and Rose City, called Camp in the Woods. I believe it may have been the Bay City YWCA camp. The smaller size made easier times, and I was able to make friends and have my first experience of a close girlfriend.

Mimi was a year or two older than I, so there was that teenage admiration and crush on her, envying her developmental stage, and being not yet there. When we were not thinking up things to do together, I enjoyed the horseback riding and swimming. Close behind were nature studies and crafts. Like many in that day, I laced a billfold together, and braided a lanyard out of plastic strips.

A camp memory of a more unusual kind was the night the whole camp got food poisoning. It started with a hotdog roast, and a couple hours later, campers and counselors alike were sick. The bathrooms were a block or so down a now dark dirt path. It was decided to bring large basins to each cabin and keep the counselors in the cabins to help their campers. We gathered around the basins for a communal experience of losing our dinners. Can you imagine being a sick counselor, being responsible for 8-12 girls who were also all sick? Fortunately, by morning, people were tired but healthy. Many years passed before a hotdog ever sounded good to me.

On Sunday, we gathered and walked halfway around the lake, to a small clearing. On benches made of tree trunks, we sat and had a Sunday service. I remember it as a peaceful time. I walked that path around the lake a few other times with friend Mimi too, and we, giggled about the possibility of visiting the nearby boy's camp, but always lost our nerve.

When I wanted to be alone, or felt left out, I had a secret place. Down the main road was a cedar swamp and woods, a magic sort of place with soft lighting and moss and mushrooms carpeting the ground. There were a few miniature ponds reflecting the beauty, and moss covered tree trunks lay like match sticks with baby trees beginning to sprout from them. Each square foot was a new surprise. The trees above formed a soft canopy, with patches of sky showing through lacy needles, and wandering branches. It reminded me of that favorite book, "Girl of The Limberlost" and my perception of Elnora's description of the Limberlost swamp. I told no one about this place, nor did I ever see anyone else near there. Looking back, I am surprised that campers had the freedom to just be gone like that, unaccounted for.

Camp songs still hide in my head, and flit through my memories, occasionally coming to the surface and even out my mouth once more. Tell Me Why, 99 bottles of Beer, What Did Dela-wear?, Stuck my Head In A Little Skunk's Hole, If All The Raindrops, and many others. Along with the songs are lines from the melodramas that the counselors used to perform for us. "Twas a dark and stormy night when my Nellie went away."

Family Matters

I want to segue back to family life. We were a family of four when we returned to Michigan. (My mom and 3 children.) In late 1945 or early 1946, my father came home from the Second World War and we again became a family of 5. Here are some memories of both.

One day there was a knock at our door, and my mom's college age sister stood there with her friend Celeste. They had hitch-hiked from Central Michigan College, about 30 miles away. People were driving less because of war time rationing, so hitch hiking was common, but not so much among young girls. My mother bawled her little sister out, put them up for the night, and took them back to school the next day. They were having a little daring fun. My Aunt

Jane is still living, age 89, and as I mentioned this to her a few months ago, we both had a laugh. She remembered the details.

My mother was basically a single mom, during the war - three kids and a household, and fortunately, my dad's pay. We were lucky to have that family and emotional support of my grandparents next door. I was in school all day, thus saw little of my mother unless she was fitting clothes on me during the weekend. She had two younger children to take care of and the household to keep up. We did not go on trips or vacations. I assume the war shortages of materials pushed everyone to travel less and use less. I imagine she had her hands full.

Mom was a stoic woman in many ways, and taught us to be the same. It was both a cultural characteristic and a family one. One day, I had written my name in many styles on a piece of paper. I wanted to show it off, and went out to the playground, expecting kudos. One of the guys started making fun of it, and ultimately grabbed it from me, ripping it. I came in the house crying and told my mom. Her response was "Never mind, Karen, maybe they were having a bad day. Just ignore it. Show them it doesn't matter" It was clearly her way to help me feel better, but it ignored my emotions, tried to explain their actions away, and basically told me to act as if it had not happened.

Every coping mechanism has an upside and a downside. There is certainly strength in acting as if nothing bothers one. And especially there is strength in not acting on emotions at the moment. However, I think I learned those lessons too well and had to unlearn them much later in life in order to validate my own emotions, and choose my actions with others. It's not always appropriate to go be nice to someone who has just messed with your life.

Another cultural factor in my generation was that women were taught to ignore their own needs and take care of others. I surely learned that too well. I grew up taking pride in being able to ignore my needs and feelings. Fortunately, eventually I learned better.

The upside of those teachings, however, stood me in good stead as a counselor. I was an excellent empathic listener, acutely tuned to the needs and feelings of others, and to find ways to help others even when I was going through difficult times. Had I learned more balance sooner, I would have been a better example for my kids and clients, and saved them some learning on the same subject.

One thing about our family that is still uncertain for me, is whether we actually all grew up as islands, which was how I felt. (With the possible exception of Becky and Charlie.) AH and I played together a lot while we were in the army. We were the constant in each other's life, and when we were apart, I remained shy and self-reliant. Then, when we came back to Michigan, we sort of grew apart. I hardly remember either AH or Becky after we came back, except for what I have written. Of course Becky was 8 years younger than I. As I grew older, I have faint memories of my sibling's friends, but not many of any of us doing things together, and no clear pictures of who my siblings were, who they were becoming, or how they spent their time. I have been known to be envious of my grandchildren's close friendship with one another. My puzzlement is whether this sense of isolation was just me, or whether it indeed was part of our family dynamics. I will be curious what the others say to this.

Dad Comes Home From War

Although I didn't sense it at the time, a strange drama played out under the surface the day my dad came home from overseas. We had not seen him for almost 2 years. He had been involved in some of the nastiest battles of World War II in the European theater. He and my mother had argued by letter, and even mentioned divorce. (I only found that out many years later, when I found the letters they had written). Dad was coming into Detroit on a train, and we drove down from Midland the night before, to stay with mother's cousins, Dolores and Welby.

The next morning, Dolores and Welby took my brother and I to the train to meet my dad, and my mother stayed home – presumably sick. It must have been a very stressful homecoming for an already stressed couple. I assume that my mother and father greeted each other back at Delores and Welby's house. How strange!

Dad had what would now be called PTSD and was then called 'battle fatigue' His hair was partly white, and he was somewhat quiet, diving behind the couch at the sound of a plane. He had been present at D-Day, The Battle of the Bulge, and the Battle of St. Lo to name a few. He had seen his jeep driver killed as a bomb exploded under the jeep. He had lost men that were under his command. When asked, he would not mention battles, or deaths, but preferred to talk about coming home to his family rather than being in the war. Even interviewed by the Midland Daily News he did not talk of war.

He spoke of the funny, the interesting, and the human stories of war. He told of searching a house, looking for German soldiers, hearing noises upstairs, and ascending the stairs with guns drawn. They quickly opened a closet door, where the noises came from, and found a large dog. The dog was hungry, whining, and as frightened of them, as they had been of his noises. Although they wanted to take him with them, they could not, and fed it from their rations, leaving the door open as they left.

Another time, around the same period, they went into what they thought had been a small enemy command center. They found large sheets of thin paper, various sizes and shapes, with notches cut out, and letters on them. They dutifully took these back to their experts assuming it was code, and not being able to decipher it. There was a good laugh all around when they were told that it was a women's dress pattern.

The rations that the army provided got tiresome after a while, and my dad felt responsible for the welfare of his men. One day, he had the time to wander around, finding a farm house that had chickens, and eggs. He traded his own cigarettes and other things, maybe even money, for some eggs and went back and commanded the men to fix their breakfast of scrambled eggs. What a feast after days of being hungry and cold, and living on rations.

These were the kind of war stories we heard.

After Dad came home, he asked if we had looked under the lining of the boxes his medals were in. Dad had won four medals: The Silver Star, Bronze Star, Air Medal, and Croix de Guerre. The article in the paper names some different medals, but those 4 are the medals our family has. He went and got the boxes, and showed us the beautiful gold cross which he had put under the lining of one. We later found that it was 10 carat gold, it was lace filigree, and lovely. My granddaughter Jillian has it now. Dad also sent back a German crèche set which graced our fireplace mantle each year. My picture was in the local paper with it. AH now has the remains of it. Some pieces have gotten broken or lost over the years.

Dad was promoted to Major Bradley just as he was being discharged. The promotion pleased him, but didn't pay the bills. He still needed a job. Grandpa Bradley, his father, wanted him to buy the funeral home, in partnership with his brother Bill. Grandpa was ready to sell, and both boys needed a job. My dad had the only embalmers license, having gone to school before the war. My uncle had only a funeral directors license, and had not gone to college. My mother became insistent that my dad should therefore own 2/3 of the business.

I am guessing that went counter to the family values, but it happened anyway. My parents fought a great deal about that issue, and my way of stopping the fights was to pretend to wake up and cry, causing them to stop talking and come in and take care of me. I probably was in about third grade. If there were leftover hard feelings in the family about the business split, I never heard any part of them.

Living In the Funeral Home

At some point, before my junior high years, we moved into the funeral home, making it easier for my dad to integrate family and work life. Grandma and Grandpa bought a small retirement house, about a mile away. Grandpa still came to work every day, while grandma became the baker of cookies for the neighborhood and grandkids.

At the funeral home, Grandpa was the constant patriarch of the business, even after retirement. He sat in the office, reading the Free

62

Press, cigar in mouth or hand, spittoon ready at his side. He generally had a game of solitaire either active or waiting. He wore his usual business clothes, with tie nearby, open collar on his white shirt, suspenders and business pants. He was as much a fixture in that office as the large ticking clock on the wall. That clock was reset remotely every day by Western Union, and in that era was an unusual possession.

Between the ticking of the clock, the smoke of the cigar, and the intermittent spitting sound, as cigar wastes flew toward spittoon, there was a definite "grandpa atmosphere" in sight, sound and smell. The smell remained long after the sight and sound was gone.

Growing up in a funeral home not only made our friends curious, but affected our lives in many ways. Just for basics, our social patterns, noise level and play activities were determined by what was happening downstairs. When there was a viewing, the visitation hours and the funeral itself demanded quiet from us upstairs. It also meant we could not go out and ride our bikes or skate around the driveway. This was an old building, built in 1911, and responded to footfalls with creaks. Creaking noises do not go well with funeral services. Friends were barred during visitation and funeral times. The rest of the time they were welcome.

A.H. and I let our curiosity lead us to hang over the spiral stairway banister when there was a rosary being said downstairs. We listened to the unfamiliar but mesmerizing sing song of reverence and respect. The words eventually stuck in my head from sheer repetition. When there was no business downstairs, that spiral staircase banister made an exciting slide with a steep and curved trajectory. Watch out for the post at the end, though!

Occasionally my dad would bring a child upstairs to play with us. These children were restless and tired of the grief of the grownups. They too were sometimes traumatized by loss, but children grieve differently from adults. They often alternate times of sadness or tears with "business as usual", fighting with sibs, playing with friends, or other normal activities. Living in the moment, as children do, has the advantage of giving moments and even hours of respite, in between the waves of loss, allowing for rest and a return visit to the state of normalcy.

Our school friends were sometimes inadvertently affected by our home. I can remember having a friend over, and my mother asking me to go downstairs and tell my dad dinner was ready. I went downstairs and my friend tagged along. There was a body in a casket in the viewing room. My friend started crying. What was familiar to me was scary to her. She went home upset, and had nightmares that night. Her mother was angry that we had let her go downstairs.

The casket showroom was in the basement. And behind that room, was another where the spare caskets were unwrapped and kept. There, folding metal frames with wheels called casket trucks stood ready to move caskets around.. When empty, they made good vehicles for us to use for races, or just ride around on a rainy day. Getting in the caskets was never done or even thought of. We had been taught that it was illegal and unethical. However, at high school reunions, 50 years later, people tell me they remember playing in the caskets. Memory is indeed slippery. That never happened! At least not on my watch, and I would guess not on AH's either.

The funeral business spawns many jokes. Our friends and even strangers assumed they were being funny when they said: "I hear you have a great lay-away plan", or "I heard people are just dying to get in". They were being funny, but we had heard the same jokes many times before. There were often questions about what "corpses" could or couldn't do. "Corpses" was the word our friends used. We were forbidden, calling them "bodies" instead. We were also not allowed in the prep room or embalming room, again with the explanation that it would be unethical and disrespectful of the family. Thus, we had no idea how bodies acted, or if they acted at all. I saw my first dead naked body on an autopsy table as I worked at the hospital, many years later.

As we approached our teens, our cruder friends wondered about, or accused those working at the funeral home of "practicing" on the bodies. I was too naïve to know that they were projecting their own curiosity about sex and the sexual act. Since my father always stressed that his work was to be respectful of the dead, and to serve the family, I didn't know what to say to such comments, even after finding out the meaning. I usually just walked away embarrassed.

Confidentiality is an issue in any family where someone works with other's private business. We were taught that no information went out of the house. My parents talked freely at home, or at the dinner table, and we heard much about what went on in the business and the town. My parents were not judgmental about others. The talk was more often factual. We were taught that "I don't know", was a proper answer to questions about others, even when it was technically a lie. It was the easiest way to honor confidentiality without betrayal. I used that same system raising our children, when my husband was also a funeral director and I worked at the hospital. Ethics and ethical boundaries have been very strong in our family, for several generations, serving me well. I am grateful for the training.

In those days, the funeral homes in small towns also ran the ambulance. There was no such thing as an Emergency Responder, apart from passer's by, or ambulance drivers and policemen. The business phone often rang in the middle of the night, and my dad, and much later my brother would get up and go to the scene of an accident, or to a home where someone was ill or hurt, and then to the hospital.

We, in junior high or younger, were taught to answer that emergency phone and get the necessary information from a possibly upset person. The information included location and directions, as well as call back number. We then relayed the information to whoever was on call, and sent them out with the ambulance or hearse, whichever was needed.

I remember a night time blizzard, with parents gone to separate places. I was in High School, my brother in junior high. We got a call and could not get hold of my dad. So we hopped in his old Dodge with the broken windshield wipers, and I drove, and my brother reached out the window and worked the wipers. We drove around, found his car, and delivered the message. At the time, it felt like an adventure, but also a necessary act. Others were counting on us.

There were still phone operators, and at times, my dad would call and ask them to call the number where they were to be that evening; A primitive personalized form of call forwarding.

The funniest ambulance story happened when my dad was taking a patient from Midland Hospital to the University of Michigan Hospital at night by ambulance. Because the patient was very ill, one of the interns from the hospital rode along. Interns are eternally tired, and this one was no exception. On the way home, by now past midnight, the young doctor went to sleep on the cot in the back of the ambulance. They stopped for gas, and an attendant appeared to pump gas. The back door opened and the intern got out of the car, stretching and yawning, on his way to the bathroom. The attendant, thinking the car was a hearse, and the man a ghost, or a dead man walking, got wide eyed, panicked, and ran back into the station, locking the door behind him. My father explained, and the still doubtful attendant finally was willing to finish pumping gas.

The State Funeral Directors Association had a family meeting once a year with picnics and entertainment for the kids. Finally we didn't have to hear any more corny funeral home jokes for a day.

At home, we were introduced to salesmen, and other funeral directors who were around our place on business. My dad was eternally and compulsively hospitable, offering lunch or dinner with our family to anyone who came. This meant my mom had to keep food in the house, keep the house picked up, keep up her activities, continue to run the household, parent three children, and have meals ready on demand. One time, a salesman left some money under his plate. My parents were both insulted.

I often get asked how living in the funeral home affected my life. I have already spoken of the physical and schedule differences it made. Let me mention the character impact. I certainly learned that life is fragile, that one cannot ever count on seeing anyone again. I was constantly around stories of those who went to work and died on the way home, or were going to a family party and died on the way there or children who drowned or got hit by cars. It left me with a strong drive to complete all personal and business transactions in my relationships. It is important to me to do what needs doing, and say what needs saying before parting, or for that matter, before going to bed in a marriage.

Later when married, at first, I could hardly let go of my husband to let him go to work if we were fighting and were not in a good space. I have mediated the rigidity of that, but I still attempt to bring things to a close or a positive sense before saying goodbye. The closer the relationship, the more important. No unfinished business, or as a friend once said about relationships , wicks must be trimmed and fuel must be clean to keep the flame burning bright. Interestingly, I also have worked around death for most of my working life.

Self-Reliance – Asking for Help

As you can see, we were encouraged to grow up fast and take responsibility at a young age. It built self-esteem, a sense of accomplishment, and being able to count on ourselves. We learned to problem solve well on our own. We were trusted with important information and actions. Above all, we were encouraged to be self-reliant and not ask for help. That teaching was also somewhat out of balance, and it was many years before I gave up being "superwoman" and started asking for and accepting help. I taught my kids a version of that too and they have carried on the job of learning to create balance in their own lives.

One day, at about age 10 or 11, I slipped on the waist high climbing bars on the playground and landed hard. My crotch area was so bruised it was soon dark black and blue. The pain and not being able to walk well, or sit easily probably lasted about two weeks. I did not even mention the incident to my parents. I saw the bruising when I got a hand mirror to look. There was not much could have been done in that case, other than aspirin and empathy. Both might have helped, but I never gave it a chance or a thought. Both that cultural and family stoicism kept me on my own.

When about 13, I had poison ivy which kept me out of school for two months and in bed for part of that. I nearly lost an arm, and was pretty miserable. Mom was gone one day, and Dad working downstairs. He came up for lunch and I asked him to help apply medicine on my arms or legs. I really could have used the help, but more than that, I wanted his support and company. I was lonely, itchy and tired of being sick. His answer was "Karen, you are such a big girl that you can do that yourself", and he went back downstairs. He may have been shy around his 13 year old daughter. He may have been busy downstairs, afraid of poison ivy, or just teaching me the same stoicism he used in his own life. I went back to bed and cried. Had I been more assertive, I could have spoken up, but I was not and did not. It was difficult to ask for help in the first place.

My sibs have all talked about not asking for help, or being told not to. For whatever reason, we all learned and decided not to ask for help, and to take care of things on our own My mother taught us a similar thing differently when she told me to think of what the other person was going through, rather than to acknowledge what I was going through. A lesson too well learned. .

My Dad had another whole side to his personality which was all about service and helping others. He, more than once, went out of town on business, took a homeless person out for lunch, listened to their life story, and gave them some cash.

One school year, there was a famous violinist coming to Midland to play for the high school students, and later do a concert in town. He was partially sponsored by the Rotary Club, and at that time my dad was the president. My friend Libby Lee, was also a violinist and was in bed with a broken back, and could not go see the concert. I asked dad if the violinist could go to Libby Lee's house to visit her. Dad quickly arranged that, and Libby Lee was both embarrassed and thrilled.

I am grateful that he validated my wish to help a friend. He did many things like that for others. He spent Christmas Day transporting others to and from the hospital so they could have Christmas with their families. At his death, many people spoke of special favors, and of their love and gratitude for my dad.

Unfortunately, his generosity was mostly for those other than his family. Before he went overseas, he had been more involved with his family, but when he came back, and bought the business, he lived to help others. He was partly the little boy who lost his mother at a young age, and couldn't ask for help, and partly enjoying helping others, with the resultant reputation and admiration

And so, we learned that strong self-reliance. There is nothing wrong with self-reliance. It can be a real strength. There is also nothing wrong with asking for and receiving help from others. It makes life much easier and freer to assume we are all connected, and that many people care, and that asking for help is a natural part of being in the human tribe. I do it more easily now, no longer feeling shame or inadequacy if I need help.

In Bob's (my youngest son) first book, and in his work as a consultant, he uses this concept in the spiritual sense, and says that self-reliance is deadening, while God-reliance is life giving. We cannot do for ourselves what God can do for us, and we also cannot do for ourselves what our fellow human beings can do for us at times. Amen.

Special

These days, when I get together with my sibs, if anyone calls anyone "special" we all laugh. It is an "in" joke. We all knew that we grew up thinking that we, our family, or our town was special in

67

ways that they were not. We learned that "special" was to be recognized and carried weight in one's standing with others, or with oneself. We were told at various times that our family was special because of ancestry, intelligence, success, or other things that really were more common than special. Our town was special for some vague reasons - I suppose intelligence and resources. I was special because I was smarter than most and thus carried responsibility for giving more to the world. This attitude of "special" was a sort of arrogance playing in the background of all our interactions and actions and was subtly pervasive in our lives.

I think it was mostly my mother who brought that forth in the family. She often mentioned how we or the family were more, better, or different from others. For her, this seemed to be a way of attempting to instill self-esteem or a sense of responsibility. But the downside was arrogance or separation from others, a setting apart. I suppose it was for her, a way of propping up her own self-esteem. Toward the end of her life, it became one of her major defenses, as she isolated herself, and criticized others. What had been subtle in her life became her main platform of self-defense.

When I was younger, the clothes my mother made for me were always "special." They were made of pre-war material, using hand me downs. Thus they were finer cloth, different patterns and bore her creative special touches of buttons or lace. As she fitted the clothes, she often told me that I would be the only one who had clothes made out of cloth of that quality, or in that style. I know she took pride in her own creativity, and in making my clothes. But it was clear that the uniqueness fed her, and that she hoped it fed me too. It did, but it also set me apart.

There was my two sided reaction to special-ness. On one hand, the pride, special-ness and attention. On the other hand, the self consciousness from being noticed as "different" by the other kids, and knowing I didn't quite fit in – the separation.

In later life, I enjoyed unique clothes and calling attention to myself with clothes, but it was always my choice as to when I was willing to get the extra attention and like it. And indeed, though the attention was nourishing, it sometimes also nourished <u>my</u> arrogance.

Here is something I wrote, as I was working out this issue in my own life:

"In my family there was a lot of emphasis on being special. This was reinforced by words and actions "Don't forget what your family has meant to this town" "God gave you more brains than usual. Its your responsibility to use them to help the world.

With "special" comes a sense of individual strength, sometimes false, With ordinary comes a sense of belonging, and the strength of community.

Without a sense of ordinariness, there is no room for true collaboration among equals, for empathy, or an honoring of alikeness. There is only a sense of being better, worse, different, more, or less than another, which equals separation from that other.

Each moment calls for the challenge of recognizing both special ness and ordinariness in oneself, and in the other. Each life situation calls for choosing whether to emphasize one or the other. Each day calls for integrity and lack of fooling oneself in this choice.

There is no doubt that feeling special can be a healthy characteristic to teach children. I'm grateful for the teaching. It's important to remember that teaching ordinariness is equally healthy." (About 1990).

On to Junior High

7th grade was the beginning of Junior High and meant changing classrooms for each class. I was a little intimidated, but adjusted quickly. The anticipation had been worse than the real thing. The building itself was right next to my grade school.

At some point, we were assigned poetry for our English class. This seemed more serious than the adventures with limericks had been. I soon learned there was a competition. Midland schools had a poetry book, Fledgling Wings, published each year containing outstanding poetry from junior and senior high students. I began to write to get published. Here are two of my poems from Junior High.

A PERFECT DAY
How wonderful to make the plans
To guide me through the day
And when that day is over with
To know that I can say:
"I've finished all I planned to do"
"I've nothing more to tend
"Today has really been worthwhile"
"I'm sorry it must end.
Don't let it end – instead let live
To shape your other days
Just use it for a pattern
To guide your future ways

DEATH
Though life is for the living
And your faith is very strong
Still it seems when a loved one goes
That something's very wrong
"They should have lived a little longer"
You say to yourself and then
One must stop to realize

That we are only human
We're given the power to live our lives
And if we live them well
We earn a life beyond the earth
Where time will never tell
So the living go on living
Although things aren't quite the same
We remember the good that the person has done,
And accordingly set our aim.

Poetry helped me express what was inside. My poetry was not very complicated, or even good compared so some of the same age in that little booklet, but was a true reflection of my growing philosophy of life, and the decisions I was making about how to perceive life. Of course the musings about death came about from being a child growing up in the funeral business. Interesting that both poems talk about using the present as a pattern for the future.

Another class brought embarrassment and curiosity, as it likely does to most Junior High or young teen students. The Physical Education locker room was the scene. I was late maturing, and self-conscious about it. I glanced surreptitiously at the pubic hair and developing breasts of the other girls, while hoping they would not glance at mine. I tried not to let anyone know I was looking. And at the same time, I imagined that everyone knew I was looking and ashamed. I suppose I was not alone. I was never sure I measured up. And of course I couldn't settle that issue for myself. Junior high is such an age of tentative self-image and bouncing emotions and tension for so many.

On the other hand, I definitely measured up on the trampoline. It was similar to jumping out of a swing, or off a diving board. It was my favorite part of 8th grade gym, even though I had a bladder which didn't quite want to cooperate. (Folded toilet paper seemed to work just fine to hide my defect). We jumped and landed on our feet, our seat, our back, and our front, and finally learned to turn flips. We were kept safe by the rest of the class lined up with hands ready around the entire edge of the trampoline. Should we bounce too far toward the edge, many hands would push us back toward the center and keep us from falling. As an adult, I was on a trampoline with my grandkids when I was over 50. I was a little more awkward, and a lot out of practice, but enjoyed feeling those old feelings. I am so glad I have had the experience and the memories. I suspect my actual time on a trampoline is over, even though it still pulls me toward attempts when I am near one.

My friend Libby Lee, the one who played the violin, broke her back on that trampoline. She was in bed in a body cast for several months. I used to go over and read to her and play paper dolls. I hated paper dolls—still the tomboy—but I did it to entertain her, and because she was my friend.

Poison Ivy and Soap Operas

Ever the entrepreneur, I was at the golf course one spring looking for golf balls in the pond and weeds. The more I found, the more I could sell. Unfortunately, I also found poison ivy, unrecognized, along with the recognized golf balls. Two days later, my face broke out, and then the rest of my body, and then defied the usual chamomile lotion and poison ivy remedies. Poison Ivy does not spread after the initial sap of the plant is washed off, but one can get a systemic allergy to it. If that happens, the immune system reacts over the whole body, and the original rash spreads. Finally I went to the doctor, with rash, and swollen arms, legs and face. He gave me Benadryl, more unrefined in those days, and more likely to create drowsiness. The itching was such that I stuck my arm or face in the freezer to stop it, crying with frustration. Or I might be soaking in Potassium Permanganate baths, leaving my skin somewhere between tan and purple. The rest of the time I was sleeping from the Benadryl. For weeks, turning into months, I could not go to school. At one point, there was worry about my losing my arm from the swelling. My fingers were so swollen and peeled that I did not have finger prints.

I was occasionally able to hold a book to read, but a lot of my time was spent listening to the soap operas on the radio. That was my "do not disturb" time in the afternoon. With not much else to do, they were addictive. What would happen next? There was Young Doctor Malone, One Man's Family, The Guiding Light, Ma Perkins, The Romance of Helen Trent and others. After school came Sergeant Preston and the Green Hornet. In the evening was Perry Mason, Nick and Nora Charles, Inner Sanctum, Baby Snooks, Dagwood and Blondie, Henry Aldridge, The Life of Riley (which had Digger Odell, the Friendly Undertaker)., and Fibber McGee and Molly. There was also the Lone Ranger, and the Phillip Morris Playhouse with Johnny calling out "Callllll Forrrrrr Phillip Mooooor...eeeeesss..!!!.

Television was in the near future. I saw my first television when I was in 10th grade. but with the soap operas on the radio, and the resulting extra prizes to order (like secret decoder rings), I thought life was as good as it could be while scratching away my days.

After the poison ivy began to go away, the doctor decided I should get poison ivy shots. It must have been too soon because I broke out all over again, and spent another couple weeks in bed.

The memories of radio bring back an evening when my brother and I went with our parents to a dinner. Dad was to be the after dinner speaker. (It may have been Toastmaster's Club.) AH and I did not want to go because we might miss the Lone Ranger, starting at 7:30. When Dad got up to speak, he looked at his watch and announced that no one had to worry about his speaking too long, because his kids had ordered him to be home for the Lone Ranger at 7:30. As usual, my control issues and embarrassment came rushing forth, since I was getting uncalled for attention, without warning. I feel an occasional twinge of that now with unexpected attention, but then it was full blown teenage angst.

Don't get me wrong, I love being the center of attention, but only when and where I want.

My Acting Debut, and Other Adventures

I loved the attention in Junior High when I starred as a minor character (Miss Persimmons), in the play, Mary Poppins. My parents had talked me into the venture.   Miss Persimmons, a prim and indignant woman, is talking with Mary Poppins in the park,. The wind catches her umbrella and she flies up in the air. I was rigged out with a parachute harness and wires, and on cue, rose up into the top part of the stage and flew across, acting very surprised and huffy. I thoroughly enjoyed it.

My social life was still scarce, but slowly beginning. One weekend I was invited to a cottage with a friend and her family. We two were out exploring the lake, and waded to a very small island, not too far offshore. I noticed that it was very deep off the other side of the island, and dove off, hitting my head on the bottom of the lake and bending my neck back. I was extremely lucky, as this is one of the common ways that young people end up paraplegic from a spinal cord injury. I just got a stiff neck.

In 1949, Midland, (and many parts of the country) had a polio epidemic. Two people I knew died. One was Linda Poffenberger. The Poffenbergers had two adopted children, and none of their own. Both children died of polio within a week that fall. Their mother never quite recovered from losing her only two children. Linda was one of the little girls who had been at my birthday parties 10 years before.

This same summer, my father, and my 5 month old brother Deke got very ill.(I have not mentioned Dekie before, but will shortly.) We were worried about polio, because, not only was it prevalent, but as you recall, my dad ran the ambulance, and therefore was around the sickest people. In later years, my mother blamed my brother's illness on my dad, and it became a wedge between them. There was never any proof of what happened to my brother, except that the doctors thought he had encephalitis. There was some conjecture about chicken pox.

I was also very ill that summer, and left with one arm more contracted than the other, and some other imbalances in my body, and so there was speculation that I may have had polio. If so, I was most fortunate compared to many others who had it. I have not had symptoms of post-polio syndrome, and other than my feet, I do not have any symptoms which could possibly be connected to polio, making it an unlikely speculation.

Deke

My brother, Deke Watrous Bradley was born January 10, 1949. He of course was named after my father, whose nickname was Deke. As before, I do not remember my mother's pregnancy, or Deke's birth. I would have been in 8th grade. Deke was a precocious and lovely, little baby, and then, at 5 months old he got ill. He was ill for a long time, and I remember the bedroom door being shut, and the room darkened. I remember the house got much messier than usual. His illness was not discussed with us. I later learned that my mother was feeding Deke with an eye dropper, and that one day she took him outside and took pictures of him, because she thought he was going to die. I remember not wanting to bring my friends home to a messy house. Typical teenage narcissism. My mother must have been emotionally and physically exhausted. I can only imagine the family dynamics that led to no sharing and exhausted parents, who were at odds about whose fault it was that their child was ill. I wish my parents had talked to us, and asked us to help with his care and the house. I am curious what AH and Becky remember about that time.

Several months, maybe even a year after Deke got better physically, he began withdrawing from others and from the world around him. Today we would recognize that immediately as autism, but back then it was a total mystery, and parents were often blamed. He had begun to talk before he withdrew. He could say "baa baa sh..." for Baa Baa Black Sheep. He could say "sis" and he would often rock and hum to music. After he was ill, he had bouts of extreme pain that may have come as he was teething, although we never knew. At those times, he would throw himself on the floor, rub his face on the carpet and scream. He stopped talking altogether. One doctor said "He found the world a hell of a place to live in, and decided not to live there" That seems unusually kind and perceptive for that period in time—mostly my parents took some blame

Deke became totally nonverbal, although still very quick and normal physically. He was unusually facile with his hands, and obviously intelligent. Because he did not talk, we could not tell what he wanted or was going to do. He often wandered off, and several times ended up in the neighbors houses, occasionally early in the morning. It was still a small town with not many locked doors. He required constant watching and Becky got the brunt of that. I don't know why I was not asked to care for him much. He was never a violent child, and our family, although frustrated, and having to keep him safe, and not lose him, did not use punishment for him. Becky has said that she got frustrated at times, as any 8 or 9 year old with responsibility for a young sib might do. Later, when my mother was older, she appeared to not be able to forgive herself for not being able to help Deke.

We took him on a family camping trip, and other experiences, hoping that between being with family, and having new experiences, something might change. It did not. My mother took him to many kinds of doctors. I remember going with her to what I now think was a chiropractor. He was manipulating Deke's head and neck, and Deke screamed and screamed. Nothing changed. Deke lived at home with us for four and one half years, and then when my mother was pregnant again 4 years after Deke's birth, she and my father agreed to begin to look for an institution to put Deke in.

That was a common thing in those years, although those who have seen the movie or read the book about Temple Grandlin know that there were exceptions. It was a long and difficult search that my mother undertook. I imagine it was also a heartbreaking decision. She traveled the entire state of Michigan, and many places out of state, to finally find what she considered a satisfactory place. The place she found was near St. Louis Missouri, across the river in Godfrey/Alton, Illinois. It was called Beverly Farm. It had been founded by a physician who had a daughter who needed special help. He wanted a place where the children could have a permanent home, and work on the farm, growing up useful and loved. It was not unlike a college campus, with many red brick buildings, and people walking around outside. At that time, there were people there who ranged in age from babies to older adults. Deke was put in the nursery building with Mama Barnes in charge. My mother left him there with a heavy heart.

After Deke had been there several years, Dr. Smith, the son of the founder of Beverly Farm, died, and the parents banded together to buy the farm, and incorporate it as a non-profit institution. My parents became active on boards and committees, helping oversee the running of the corporation. They visited as often as they could. My father died in 1968, and my mother continued to go to Beverly Farm, and be active there. My mother had her own difficulties in the years after my father's death. She went through some mental illness, which I now think may have started around menopause. She and my father also had been drinking excessively before my dad's death, and my mother continued that pattern unchanged. As her life became more unmanageable, she became less competent, and eventually stopped going to Beverly Farm. We children were raising our families and oblivious to what became a sad situation. When our mother's life necessitated us stepping in, we realized that she had not been to see Deke in several years. In about 1987, I went by Beverly Farm twice within a year, and visited on my cross country trips. I had no idea that at that time that he was listed as an orphan, with no one from the family looking over him.

I had not seen Deke for maybe 20 years. My visit affected me profoundly, and I cried for several hours off and on after I left. Here is what I wrote:

"After seeing my approximately 39 year-old autistic brother for the first time in several years. I was extremely affected. I was startled at the look of fear on him, startled at the family resemblance. I cried and grieved for what had been lost- for me—for him,- for our family- for the world. (About 1987)

Little brother – long gone
Frightened
No where to run
"They" make him stay
He rocks far away.
We eat cookies,
He and I
He, ravenous and greedy – for cookies
I curious and greedy – for a brother
I cry
I talk to him
I show him pictures
Mom, brother, sister
He puts his thumb over their faces
To make them go away?
He runs
I say wait
He waits
He has learned to obey
But no one taught him
To kick at the sidewalk,
Looking like his brother
Or to look pensively at the trees
Like his sister
Or to set his jaw just so
Like most of the family
I am his kin
He is my brother
Scared
In the world but not of it
Trained
Broken
Not happy
Hungry
Move fast
Don't look back
Swing

Rock
Grunt
Sensitive and knowing eyes
When not haunted
Sure feet
When not running away
He is the small fox of my dream memories
Unprotected
Kept in captivity
Always wild
Inhabitant of another world
Wearing his soul on his face
My brother
Echoes from long ago
"Sis"
"Patty Cake
Baa Baa Sh…(his past words for Baa Baa Black Sheep)
The aborted person echoes through time.
Gone since four years old
Never to be found again
Only remembered
And reminded
By his shadow and his echoes
Now present
My brother"

This writing may sound as if Deke was not happy, or Beverly Farm was not adequate. He was not happy, but Beverly Farms was adequate and more. It was an institution taking care of many people; necessitating guidelines, rules, and structure. But I never saw any signs of inappropriate care or of lack of care or caring. I believe that Beverly Farm has always cared about its residents as much as possible given the circumstances. Eventually, my siblings and I started regularly visiting. We were now the ones on the boards and committees. I know that the place has overcome many obstacles and changes over the years to keep it a caring and individualized place for the residents.

As for Deke being happy, he might have been happier in a home with a caregiver or family where he could be alone a lot, and still be safe. It seemed to me that trapped in his body was a sensitive, intelligent person who was frightened by other people and had lost the means to express himself in normal ways. And now he was, constantly around others, many of who were noisy, screaming, making loud noises, attempting physical assaults on those around them, and of varying degrees of "normal" It must have been a nightmare for a boy/man who wanted quiet and little contact. He also had been put on medications, with my parent's permission, because he got violent and angry when he went through adolescence. It has been hard for us, and must have been hard for his caregivers, to try and figure out what to do with a child, and then an adolescent, and finally an adult who could not tell them anything.

My siblings and I have gone to Beverly Farm twice yearly for many years. AH felt compelled to take my mother there once more before she died, and we did. It has been good for us to be together as a group, and good for Deke, as he knows us instantly, and has often enjoyed car rides, ice cream, new shoes, and walking or just sitting and watching trees. With us, he can have a measure of solitude and quiet with people who care, not often available in his living situation.

I have agonized over the years, as have my siblings, attempting to find ways to provide quality and satisfaction in his life, with a little peace thrown in. The last several years, medications had to be changed because they were no longer manufactured, and he grew increasingly tense, obsessive, frustrated, and often self-injurious, picking at his hands

Deke died suddenly and unexpectedly while I was writing this, in 2012. He stood up to go somewhere and collapsed, the day after a tooth extraction. He died immediately. They are guessing it might have been a pulmonary embolism, I am guessing it was a heart attack. We had made the decision a few years ago that he was to have a standing Do Not Resuscitate order in this kind of circumstance. We were all grateful that we had done that. He was 63. He died July 28, 2012. Rest in peace dear brother. I am still grieving these months later. I still cry as I edit this part of my story.

I had often wished and prayed that his life could either be helped, or that he could have an early and quick end. It was the latter that happened. I cried not for him, as it felt to me that he was finally at peace. But I cried because I loved him, and because there are now only 4 siblings, and because going to see Deke was something that drew the rest of us together, and because while he was alive, there was hope of help. The hope was never fulfilled. There is a brother shaped hole in me.

I would like to believe that he is now talking and with my parents, and that everything is beautiful. That belief is not solid for me. I have only question marks, and hope. What happens after death is, for me, part of the mystery of life and death But I do know that I am grateful that he is not unhappy any more. And I am grateful that I loved him, and that he knew we loved him.

Earlier in my life, I had little to do with Deke while he was still home. I was an individuating teen ager. And then I was in college. And then I was married and had three children of my own in rapid order. I said before that I had no idea that my mother was caring for a child that she thought would die. And that Becky was carrying the burden of care at a young age. I was little affected back then, but I have been greatly affected in the past 25 years.

Below is something I wrote when Beverly Farms was defending its position as a good care agency. There are people who think that all residents need to be taken out of this farm campus- like setting and put in group homes in the community. It became a legal issue at the state level, and Beverly Farms asked for letters and opinions. We were not to mention our resident's name. so I used his initial. It is written about 5 years before I wrote this.

"The search for the right place started nearby, and widened. My mother, who did most of the searching, was looking not just for a place, but for a home, and surrogate parents for the son that she was grieving for. Her grief was that there seemed no help or cure. Her love drove her to find a loving place.

I do not know how she came upon Beverly Farm, but I do know that with some joy, and many tears, she decided on Beverly Farm as the home where D could be happy, be surrounded by other loving people, have a defined community to relate to and get whatever care and treatment he needed. She even found a surrogate mother for him in Mama Barnes, who took care of the nursery back then.

. Over the years, things changed, and state and federal laws played a bigger part in facilities for people like D, than love and community did. Planned treatment and educational goals moved in. Each step was monitored and gradually the monitoring and documentation seemed to take more time than the care of the residents. Beverly Farms weathered those changes and continued to provide a home, family and community for D. When we visit, the staff knows him and can tell us about his activities. They know, and they care.

D is now in his 60's. He is retired from work and school at Beverly Farm, and is spending time at the Senior Center where there are activities for him, and his beloved rocking chair to rest in. We are the second generation to visit him, and starting on the third. He knows us when we visit, but the time in the visit always comes when he wants to go "home" to his family in his building. He enjoys our visits for the ice cream, and the new shoes, and tentative kisses on our cheeks, but it is clear that we are not his family, except by biology. Beverly Farms has been true to my mother's hopes and choices for her beloved son. It has provided love, structure, and development through more than a half century.

From time to time, we look around to see what else is available. We have listened to the arguments of those who say that Community Living might be better, and we maintain that Beverly Farms is a Community, and provides the best possible place for our brother D to be living."

As I write this book, we will be going this month, September, 2012, one last time to Beverly Farm to have a memorial service with the people who have cared about and for Deke all his life. And then he will be interred next to my parents in the Midland Cemetery. He was cremated.

We interred him on June 4, 2013, surrounded by our cousins and friends. It was a beautiful late spring day, and the memories were real and deep. We loved and were loved, and so was he.

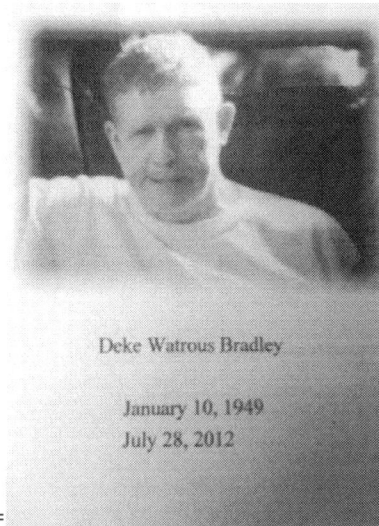

Deke Watrous Bradley

January 10, 1949
July 28, 2012

Becky and Deke   Karen and Deke   A happy guy swinging

Me
From Kindergarten to Junior High

Easter in Caro-Playhouse that
Grandpa Dutch built in back.

Family Portrait –probably 1950

Me, second row back, on right

A.H, tap dance
costume

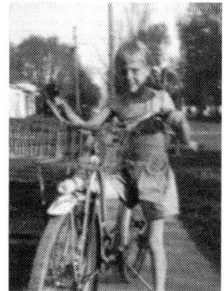

Becky

HIGH SCHOOL AND COLLEGE – 1950-58

Ages 15-23

Moving Our House

The year I entered High School, we moved – house and all. One day we were living on Buttles Street, and a few weeks later we were in the same home but now at 118 W. Collins. The funeral home needed more parking spaces, and the house was in the way.

My parents talked of many options, although I don't believe children were included in the talks. My mother didn't like living in the funeral home. There was that bit about keeping kids unnaturally quiet, and preparing meals without notice for sales people. But I suspect she thought my dad might spend more time at home if business and home were in separate places. He often found one more thing to do downstairs, and then spent the evening at work after a full day at work. Deke was either newly born or on the way. And the next year, I would be in high school, and AH in Junior High, with more opportunities and even necessities for a social life as teens.

Whatever it took, someone came up with the idea of moving the house. I am assuming it was financially useful too. It would also be of advantage to have a home with a known history and repair records.

Once that was decided, the work commenced. The lot on Collins Street was purchased. With now four children, we needed an extra bedroom. They decided to put an addition on the house, consisting of a master bedroom and bath downstairs, along with back entry way and breakfast nook. There would be a new basement dug and a new garage. This was a complicated project.

When this sizable two story house was actually moved, I can remember it going down the road. Wires had to be unhooked in its path, and trees trimmed. I suspect they went about 2 blocks down Buttles Street to Ashman, and then out Ashman to Collins, turning left on Collins.

(I realize that these directions are meaningless to non-Midland people, but fun to contemplate if you know the town.) My memory is blank about whether the furniture was in the house, or moved out. Certainly breakable or easily movable things would have had to come out. I know they took down the large brick chimney.

My sister says the house was moved during the school year. But she did not go to a school where she would have seen it, and she thinks she remembers seeing it being moved. I think it was moved during the summer, but I am at least sure we moved in during the summer. I remember meeting the new neighbors: the Brooks kids down the street, Marleigh, Audrey and John, the Prills across the street, Sonny and Joanie. The Asch's down the street, Myrna and Ellen, and many others. One of our first introductions to the neighborhood was going over to the Brook's home and seeing their TV. This would have been 1950 or 51. None of us had seen a TV before, and even the snow on the screen, and the test patterns were interesting. This new neighborhood was going to be fun! With my adolescence, and assurance that the new neighborhood held potential friends, it was not so hard to leave the playground behind.

So there we were – same house, different address and different views. It is interesting that when I picture the views out the windows of that house, my younger memories are of the Buttles Street neighborhood, and my older ones of the Collins Street area.

I lived in this house for more years than any other. This includes up to the present time. It holds memories for me from before the army days, as well as through grade school, and up through college visits back home. I want to describe a couple of the strongest memories of parts of that home.

My bedroom, shared for a time with Becky, surrounded me with my own choices for colors and design. My mother had asked my suggestions and I had asked for a dark blue ceiling with shine-in-the-dark-stars, white walls, and a blue bedspread. Instead of arguing with my unorthodox choices, she followed through, and I loved going to bed at night, seeing the Big Dipper and the North Star shining. Mom finished it off with blue and white striped curtains. I loved that room! Being accepted for my ideas, and having them turn out so well, set me up to try my own decorating as an adult, even when it was not always similar to most people's.

One day, maybe while mom was pregnant for Charlie, or maybe when they were to put Deke in his own room, she approached me and told me I would be sharing my room with Becky. This was the first time I had ever been asked to share a bedroom. I felt entitled to a room of my own, and was not at all happy. Entitlement or not, Becky moved in.

Becky was probably around 7, and at her age, wanted to copy her big sister. She wanted to go where I went, wear what I wore, and do what I did. If I got out a plaid skirt and white blouse, she would find one too. I was having none of that. I am sad to say that I was not a kind sister, and did everything I could to discourage her company and interaction with me. I suppose I needed my own identity at that time. Too bad I was not a little more mature. We both might have been different now.

I proceeded to establish my own half of the closet, and let her know that there was an invisible line down the center of the room. She could only cross it to go in the closet, the rest of the time she had to stay out of my half.

Becky and I are very different in character (and she would not want to copy me anymore).Even then, she loved dolls, and girly things, and I was still quite the tomboy. She probably kept things in order, and put to shame my messy habits. If our lives now are any indication, it was most likely. However, we don't draw lines down the middle of our relationship any more, and though we might not agree on many things, we would defend each other and care for each other at the drop of a hat. We have shared the trip to Beverly Farm twice a year for years now, and the 9 hours in the car each way has helped us forge a strong bond, which does not dissolve when we get back and resume our separate lives. I am grateful.

There was one more space in that house which made me curious and explorative. The upstairs bathroom (the only bath in the house until we added on), was big – probably about 10x13 feet. Along one side was a closet with a door at one end. One bare light bulb lit the full length, showing hooks and shelves along the side, and a dark and deep set of shelves at the back, full of interesting things. This was the space I often explored. There were the usual towels and washrags, but then there were these other things. They were the sort of things that kids wonder about and only grownups know the answer to. I learned what some of them were called later – enema bag, a heating pad, a vaporizer, and an old ultraviolet sun lamp. And then there was a funny round rubber disk in a little case. As an adult, I knew what a diaphragm was, but back then, I had no idea. And as you can guess, I didn't ask.

I only explored that space when no one was home. I instinctively knew that some of the things involved body functions and possible uses that I had no idea about. I had to use my imagination, and it was not always accurate. I was naïve, and curious. Even the smell of that closet is stored in my memories.

Midland High

In 10th grade, I entered Midland High School. A new neighborhood and a new school in one year. Now I was growing up! One year after my graduation the building became Central Middle School and a new high school was built. There are now at least two high schools in Midland.

There was no Catholic High School, so the Catholic students entered the public school system in 9th or 10th grade. We noticed right away how differently their behavior toward teachers was. They stood when called on, and said "Yes, Mr. Black" or Please Miss Smith". In Latin class, their pronunciation of words sounded very different, and we learned that they studied "church Latin". We were curious about these differences, and even made fun of them behind their back. But within a few weeks, the differences were unnoticed, and we became just classmates. I had Roman Catholic cousins, so knew a little about Catholicism, but unless the differences affected our time together, it didn't much matter. If it was Friday, I had to remember, or be reminded that there was no meat for lunch or dinner at family functions. If it was Lent, the topic of what to give up was discussed, but didn't involve me. At school, there was little attention paid to these differences, although it was still notable if protestants and Roman Catholics dated. High School is, however, mostly about social life and studies, and we were all on a level playing field with those.

Indeed I was getting more social, although still somewhat shy. Fortunately, my grades and study came easily, so I had plenty of time to do other things. I write here about academics first, and then the social parts of high school.

The curriculum at Midland High was influenced by Dow Chemical Company. A common saying in town was "There are more PhD's per square inch in Midland than anywhere else." That was the nature of Dow employees. These people insisted on a good curriculum in the schools. Science and Math were especially stressed. The school was similar to today's magnet schools, but the concept had not yet been named. Advanced classes were offered.

I took three years of biology and two of chemistry. I also took physics, geometry, solid geometry, and trigonometry. There was a second year physics class and I could have taken calculus. There was a big Science Club and a Science Show every year. There was a photography club featuring developing and printing, not just taking pictures. When I went to college, I realized how unusual much of that was.

The school had the usual business and technical classes, Home Economics, Typing, Shorthand, Auto Mechanics, and Shop. The student body was separated into College Prep students and otherwise, although I did not sense a negative comparison. It was pretty natural to hang out with and be close friends with those in the same classes, but I eventually had friends and dated from both groups.

One advantage of a high level of education in that town was the expectation that the women would be smart also. Among my parent's friends were several couples where the woman also had a PhD, or other higher education. My mother's stock broker was a woman. Thus, I did not grow up with the pressure to hide my intelligence or good grades. One of my Science Fair projects was on the various kinds of plastics – differences, uses, and qualities. Of course one of our friends got the samples from Dow for me. I got very good grades, and while I didn't brag, I discussed grades with my boyfriends and girlfriends alike.

Teachers and Classes

I mention here some highlights, both classes and teachers who especially contributed to my growth or were outstanding or especially influenced me.

Our Chemistry teacher, Harold Tweedie, was also the father of a friend of mine. He made Chemistry interesting. He was a photographer and had a darkroom both at school and in his home. He sponsored the photography club, and was an excellent teacher, both for the club, and in the chemistry classes and labs. The labs had equipment similar to my college chemistry labs. He was, I believe, the only chemistry teacher, and so taught both first and second year classes. He also did private photography, and at some point, I took my little sister, Becky over there to get a portrait as a surprise for my parents. Mr. Tweedie hand colored his portraits in those days. I often visited their home to see my friend, Luanna, his daughter.

In biology, we had both lab and lecture. My first year teacher was Miss Harter, later to become Mrs. Beatty, and my second year teacher was Stanley Kuick. (In writing this, I found a Stan Kuick on the internet and wrote him. It was his grandfather who taught me, and he was happy to be reminded of what a kind, strong, and knowledgeable man his grandfather was when they went camping together.) We dissected earthworms, and frogs, we used a microscope to study pond water, and grew organisms in Petri dishes. We had a natural balanced aquarium in the room, and guinea pigs. Our active Science Club sold candy bars after school to earn money for the Science Fair and for Field Trips. The studies put me in good stead for college, and the candy bars helped me enjoy my after school hours. I fondly remember Valo-milk.

There were three teachers at least, that had been there when my father was in high school. Barbara Smith was an English teacher. She was a no-nonsense, but fun loving person, with a ready smile, and a teaching style combining business and fun. She taught everything from grammar to Shakespeare. She was big on diagramming sentences, which I hated, and remember not one thing about.

She asked us to write many things – our experiences, book reports, essays and poetry. At some point, I entered a Civitan Essay Contest. "The Duties and Privileges of a Citizen." I won first place and had to read my paper out loud as I accepted the prize. Although I was still shy, I had several opportunities in High School to be the focus of attention, and became able to do that more easily. This was one of them.

In some high school English class (Not one of Ms. Smith's), one of my poems received a sound criticism from a teacher who thought that I had not lived enough life to know what I was writing about. It is interesting to remember that the criticism hurt, but I instinctively knew it was her problem, and did not take it seriously. I did get a bad grade on the assignment..

Jessie Duncan was an institution all on her own, and another of the teachers who had taught my dad. She was my math teacher, and although she was also a friend of our family, there was never a question of favoritism. I followed the rules just like everyone else, and believe me, she had rules. They were designed to instill carefulness, attention to detail, accuracy, promptness, organization, and neatness. If you did not turn in your homework, you got an E for the day. Even if your homework was down in your locker, home and done, or folded in your pocket, the days grade was E. (Folds were not allowed either) It was to be handed in during class, and that was all. No erasures either. If there were mistakes, we were expected to recopy the paper. No second chances. Miss Duncan's classes were the only class in school that had regular nightly homework. There was no talking in class unless called on. It is interesting that most people liked Miss Duncan and respected her teaching, although they didn't like the rules. As I wrote earlier, I was a person who wanted to get things done and go on to something else. I may have been accurate in my thinking, but I was neither neat, nor a detail person. Being left handed also made it easy for me to smear my papers. However, I shaped up quickly in Miss Duncan's class. My grades were important.

When Miss Duncan retired, my mother and I helped do her retirement party. Here is the poem I wrote and read for her. By that time, I was well out of school and had children of my own.

A math teacher teaching Philosophy?
How could that be, you say.
And yet I know of one that did.
She's with us here today
Along with math she taught me this:
To always do my best.
To do things right the first time through
To not let errors rest
To be on time and be prepared
To be exact and neat.
Not just in math, but all of life
Her teaching was elite.
Thanks Miss Duncan for being you.
And in retirement days,
May the help that you gave and the joys you shared
Be returned in a thousand ways.

The last teacher who had taught my dad was Agnes Gaughan, the Latin Teacher. She was also a family friend, and came to our house for dinner several times. I remember her as a woman with grey hair, and bright red lipstick. Latin may have been a dead language, but Miss Gaughan was far from being a dead teacher. We not only translated the classics in class, we sang Christmas Carols (Including Rudolph the Red Nosed Reindeer) in Latin. Each year there was a Latin Dinner to which we wore togas. She made up a crossword puzzle in Latin. She did many things to bring a dead language to life. I suppose everyone who ever took Latin remembers this ditty:

> *Latin is a dead language*
> *Dead as it can be*
> *First it killed the Romans*
> *And now it's killing me.*

Of all my high school classes, Latin has probably served me in the rest of my life better than most. It is the basis of much of the science and medical language that I used in my work. In addition, I am a better Scrabble player because of it, and know the meaning and spelling of many words I have not seen before, because they are derived from the Latin. Thank you Miss Gaughan.

Speech Class and Stage Fright

Miss Perkins was our speech teacher. If I were asked to think of the most embarrassing and shame filled moment in all my high school days, it would be part of speech class. It was years before I could remember and think about that moment without shriveling inside, and remembering that feeling of wanting to disappear into the floor.

My mom insisted I take the class, meaning well, as always. I was a shy person, and she thought it would help. She had been on the debate team in her own high school days. She felt it important that I learn to speak in front of others. I understood, and agreed to take the class.

Each year, there was a speech contest involving high schools from a large area of Michigan. In our high school, all first year students had to enter in the Declamation section. Declamation involves memorizing a piece and reciting it.

One of the ways that my mind has never worked well is in exact memorization. Even in the Mary Poppins play, I remembered the meaning of my lines, but not the exact words. Faced with exact memorization, I look much less capable than I am. I could have done extemporaneous speech, or dramatic reading much more easily.

I felt cornered, and forced into doing something that was not me. The situation played up and exaggerated several of my weaknesses. The day of the contest, I was one of 26 entrants in declamation, and as I spoke, I froze repeatedly, forgetting the words. The prompters prompted me again and again, and there were times they had to repeat their prompt several times. My embarrassment and tension continued to dull my hearing, my memory, my voice and my mind. The longer I spoke, the worse I got. I wanted to just quit, and walk off the stage. There was no reprieve. By the time I was finished, I walked off the stage crying. I came in last out of 26 contestants. I went home and asked to quit speech class, not wanting to go back and face the shame. Luckily, my parents did not let me quit.

Miss Perkins was not an empathetic teacher. I could see her displeasure when I attended the next class, but she said nothing. Her silence was easier than harsh public or private words. It was not that I had not put the time and work in. I didn't slack off on preparation. That particular work did not fit my skills well, and everything combined to create the perfect failure.

For years, I was unable to get up in front of a crowd. I could answer questions in class if I held my hand up, but if I was called on unexpectedly, I froze. Only in college did I force myself to take another speech class and get over my post traumatic difficulties. The speech that made the difference was a speech that I gave about my brother Deke, and his difficulties. I felt emotional about him, and I was able to be vulnerable and truthful in my speech and got a high mark on it. There were other speeches after that which came more easily. I passed the class, and got over the greater part of my fear.

Later, in my career, I did a great deal of public speaking, conducting classes and workshops effectively. Had I not had that experience which felt so terrible at the time, I might not have worked on remediation, and become a better speaker. As I have aged, my speaking effectiveness has gone up and down with my confidence, but I am presently teaching an exercise class and am repeatedly told I am a good and clear teacher. When I first started teaching again, I felt as if I had lost my edge in communicating to a group, but within a few weeks, it came back.

I can sum up my high school academics by saying that I graduated within the top part of my class. We had 300+ students in our class, and I was within the top 25 students. I am eager to tell you about the rest of my high school life. Because my studies came easily, I was not as much involved in my studies as I was in friends and social activities.

My Dog – Timothy Jones Bradley

First, however, I shift backwards a year or two to speak of my best friend in late Junior High and early High School.

A friend of mine got a stray dog which her parents would not let her keep. My parents also said no. I then asked if I could keep him for a few days while I found another owner, and they agreed that he could stay on the front storm porch. I intended to look for a new owner, but fell for his soulful eyes, and the way he responded to our care. My parents must have been influenced also, as they changed their decision, and the dog became my dog and my most trusted companion for many years.

Shirley, my friend, said his name was Timmy, so that's what I called him. It may have been my sister or brother who asked what his middle name was, and on the spur of the moment, I said Jones. Thus, Timothy Jones Bradley came to stay. For the next many years, his was the friendship I could count on and the presence that would comfort me. He was my companion on bike rides and walks. And although I was still hesitant to talk to friends and family, I could talk to Timmy. I cried my teenage angst in his fur many times. Later in life, he was the early companion of my first two children, Pam and Jim.

Timmy had one small downside-disliking men in uniforms such as meter readers, postmen, gas station attendants, and construction men. Over time, he improved, although I kept a good eye out to keep him and others from harm. The postman learned to keep a good eye out also. Leash laws were not so strict back then, so he was not leashed or tied.

One day, after a year or more, Timmy ended up missing. I walked and drove around looking. No Timmy. He didn't come home that night either, so the next day, Saturday, I looked some more, and finally drove out in the country to the dog pound. With trepidation, I pulled up, and saw him there behind the fence in one of the dog runs. There was not only a high chain link fence between us, but a lower fence which formed the wall of his dog run. I was immediately worried that if I waited until after school Monday to get him, they might put him down. It was getting late in the day, and I reluctantly left and went home, with both of us feeling the pull to be reunited. I knew the pound would also be closed Sunday. Sunday, so Sunday morning, I drove out there. I parked, got out, and still not knowing exactly what to do, I started inventing the solution moment by moment.

My camaraderie and time with all the guys on the playground stood me in good stead. I was strong, creative, and not afraid to sneak around and get away with stuff. I carefully climbed the chain link fence, probably around 8 feet high, and luckily no razor wire on top. I climbed down the other side, went to the fence of the dog run, and climbed that one. It was only about 5 feet tall. I jumped down into the dog run and Timmy and I had a joyful reunion. I had a moment's hesitation, as I remembered jumping into that ditch in Oklahoma, with no way out. I knew I could climb back over the fences, but also knew I could not climb those fences carrying Timmy. He weighed probably 30 pounds or more.

We both crawled through the shelter inside his dog run, and came to the front gate of the run, which went into the main room of the building through a latched gate. I carefully unlocked that gate from the inside, letting us out into the main office space inside the pound. I relocked that gate behind us. We walked past the offices and toward the front door. We were almost out. One more door to go. Could I unlock it? I let my breath out with relief as the lock on the front door unlocked easily from the inside. We went out the front door, pulling it shut and relocking the door behind us. We got in the car and went home. I have no idea whether I told anyone about it. I wonder what the animal control people thought when they came in on Monday?

Speaking of that pound, there was little public knowledge or outcry about animal cruelty back then. I went out there another day when Timmy was again missing. (This time he was not there). I walked over to some barrels in the yard, and heard movement although they were covered with heavy pieces of wood. I moved the cover, and inside were puppies and kittens and small dogs, some dead, some wounded and alive. There were a multitude of bullet holes in the barrels where the officers had shot through the barrels time and time again, and then walked away; hoping that all the animals inside would soon die. I was feeling shock, and too traumatized to do anything. I can't help but think that it hardens the heart, and hurts the soul of the people who do such things. I felt powerless to do anything about it then. I did tell my dad, and I am not sure if he did anything. I was hoping he would go to the police. I just tried to forget it.

Remember that Timmy was the dog involved in the "dog back" riding memory of my sister so he is preserved forever in the family legends, as well as in my heart. He lived about 10 more years, and died about 1961, as I was pregnant for my third child.

High School Social Life and Me

I was late maturing socially as well as physically. The social immaturity kept me from dating until my mother practically insisted. My first date was painfully self-conscious. The Country Club, where we were members, was to have a teen dance. My mother asked me over and over again to find someone to take. I finally agreed to ask one of the identical twins living a few blocks away. I really didn't know him well, but he was quiet, and seemed to be nice. I was probably a freshman in high school. We went to the dance; both of us nearly mute, and embarrassed to be so. We danced, had refreshments and awkwardly got through the evening. We never went out again, and stayed shy toward each other in school, furtively glancing at each other as we passed in the hall. That was the extent of our friendship.

It was also my mother who later talked me into trying square dancing at the Community Center. My mother's supervisor in Social Work had been Guy Shipps, and his daughter Barbara was the teacher and caller of the dancing. She was patient and smiling as she taught. I had gained back my coordination, and loved the dancing, though still shy. That square dancing was really the beginning of my social life, and most of my later friends and activities grew from it.

The first night I was there, a boy by the name of Chuck Supinger asked me to dance. He was tall and skinny, not handsome but very nice. He was older than I, and sometimes held my hand while dancing or talking. He was a graceful dancer, and I found out he was the only male cheerleader at high school. I didn't really know how to act with only one date behind me. I was, at that age, secretly looking for romance, or my prince, or something like that, but had no idea what that meant. My parents were occasionally affectionate with each other, and watching them was my only example. We switched partners several times that first evening, so I met several people and enjoyed myself. Chuck remained attentive to me.

To my totally inexperienced astonishment, Chuck came over to me when I went back the next week and asked me to dance. A couple weeks after that, he asked me if I knew how to roller skate. Of course I said yes, as those sidewalks around the funeral home practically had grooves worn in them from my skates. I found out that he meant a roller rink. I had never skated indoors. Chuck told me that the church youth groups got together once a month and went to Brockway Roller Rink on a Friday night. He asked if I would go with him. My parents met Chuck and said yes. I had little idea how relationships developed, and was continually surprised when he kept reaching out to me. I thought he was just being nice to a new person. But he kept reaching out, and I kept accepting his invitations.

After that, we became an "item" as one might say, although there was no talk about "going steady" or any other label. One night he asked if I wanted to go to the drive in movie with another couple from square dancing. Within a few weeks, there were 6 of us just sort of hanging out together in various combinations. One of the other couples was Mary Carney and Walter Bennett. When there were only four of us together, it was likely to be Chuck and I, and Mary and Walt. We became so much a 4 part item that one day we went to the store, bought material, and made matching shirts. Then we wore them to school the next day. The guys wore theirs square dancing, but we girls had the usual crinolines under full skirts and peasant blouses for dancing. I remember that I was married with children before I could bring myself to get rid of that shirt. It signified Chuck, but so much more. It was about friendship, acceptance, and many memories of fun, events and people. It was about belonging, and feeling secure. (When writing this, I saw a Walter Bennett on Facebook from Midland. He looked like Walt's brother Bob, and I messaged him and asked. I ended up sending him pictures of his uncle and dad and his dad's high school girlfriend. So fun to make these new connections growing from the old.)

Chuck treated me like someone he enjoyed and cherished. I almost forgot to feel awkward; I finally accepted that he was not just being nice to a stranger, and that we were going together pretty steadily. He taught me to skate dance at Brockway, and because he could skate backward, he made it easy for me to follow him by skating forward. He not only made me feel less awkward socially, but he made me look beautifully graceful on the rink. He was strong enough to catch me if I stumbled, and held me so that I felt solid. Chuck eventually bought me a set of semi precision bearings for my skates, and put them in for me, teaching me how to take care of them. They were easy rolling and quiet compared to the regular bearings. I only gave my skates away when I was over 60. By then both the skates and I were antiques. I tried skating with them about that time, and found that wooden wheels were no longer known and did not work on modern skating floors. I rented a pair of rink skates instead. My body did not work as well, but I loved skating again, and enjoyed sort of a trip back to my past, without Chuck, but with good memories and no falls. Meanwhile, back in high school, the four of us, and the rest of the square dancing gang continued to coalesce into a group that really enjoyed each other and did other things together. There were the four of us, and Mary's sister Charlotte, Charlie Longsdorf, and Walt's brother, Bob. On the edges were Victor Hickman, and Floyd McWethy. We danced, went skating, and went swimming at Sanford Lake. We went to drive in movies, one night contemplating how many people we could put in the car, since they charged by the carload. We considered putting people in the trunk and then letting them sit on the hood and roof to watch the show. Fortunately that never became a reality.

Back then, teenagers seldom owned their own cars, borrowing from their parents instead. Only one of us owned a car. Charlie Longsdorf lived in the country, using his little Henry J. to get to and from school A couple of the parents in the group had stipulations about how many miles we could put on the car in one evening. We discovered that one of the cars could be put in reverse to take miles off the odometer. Hmmmm... One night we backed up on so many small streets that we had to go forward again to get the number of miles we started with.

Saturday night occasionally found a few of us at one of the Grange Halls, at someone's wedding reception. The music was great (usually Polish). We loved to dance, and no one cared whether we knew the bride or the family. The food was good if we wanted it. None of us ever drank, and we danced the polkas and schottische until we could not dance any more. One custom was a dance where the men pinned dollars on the bride's dress for the privilege of dancing with her. Our guys always took part, as we felt that we could at least repay the couple for all the fun we had at their wedding reception. I never could quite get the hang of the way the local people danced the polka. Their feet moved much more intricately than mine, but I suspect I had as much fun.

When I spent a few days in Midland in 2013, I looked up Charlie and Fran Longsdorf, and Chuck and Char Supinger. Boy they sure have gotten old! It was wonderful to see them! It is interesting to see people my own age 50 years later.

Chuck's family is worth writing about here for their influence on the town and on me. They were involved, and caring toward the youth of Midland, especially the sports teams. Chuck is carrying on the family interest in youth. He would be 83 as I write this, and is a school crossing guard, knowing each child by name, and enjoying his contact with them.

No one knew Chuck without becoming part of his family who lived and breathed kindness and hospitality. His parents, Cletus and Mary Beth Supinger, had a local reputation, cheering loudly at every high school athletic event. They knew each player, and the players knew them. Mary Beth also had a reputation as a knitter and while she watched the games, she knit. The more exciting the game, the faster she knit. She knit me my ankle socks while she watched those games. She also made a dessert called "Congo Bars" which became one of our family recipes. The Supingers were like second parents to me, and I stayed connected with them, even after I was married, and had Pam. Chuck was the youngest in the family, and the only boy. He had two older sisters, both dead now.

Chuck went in the army after graduation, and was sent to Korea. That was my junior year of high school. He was much more serious about me than I was about him, and he sent me gifts from Asia, and nearly daily letters. I have a lovely moonstone necklace and earrings received from him way back then. . I wrote him and broke up with him while he was overseas, not being cognizant of how difficult that would be for him. I wanted to date someone else. It was another example of my being emotionally insensitive or naïve. Not dealing in emotions while growing up certainly put me at a disadvantage later.

Because Chuck and Walt graduated two years before I did, and then Mary and Charlie Longsdorf graduated one year before, it meant that my last year of high school felt a little lost and anti-climactic. I was left without the gang, without a date to the proms, and dances, and without my best friends. It was like starting over.

I hung out a little with my neighbor, John Ladd, who is now a physician. I also started dating Butch Blue, actually Robert D. Blue who was a ham radio operator and wanted to be a nuclear physicist. I believe Butch is still living in the Midwest somewhere, and is still connected with ham radio. He taught me a little about that world and used to sign his letters to me with 88's, which means hugs and kisses. I also learned Morse code from him. His call letters then, were W8NDH.

I was not very kind to Butch, who was also more involved with me than I with him. I now regret my lack of depth and sensitivity emotionally. He was kind to our family, taking care of the yard when we went away, and even doing some landscaping. He had twin younger brothers who were slightly developmentally delayed and his father had set them up with a lawn care business, so Butch knew how to work with lawns and was a perfectionist. Our lawn looked beautiful when we came back from vacation. Butch attended U of M, after graduation, and I did visit him one weekend when he was a freshman in college. I lost track of him after that.

After the departure of "the gang", I also longed after the school basketball star who owned a woody station wagon, and drove past our house every morning on his way to school. I timed coming out the door, hoping he would offer me a ride. If he did, I was then star struck all the way to school I never dated Jim, but I sure had a crush on him. He had a steady girlfriend whom he eventually married. I suspect he knew I was drooling about him, but to his credit, although I did not get my way and go out with him, he never made fun of me, or took advantage of my vulnerability.

Speaking of basketball heroes, Friday was "jean day" in high school, and the girls got to wear jeans.(as opposed to skirts). One Friday, the basketball team decided they would get even, and all came to school in skirts. Only the macho could have gotten away with that. The school was in a dilemma: whether to let them stay, or make them go home and change. I believe they spent the day in their skirts. Those hairy legs sure looked funny below the skirts and above the bobby socks.

Then there was the time the whole varsity team got caught partying after curfew. It was the night before a big game. They were benched, leaving the junior varsity to play the game. I believe this may have been a first round in a state tournament or some other very important game. Our JV boys played their hearts out, and nearly won, but lost at the last minute of the game. The tension was so high, that many of the students, including me, started crying. It was mass tears and high emotions in the stands, as the heroes sat on the bench helpless, while their second string almost won, but couldn't quite pull it off. The coach had the integrity to decide that rules were rules, and followed them. It was a brave call and a good example for all. I remember coming home still crying and trying to explain to my parents what I was crying about...much more than a lost game. It was about courage, and hope, and school spirit, and contagious emotions.

I attended the Methodist Church in High School and went to MYF (Methodist Youth Fellowship). Of our square dancing group, several of us went there, and I didn't want to be left out. All the high school

94

youth sat in front right under the pastor's pulpit. That gave us social contact, and kept us attentive. Dr. Orville McKay was the pastor, and gave excellent, clear and interesting sermons. I later wrote a paper using one of his metaphors. He had asked the question: "are you a thermometer, or a thermostat? Of course, the thermometer simply registers the temperature, while the thermostat sets and controls the temperature. (God being the furnace or the heat) That metaphor became life-guiding for me. I just looked it up, and Dr. McKay died in 2010 in Midland at 96 years old.

Mary Carney and I both played intramural tennis, singles and doubles. Although I was only a mediocre player, I took the game seriously and had a good tennis racket, caring for it well. (In those days it was important to keep wood rackets in a press so they wouldn't warp.) Later on, as a psychotherapist, I had that same tennis racket in my office to help with catharsis by having people beat a pillow with it. That was a very common technique in the 70's, and a fitting end to my tennis racket.

Maybe my real glory came through the annual magazine subscription selling contest. This supported some of the extracurricular activities in school. My "inner entrepreneur", plus my competitive bent grabbed on to that opportunity, and in spite of my shyness, I found it easy to go door to door to sell those subscriptions. In fact it was so much fun, and so easy that I ended up winning prizes every year.

My sophomore year, I sold enough subscriptions to come in second in the school. We could choose our prize, and I chose a Smith Corona Portable Typewriter. I used it during college, and for many years afterward. The second and third year, I came in first, choosing a stereo set, and then having already won the two main prizes; I chose a watch which I wore for many years. I am sure my relatives and my parent's, friends, (and again my supportive pediatrician) hardly had time to read all the subscriptions they bought.

Earning Money in High School

I added babysitting to my High School income sources. The going rate was 25 cents/hour, later to go up to 35. I started at home with my younger sibs, and because I then had experience, others asked. It was much easier to care for other people's children than my sibs. My brothers and sister wouldn't mind me, and got mad if I bossed them around. They also could tattle if I spent time reading instead of playing with them. The worst time was the night my brother and I had a pumpkin pie fight while we were babysitting the younger ones. My mom discovered pie on the wall and ceiling, and we were told that the next time they went out, they would leave Becky to baby sit with us. They did, and she did, and she was a tyrant.

One family had 2 children when I started babysitting for them and 5 when I stopped. They began alphabetically, Ann, Billy, Cathy, David, and then broke the string with Charles Edward. That was the house where I read "Obstetrics for Nurses" thus getting part of my sex education. It was filled with graphic illustrations of birth, so I learned how babies got out, but not how they got in. My mother bought me a book for teens that explained some of it, so I was not completely ignorant. Of course I had no need for details at the time, but that didn't stop my curiosity. I can remember having learned some basics, and wondering if my legs would stretch far enough apart for my husband to do what he was going to do. Ah, the worries of young teens!

When I got a work permit, our neighbor, who was the pathologist at the hospital laboratory, and a friend of my parents, offered me a job. I wanted to be a doctor and at least could be around a hospital washing dishes in the lab. Back then we washed Petri dishes, syringes, and even the blood drawing needles. There was no such thing as HIV and we carefully washed and sterilized, and then sharpened the needles. It was a very different world.

The second year I worked there, I was assisting in doing urinalysis. That meant I dipped the sticks in the bottle and put tubes in the centrifuge to spin. The Technologists then looked at the spun sediment, to identify infection, bleeding, and other problems. I was closely monitored but satisfying my desire to learn more. Eventually I also learned things like EKG's, and finally drawing blood. By then, I was probably in college.

Unfortunately, before then, my boss, the pathologist, and my pediatrician had both talked to me about giving up my dream of medicine. In those days, women doctors were almost unheard of. And women who got into Medical School were disdained and given a very difficult time. I listened to both doctors because I liked and respected them. Their argument was to appeal to my responsible nature: "Karen, you would not want to be responsible for taking money from the state, and from the university and then not use it, would you. You would be wasting their money when you got married and had children instead of working." How things have changed!!

I worked at the lab during all of high school and college, coming home summers and occasionally working even vacations. And finally, I was employed there off and on as a full-fledged degreed Medical Technologist after my college graduation.

A New Brother

I had no idea that my mother was pregnant when I was a junior in high school. My first clue was the note on the dining room table from my dad saying mom was at the hospital and we had a new baby brother. I stayed home from school to take care of the other kids, and get them off to school.

One would think I would have noticed the pregnancy. I didn't, and none of my friends did either. They were just as surprised. What I suspect, is that, particularly with this pregnancy, my mother had very mixed feelings because of Deke's illness and the resultant disability. I do remember that during her pregnancy this time, I never saw her eat much besides bread and milk. She was 42. In that period of time, it was most unusual for a woman to be having a baby after age 40. It was thought to be dangerous, with much more chance of producing a problem delivery, Down's Syndrome, or some other genetic problems.

My brother, Charles MacLean Bradley was born January 3, 1953. I think my mother started bleeding after he was delivered and may have had to have a transfusion, but I am not clear if that is an accurate memory or not. I occasionally remember changing diapers, or baby sitting with Charlie, but otherwise have little memory of him as a baby. As a teen, I was horribly embarrassed that my mother had a new baby, and even more so that I didn't know about it so I could warn my friends. I remember one time taking him for a walk in a carriage or stroller, and someone asked if he were mine. I was mad, and didn't want to take care of him again. Another typical teen reaction.

As with Dekie, I do not remember being asked to take care of Charlie much. Maybe my mother was still shepherding my social life. I left for college before he was 2 years old. Becky got the brunt of taking care of Charlie, just as she had Dekie. Consequently, Charlie and I never got to know each other much until more recent years, when I was traveling around the country after Hawaii, and as Charlie has reconnected with our family more in the last few years. I often have had the sense that he is the sibling most like me in many ways, but by way of a very different background and parents.

I was the first child, and probably got the best and the most of my parents and grandparents attention. Charlie was last, and had actively alcoholic parents, and my sister as a surrogate mom. We both turned inward under stress, and both have used writing to express ourselves. He has much more of a sense of humor than I, both in writing and everyday life. I am the serious oldest child, his writing uses lightness and humor to make a serious point. We both have sharp and curious minds, although mine has faded a little in the dawning of my older years. We are both aware of our surroundings, somewhat hyper-vigilant, and have a large sense of responsibility. My other sibs also have much of that sense of responsibility. I suppose, it goes along with being a Bradley and being "special"

My high school graduation was not much of a milestone for me. I was mostly eager to get on to Michigan State. They had one of the best Medical Technology programs in the country, and since I had given up medicine as a career, I settled on being a very good tech.

97

The graduation was most notable for the disagreements between my mother and I about lipstick and heels. She wanted them for me, I didn't. I was pretty rebellious, but ended up giving in. The time between her suggestion and my surrender was filled with disdainful distance and pouting on my part, and a firmness and stiff upper lip on the part of my mother. I think I went to the prom that year with Butch Blue. I have no kinesthetic or visual memories of my graduation. I only have the certificate. There is a photo to remind me.

My summer was spent working at the hospital laboratory, and baby sitting, and then I was off to East Lansing in the fall. I had a partial scholarship based on my grades.

I was eligible to take comprehensive exams. If I passed, I would be allowed to skip some of the required freshman courses. I took 6 exams and passed three of them. Thus I started my freshman year with 11 credits. Michigan State had terms instead of semesters, and a full term of credits was 16. I was able to take some electives and took advanced swimming and General Chemistry. The Chemistry was required for my major, but most took it the second year. In swimming, I ended up getting my lifesaving certificate.

I spent my first three years at Michigan State living in West Landon dormitory. That first year, my roommate was assigned and was a totally inappropriate match for me. She was a sophomore, a party person, a drinker and from the big city. She loved to stay up late, and sleep in. I loved to go to sleep at 9 and get up at 6. She had parties in our room, and I crawled in bed in the middle of them. We had no common interests. She seldom exercised; I was always playing tennis or walking. She was majoring in Elementary Education, considered an easy way to get through college and find a man; I was in one of the hardest curricula on campus. We were lucky to make it through the whole year without more fights. The next year, she moved into a sorority house, and I was grateful to see her go.

That first year was also a big one for the college. Our football team ended up going to the Rose Bowl and winning!! (I asked my parents to go and they refused, probably because of finances.) Michigan State College was also renamed Michigan State University that year. Everyone celebrated!! I went through a short time of homesickness that year, but it was soon resolved.

My next roommate was Sally Shively, the daughter of a tire executive from Akron. She was, in some ways, as different from me as Bev had been. She had a coming out party in Akron, had lots of cashmere sweaters, and was very upper class. She was also very down to earth, not arrogant, and a lot of fun. She even let me frequently borrow her sweaters. Everyone liked her. Her boyfriend, Ben, was also from a tire family, and they eventually married and had two children. I have seen them a few times. Sally had been an only child and wanted to go to Veterinary school. And at one point, she and I and two other girls from the dorm had gone on a road trip to her parent's house in Akron.

That sophomore year with Sally as roommate was when I got in trouble for that issue of being "special". Sally was more inclusive and friendly than Bev had been, and so I was more naturally included in dorm activities. A few of the girls knew I had not had to take all the freshman classes. One knew that I had been solicited for a research study for very intelligent students.

However, that was not what got me in trouble. Whatever we talked about, I seem to have told people how that was done in Midland, or what I knew about the subject. I spoke with an air of authority. In hindsight, I acted as if I was entitled to be special. I talked about the wealth in Midland, about all the recreational facilities. Of course I assumed and believed that Midland's way was the best way.

My friends cornered me one night, and threatened not to speak to me again if I did not stop talking about Midland. It probably didn't cure my arrogance, but it sure made me quieter about the town I grew up in. I did not have much practice in feeling ordinary, or simply fitting in with others in a group. What confidence I had so often took the form of speaking like I knew my way, or that my way was better. It was not consciously bragging, but more an innocent superiority, born of family training, being intelligent, and being brought up in a town that really was special in many ways. All this, resulting in a pretty low emotional I.Q. must have made me difficult to be around. I am thankful that I had some saving characteristics which encouraged some to be friends with me, spend time with me. Later on in my life, having learned some options, and even ended up writing an article on Collaboration.

Meeting Clark

General Chemistry was a huge lecture section with an instructor with the name Birdwhistell. Remember that I took that my first term freshman year. In our first lab session, we were asked to choose a lab partner, and I was standing next to a young man and asked him if he would like to be partners. His name was Clark Hamp, and we would eventually end up getting married. We were both quite shy. He was from the small town of Elsie Michigan, and was the first in his family to go to college. We became friends, started doing some things together, and slowly realized that we were dating pretty steadily. Our time mostly consisted of long walks down by the river, around by the barns of MSU or through the woods. In the spring we found the baby animals and the Sugaring shack where the maple syrup was made. I suppose that wasn't much like most couple's dates, but it suited us. Clark had a hometown friend that he roomed with, but otherwise didn't know many on campus. I imagine that I felt out of place on a large campus too.

Clark lived at West Shaw Hall, and when the next dance was announced there, he asked me to go. I think the Shaw dances were twice a year. There were big name bands, and semi-formal dress. I went to that dance and many others with him, and eventually we danced to Duke Ellington, Benny Goodman, Glenn Miller Band, and Tommy Dorsey, among others. By the time I graduated, I had autographs of those people on dance cards. Many years later, after Clark and I divorced, I threw away my college souvenirs. I am sure, had I saved them, those would have been of interest if not of value to someone.

Roller skating was a shared familiar high school activity, so naturally we ended up at the rinks around Lansing. . Clark was not nearly the skater that Chuck had been, but I enjoyed skating again, and in fact still have my skate case with the stickers from many of Michigan's rinks. As time went on, and especially as the weather got chilly in fall and winter, we cuddled over the steam vents on campus, or sat down by the river and "necked". Neither of us were drinkers or party people. We enjoyed each other and occasionally double dated with Sally and Ben or Clark's hometown friend, Gary and his girlfriend Doris. It was, in some ways, a typical college romance, and in other ways, more like an insular small town romance.

During this time in the culture, people were not yet conscious about their relationships. I was not unusual in "just letting our relationship happen" instead of looking at the process of us together, and consciously choosing. When that kind of relationship consciousness started in the late 60's, people began to explore the dynamics of their partnerships, and a divorce epidemic ensued. Clark and I were part of that, but that is getting ahead of the story. It is interesting that I was a person who often thought about my future jobs or education, but not marriage.

I did occasionally date other men A graduate student from Egypt, some of my square dance partners, and an intern from Midland Hospital.(Who I met when we were both assisting with an autopsy.) I knit him socks, and he gave me records for my collection. He wanted me to quit school and finish putting him through med school, and for us to get married. Fortunately, I was astounded that he thought about getting married. or about my quitting school. I didn't even think that much of him. Good choice on my part. I later learned that many medical students at that time tried to find a woman to put them through medical school and then divorced afterwards. He said to me, "I thought you loved me, after all, you knit me socks." My process was that I enjoyed knitting and found a pattern with the caduceus on it, (a medical symbol). I thought of it as a good challenge to my knitting skills and a good gift for him. It had nothing to do with loving him. Clark also dated other women while in college, especially when he went home for holidays.

My Parents Object

I told my parents about Clark. I eventually invited him to Midland to attend an alumni dance. My mother did some sleuthing, and unknown to me, considered him beneath me, and trouble. She found that his parents didn't have auto insurance, and I am not sure what else. Consequently she told me he could not stay at our home for the dance. You would have to know our family to know how shocking that was. Our family had always been about hospitality to friends and strangers alike. It was a strong, many generation value to be open to others, and is still one of my strong values. Remember the homeless people my father picked up, and the many salesmen who came to dinner at our house, or children who played with us because they happened to be at the funeral home. There was always spare food or a spare room at our house.

This was a strong departure from what I had expected. I reflexively went into an oppositional state. If she didn't want me to, I surely would. A terrible start to a relationship, and terrible reason to continue it. And I did.

I suspect that mom was going through a great deal of stress and guilt about putting Dekie in an institution, as well as having a strained marriage and a very young child at home. And of course what I had no clue about at that time was that she probably also was dealing with memories of her first marriage, feeling scared for me, and wanting to have control about who I hung out with. She may have been actively alcoholic already. If so, I was oblivious.

When she said Clark could not stay at the house, I went and asked my Great-Aunt Honey if he could stay there, and she said yes. I have no idea whether Aunt Honey knew my mother had turned me down, or whether she simply thought my mother thought it improper to have Clark stay at our house, but I do know my mother was furious.

Thus the stage was then set for my mother's strong feelings that I should not be dating Clark, and my determination to be rebellious. Little did I know that we were nearly repeating the history of her first marriage step by step.

More College Activities

Back at college, I was also square dancing with the college club, the Promenaders. I was enjoying it as much as I had in Midland. We danced weekly, and traveled to exhibitions, festivals, and places that we were invited to dance. I was definitely embarrassed one night when I slipped and fell in the middle of a show. I got back up, and both the audience and my co-dancers were undisturbed about my error, and caring about my fall.

I also was in the Block S section at football games. We held a pack of cardboard squares of varied colors, each one numbered. We then flashed the right number at a signal, forming a picture or a message visible from across the stadium. I was not an enthusiastic football fan, but it allowed me to feel part of the action and excitement of the games. There were pep rallies the night before the games, and I remember Paul (Noel) Stooky, later a member of Peter, Paul and Mary, who was entertaining at one of the rallies. He later became a friend of my roommate Sally. Between Clark for my security and Sally for fun, my college days were good. I found the academics challenging, and learned a lot. Sally remained a good friend even after she moved into the sorority house.

My grades qualified me for inclusion in the Med Tech Honor Sorority. I joined, but was never interested in the traditional Greek life on campus. My only envy of Greek life was the ceremony that happened when a fraternity man gave a woman his pin. This was a forerunner to engagement, and was celebrated by the entire fraternity going, at night, to the women's dorm or sorority house, and serenading her. There were candles and flashlights. It was very romantic, and watching it, I felt envious, and wished it for myself. That was never to be. I never dated a fraternity man.

Another high school activity continued in college was tennis. Sally and I played often. One day we used tennis as an excuse to push one of the boundaries on campus. She loved pushing boundaries harmlessly, and I loved going along with her, though I didn't have the nerve to do it by myself. One of the campus rules was no shorts on campus without a coat over them. We decided to walk to the tennis courts in shorts with clear plastic raincoats over the top. We missed out on the fun, when no one challenged us.

So, we tried again with another boundary. It was fine for the guys to pick us up at the dorms, but there was no touching allowed. We let Ben and Clark in on the deal, and when they came over that night, they sat down; we put newspaper on their lap and sat on the newspapers. The housemother came running over, and we argued with her that we were not touching. After all there was paper between us. That kind of rebelliousness was fun, but my rebelliousness proved more serious and destructive when I used it against my parents in the relationship with Clark. I seemed not to be able to help it.

Meanwhile, my studies were doing well. There was no school of Human Medicine at MSU, and so the Med Tech program was taught in the school of Veterinary Medicine. It was said, and became obvious later to me that the association with a Vet school added to my education, rather than taking anything away. We were taught by anatomists, bacteriologists, and physiologists, who also knew and could give us a perspective of inter species data. I can remember looking at slides of chicken blood, and dog blood, along with human blood. I got an excellent education there. When I took my internship, my senior year, I found I was much better prepared than my fellow interns

My final year of classroom work, we had a class celebration, and I wrote a poem for it. I put as much of our medical terminology in as I could:

MED TECH DREAMS

It was late Sunday night on the campus
And everywhere quiet was heard
The weekend was over and all were asleep
As I walked thru the night, no one stirred
But all of a sudden in one of the rooms
Oh what a sight to behold
Twas hovering over a med techs bed
Twas a dream of the learnings of old
Of tissues and cells and of organs it spoke
Of agar and sucrose and starch
Twas passing before her in cinemascope
Look, up popped a giant sized arch!
Through the arch came the first of a sightly parade
It's the king of the body controls
King Heart with his flowing pericardial sac
And the blood vessels formed his patrols.
Look now! Sound the trumpet! Here comes Princess Skin
She's stratified Squamous bedecked
And young Prince Nerve Ending is riding beside
Her feelings to choose or reject.
Here comes a great row of columnar guards
Their cilia waving on high.
As they toss out all would be intruders so fast
That no stranger or foe dare draw nigh.
Behind this for microns and microns on end
Stretch the white fibrous bundles you see.
They form Ligament #1 of the king's body guards
They are versatile, tough as can be.
Here come the chief and parietal cells
Adorning the glands in the wall
The stomach is home to these secreting mites
They split foods in their tubular hall.
Look out, these may bite you, here come the teeth.
Their enamel is shiny and bright.
They're rough and they're tough. They tear and they grind.
And like stars, some may come out at night.
Catch that kidnapper, after him quick.

He's running away with that bone.
Whoops, my mistake, it's a skeletal muscle.
Look at him work, Ugh, Grunt, Groan!!
I guess he was last in this best of parades.
The music and fanfare is through.
These parts that you've seen are the parts of us all.
Of you, and of you, and of you.
These are the dreams of a future Med Tech.
They're visceral, wild, and rough.
But we study to learn and pass out exams
So the labs will be run good enough.

Internship Year – Personal Choices

The Fourth year of the Med Tech program was an internship. There was a list or booklet of approved placements all over the US, with most students choosing a place close to home. We would be trying out our knowledge and skills under the direction of experienced techs, and practicing our work under supervision for an entire year.

Because of the emotional bind I felt myself in about Clark, I thought about getting away from both he and my parents. I knew that I was not really in love with Clark, but because of my mother's objections, and my obsessive opposition to her on this issue, I was caught. I was hemmed in between my determination to be right about my choice of a partner and my own uneasiness about it. I started applying for hospitals away from Michigan.

I was accepted at Tacoma General Hospital in Tacoma Washington. That was about as far away as I could go. They had a house across the street from the hospital where I would be living. I had no way of knowing that I had picked a hardnosed but excellent program. Because I had traveled the country before, but never seen that part of it, I was curious about Washington. I would be taking a bus there.

By the time I got on the bus, my relationship with my mother had deteriorated. She took me to the bus station, barely saying goodbye, let alone hugging me, or wishing me well. I felt abandoned, alone, uncertain, and uncared about. I had known I was leaving my family, but I didn't anticipate them leaving me. I cried when she left.

My enjoyment of travel and my excitement about seeing new things, kicked in once out of town. The cross country bus ride was long but fun, and instead of the Route 66 of my youth, we took the equivalent of Route I-90. There were occasional stops where we could get off and walk around, or get a meal. In Minneapolis, I got out stretching my legs. When walking by a dumpster, I caught motion out of the corner of my eye. I turned and saw a small flying squirrel trapped in the dumpster. I reached in, picked him up, and put him in a small tree nearby. That was the best I could do, given the situation.

One other thing on that trip stood out. When we went through Montana or Wyoming, or somewhere in that part of the country, silver dollars were used instead of paper. I was fascinated, and used up all my bigger bills so that I could get change. I got to Washington with over a dozen silver dollars.

Tacoma

In Tacoma, I joined about 7 or 8 other interns, several of which were sharing that house across the street with me. Most knew the area, all new to me, so my first few days were those of exploration. For the first time in my life, I smelled the awful smell of paper pulp mills. With no car, I got to know the town on foot. The Frisco Freeze, similar to Dairy Queen, was a favorite find.

The Pathologist in charge of the lab was Dr. Charles Larson. His daughter, Lucille Larson, was the chief tech and head of the internship program.

I had difficulty with Lucille the first weeks, although I could see that the program was excellent. Lucille seemed emotionless and hardnosed. I soon learned that by luck, I had picked a place which would prepare me in all ways for my career as a tech. Lucille was strict, and detailed, and our rotation through the departments was well taught. I learned that Lucille did care, but was focused on teaching us well. The first 3 months were spent rotating through the departments and learning theory, routine, and skills of various tests. In addition, my own curiosity led me to attend the CPC or Clinical Pathology Conferences at the hospital once a week, where physician and interns gather and discuss puzzling cases. There I silently listened and practiced the skill of diagnosis, pitting myself against those more trained. I may have been the only med tech intern that ever attended.

After 3 months, we began night call, and got paid the grand sum of $3 per night. I was so frightened that I had the experience of waking up thinking the phone had rung, and could not tell if it was a dream, my imagination, or true. A couple of times, I had to call the hospital switchboard to find out. We had been instilled firmly with the idea that when we got called out, lives were in our hands. I felt the responsibility and the fear, even knowing that each department had procedure notebooks in case I forgot anything.

Meanwhile, on a personal level, I was in trouble. We had coffee hour daily, and I ate two donuts every day, and for the first time in my adult life, gained weight. I went from 110# to 130# within 3 months. I had been considered skinny before and never had to limit my appetite. I had a good sense of hunger and fullness. I also had always been active. Suddenly, I knew no one, was not physically active, and was estranged from my family. Donuts tasted good and filled the voids in my life. I was 22 years old.

Another clue to my troubles was an exceptionally messy and chaotic living space, my room. It was so bad that one of my colleagues sneaked the door open and took a picture, later showing it to me, and threatening to put it up on the public bulletin board at the lab. I believe she was trying to help, but it served to embarrass me. I cleaned up my room for the time being, but it soon was messy again. I am not a particularly neat person at best, but I had never let things get so out of control. The only other time that happened in my life was when I had three small children, and was working full time, exhausted and overwhelmed.

Clark Appears Again

Clark and I had been in touch by letter and phone. One night he called and told me he was on a bus on his way to Tacoma. I had no idea he was coming and immediately had a sinking feeling, as I went back into that internal bind, and thought of him being there. However, by the time he got there, I had found him a room to live in, and felt a measure of relatedness and security to see him again. I was still feeling estranged from my family, and terribly alone. He was to stay in a third floor walkup in a rooming house. The other renters were older men, and the bath was on the second floor and shared.

Between my loneliness, and knowing that my mother was not right, but neither was Clark right for me; and my not wanting to let go and be alone again, our relationship picked up where we had left off, but without the constraints of having family around. We were soon hanging out at his place, and it was not long before we became intimate. He was my first sexual partner, and although I had never intended to be sexual before marriage, this was the perfect storm and set-up. I was 22, I felt like my family didn't like me and didn't care, and Clark showed up without asking. It was a cold rainy winter in Tacoma, and I grabbed on to his company. I thought I was in love, or at least that I could love him. I was still naïve enough to think that most people thought like I did and that we would collaborate and build a life together. I moved from the house across from the hospital, he found a job, and we were creating a life. Our rent was twenty five dollars a month.

I got pregnant within a month or less. We felt a little scared, but also excited and happy about having a baby. Aside from some initial morning sickness, I continued working, and felt good. We planned a March 6th wedding, in the Methodist Church down the street. One of my fellow students and her boyfriend stood up with us one evening after work. The minister was nice. Two of the other interns, both men, came to the wedding. I was totally surprised, but very pleased to see them there. I did not speak of my pregnancy to my boss or co-workers although I am sure many guessed. I imagine my maid of honor had told some of the other students about the wedding. I had not felt judgment from either the other students or my teachers, about the pregnancy or the wedding, but I certainly felt shame. At the same time, we still continued to feel expectant and happy about our coming baby.

Before the wedding, I called my mother with much trepidation, and told her I was pregnant and getting married. She was, of course, sad, and shocked. I only know after having my own children and loving and caring about them, how difficult that must have been for her. I was, after all, the oldest and first. I am certain, in hindsight, that I hurt my parents greatly. I must have dashed their dreams in more ways than one with that decision. My mind was fixed on the alienation, not on how they might feel. I think I actually believed that they did not care. That is, my mother didn't. My dad had been silent. Clark and I had a picture taken of us at the wedding, and sent out wedding announcements to friends and family.

Married, Now What?

There was a financial recession in that area of the country in 1958, and I continued my internship, (not getting paid, except for call nights) and Clark found odd jobs. We barely managed to pay our $25 dollar a month rent. I could eat lunches at the hospital and those donuts in the mornings, and attempt to save something for Clark.

Aside from that, I was not much of a cook. I knew how to cook steak, but that was of no use on our budget. I also knew how to make tuna noodle casserole, and tuna salad. That was about the extent of my cooking. I could make toasted cheese sandwiches too, and we ate a lot of those. Clark's grandma sent us some of her home made noodles, and I asked Clark how to fix them. He said, "I think you soak them until they are soft" So we soaked them 2 days and threw them out when they smelled rotten. In spite of all the odds, we managed, as many young couples seem to do. And I was physically healthy, so my pregnancy proceeded naturally, and was no problem after the morning sickness subsided.

Back to Michigan Again

In June, my internship was over, and I graduated with honors from Michigan State, in absentia. We went to the St. Vincent DePaul store and bought a big old steamer trunk. We put everything we owned in it, and shipped it back to Michigan by rail. Then we got on the bus for the long ride back. I remember my ankles swelling because of inactivity on the long ride, but no flying squirrels, and no more silver dollars.

We got to Michigan, and went to the cottage at Half Moon Lake where Clark's parents were for the summer. Up to this point, I had not seen a doctor, other than when I had been morning sick, nor did I feel a need to, as I had great faith in my health and in the natural process of childbirth. I just enjoyed the summer, picking elderberries and swimming. It was a good and healthy respite, to be where there were parents again. Paul and Delilah, Clark's parents, were always kind to me, and to us. They were thrilled about a grandchild, and totally non-judgmental, at least out loud, about our marriage and pregnancy.

HIGH SCHOOL

Timmy at my side

1950's glamour picture

Prom – Chuck and I

High School Graduation picture

Square dancing

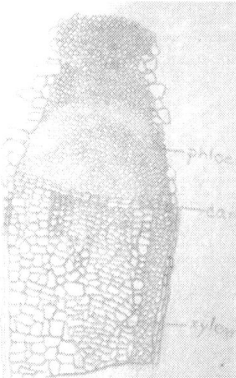

Biology Drawing

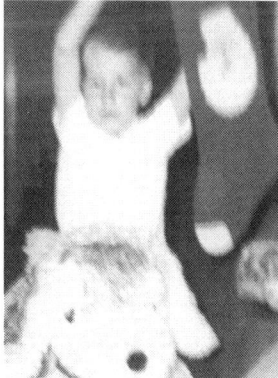

Charlie

Becky and A.H.

COLLEGE

MORE COLLEGE

Me upper left – square dancing again

Roommate Sally Shively

On the banks of the Red Cedar Skinny me

Tacoma General Hospital

A WEDDING !

MARRIED LIFE AND CHILDREN – 1958-70

AGES 22-35

Moving to Midland –1958

Toward the end of the summer, I got a call from my mother, wanting us to come see her obstetrician. (Dr. Irvin Howe, who had delivered my younger brother Charles 5 years before.) Her call surprised me, as I still believed she did not care and had written me off. As far as seeing the doctor, I thought one just waited until going into labor, and went to the hospital. I really had not thought of prenatal care, not realizing it was necessary and still taking very good care of my health and diet.

I was longing for reconciliation with my mom and dad, and as she talked about an exam before delivery, it made sense, so I talked with Clark and we agreed to go.

While there, my parents brought up moving there for the delivery and to live afterwards. Pam was due in October and this was September. My father told me he owned a small house on Ashman Street, and would rent it to us. It was only years later that I figured out that he probably bought it for that very purpose, so that they could be sure that their grandchild, and I were taken care of. My situation certainly must have brought back my mother's fears from her first marriage – that of living away from home and no family to see what was happening. As I look back I feel so much more grateful and heartful toward my parents than I did then. The pain of the rejection kept me from seeing past my own life then.

Clark and I had decided long ago in college, if we ever had a girl, we would name her Pamela Jo. My roommate was Sally Jo, and Jo was the name of one of the characters in the book, Little Women. I thought it was a feminine and strong name. Of course we had no way of knowing whether the baby was a girl or boy. Yet I was quite certain, and indeed had a strong sense of probability about the sex of all three of our children.

Pam

While pregnant, I spent a lot of time knitting (thank you again Miss Ritchie) I knit at least two outfits for the baby. One, a mint green one piece outfit with snaps at the crotch with a little elephant overstitched on it. I also knit a sweater. I enjoyed the knitting and talking to, or thinking of my unborn baby as I knit.

My sister Becky made me a maternity skirt and top. I had been wearing Clark's jeans or khakis with a long piece of elastic, or rubber bands at the top of the opening, leaving the zipper open. Baggy shirts or sweatshirts covered the open zipper. I was so

111

grateful for Becky's gift, as we had no income and I had not been able to buy clothes. Now I had a pretty outfit when I needed it. I felt good during my whole pregnancy, although I missed swimming after we left the lake.

We did move to Midland, and I even went to work at the hospital lab until the baby was born – this time as a full-fledged technician. Luckily, I was there the day I went into labor. I was hurting, and checked with some of the women who had children, and we decided that yes, it was probably labor. So I walked down to the OB floor, where my doctor was scheduled to make his rounds in an hour or so. He suggested I admit myself, although also saying it might be a while before the baby was born. Indeed, about 10 hours later, our Pamela Jo made her entrance. It was around 9:30 pm I believe.

It was a normal delivery and I was so fortunate. Dr. Howe had set up a mirror, not a usual thing. I am not sure if he did that knowing I was familiar with medical events, or just because of his friendship with our family. I watched her emerge from inside of me, watched them clean her face off, and then saw and heard her first cry. It may be an overused phrase to say that watching my daughter born was a miracle, but indeed it felt like one. She was a healthy baby, somewhere over 8 pounds. No fathers in the delivery room in those days, but Clark saw her as we left the delivery room for my room. We were both so thrilled, and I was in love with my daughter.

Pam was a perfect child to have for a first baby. She was calm, ate well, slept well, and developed normally. I nursed her (and each of the boys), for at least three months, and I think more like four or 5. Looking into her eyes, and watching her look back at me while she snuggled against me nursing, several times a day, was the highlight of my life at that time. Within 6 weeks, I unfortunately went back to work at the hospital, and continued to nurse her for awhile, exchanging one breastfeeding a day for a bottle. We needed the money from my job to pay off the doctor and hospital bills. As I remember, the doctor charged $350.00

It had only been 5 years since I took care of Charlie as a newborn, so in a way this was not a new experience, but I must say that having my own child felt very different than taking care of a younger sib. I was so in love, and so aware of the large responsibility. Charlie was still in Pre School when Pam was born, and went to school proudly proclaiming that he was an uncle.

Pam was no more than a few weeks old when Clark brought home a puppy. I felt immediate overwhelm thinking of potty training a puppy, taking time to pay attention to both the pup and the baby, and also working. Somehow we managed, and our dog Freckles, even had a litter of pups when she grew up. She was not one of my memorable pets, and I don't remember her fate. I suspect she may have been given away when we later moved to Detroit.

One incident I remember was the coal furnace in that house rented from Dad. We didn't know it, but the firepot was cracked. Thus the temperature was barely controllable, and at times it would get very hot in the house, and at other times the fire would go out, and it would get cold. One morning we woke up and Pam's bottle, given in the middle of the night, was frozen on the floor. We had no idea how dangerous that condition was, and luckily nothing more happened before we moved. We were fortunate

Pregnant Again

Even re-reading this it seems like I ought to write a lot more about Pam before another baby enters the picture. That is how I felt then, also. There should have been a lot more time, more firsts, more events with Pam before it was time to think of another child. But at times, nature intervenes despite our best plans and precautions, and here I was pregnant again. It was commonly thought that nursing mothers did not get pregnant, but we clearly disproved that. Obviously, this baby really wanted to be here. We were using proper prevention besides the nursing.

I was working the 3-11 shifts, in order to be with Pam as much as possible. One of the interns at the hospital, when noticing my second pregnancy approached me in a kidding way and asked: "Do you know what causes that."

Clark and I were a little scared – No, make that a lot scared about the financial aspects, and a little scared about two small children to care for. I was the main breadwinner, our hospital bill was not paid yet, and our money was barely paying our present bills. I went back to Dr. Howe, still distraught about being pregnant again so soon, but he assured me that his fees were the same whether I saw him early or later in the pregnancy. He also assured us we would have time to pay him. He was so positive about things working out, and I left him feeling more hopeful. He affirmed that I was physically fit and healthy. Knowing my parents, he may have thought they would help if needed. I am not sure they would have. However, he was right, things did work out. It was just difficult physically and financially for a year or so.

When my mom learned of the second pregnancy, she got angry, and in fact, ended up in the hospital for depression and psychosis within a few weeks. I apparently had put her plans out of commission again, and that was the straw that broke the camel's back on her fragile mental health. It turned out she was planning that once Pam was a little older, I would divorce Clark. I had no such idea. She had done things like invite me over for dinner with the baby, but not invite Clark, and of course I refused. I carried some sorrow and guilt about being the cause of her hospitalization, even though I realized I had done nothing wrong. I was eventually able to move on, resolving my confusion about that.

Thinking back, my mom would have been about 47, surely near or at menopause. There was little done then for women who had a difficult time with their hormonal changes. I suspect that "there but for the grace of God, and advances in medicine, go I". At the time I was judgmental, as if she could have done better, but surely she could not have, given all of what went before, including her drinking.

I certainly have changed over the years. I don't know what happened with her, and I wish it had not. It would have been nice to have a different kind of mom, both for me and for the younger kids still at home, as well as a different kind of grandma for my children, but it was not to happen.

I was certain about this baby being a boy, and we chose James Clark for his name. The pregnancy was easy, and Pam continued to be an easy child. She was being rocked to sleep nightly by her dad while I worked. Clark found part time work at a photographic lab during the day, and was learning color processing. I was on call once a month for the weekend, at the lab, which meant it was possible I would work 36 hours straight without sleep. I was fortunate that I could almost always take a 20 minute nap before going to work for my 3-11 shifts. On those call weekends, I slept on the blood bank cots in the lab. I was constantly short of sleep and tired.

Lab Life

I was sole employee on the afternoon shift. My work consisted of doing routine blood and urine tests on all next-day surgical patients. There were extra tests for those at risk—the anemic, the diabetic, etc. And then there was lab work from the medical floors or the emergency department as needed, and it was needed often. Working alone made things easier in some ways. On the other hand, I had no one to share the work with when busy, and no one to share the responsibility with. It was a heavy load at times.

Sometimes I finished early, and visited my colleagues or helped out somewhere else. Other times, there was extra lab work, or an ongoing urgent situation, and I got home at one or two in the morning, rather than 11 pm.

One night, there was a horrible accident. A hot water heater exploded in a home and burned the father terribly. He and the mother were able to rescue the children, but all were burned. I had finished my work for the evening, but stayed all night that night setting up blood for the family, doing other lab work, and helping out in ER when I had time. There were no special burn centers then, as there are now. The husband and father eventually died, and the others were scarred for life, even with many skin grafts. Events like that widen one's scope of how life can happen. It also gave me some idea of the things my father had seen and been part of at the funeral home and ambulance business. In fact, our ambulance brought some of that family in that night.

114

The most responsible and critical task for a med tech was typing and cross-matching blood for a transfusion. People could die from small mistakes, and there was no room for error. The techs who handed the blood to the nurses the next day had to trust that the work and the labeling was accurate. I felt most alone in those times.

In Midland, the ever present threat of a large hospital emergency came from Dow Chemical with its potential for explosion or chemical accident. This situation might mean multiple patients needing blood, or lab work, even worse than the family accident above. . When I was already tired, I dreaded the possibility. I used to dream about it. Fortunately it never happened while I was there, but there were times when my fatigue left me vulnerable, and I would talk out loud to myself as I set up transfusions. That way, my voice was a check on what my hands were doing as I could see and hear myself work. I was most fortunate that I never made a mistake which hurt or killed someone.

My old longing to be a physician still existed. I often ate with the interns and tried to outguess them on diagnosing their difficult patients. I did fairly well, and it was fun, stimulating and educational.

Over time, I got to know people who were frequent patients. I was skilled at drawing blood, and was assigned the pediatric ward among others. Thus I got the "privilege" of sticking needles into the vulnerable kids with chronic diseases. I could only justify my actions by their necessity, and also by knowing that someone else may not have done as good a job.

A vivid memory of a young girl, Elizabeth, comes back to me. She was 9 years old and had cystic fibrosis. She was back in the hospital with yet another lung infection and I went to draw her blood one Friday afternoon. I said "Elizabeth, I will see you Monday night" She looked at me and said "I won't be here". I asked if she thought she would be going home before then, and she said no. She was prophetic. I came to work Monday, and she had died during the day. I was often humbled by what we don't know and can't explain in medicine and in people's lives. I learned to listen to the patients as carefully as I listened to the doctors.

Jim

Meanwhile, every time I ate during this second pregnancy, the baby got hiccups. I used meditation and relaxation techniques, knowing I was stressed, and not wanting to stress my baby. However, that did not stop the tiny little jerks from inside my uterus. The little guy may have been sensitive to some food, or something. He was much more active than Pam had been while I carried her, not even counting the hiccups.

I went into labor this time in the middle of the night like most people, and had about 6 hours between the time I got to the hospital and the time Jim was born.

Jim was born two days short of Pam's first birthday. October 26, 1959. He was a healthy baby with dark hair, as compared to Pam's red hair. There were no APGAR scores then, but I don't doubt he would have scored within normal range. It was clear within a few days, that this guy had a very different energy and character than his sister. He was active, not so cuddly and had difficulty sleeping.

Within a few weeks, he had developed colic, as they called it. I suspect now that he had celiac disease as an infant, but that was not on anyone's radar then. If so, he has apparently outgrown it. From 10:00 pm to 2 or 3 am every night, he screamed and cried uncontrollably. We tried different temperatures in the room, different foods, and different positions. We tried swaddling him, walking with him, taking him in the car, holding him various ways. We tried everything we could think of, and both he and we got more tired. Because I was nursing him, I slept in the rocker/recliner, holding him on my shoulder or belly every night for months.

I can remember one night when nothing would stop the crying and obvious distress. I was strung tight inside with the struggle of attempts and failures to help my son feel safe and peaceful. I felt like a failure as a mom, and I was exhausted. I took him into his bed, and laid him very gently in it, carefully controlling the growing storm inside myself. I shut the bedroom door so his screams were not so loud, and walked out the front door. There I began to cry and scream. I was as helpless in my way, as he was in his. I could not seem to help him, and he was my son. That incident made me understand parents who throw or hit their child. I had felt the urge. It certainly was not his fault, but there were times when it bruised my psyche and self-esteem and I did not know what to do with my own frustration or his. I didn't know how to love him so he felt it and was helped by my love, and the doctors were not much help, simply saying he would outgrow it. I felt inadequate, helpless, tired, and hurting for him, and for me. In time, things got better, but it was a very difficult time.

His lower legs and feet were turned inward, and bowed when he was born, and massage and care did not seem to change that. The orthopedist suggested leg casts. Those were applied at about 10 months old just as he was pulling himself up to walk. More frustration but no good alternatives in sight. The casts were adjusted about once a month, sort of like braces on teeth. He had them on for 6 months. As soon as they came off, he was walking within a week or two.

On looking back, I know that I, and possibly Clark, were just putting one foot in front of the other and doing what needed doing. We were short of money, energy and time. One example of our state

116

was our aforementioned coal furnace, which we sometimes had no money to purchase coal for. We would go to the railroad tracks, where the trains still hauled coal, and pick up the extra from around the tracks. There were occasional times that we chose baby food and milk over food for us. I suspect, if I thought at all, I thought it was just part of getting started in family life, and would get better. I continued to work full time, and wished that Clark could find full time work. I remained chronically tired. And of course, eventually it did get better – after several years of scarcity.

I often came home to a very messy home. Clark was taking care of the children, and as I walked in the door I started picking up dirty diapers and whatever else was on the floor. I then did the wash, fixed the dinner, and got my clothes and uniform ready for the next day's work. I can remember holding two children, spoon feeding one, and nursing the other. I did not have the skills or practice in clear, direct, loving communication between Clark and I. The best I knew was to behave in loving ways until my anger built to the place where I could not contain it. I then had a stack attack, (angry about a whole stack of things) and yelled at him. He responded like a chastised child, getting out the vacuum, or doing some cleaning until I calmed down and the cycle started over again. I felt like an angry mom, and he responded like a bawled out kid. I didn't know how to break the cycle. Unfortunately, I did the same with the kids at times.

In today's world, counseling, or books on relationship would be plentifully available, and I might have taken advantage of them. These things came 10 years later or so, and indeed I did take advantage of them, but at the time, they were not culturally widely available.

It is amazing how much I missed, or do not remember about the children's young years. I remember reading to them, holding them, cooking and cleaning, but I hardly remember restful or fun times when they were very small. My sister was babysitting for us part of the time and fortunately was a neat person and cleaned our house a lot. If she judged us, she did not say anything, and I was thankful.

Clark then began to work for my father at the funeral home. It was a mixed blessing, as my dad paid low wages and then magnanimously offered extra money to "go out to dinner". We needed the steady income more than the nights out spending lavishly. However, we were both thankful for steady work and income.

Moving To Detroit – 1960

Clark came home one day mentioning the possibility of Mortuary School., a two year program at Wayne State University in Detroit. He would then have a funeral directors and embalmers license, and his job opportunities would be wider. When I was in college, my dad had asked if I wanted to go to Mortuary School, and he also asked my brother. I think he really wanted a third generation in the funeral business when he retired. He may have thought Clark was his hope for that.

After some thought, we decided to go, and packed up our two small children and household for the move. Pam was 2 1/2 and Jim 1 ½, casts still on. We moved to a 4th floor walkup apartment at 683 Prentiss, a few blocks from Wayne State University Mortuary School, in a seedy part of Detroit, not too far from downtown. Seedy meant that we were near the Jeffries projects, now abandoned, but then a large poverty level apartment project. It also meant we were near a bar where it quickly became obvious that there was more than just a bar business being run. There were expensive cars with expensively dressed men picking up and dropping off scantily dressed women, all day and presumably all night. It was pretty clear that sex was being peddled for money. We often walked that way on our way to the neighborhood playground with the children, and although I was friendly and spoke with the women, we kept our distance. I was unfamiliar with that side of life, and wanted to stay that way, even though there was some curiosity. As I have grown and learned a bit about human trafficking, it makes me wonder more about those women and their lives.

A 4th floor walkup apartment meant a lot of steps, carrying groceries, children, and anything else that needed to be carried. One day, Clark leaned way out on that porch railing 4 stories up, and nailed a board to one of the porch posts on our back porch. We then attached a pulley and rope and rigged a way to pull things up to the apartment in a laundry basket. Groceries of course, not children.

Ah yes, that was also the place where the Cockroach Adventures took place. First came the children's delight at coming in the door in the evening, and seeing who could stomp the most cockroaches, as they skittered back to their dark cracks. Then the problem got worse – too many to stomp. I suspect the whole building was infested, although it seemed our part of it was one of the worst in spite of our carefulness. We had difficulty not eating the ones who invaded our food, and the thought was not appetizing. The little ones were hard to see. We found them in the clean laundry, and certainly they were in the dirty laundry, embarrassing us at the Laundromat. It was quite gross to sort out the roaches from the raisins in the cereal every morning.

We decided something had to be done, and although we were at least partially conscious of the danger of sprays, Clark and I put on masks and shut the bedroom door to the kids' room, and totally soaked the apartment with bug spray. It certainly cut down the population, and we are fortunate that it did not seem to injure any of us. I may even have been pregnant then.

When we packed to move, we carefully packed one item at a time, and when the box was full, sealed all the seams and took it to the storage room which seemed cockroach free. Even so, when we got to our next home, we found over 200 roaches as we unpacked. We had missed the ones that were inside the toaster, and in the cracks of the kid's rocking horse, among other places. Those guys concealed themselves anywhere sticky fingers, skin cells, or a crumb of food might have been. We unpacked very carefully, stomping and squishing live roaches as we unpacked outdoors. Fortunately, we won that war. Although we saw an occasional one, they were not thick enough to reproduce, and we gradually stopped seeing them.

Returning to the Detroit time, I found a job at Parke Davis Pharmaceuticals very soon after we moved. I would be doing antibiotic research, testing soil samples from all over the world under the direction of a Dr. Hillegas. I was working in downtown Detroit, by the Detroit River. Our lab had two professional techs and one lab assistant who was a member of the union. Fortunately, neither she nor we distinguished between union and nonunion duties, simply helping each other and getting the job done.

Our job was to preserve and freeze dry those soil samples, and then test them for antibiotic activity. We tested against both bacteria and molds, always hoping to find the next penicillin, or tetracycline. It was interesting work, and required good technique and exact record keeping. Noon hours, we relaxed, eating our lunches down by the river, and watching the boats go by. As a byproduct of that job, our house sported an old oak roll top desk for many years that came from the company surplus store for $20.

One of our favorite weekend family activities was to walk from our apartment to downtown Detroit to wander around window shopping. We enjoyed watching the Vernors' bottling plant, and hoping to eat some day in Greenfield's cafeteria, both long gone now. If we window shopped at Hudson's on Sunday's, we occasionally came back there to wander through the inside of the store when it was open. We couldn't afford much, but there were several floors of merchandise, and looking around was an adventure all its own.

Belle Isle was our city escape from hot weather. It is an island in the Detroit River, made into a park, and still viable. The apartment had no air conditioning and even if it had, we might not have had the money to use it. There were breezes coming through those windows, high off the ground, but for the most part, it was like any inner city apartment in summer – fairly warm. We often went to Belle Isle for dinner, buying hot dogs there, and then swimming or watching the herd of white deer. Some weekends we visited the aquarium, or watched people fish for and barbeque carp from the river.

Belle Isle was also our viewing place for the unlimited hydroplane boat races. Clark and I had been fans in Seattle before we moved

119

back. We had our favorite boats and drivers (Miss Budweiser, Bill Muncey who drove the Atlas Van Lines boat) Now we could watch them in Detroit. Those huge Allison engines with their loud and throaty roar, were thrilling to hear and to watch, as they spouted their rooster tails, using the river water to cool the engines.

My innocence about life in the big city showed when we were downtown one hot humid summer day. There was a man lying on the sidewalk with flies all over him. People stepped around him, appearing not to notice. I was scared for him, and appalled at the lack of response. I found a policeman, and asked about the man, and the policeman chuckled under his breath, and said that the guy was probably a drunk. I was angry, and responded that I was concerned that the man might be diabetic, or have had a heart attack or some other medical condition. I badgered the officer, until they called an ambulance, which took the man away, I assume to Detroit General Hospital, not too far away. I still have trouble when I see obvious needs for medical or mental health care, and non response of fellow human beings. I have the most trouble when I feel myself not wanting to respond, when I am tempted to become "one of them"

With the certainty of working at Parke Davis, we needed a baby sitter. An ad in the paper brought us a wonderful find in the person of Mrs. Mildred Hardison, who the kids, with her permission, called 'Hardy". She took the kids outside every day, up and down those flights of stairs. She was not well at the time, but did not tell us, nor was I there to see her struggle. She was on time and consistent, as well as so good with the kids, earning my implicit trust.

One day after work she met me at the door with the news that she was quitting, starting now. With no relatives and no backup, this was a crisis! I asked what was happening, and found that she thought Pam had called her a nigger. She was not staying around for that. I was immediately doubtful, as our kids had never heard the word at home, and had little contact with other children. I had never heard it from them.

I begged Mrs. Hardison to stay, explaining my doubts, and promising to get to the bottom of the incident. That very weekend, Pam was playing with her dolls and I heard her say what sounded to me like "nigger". I asked her to repeat it, and was relieved to hear her two year old little girl voice, talking to her doll, calling her "little girl", with it sounding very much like nyi-gir, and translating easily into "nigger" When Mrs. Hardison came the next Monday, I had Pam say it for her, and the crisis was over. She was with us for the entire two years. After we moved away from Detroit, we came back to visit one weekend, and attempted to look her up, finding that she had died.

My father's sister, my Aunt Lucile, and her husband, Morley Warren, lived in Indian Village not too far out Jefferson from downtown Detroit. Aunt Lucile was the beloved favorite aunt of all her nieces and nephews. She loved children, and it was a dream having her live close by. It was like an extra set of grandparents. Lucile had frail health from an old case of tuberculosis when she was in college. Morley was a binge drinking alcoholic, so they were not candidates to take care of the children if needed, but they had us over for dinner often, and went several places with us, including Bob-Lo Island Amusement Park. They were kind and generous, and Aunt Cele was fun to be with.

She had acquired her tuberculosis when in nurses training, and left school to go to Saranac New York to live in a Sanitarium. Her mother had died of TB when the kids were young. After her treatment, Lucile had only one working lung. She was an amazing lady of limited energy, but unlimited love and generosity. She loved all children, and made all people of any age feel special. She had a marvelous sense of humor, and looked on the bright side with a twinkle in her eye. She was compulsively generous, pulling bills out of her apron or pocket and tucking them into the hands or pockets of her nieces and nephews. She lived her later years at Higgins Lake, and everyone from the postman to the neighbors loved to spend time in her company, and cared about her. I always thought of her as one of God's angels in human form. Her home was like a museum with a sense of humor, - good natured, often political cartoons pasted around and a sign that said Skunk Hollow out in the yard.

Besides being an angel, her best characteristic to me, was her joy at being my co-conspirator in scouring the second hand stores in the Detroit Area. It was our passion and our spare time fun. It was often even our Christmas Shopping trip. We found things we needed, things we wanted, and gifts for others, both funny and serious. I discovered the stores in my section of town, and she in hers. She had been around Detroit longer and also knew the fancy consignment stores in Grosse Pointe and area. There are still things around my home, or my cousin's home, found in that era. (My cousin lives in Aunt Cile's former home at Higgins Lake.) Many of us in the family carry on the tradition of enjoying second hand stores, and getting our furniture, knick knacks and sometimes our clothes there. Pam has a large round frame with a picture of a lion in it that came from that era. That was almost 50 years ago, and so that frame, old when I bought it, probably is over 100 years old.

One night we went to Aunt Lu's for dinner. Morley was drinking and Aunt Lucile busy fixing the spaghetti. Morley announced that he would test the spaghetti to see if it was done. He proceeded to take a strand out of the pot and throw it at the wall. He announced "When it sticks to the wall, it's done. Their walls had recently been painted, and it was clear that Aunt Lucile was dismayed. . She promptly one-upped him as she left the room, and came back with an empty picture frame. She pounded a small nail into the wall, and framed

121

the spaghetti. Aunt Cile's life was not easy. Uncle Morley used to take the car to Detroit, and lose both his money and car. He then took a cab home, leaving Aunt Cile to hire Joseph, the apartment maintenance man to go to Detroit and search for the car. There were also out of town business trips when Morley spent his entire paycheck and Aunt Lucile had to skimp until the next one. His employer sent him to dry out several times to no avail. He remained a drinker to the end, with brain damage which made his temper tantrums dangerous. In spite of that, his nieces and nephews found him fascinating, hearing about his times in the Navy, or on assignment for the newspaper, or his attempts at becoming a writer. The sad ending was that he drove the wrong way on a freeway one night, crashing into and killing a mother and daughter, as well as himself. That happened many years after we lived in Detroit.

In the fall, the Detroit Thanksgiving Day Parade was a stand – out. It was something like New York's Macy's parade, but I suppose not as big. There were huge balloon figures, stored carefully from year to year, and numerous floats, bands and horses. It was a big deal for children, and ours were no exception. We put on winter clothes, to stave off the late fall cold, and waited in our place on the curb for what seemed like hours. We took blankets to wrap the children in. When the parade finally came, the kids clapped and eagerly waited for the Santa float at the very end. They raced to pick up the candy that was thrown from other floats. One year, my mother brought Charlie down, and they stayed in a nearby motel, where we all watched the parade in relative warmth from their window or balcony.

Charlie, who was only 7 at the time, also came to stay with us and see the play, "Hair". He flew to Detroit, and it was only years later that I knew he got off the plane at the wrong airport, and someone chased him down and made sure he got back on.

Another Aunt Lucile adventure was Eastern Market, a large outdoor-indoor market where restaurants and individuals bought produce, meat, and fish. It has survived the downfall of Detroit, and still operates.

The Detroit Zoo in Royal Oak was a must. Our kids were the third generation in our family to enjoy that. Zoo philosophy has changed over the years and I have not been there recently to see how this zoo has changed, but I still hear friends talk about going there. When I went to the zoo as a little girl, I spied the first black person I had ever seen. I excitedly shouted, "Mommy, look at the big ape!" thinking he was a gorilla. Sheltered kids = no social manners. (And probably embarrassment and hurt feelings.)

Our two years in Detroit were fun, relaxed, and with enough money to be comfortable. The watchful and twinkling eyes of Aunt Lu, along with Uncle Morley, were such a gift. I spent much more time with the children than I had been able to in Midland, and was away from the stress of my mother's disapproval of my marriage. Those were good years for us all.

Moving back to Midland – 1961

After Clark graduated from Mortuary School, we moved back to Midland (As aforementioned, carrying a few unwanted cockroaches across the Detroit and Midland border with us). Clark would now be working as a licensed mortician for my dad. We had talked about having another child and were pregnant with our planned child, but had planned the timing so there was plenty of time for Clark to graduate and us to get back to Midland. I finished my job at Parke Davis, and we packed. At the time, we had a 1957 Chevrolet, and packed some in that, and then rented a truck to move. As usual, the natural order of the world was smiling on us, and my pregnancy was healthy and good. What a turn our lives might have taken had anything happened to me, Clark, or one of the babies during pregnancy or delivery, or beyond. We were most fortunate.

It was 1963, and we found a small home out on Waldo Road in the country. I settled into being a mom and housewife, waiting for our baby, which we assumed would be another boy. Clark was continuing work at the funeral home. We probably moved in June or July, and Bob was born the following February.

My only claim to fame became the Science Radio Program sponsored by Dow Chemical. At the end of the program, there was a science question, and the first to call with the answer won a prize; products of Dow Chemical. Science was my forte, and I ended up with more Saran Wrap than we could possibly use. I quickly learned to dial all but the last number of the radio station, and then if I knew the answer, I dialed the last number. That generally made me the first caller. The Midland Daily News came out and interviewed me and took a picture of the children and we ended up in the paper. The town was still small, the world news quieter, and someone who won the radio show a lot was deemed of local interest. The kids enjoyed seeing their picture.

During that time, Becky got into more conflict than usual with my dad. I will let her tell the story some day in her way, but she decided to move out and come to live with us. It only took about a week before she moved back home. She could not stand to take a bus to school, and she had to carefully pick up the pins when she was using the sewing machine because of the babies and the dog. Timothy Jones Bradley was back living with us again.

Bob's Beginning, Timmy's Ending

In fact, about that time, Timmy began to wake me at night, obviously in pain. He, of the dog pound rescue was getting old. He was by now about 14 years old. A trip to the vet uncovered cancer which had spread to his bones and his internal organs, causing the pain. I took him home, but not for long. He was soon in so much pain that it was cruel to let him continue living with it. I sadly, and with about 12 years of history with him, took him to be euthanized. I might have prolonged his life had there not been two small children to care for and a third on the way. He was getting cross with the kids, and I was having difficulty being waked up many times a night when he wanted comforting. He was gently nosing me awake when he was hurting, seemingly not wanting to be alone in his pain. It was a sad time for me. Losing a long term pet is always difficult. Making the decision to end their life even more so. Having the children around softened the blow for me, but I had a lot of feelings about him.

Bob was born February 25, 1962, a whole month overdue. My doctor seldom induced labor. He felt that as long as the baby sounded healthy, and the mom was doing well, nature knew better than he. Clark had been out on ambulance calls nearly the whole night before, and was getting a good night's sleep, and now I had to disturb him. We got to the hospital with about 45 minutes to spare. When Bob was finally born, he was a precocious infant who, in many ways, really did act about a month old. He smiled real smiles, and shed real tears from the day he was born. He slept through the night from about 4 days old. He had a voracious appetite, such that I began to feed him cereal within a couple weeks, along with nursing him. He was so laid back and content, and required so little care, that the first time we went over to my parents with him, (he was a week or two old) we forgot him. (Sorry Bob) He was sleeping in the bedroom, and when we were ready to leave, we bundled up Pam and Jim and started to walk out. We got almost to the car, and I said, "Wait a minute, we forgot Bob" It slipped my tired mind, and everyone else's. After all, we had cared for only two children for 2 ½ years.

Bob was an unusual baby. He not only seemed mature, but somehow aware and innately wise from the time he was small. All of my children had obvious gifts, strengths and individualities. Bob seemed different in a way that I did not fully understand, except that I always had the feeling that he was somehow more than most people, and it had nothing to do with that "special ness" of my family, or an ego thing. He seemed to take in and understand more about his world than any other baby I had seen. I had a premonition that he might die early, and it scared me, but as time went on, without incident or illness, I felt more relaxed. There came a point when I realized that if something happened to him, I would do what I could, and other than that, I had to trust God to care for him., and the others too. That freed me up to enjoy the children and not be hyper-vigilant about him, or any of them.

124

By the time Pam started school, Jim was almost 4 and Bob 1 ½ We bought our first house. - a house on Indian Street in Midland. When we left there, we sold it on a land contract and moved to 1116 W. Park Drive. That was 1965 and Bob was about 3 years old. It is amazing to me as I write this how time gets stretched out in my memory. For instance, my memories make it seem that we lived in each home for several years, but when I think of the ages of the kids when we moved, we did not live anywhere nearly as long as I thought.

It was one of the fortunate things of our marriage that Clark and I agreed about money. We never had fights about what to spend, how to pay bills, or what we needed for material goods. Together we decided that we would never again count on my income to pay bills, thus I would have the freedom to work when I wanted to, but to full time parent when I wanted to or needed to also. If I was asked to do something I particularly liked, I was free to work, and then stop when finished. It gave me good control over my individual time, rhythms, and judgment about the children's development.

Besides work, I indulged my joy of writing and the dream of being a free-lancer. I took a writing course at Delta College, (now University). We were given a little sign that said "Write to express, not to impress." I hope I have stayed with that in this writing

Here is one of the poems I wrote around that time which I submitted but never was published. I did not succeed as a free-lancer, although I enjoyed writing tremendously. Many years later I came closest to being a "writer" when I was making several hundred dollars a month from my writing. Here is that poem from back then.

That's Cats

Baby kittens snuggled close
So innocent and sweet
They seek the warmth of food and love
Between their mother's feet
Their antics are a source of joy
With all their spits and spats
Too bad that kittens soon grow up
And end up just plain cats.

The Animals We Owned

(I am going to skip ahead here as well as talk about animals we owned during this time. Pets figured heavily in our lives, especially later when we no longer lived in Midland.)

Obviously I liked cats. I seem to have owned them, or rather they have owned me most of my adult life. My mom didn't like cats, so my childhood was cat-less, but when the kids were young, cats found us wherever we were. Bob was allergic to them, although I did not realize that for several years after he developed the allergy. We had at least one cat most of the time, and I still have cats. We had a couple batches of kittens while the kids were growing up, and so they were exposed to baby animals, and birth through our cats, as well as the puppies mentioned before. We also had our share of accidental deaths, or cats that ran away, exposing the children to the realities of death and loss.

I find cats a satisfactory companion – smarter than most think, more trainable, and seldom co-dependent. They have a mind of their own, and do not pay attention to me unless we happen to connect. They want what they want when they want it, and ask directly. They are just as plain about what they don't want, whether it is petting, or a brand of food. They enjoy being loved, and enjoy independence. Generally, it is better to have two to keep each other company. They learn from each other, and collaborate in play and hunting. Although they are a hindrance to us when we want to travel, we continue to get pleasure out of having them around. The density of pets, both cats and dogs in the senior co-operative where we now live is high. We have been tempted to get a dog, but they are "care intensive" compared to cats, and neither of us wants the responsibility or the disadvantages.

As our children grew up, we owned dogs pretty consistently. After Timmy, there were several. We inherited two dogs from Clark's parents when they died. There was a beagle named Snoopy, and an English Setter named Cindy. We quickly found a home for Cindy. We had Snoopy for several years. We had a dog named Curly, who accompanied us on many of our camping trips along with Snoopy. In the car Snoopy often got car sick. Curly thought that was nonsense, and would turn around and bite him, attempting to change his behavior. It made for chaotic moments in a closed van, and the kids learned to get their feet out of the middle of the fight pretty quickly. We also had two geese for a season. We came home one day to find that they had been slaughtered by a neighboring malamute. We were all sad that we had not been there to protect them.

Another experience with death was the pigeon which had fallen from an eaves trough nest and was not being cared for by the parents. Since pigeons eat from the parents' gullet, we learned to form our fist into a funnel with an opening at one end, and let our baby eat from that opening, sticking its head down into the fist, as it would have its mother's throat. That adventure ended in a tragedy, when just as the baby was ready to learn flight, we put it in its cage one night, put the cage in a closet so the cats would not get it, and went to bed. Somehow the closet door did not shut tight and the cats killed the pigeon through the cage bars during the night. We all cried for Homer's death.

Our most unique pet was our baby raccoon, Igor. Igor taught us how to make him into an indoor/outdoor pet, as well as teaching us a great deal about raccoons. He had a spot in the house which he used for a bathroom, and we learned to put papers there and change them daily. A pet raccoon seduces one with cuteness and affection. They are intelligent, curious, affectionate, and mischievous. Their little hands are velvety soft, as they feel and explore one's face or arms. Their curiosity leads them to explore many things. Igor got into a box of Oreos one day and became an instant addict. It is not true that raccoons dip all their food in water. He did not care whether he had water with his Oreos or not. He did however love to play in water, and a pan of water with a leaf, a frog or a hard dog biscuit in it kept him interested for a long time.

Igor was also seemingly addicted to the smell of lighter fluid. Clark smoked, and as he walked in the door after work, Igor came running, continued running up his pant leg and started searching in his pocket for the lighter. He worked the lighter out of the pocket, and turned his treasure over and over, as if it were precious gold, or the best food. He felt, and smelled, and seemed to be in a trance. Igor and the dog were buddies, playing together with great glee. One of Igor's mischievous tricks was to sneak up in back of the dog, or one of his people, and grab their ankles with his front paws. Scared us every time.

We eventually had to make a decision to let him go when he matured. He began getting nasty, and aggressive toward us. Also, if he got left in the house, he now created chaos, pulling things out of cupboards, and tearing them to shreds. After a sad interlude, we took him to a place where we knew there were many raccoons and a good food source and hoped that he could adjust.

I wish we had one of those "happy ending" stories where we saw him two years later, and he came to us in answer to our special call, but the truth is, we never saw him again, although we looked a few times. We could only hope he had a good life. I suspect we did him a great disservice by raising him as we did. It was good for us, but I am not sure it was good for him in the long run.

We also had our share of guinea pigs, hamsters (had to have "hampsters" with a name like Hamp), rabbits, and pet mice. And of course frequent gold fish, or guppies. And although not exactly pets, we provided a place for quite a few caterpillars to spin their cocoon and hatch into beautiful butterflies or moths. The cats invariably learned what belonged to the family and what was fair game, and never killed one of the smaller pets, considering them siblings, or at least to be ignored.

West Park Drive

I worked in a private laboratory for a while while living on West Park Drive. One of my friends and former co-workers called, and was

127

setting up his own lab. He wanted me to set up and manage the bacteriology section, my specialty at the hospital. This was very part time work, but very enjoyable, working with friends in a no-pressure situation. At the same time, I was taking call at the hospital laboratory some weekends and once more found myself working more than I wanted to.

We were also in a child-care dilemma. Clark was at the funeral home, and on night call for the ambulance. We even had an extension of the funeral home phone in our home. I was on night call for the laboratory. Often, when he was called for an automobile wreck, I would also be called to set up transfusions for the victim. Someone had to be with the children.

For a while, we had to be very careful not to take call on the same nights. We finally resolved this dilemma by finding a young woman, Connie Grinnell to come live with us for a year. She was going to college, and her parents lived several miles out in the country. It was more economical for her to live in town. The Grinnell family had taken in foster children for years, and so Connie was experienced in child care, and truly loved children. She moved in with us for a year, and it was a winning situation for all of us. We felt comfortable with her when we were not there to care for the children.

We were not always so fortunate with child care. Some of the people or places that we later used for daycare were not good. And we did not always find out right away. I only knew after the fact that all the children were forced to watch T.V all day at one of the places, and were told not to get up and run around. This was the same place that humiliated one of the kids for wet pants. I tried to monitor each place. I was not always successful.

Although I enjoyed my work, I often felt the ambivalence of working. The money was nice, but not often necessary, so work was not necessary either. On the other hand, there was also this, (Should I admit it?) I was not happy as a full time, long term stay at home mom. I got bored, and burned out. After the children were in school, there was not that much to do at home, but if I worked, I was not there when they got home. It so often felt like a dilemma. – How to nurture the children and be there for them, and also nurture myself as an individual. I know I was not alone among young married women with small children, then or now. I am just glad I had the choices. I may not have made the best ones, but I attempted to strike some balance, choose wisely and make sure my kids felt and were cared for and about.

We developed, for the first time in our marriage, a lovely and active social life. We had wonderful community fun and feeling when the people at the hospital lab got together at various homes to make music. Norabelle Willians, a very bright chemist with post-polio syndrome worked with me, and she and her husband were early role models of mine. Her husband played several instruments. Clark played piano and accordion. I loved to sing and played the accordion a little, in fact took lessons on it. It was an antique 120 base accordion that Clark had gotten from his music teacher. Bill Williams borrowed the accordion one time and dropped a cigarette ash on it. It was made of highly flammable cellulose, and started burning. He had to pick up a flower can full of water and dump on it. He later took it apart, drying it out, and regluing the reeds which had been hurt by water.

Several other people enjoyed playing instruments, or just singing along. Those were fun evenings. We had a couple of "fake books" with lots of old fashioned songs in them. They were called Fake books, because they went against copyright laws, and had just the melody and the chords with the words. One ordered them mail order and they were quite expensive, but fun to use in a group. I still have them.

The children were getting older and a little more independent. I was less tired, and we had a lovely house that we could entertain in. Ron Klump was a pharmacist in town, and they had 3 little children. We also met the Alexanders, Phil, Elaine, Susie and Greg. I am still friends with Phil and Elaine, after not being in touch for many years. They are in their 80's now, and I still feel privileged to know them. Phil started a business in Organizational Development in Ann Arbor, Elaine worked with him and also did some writing of children's books. She is now working in politics, and calls herself "69 and holding". She is another one of my current role models on aging.

I am not sure how we found Holy Family Episcopal Church. We were not church goers, and neither of us had any Episcopal background. I think it possible that through Phil Alexander, we learned of Sensitivity training and attended our first session at Holy Family. But however it happened; we joined that church, went regularly and became well integrated there. This was the late 60's , and true to the counter culture of the times, the church had guitar masses, slide shows, and a pastor with a rebel wife. Bruce Bailey was the pastor, his wife, Madesta was the rebel.

We found friends for the children and for ourselves there. This period stands out to me as one of the most cohesive and best of my married life. Our family had a nice home, a church home, and some people that we were regularly involved with. We were knitted into a warm and enjoyable fabric.

This was a season of change in the culture everywhere. In Midland, it took the form of protests over Napalm, used in Vietnam and made at Dow Chemical. Napalm was a flammable substance used in the Vietnam War, with disastrous results for the natives, and later for the soldiers exposed. Dow eventually became the sole manufacturer of it. Some of the protesters were children of Dow Executives, embarrassing their parents. The Vietnam War was being protested throughout the country. Currents were stirring. (our children were approximately 7, 6, and 4 at the time). John F Kennedy had been shot in 1963, and his brother and Martin Luther King were killed in 1968. There was idealism and tumult affecting all ages. Protest became a common and somewhat effective tool throughout this era.

In 1967, Dow Chemical decided with Consumers Power, and Bechtel, to build a nuclear power plant in Midland. I got involved in attempting to stop the plant, along with Mary Sinclair, and the Nuclear Study Committee in Midland. It felt good to have an interest outside of work and children and to think I was helping with a cause I believed in. Our main concern was nuclear waste, a problem which still has no solution. And we, as a small committee of people, were able to organize and get information to the people of Midland. Here is the letter I wrote to the Midland Daily News during that time.

Concerned Over Nuclear Plant

Dear Editor,

Yesterday I attended a hearing on the proposed nuclear power plant for Midland. Today I am very concerned.

It seems as if there is some soul searching and much fact finding to be done yet before the plant and others like it are built.

Yes, it is a good source of electricity and power. Yes it is clean – no fly ash or coal dust. But – yes, it puts radioactive substances into the Tittabawasee River and into the air. Yes, these substances are concentrated in the animal and plant life of the river. Yes, it will raise the temperature of the water - as much as 5 degrees.

Are these changes in the river safe?

There is a great deal of controversy on this point. Some of the nation's top radioscientist's disagree.

Can we, can I, can you, afford to make the same mistake with radioactive "runoff" as has been made in the past with DDT? Because "safe" levels are simply not known.

There was a statement read at the hearing from the city council. I cannot quote it exactly, but the words were something like "a majority of the people of Midland support the project. " Where this statement came from, I do not know. I do know that the majority of the people of Midland were not asked.

There are alternatives to this project. Become informed and don't be part of the silent majority. And then decide for yourself and the future generations of Midland.

For more information, write to the Citizens Committee for Environmental Protection. Box 1201, Midland Mich. Or to me.

KAREN HAMP

1116 W. Park Drive.

130

Our thrust was education, rather than active protest. At meetings where either Dow or Consumers attempted to sell the idea of the plant, we asked hard questions, and had hard facts to back up our opinions. Other members of our group also wrote letters to the paper. Eventually there were construction problems at the plant, and both the time and the money were way more than expected. Both Consumers Power and Dow Chemical backed out of the project. During the whole process, our committee made it much harder to go forward. We took the high road, did not get nasty, and maintained our educational focus. We reached people with facts and rational arguments. We encouraged people who questioned, and gave information to answer their questions truthfully. I later interviewed Mary Sinclair when she was quite old, but still feisty.

In family life, meanwhile, our children were baptized at Holy Family, and Pam was confirmed with Margaret Whittaker as God mother. At one point, Clark and I took over the youth group, and did activities which our kids were also included in. The Youth Group sold donuts each Sunday at Coffee Hour to support their activities. That meant we picked up the donuts before church each week. One Sunday Bob looked up at the figure of the baker on the very tall sign hovering over the donut store, and with all seriousness, asked if it was God. I suppose the imposing height of the sign and the every Sunday routine prompted the question.

One winter during this time period, skiing became our new family interest. It was a popular activity among many of the families in church. We decided to take our kids over to Apple Mountain, or Bintz's Apple Orchards near Freeland, and take ski lessons. It was a hit, and we all learned to be amateur skiers. At one point, the kids stayed with one of the church families for a weekend and Clark and I went skiing up north. I tore a pectoral muscle on a rope tow, but it was at the end of the very enjoyable weekend. I did a small amount of downhill skiing and some cross country, for many years after that, stopping the cross country skiing only in my late 60's or early 70's when foot trouble made it uncomfortable. I think that season of our life was a good and positive time for all of us. Not just the ski season, but the season at Holy Family. Bob later skied in Colorado with his church youth group. But that was 10 years in the future yet.

Getting Involved in T-groups

Whether we got involved in Holy Family through the T group movement, or vice versa doesn't matter. They were inextricably combined in our lives for a time. I know we attended our first group at the church. I was very interested both because Phil Alexander had described the T groups at Dow Chemical and because I had taken nearly enough psychology at Michigan State to get a major and had a continued interest in personal growth and psychology. At the same time, personal growth was a growing interest in the culture.

The Alexanders were members of the Methodist Church and Phil took his experience from Dow into that church. Our pastor volunteered Holy Family through the diocesan connections. This must have been around 1967, and Clark went because I did, and because it was at our church.

There were some leaders who had been trained at the "mecca" of Leadership Training, NTL (National Training Labs) Bethel Maine. It was the go-to place for aspiring trainers. I was impressed with their skills and knowledge and immediately wanted to be more involved. I realized that some trainers were better than others, but it was only years later that I realized how many people were being hurt through those groups by bad trainers or bad techniques, and the "one fits all" formulas. The idea was to be more sensitive to others and aware of oneself., and to communicate honestly and openly. The T stood for Training, but also Trust. The idea of T groups in the church became to be more Christ like, or able to better follow Christ. Many denominations espoused this movement. A couple of our first trainers were Clyde Reid, and Bill and Kathie Dannemiller. Clyde wrote a well read and popular book back then called Celebrate the Temporary.

I was exhilarated by my first experience. This shy person who had suppressed emotions all her life was now being encouraged to express herself. Asking for what I wanted and saying how I felt was a kick start to a richer life at the time. My intuition said "go". Between not wanting to repeat my mother's parenting mistakes, and my sense of discovery of self, I celebrated. It was my first foray out of my family "don't touch, don't feel, and don't express needs"..

. (From the distance of time, I see that what I experienced as a huge change was really only baby steps, and in addition, made me think I knew more than I did.) I am quite sure I hurt as many of my friendships and relationships as I helped with my new "self", and may even have contributed to my later divorce with the way I used that newfound "self".

I joined the Michigan Episcopal Training network to learn more, and fuel my passion and excitement. We met at Emrich Conference Center in Brighton. This group, under the Episcopal Diocese of Eastern Michigan, and the Adult Education Director Josephine Kelsey was composed of ecumenical clergy and lay people. Its purpose was to train people as consultants to churches or other organizations, to bring forth those values of openness, compassion, kindness and love. Some put it in more religious terms and spoke of it as becoming more Christ-like, and helping organizations do likewise. Our group used both theory and practice, working hard on planned change within organizations, and within ourselves. Jo Kelsey still lives in Ann Arbor.

These developments happened concurrently with the Vatican II Council in the Roman Catholic Church, so the nuns and priests of that denomination were feeling a new freedom and excitement, and actively took part in ecumenical groups and trainings.

For me, raised in a family where emotions were secret, intimacy was nonexistent, and collaboration was barely known, it was like Christmas and my birthday all happening at once, and I soon considered myself an expert, when in actuality, I was barely touching into skills that take a lifetime to put into practice well.

The culture was encouraging a letdown between work and spirit, and between the churches and psychology. Techniques of openness, catharsis, compassionate confrontation, and self-responsibility seemed to lead to intimacy, trust, and a greater sense of closeness and belonging. Honest self expression, accepted by others led people to feel love and compassion. That was the ideal. Some of us "wanna be" experts were more integrated and emotionally mature than others. Ego-bound leaders injured people in such groups. On the other hand there was real progress and growth for many.

On the West Coast was Esalen Institute, where notable people such as Fritz Perls, Barry Stevens and Hugh Prather, Abraham Maslow, Carl Rogers and Jack Gibb were doing and teaching similar principles. Some of these people left their institutions, and took these programs to the mainstream, going to work for corporate and church cultures. It was Jack Gibb who had been hired to do the trainings at Dow Chemical. Jack had written a book called "Trust-A New View of Personal and Organizational Development". California was a center of activities in the West, while Bethel Maine held sway on the East Coast, and in the middle was the meeting, melting and coming together of Academic, Corporate and Religious institutions, both in cities and small towns.

Many of these people were able to put ideas into theories and models which made sense intellectually as well as to the heart and soul. Some leaders linked directly to Christianity, and others only linked metaphorically. What I knew about myself was that I was feeling more deeply than ever before, and was more sensitive to my needs and feelings and those of others. I felt alive. And I felt a profound sense of gratitude. I felt close to God, and my spirit was lifted into joy. I continued to use Jesus as a role model, and find the means to come closer to living up to it in the T groups.

If I had to name the one tool that came out of this period of my life that has most influenced me, and been most useful, I would name Josephine Kelsey's translation of Erickson's stages of development. Jo did this translation in order that Christian Education leaders would understand age-appropriate tasks of development, values, and spirituality. Erickson teaches that children must learn certain things at certain ages in order to develop into mature human beings. Each stage builds on the others, and missed stages leave a hole in the personal and social self. Dr. Kelsey simplified this work, into what I always thought was a way that Jesus might have taught these tasks, though he might have made a parable out of it.

I have used this chart in parenting, counseling and consulting. (Groups and organizations go through developmental stages too.) Here is the chart:

Age	Task	Questions
0-2	Trust	Who or what can I trust? Is my world trustable?
2-5	Hope	Is there hope if I reach out, or act, or express myself?
5-9	Belonging	Do I belong? Where do I belong?
9-13	Accomplishing/ Doing	What can I do, or accomplish? Can I be successful at doing things?
Teens	Believing	Who/ what can I believe in or rely on?
Young Adults	Committing	What will I commit to move toward? Will I stay consistent with my beliefs?
Adulthood	Caring	Beyond the self to care for others, And the earth (As well as self)
Older Adulthood	Affirming	Affirming that life is worthwhile. Wisdom.

Since the time that this chart was set up, the functional lifetime of adulthood has increased dramatically Where people used to be "old" at 60 or 70, many are now functionally learning, driving, and using computers into their 80's or 90's. There are more centenarians than ever before.

In the book "Composing a Further Life, by Mary Katherine Bateson, she proposes that we divide adulthood into two stages: Adulthood One – The traditional time of raising children and making a living and eventually retiring. And Adulthood Two- a time of active wisdom, where one is mentally and physically functional, and can construct a different life based on strengths, unused talents, priorities, or a bucket list. This might follow a traditional retirement, and might last as long as one is functional and capable of caring for oneself. Old age, or older adulthood would not start until one is unable to fully function, and may need help from others, either cognitively or physically. Following Bateson's model, a stage would be added between Adulthood and Older Adulthood. It could be called Active Integration.

You will see, as my story progresses, that my own life somewhat followed that path with an extra stage. I have, like many, reached turning points, and after a period of letting go, begun to construct a different life. I am again in that process while writing this. I am hoping my next moves still fall into the Active Integration mode.

To return to my life, at about 32, I was learning and growing, following something which was important to me both personally and professionally. It was exciting and energizing. However, as I got more excited and enlivened by this process, Clark got less so. He lost most of his interest in the groups or the movements. This could have been taken as a warning sign for our marriage, but neither of us talked about it, and I remember only wishing that he was more interested, and judging him for the lost interest.

Shifting Sands -- 1969

At the high side of this shift in me, my life changed forever in August 1969 when I went to a week-long T group at Adrian College and opened up parts of my character which I had no idea existed. My life became forever more loving, fun, and richer. I let myself fall in love and be loved in a way that I had never experienced before. My femininity was strengthened and called forth beyond my past knowledge or experience. My sense of partnership and joy was forever increased.

I did not have an affair, although I entertained the question long enough to say no. I had strong moral boundaries, and though I felt desire, I had been well steeped in drawing lines between emotions and actions where ethics and morals were concerned, and did not, for long, consider acting physically on that desire. What was so enlivening for me during this week was letting myself feel the emotions, and the desire in ways I had not before. I interacted with a man who was both assertive and responsive in relationship, stating desires and emotions honestly and clearly, yet still honoring my being and my decisions without backing away. It was truly a life changing relationship and week. I have continued gratitude for that experience and for the group, leader and person who helped provide it.

I went home as more of a woman, partner, and human being than ever before. I wrote it this way: *"I felt reborn in my femininity. For the first time in my life, I felt soft, loved, receptive, beautiful, sensuous and wonderfully womanly."* It was very interesting that the shape of my body actually changed to a more curved and soft shape over the next year. I didn't throw away that tomboy, but I also became a woman.

I was full of wonder and questions- that I, a married woman who had three children had not been awakened to that state before. I began valuing myself and others around me. Clark asked me if I had been with someone else, and in that spirit of truth and love, I told

135

him no, but that I had felt love and been loved, and that I was back home to bring all that back to him. I made it clear that I had not been untrue to him in action. I made it clear to him in words both spoken and written that I was feeling incredibly close and loving to him. (and to the children, and everyone else I contacted). He was nonetheless shaken, and because he had not been the one to awaken this in me, he probably felt inadequate, but whatever he felt, he turned away from me, later saying that he had lost the woman he married that weekend. I was devastated by his reaction. He could not see the woman he married, inside the woman I had become. We were about 33 at this point. I am not sure how I might have felt had the tables been turned. At the time, I did note to myself that I was about the same age as Jesus had supposedly been when he died. My old self, in many ways died. And I was resurrected.

My response to Clark's withdrawal was sadness, but that well learned arrogance of mine was present. Although I didn't speak it, I began to blame him because "he didn't want to grow", or "he didn't want my love", or whatever. I look back on myself, seeing the over confidence and the shallow thinking of a 30 something woman, who "takes pride in her way of doing things, knows she is special, and is quite sure she is doing the right things." I had grown larger, but not so large that I could see "the other" with compassion and love, when he got scared and moved away from me.

I attempted to be supportive, compassionate and loving toward Clark, but that same old pattern of anger building up in me was recurring, along with the arrogant cover up. Years later, when he came to me to explain the expansion he felt in his life from smoking marijuana, I could sense that he was as excited by his discovery of himself on pot, as I had been by my discovery of myself on openness, awareness, and my budding emotional life.

I tried every way I could think of to bring Clark toward me, or bring us together. As those actions failed, I begin to feel the cracks in my excitement over my own growth. I felt the beginnings of a sort of depression even in the midst of my joy. This did not bode well for our relationship.

As time went on, I began to see that if I got really discouraged or depressed, Clark would move toward me and take care of me. I would, of course, then feel better and want to do things with him, at which point he would back away again. Then I would start feeling discouraged and depressed. He was only available if I "needed" him, not if I "wanted" him.

At some point, a few years later, I made a decision to keep that depression and discouragement out of our relationship. I realized how easy it would be for me to move toward depression, or to act discouraged in order to get his closeness. I developed more of a support system, and different coping mechanisms. At no time did I consider other men. I say that, because eventually I found that he indeed was considering other women.

Meanwhile, we were still surrounded by our church friends, Baileys, Struthers, Bons, and many others. Among them, Betty and Preston Jones, one of the first African American families to live in Midland, came to our church, and we started a long friendship. They both have done great things for themselves professionally and personally. Also as part of a small community of African Americans in Midland. I interviewed Betty for the Michigan Women's Times, a women's newspaper that started. Betty has been my mentor and sister when it came to discussions on race relations, relationships and cultural differences. I value their friendship immensely. We lost touch for many years, and picked it up again when I came back to Michigan in 2006. I admire them both.

Clark and I were not openly hostile to each other until much later in our relationship. One of the first times I can remember being irreconcilably hurt and hostile was an evening when we had another couple over for dinner. The husband had diabetes but did not know it yet. He just didn't feel good. After dinner, we talked, I put the children to bed and the husband of the couple fell asleep on the couch. His wife was angry and eventually suggested that the three of us go out dancing. I could not agree without a baby sitter for the children, and her husband was obviously not then capable of watching the children. Later we would realize that his blood sugar had probably been way out of control that night. Either Clark, or the wife of this couple suggested that the two of them go out dancing. I fell silent.

They actually went, and I felt abandoned, angry, and agitated. I hid it all, reverting back to my younger self, when I didn't feel the right to interfere in other's decisions. I did not even protest as they walked out the door. I got out my sewing machine, and started making something for one of the kids. When the man woke up, I made sure he felt good enough to drive, and he went home. I was livid, scared and mute.

At about the same time, Clark bowled one night a week, and began coming home much later than usual – sometimes 3 AM. I was scared at first, and called the police. I even called one of his bowling teammates who I knew well. This was probably when he began to be unfaithful to me. I am certain that I was being both naïve and in denial. My family history and our friendships did not contain unfaithfulness that I knew of, and so I had never heard those dynamics or seen them. With my usual deprecating ways, I leaned toward trust, and didn't fuss or ask questions. I assumed he was like I was and would not be unfaithful. I assumed he was committed to our marriage in the same way I was. I continued my activities.

For a couple summers around that time, I took the children to the Communicating Arts Seminars put on by the Episcopal Diocese.

These too were at Emrich Center in Brighton. Clark would not go, mainly because the man who had awakened my deep femininity was part of the staff, along with several other people from the Episcopal Training Network. He did not realize that although I still felt attracted, I almost never interacted with that man, nor he with me. It would have been like playing with fire for me, and I would not. The kids had a good time. I remember them helping paint a Volkswagon, and I remember Pam helping make a film. The facilitator for the film was Jim Galbraith, from Howell, a well known photographer. Josephine Kelsey, and Richard Han, later to marry, were facilitators. Also a man named Evan Sherrard. We did lots of intergenerational creative activities. There was a Walter Mitty talent night, we made a mud slide on a steep bank of sand and dirt, and slid down it, we made pottery out of clay we dug, and fired it overnight, in an underground kiln. Josephine's sister Candy was there and helped out. Wonderful family creative fun.

A friend loaned us a small motorcycle for one summer. He had nowhere to keep it, and I rode it all summer – to work, to the store, and just for fun. I have always liked the wind in my face, whether from bicycling, roller skating or that motorcycle. It was a sense of freedom and fun. My younger brother Charlie now rides, and owns two motorcycles. He has ridden cross country, and recently took me for a ride on the back of his bike.

Our house, back then, became a center for people from various groups around town. Some people had gone to the T groups; others were just people we met who didn't have family in town. We were still somewhat estranged from my family. One Thanksgiving saw 20 people at our house. This was the "hippie" era. However there were never drugs or drinking at our home. We had an ongoing communal project, a large 3' x 6' rug being hooked, and lying in front of our fireplace. People came over, sitting in front of the fireplace hooking on the rug, and talking. The kids were accepted as part of this crowd and people treated them as if it took a village to raise them, and all were part of that village. The finished rug was in our homes until the children were grown.

A memorable New Year's Eve around that period was a blizzard filled night, when our friends Preston and Betty came over, bringing their boys. We put the children to bed behind the furniture when the time came, and the 4 of us talked and sang the evening away. Eventually, we showed our guests to an extra bedroom, as the snow was too deep and the wind too strong to go out safely.

Our children did well in school. Summers were for playing around the neighborhood and for camping vacations. We sometimes took my young brother Charlie along. Remember, he was only 5 years older than Pam, and fit right into the family. It's interesting that my mother was still cool toward us, but let Charlie join us. He went with us to the Upper Peninsula where we hunted agates and native copper, with Pam finding the prize. We called it her potato, and it was a piece of native copper. That may have been when the family legend of the "pink plate" was started by Charlie. Nobody wanted the pink plate until Charlie made it special with his story, and then they all wanted the pink plate forever after when camping.

One of our fun and repeated camping trips was to Ocracoke Island on the south end of the Outer Banks in North Carolina. We also went to Deep Creek Lake in Maryland, and in fact I took Mark back there this last year. (Yes, Mark figures in my life now, and will figure prominently later on in the book.) Finally, when the kids were young teens, we went to the west coast. That trip took us many miles across the trans-Canada highway on the way out, and across the US on the way back. I suspect, and have heard from the kids, that camping was their favorite time, growing up. Although I did not articulate this until years later, we spent our money on experiences, not things. This had been true of my parents also, and is still true of me.

Because of the changes in me, I was more people oriented than ever. I was involved in creating a slide show for the annual meeting of the church, using my favorite hobby, photography. Slides were the medium for most back then. I just converted all my pertinent ones to digital images.

My father died in 1968 at age 57. We were just getting closer, and I look back and wish he had lived longer. He had a heart attack, was scheduled to come home, and had another one which killed him. I had gone to see him the night before he died, and felt sad because he had been grumpy, and I left disgusted with him. It was a week after Easter. My mother gave me his camera for Christmas the next year.

Half Moon Lake, where Clark and I had come to before Pam was born, continued to be a vacation spot for us. The kids learned to fish for bullheads using bread balls for bait. They sat on the rickety old dock that Clark's grandfather had built with slab wood brought up from the bottom of the lake. They swam, rowed a boat, and enjoyed the company of their great grandparents, Clark's mother's parents. The plumbing was an outhouse, the well about 8 feet deep, basically lake water filtered through the sand. We all enjoyed the simple and slow moving life. We walked through the woods, explored the marshes and swamps, and chased down our pontoon boat, made from old oil barrels with a deck over them. It frequently got loose from our dock.

A family back packing adventure was an outstanding success one summer. There was a trail across northern Michigan that went approximately from Tawas on the East coast, to Traverse City on the west. The children were about 10, 9 and 6.. We made pack frames from plywood for the kids, and got some inexpensive frames from the second hand store for ourselves. I even made the dog some pack sacks so he could carry his own food. We asked my cousin, Steve Alguire if he would pick us up at the end of the week. He agreed, and we set out at a very modest pace, starting at Kalkaska. We probably went less than 20 miles that week. The children carried no more than 10 pounds, and Clark and I carried about 30 apiece. We were able to take our food, and even made June berry syrup for pancakes one morning. The first couple days, everyone was tired, from the unaccustomed work, but after that, it got easier, and we marveled at the newly appearing muscles. One morning, one of the sleeping bags fell into the camp fire as we attempted to dry it out. It got a big hole burned in it but was usable. Wonder of wonders, we had no rain all week. Our dog became very primitive, and when we came to a store,(which we had not expected) , he stayed outside guarding our packs. One of my favorite pictures from that trip is Bob with a butterfly on his shoulder.

Looking back from another 45 years' experience, I would say that it took a lot of courage to take the children into that week. Maybe it was just a lack of life experience – naivete rather than courage. What if they had gotten sick or hurt? Worse yet, what if one of us had? There were no cell phones, and certainly no pay phones in the woods. Luckily there were no accidents or injuries, and both Clark and I had an overall trust in being able to handle life, especially out in nature. Clark had wonderful improvisation skills, having grown up on a farm. I learned that kind of creative thinking and skills from him during our marriage. The next summer, we went back to that little store where we had gotten ice cream—this time in a car. They immediately recognized the dog.

I mentioned my dad's death, but did not mention the stories I heard at his visitation. Person after person told of my father's extraordinary kindness, and of him going out of his way to do something for them. It was bitter sweet, as he did not treat us that way. There was a time in my life when I was angry that others got such a wonderful friend, and his family did not. In following years, I cried many times for my dad, including as I was writing this. The night he died, I went out at night, lay on the ground and looked up at the stars, hoping he could see us, and was happy. For years afterward, when I was near his funeral home, there were times when I saw someone walking down the sidewalk and thought it was him, only to remember that he was gone.

The following Christmas, as I mentioned, I got his camera. It was a non-interchangeable lens Nikon camera called a Nikkorex. It was my prize possession for many years and I took many a memorable picture, some of which I eventually entered in art shows and won prizes with, or sold. Clark eventually got a camera also, and we both enjoyed photography for several years.

Clark's parents died close to that time also, and were also both 57 when they died. His mother went first, very unexpectedly, his father a year or two later. When our children were born, all the grandparents and great grandparents on both sides of the family were alive. Within a few years, the kids lost all their great grandparents and three of their grandparents. Clark was an only child, and so he was left without family except for a great aunt, another aunt which he hardly knew, and two distant cousins. I suppose that may have helped destabilize his life a few years after that. At least I had siblings around, and my mother was still alive for many years.

Because my life was tied up with my children, Clark, my activities and my work, I did not pay attention to how things were for my younger brothers and sisters. I knew that my mother and dad drank, but had no idea that it was a full blown alcoholic home by then. It was a very different life for my younger sibs than it had been for me, a very different family. It had become the normal for them, and they didn't talk about it.

There was a wake-up call for me, just before my dad died. I had offered to help my mother host a party for an out of town friend who had recently lost his wife. I went to help, and my mother was totally drunk. My father was snoring loudly on the couch, in the way I had heard him snore when he was drunk. I got my dad up and made him go into the bedroom to sleep. It was the worst I had ever seen my mother, and I leave out the details out of respect for better days. The guests started coming, while my mother was flirting with the guest of honor who was very uncomfortable. I took over, terribly embarrassed for the sake of our guest and his friends. I realized how far out of control things were for my parents. I attempted to talk to them at a later date, but there was little response, or willingness to get help. By then, my father often had acute chest pain, and my mother was losing the ability to reason. What a sad situation. She, who had been valedictorian of her class, was no longer very smart. I did note that neither of my parents was physically abusive to the kids, although my father was sometimes verbally abusive to Becky. It was one of those incidents that triggered her short stint of moving in with us a few years before this.

With all the loss of parents and grandparents, both Clark and I absorbed a lot of change in our families and ourselves. I suppose neither of us were aware at the time of how all the changes were affecting us. Looking back, I am certain that all this destabilized both Clark and I, and eventually turned our future directions in ways they might not have gone otherwise.

As my father's post death financial affairs got straightened out, my mother offered Clark the funeral home, or at least my father's share of it. We turned her down. Despite the license, Clark had neither the skills, knowledge, nor motivation to run the funeral home, and I did not care to help. I had grown up in the funeral business, and did not want to be back into it in a way that would require my work. Neither of us was eager to be business owners.

The funeral home was sold, and because the younger men who bought it were licensed, they did not have money or need for another embalmer. Clark began looking for another position, and found it at Voran's funeral home in Allen Park, near Detroit. Once more we picked up and moved to the Detroit area.

PAM 1958

Happy Parents and Pam

JIM 1959

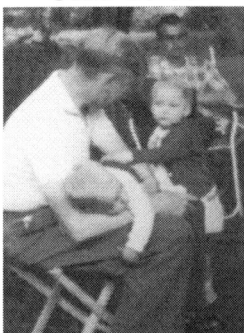

Grandpa Deke and Jim

BOB 1962

Bob and Pam

See my sis ?

Love my Millie doll

Pam and Grandma Dee

142

Aunt Lu, Uncle Morley and Pam

Family Portrait 1963

Dad and the kids

Mom and kids – just before Bob

A growing boy!

Camping

143

Camping again

Halloween

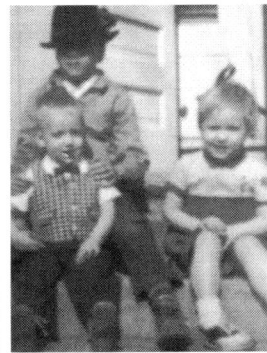
Uncle Charlie and his niece and nephew

Buried in sand

Curiousity

Fun in sun and water

Canoe on the pond with Dad

Camping again

Pam and friend

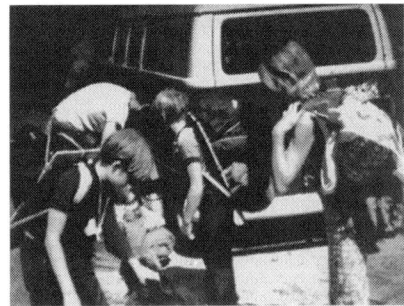
Back packing preparation

BACK TO DETROIT -- 1971-1984

The Next Years in Summary

The kids were about 12, 11, and 9 when we moved this time. It was about 1971. Part of the next several years will sound chaotic, but from the distance of time, I see a more orderly process, or processes at work. It was an intensely destructive time, and yet out of the destruction came the foundations for who we were to be for the rest of our lives, and for what our family was to be. The children's lives, already changing rapidly through their adolescent process, changed more as they lost their foundations and built new ones. The forces of destruction, reconstruction, and healing worked back and forth in our lives, never in a straight line.

In writing this part, I will alternate, as I have before, between family matters and professional matters, between family matters and personal matters. At the end, I attempt to sum it up, but that is many pages away from here. We start this part in 1971, and end it in 1984.

More New Beginnings

We found a temporary rental house in Taylor for a month or two, facilitating the kids starting school, and Clark starting work. It was reasonable short term rent, and close to his work. While he worked, and the children were in school, I looked for an area to buy a home in, and for a home to buy.

Using my habitual "out of the box" explorative bent I found Grosse Ile. It really was an island, with a bridge at either end, located east of Jefferson Avenue, in the Detroit River, not too far from his work. One of the first things I heard from residents was "In case of more race riots, we can just raise our bridges". The riots in Detroit had been four years before, and were close to the surface in memories for residents. It was less meaningful to me, as I had not been here. I was ever the water person, and wanting to be near water, and the amenities of living, but away from city life.

The large metropolitan area seemed overwhelming at first to us even though we had lived in the area before. The kids were older now, with more activities over a bigger geographical area. We had more money and better transportation, and thus more freedom. We had to consider schools, travel, shopping, and other changes from a small town.

As I thought about a home on Grosse Ile, it felt peaceful and exciting. It was a delight to know that from the shores of our island we could look across to Canada. From the opposite shore we could see the steel mills pouring steel at night, emptying out the pouring pots – the molten steel glowing in the night. I envisioned Grosse Ile as an island oasis in this large metropolitan area, only 15 minutes from Clark's work. It seemed somewhat like a permanent vacation.

My vision ultimately turned out to be somewhat distorted. It was an oasis, but many of the people who lived there embraced a different island lifestyle than I had imagined for us. I had not paid enough attention to the wealth, yacht clubs, sailing, boating and golf courses. I had only seen the deer and other wildlife, the views from the shore, and the idyllic distance from a big city. I found a very modest home on the west side of the island, the opposite side from where the large homes and wealth that characterized this island were located.

The children soon found it complicated to fit in, since they could not reciprocate the social life, or mindset. As with any children, the older they get, the more important fitting in becomes. We did make friends, and so did they. We also started attending the Episcopal church on the island. We even became leaders of the youth group there. It was not that people on the island were unfriendly. It was simply a lack of commonality. We found some neighbors close by that we enjoyed, and that we kept in touch with for several years after that, even seeing them when we vacationed in Canada several years later.

We, or at least I, often went running through the hedge to get to the shore to get gorgeous pictures of the sunsets over the steel mills. We walked to the shore at night, and watched the glowing steel pouring like a waterfall on fire.

We were invited to a Halloween party, and because we were new and the name of the island was still fun and new to us, we decided to go as a pair of Gross Eels. It was just the sort of thing that newcomers might think of, and people who had grown up there would not have. Our friends enjoyed our humor, and we enjoyed the party. Life seemed good.

I was not working, but soon started teaching Yoga at the YWCA in Wyandotte, just upriver from us. I had taken a Yoga Class in Midland, and enjoyed it a lot, and knew I could teach a simple form. Clark seemed to like his work, and was bowling again. I mainly stayed home to make sure the kids got adjusted well, and to put our home together after a move. I continued my activity with the Episcopal Training Network. Things seemed to be progressing smoothly.

An Unexpected Schism

One day, having been in that house a year or so, Clark came home and told me he was in love with someone else. Immediately I thought back to very late homecomings after his bowling. I had thought he just needed to adjust to our changes from the deaths of our family members, and my interest in personal growth. He did not mention my experience in Adrian further, and I assumed that was behind us. I was startled and shocked at his admission, and very frightened. Nothing in my family of origin, or my thinking about us had prepared me for this turn of events. He said he wanted to spend time with her to decide his future. I was obviously naïve about the world in general to not have even considered such a possibility, but right then, I had to figure out how to respond.

My "growth" experiences of the 60's had taught me to be honest, and to accept my feelings and needs, but my upbringing on being conscious of the other person, and considering their needs took over, and I mistook that for love. I remained silent about <u>my</u> needs and my devastation, and even my fears about our marriage. I reverted to what I thought was "unconditional love". I decided that the most loving thing to do was to tell him to spend as much time as he needed with her, and decide what he wanted, being totally accepting of him and his wishes. In hindsight, this is a clear example of doing what might be loving and accepting toward him, but not to myself, our marriage, or the children. It was a clear example of being "selfless"—acting as if my "self" did not exist. And I saw in hindsight that it did not let him know who I was or how I felt either. It was incredibly co-dependent, but I did not know that. At that time, it was the best I knew. I felt like I was falling down a bottomless pit and it was up to me to hold our family together. I went into superwoman mode, and took on the task alone.

Over the next months, Clark was in and out of our house, and our relationship. I got very manipulative, and very seductive, hoping to win him back. It worked, and eventually he came back home to stay. I was relieved, although life still felt tentative. At least there were two of us, although there was less automatic trust on my part. I tried to talk about what went wrong with us. He would not go to counseling and he would not talk. So we went on, much as if nothing had happened.

Moving To Trenton- 1972

We sold the Grosse Ile house and moved to Trenton in 1972 or 3. Partly, I needed to get out of that place of our separation. I also thought that if we lived in a place which was more suitable and larger, Clark might be happy and our relationship would be stronger. Bob was in fifth grade, Jim in seventh and Pam in eighth.. We were on the edge of town and it was like being out in the country. We made a garden, and acquired 2 dogs, a cat, and eventually two geese and a baby raccoon. We put up a portable swimming pool in the back yard, and became the go-to place for swimming in the neighborhood. Life seemed to be progressing in a positive direction again. My photography was winning some prizes in a couple art shows, and I was enjoying that. Clark and I had gone to Photography Club in Midland, both enjoying it, and continuing to enjoy that hobby together.

Sometime before that, after his parents died, but during the years of all those funerals, Clark had lost his great aunt, Carolyn Godreau. He was her only heir, and had inherited $120,000 dollars, a huge fortune in those days.

I want to say a little about Caroline, an interesting person, and influence on our kids. She had gone to college and gotten a masters degree, and taught in a one room school. Keep in mind that this was before 1900. I think Pam still has the school bell from her classroom. Her only sibling, Clark's Grandpa Henry, repaired lawnmowers all his life, and lived in a very small run down home. Caroline was a misfit in the family, but put education, sophistication, and quality into her life. She was, when younger, a singer with a beautiful voice, and at one time we had some records of her and some photos of her in stylish, elegant clothes. She spoke Spanish and Puerto Rican fluently, and was married to a Puerto Rican man named Gregory Godreau. (Or we assumed she was married) It was a curious relationship, which I think started when her parents rented Greg a room when he came to this country, maybe to the University. All we knew of Caroline and Greg was that they lived (and slept) on different floors of the home. After Greg's death, Caroline's life was her cats, all 13 of them, and her house smelled of cats. She, over time, convinced the butcher that she was poor, and he responded by saving scraps and bones for the cats, which she ate, and also gave to the cats. She taught our children some Spanish when they were very young. She was a remarkable woman for her day, even with her eccentricities. The whole town thought she was poor, and even we didn't know she had that much money.

Anyway, Clark inherited her money, and we had used none of it. We eventually decided to use part to put an addition on the house, and I designed a family room with a basement under it, a large fireplace, and hardwood floors. It served us well for entertaining family and friends. It was a great teen age hangout. We also bought a van out of that money, so that we had a good car to camp in. I put Clark's affair behind me. It was what I wanted, and so I acted as if it were so. I suspect it was so, at least provisionally, at the time.

I was more at ease in a different house. We were taking walks in the evenings, and it seemed an enjoyable life. One art show I entered both photos and some mobiles made from Lake Superior driftwood. The mobiles were a great hit, and I brought home many orders for more. We were irregularly attending the Episcopal Church in Trenton. I was still teaching Yoga in Wyandotte. I was still not working.

148

A Mysterious Letter

One day, a letter came addressed to me. It was letters and words cut from our Trenton church bulletin, and from newspapers and magazines, pasted on paper. As I remember, all it said was "Take care of your own family first" I do not remember the exact timing of it. It felt scary, so unexpected, and I did not know what it meant. I gathered Clark and the children together and showed it to them. I asked if anyone had any clue what it meant. I asked every question I could think of to try and figure out its meaning. I asked the kids if they were feeling neglected or in trouble, either in school or outside of it. There were no answers or clues forthcoming.

Clark said he knew nothing that would lead to a letter like that, although in hindsight, I assume he was seeing another woman, or other women, and someone knew it and was trying to warn me. A thought came to me 20 or 30 years later that he may have done it himself in an attempt to shake me into paying attention. I never found out any more about it. I was again not considering the idea of another woman, even after the affair. I assumed that since he had decided to come back, he was committed to our marriage. When he came back, I had asked him to please let me know if things were not as they should be, and he had said he would, but nothing since then. I now felt wary, but went on with our life with no major changes.

Going Back To Graduate School

Well, there was one major change. I thought about going back to graduate school. As a result of my growth, learning, and activities, my thinking toward my work shifted and I started wanting to work more directly with people.

I had focused on communication, relationship, and all things interactive between people, I wanted more of that in my work. Patient interaction had been an indirect but important part of my job as a med tech. Now I wanted it to be the main part of my work.

The intellectual exercise of putting symptoms, lab results, and other evidence together for diagnosis still fascinated me. My skills of analysis were good, and I was able to combine that with thinking widely, and sometimes outside the box. So I was good at diagnostics, as well as efficient and accurate at the actual laboratory work. However, I was eager to use my strengths and skills more in the emotional, relational, and spiritual realms of life.

I thought for quite some time about the possibility of graduate school before I mentioned it out loud. I had listened to people in the sensitivity groups, and the Episcopal Training Network, and knew that Social Work was a versatile degree, and would allow many kinds of employment. I then talked to Clark about it. The children were either young teens or almost teens. They were 14, 13, and 11. Thus they still needed guidance, but not a lot of physical care. They were in school when I would be and I would be home on weekends, and for summer vacations and holidays. I suppose the idea of our marriage not working must have been in the background, however, I do not remember thinking about that. At that point, it would have been a minor issue. A social work degree would give me the credentials for that direct interaction I was interested in. Clark had no objections, and the kids seemed ok with the idea. I applied to the School of Social Work at Wayne State University in downtown Detroit. I was easily able to get letters of recommendation and grateful for them.

Incidentally, when I told my mom I was going to go to graduate school, her response was that I was going to waste all the education they had given me, and give up my career. Looking back, her generation finished their education, and then stuck with their decisions all their lives. My generation was possibly the first one which made major career moves in the middle of adult life to satisfy changing needs. As I write this, many people have 3 or 4 different careers during their working life. My mom was wrong. I do not believe that any education or life experience is ever wasted.

I got no reply from Wayne State, despite a phone call or two, and then, a week before school started I got a letter of acceptance. My first thought was to refuse rather than to turn our lives upside down on the spur of the moment. I could go the next year. But then, I talked it over with Clark and the children, and decided to enroll. The money was there from my Yoga Classes, so the family budget did not have to stretch to pay for school or text books. Graduate school was much less expensive in 1972 than it is now, and I was able to use my small income to pay all my school bills, with the exception of the gasoline to drive there. (At that time, gas was less than a dollar a gallon.) So I began the commute to Wayne State University for a two year program leading to a Master's degree In Social Work (MSW)

I also taught the children how to plan meals and how to figure out the family bills, and rotated those jobs between them. They were now 10, 13, and 14. They were supposed to keep the house clean also, but that became less of a reality as they grew into their teen attitudes and activities.

Should I have put more effort into our marriage or the children at that point, rather than going off on my own path? Hindsight is tricky, and looks at questions that did not seem pertinent at the time. I am not sure I even knew what it meant to put more effort into our marriage. Answering those kinds of questions later cannot change what was, but thinking about them helps me to see the patterns of my life, and also how I have made other decisions throughout my life. I know I was excited about school. There is no way of knowing if choosing to stay home would have changed history. I certainly considered things like whether my kids would get enough supervision and attention. I took my marriage for granted, even though there had been problems. I don't mean I didn't attempt communication and affection. I just mean I trusted the marriage as a matter of course. In my defense, that really is very much what the culture was like in those days. In my mind, my commitment to my marriage meant I was in a partnership and would do what I could to help make the partnership work. There was little emphasis on conscious relationships then. The emphasis was more on personal growth, and only later, when the culture became a disaster of divorce was there more emphasis on relationships. This may have been when the narcissism of today's world took root, or the split between self-satisfaction, and a satisfactory life for all began. One of the widespread cultural sayings in those days was called the Gestalt Prayer, by Fritz Perls of Esalen: It went:

I do my thing and you do your thing
I am not in this world to live up to your expectations
And you are not in this world to live up to mine.
You are you
And I am I
And if by chance we find each other, it's beautiful.
(And at the time, the version I saw added: "And if not, it can't be helped")

In school once more, the classes were of less interest to me than the degree and what it would allow me to do. I was there in order to fulfill what seemed like my next marching orders in life - doing counseling, and becoming more Christ-like. At the time, Social Work students at Wayne State were not trained for or expected to go into counseling. In fact, it was discouraged by the school, and there were no classes, curriculum, or discussion of that possibility. It was expected that we would work somewhere in the Social Welfare System, or in Community Organizing. Those who wanted to do counseling were on their own. So when I saw my first client, a few years later, I did so with little preparation or theory, and lots of good will, caring, and determination.

I contrast this with my son Bob's college education in counseling many years later. He had very specific techniques, practices, and theories to learn, and was encouraged to be active in his own growth process, and that of his marriage. I wished that I had gotten that.

A story here from non-academic grad school years: Wayne State was near downtown Detroit, and not in a safe part of town. I was used to walking with my car keys in hand for possible defense. One evening, while attending school, I was walking to the parking garage after class.

We had been told by the school that there were some recent rapes in that parking garage and warned to be watchful and careful.

Our Volkswagon van was parked on the third level of the garage that night, and the garage closed at 10 pm.

Our car had a pretty consistent mechanical problem any time there was moisture around. The coil (?) got wet, and the car would not start. We carried a Bernz-o-matic torch in the car for that situation. It was handy for drying off the engine parts. That particular night was humid, and there had been rain during the day. I turned the key, and the car didn't start.

I got out, opened the tool chest and happened to glance to one side, only to see three young men watching me. They did not look like students, and in fact appeared somewhat furtive. Actually, two of them were watching me. One was messing with the overhead light, the only light in that area of the garage, the only light between the growing darkness outside, and total darkness inside the garage.

I was immediately tense, remembering our warning, and seeing that I was the only person in sight except for the young men. I quickly and intuitively made the decision to choose assertive action over fear and walked toward them. I explained my dilemma, asking if any of them might help. I also told them that my husband was on the way, although that was a lie. I had called him, and he was not home. One of the men said "You have a lot of nerve asking strangers to help you down here." I continued my purposeful proactively and mask of trust and said something like, "Well, we are all human beings, and you were the only ones around that I could ask, and I appreciate your help. I again added that my husband should be there soon.

We still could not get the car started. I began to realize that none of them seemed mechanically competent, and I also had the thought that they might sabotage the car if they had bad things in mind. So I asked them to help put the tools away, and help me push the car over to the entrance to the ramp. I knew the car would coast down the three levels, and also knew I had to get it out of the garage before the garage was locked for the night. I would feel better even if the car wouldn't go, to be at street level

That worked. The car coasted down the ramps, and I got it out of the garage. Apparently the coast down three levels dried out the wires, or jiggled something, and the car started on the second try. I thanked the young men, who by now had walked down out of the garage, and I thanked God for their help and my safety. I believe they had targeted me when I walked into that part of the garage.

I could second guess the situation, and wonder what might have happened if I had been totally honest and told them I was frightened, but willing to trust them. However, I was grateful for the impulse to do what I did, and for the results. The only thing I might do differently now would be to take a moment and pray for guidance. I suspect God got in there somehow anyway. Nowadays I often have more faith in God than in myself, and try to live in partnership with

Him. My life has expanded to include that dimension much more, and that growing faith seems to make life easier, more content, and happier.

So, here I was, having worked for many years, older than most of my fellow students and with three children and a lot of life experience. My interest was in counseling, rather than conventional social work, and when it came to writing papers; my inclination was to write on things that really interested me. My first paper was on "The Value of the Christian Church as a Social Welfare Institution." I was going through a time of integrating principles and theories of psychology and Christianity, and carrying that integration through to school seemed worthwhile. I was convinced that the church had great potential to help people in many facets of their lives, and that I could help with that as a Social Worker. I framed it in the paper as the value of community, love, faith, redemption, and action. I left the overtly Christian parts out, assuming that they would not be appropriate in a paper for grad school.

Another notable non-academic happening was studying together with a group one night, and trying marijuana for the first time. I rather enjoyed it, and especially got captivated by the music playing in the background, as my heightened senses sorted out one instrumental part after another, and heard music like I had never heard it before. It was the heightened senses and the slowed down time, resulting in more mindful attention to everything that I liked. This was also true in interaction with others. Careful attention, and open curiosity during interactions, as well as paying attention to nuances seemed very healthy to me. Despite marijuana being culturally popular, and personally pleasant, I cannot say that I smoked more than a few times in my life. Many years later, I took "ecstasy" (MDMA) once, and experienced several hours of close personal interaction with seemingly no barriers and perfect agape love. It carried over into the rest of my life, and in some small way, became a template for part of my personal growth. I can truthfully say that it changed my life in a small way, especially in attentiveness and focus.

I am not advocating either drugs or alcohol for any reason or any person. I think they do far more harm than good when used as escape or addiction. Frankly, I was lucky, and I was not addictive, at least to those things at that time. I was integrated and healthy enough, mentally and physically, to learn some useful things from trying them, and to enjoy them without wanting more.

Each semester of school we not only had our class work, but our field placement. We chose the field setting, and I tried to choose settings which would propel me toward my goals. My first was a large psychiatric hospital.

Wayne County General Psych Hospital was then at the old TB Sanitarium of Eloise. It was a long and short term psychiatric setting, with many having been there for years. Medication, and time on the wards, either taught patients to be good patients, or made them want to get better and get out of there. A few years later, places like that were closed all over the country, and the people who had been there a long time had no safe shelter to go to. Many ended up on the streets homeless. Today's mental health system, or lack of it, stems partly from that.

The following year, I chose Detroit General Hospital. I was in what would now be called the old DGH near Greek town, where the poorest and most desperate Detroiters went for medical care. In fact, as I walked up to the doors each morning in winter, I had to be careful of those sleeping on the steam vents outside the entrance, trying to keep warm. Hospitals and medical focus were familiar to me, but doing discharge planning, and helping patients access social services was all new, and through these new lenses, I saw people, health care, and poverty much differently.

My Final Master's Paper -- and Graduation

My final paper, at the end of the two years was on "A Planned Process of Change". It described an original circular process of change for both individuals and organizations. My professor thought it should be published, and added her name to it to give it weight. It was not published, though many of my fellow students began to use it.

The whole paper was the result of integration of my learning from the Human Potential movement, the Episcopal Training Network, the T-groups, Christianity, and conventional Social Work. It was focused on the process of change in doing therapy, or consulting. I wanted to know how people changed, and could not find pertinent literature which seemed helpful, or complete.

In today's world there are far better explanations, theories, papers or books on change. My son (Bob Hamp) has written a book called *Think Differently Live Differently,* which is also a book about how people change through changing perceptions and beliefs. — becoming fully who one was created and redeemed to be. It is an overtly Christian book with a central theme of letting God be the source of your life. Using God as source, and self as servant, the Holy Spirit as companion guide, and Jesus as example and the one whose life made forgiveness complete, seems to keep people on track for a life of integrity, freedom and love – the way we were created to be. (I am paraphrasing what I understand of his work,).It works, as many of his readers can attest to. He is about to publish his book on church leadership – *Think Differently Lead Differently.*

In the era when I was in graduate school, the field of purposeful change, and self-awareness were newly developing, and my paper was as innovative then as his book is now.

154

I graduated from the Master's Program in Social Work in 1974, and our whole family celebrated. Clark and the kids gave me a microwave. I suspect the meals around our house had not been too well thought out for the last couple years. I was eager to get a job, and Clark agreed with that idea. Pam was very disappointed, thinking I was going to stay home now that school was over.

That gave me pause. She would be going into 9th grade and wanted me home. I wanted to honor that, but also was excited about my future. Pam and I talked a little about what she wanted. About this same time she was concerned that her dad didn't seem to pay much attention to her, so she was evidently feeling somewhat deserted by both her parents. I did stay home for a few months, and then was eager to get a job.

Wyandotte General Hospital and Phyllis

My first Social Work job was in both Physical and Psychological Rehab, at Wyandotte General Hospital. My supervisor was a man named Tony Bandyk, who hired strong assertive women and then balked at their strength and assertiveness. Later on, a group of us got together as "alumni" of his system, to lick our wounds and make fun of Tony. Not very nice, but therapeutic. I enjoyed the work, but was still doggedly headed toward counseling and private practice. I hired a Social Worker who was already a certified counselor for supervision. I needed two years of supervised work in order to write the Academy of Clinical Social Workers exam, qualifying me to do the same.

(At that time, hiring supervision was acceptable. Now one must actually have a work supervisor who has that credential. The credential still exists and I renew mine each year, but like many fields, there has been a plethora of new, advanced, "necessary" credentials. These serve to divide the field into many splinter specialties, and make lots of money for those who supervise the credentialing and collect the extra fees. The ACSW is not as prestigious as it once was.)

One day at work, I was seeing a young teenage girl who I sensed was intelligent and had lots of resilience. I felt a sense of connecting to her. She had been hospitalized several times. She was being discharged from the psych ward at that hospital, and was not supposed to go back to her home, and had nowhere to go. I was doing the discharge planning. On the spur of the moment, I, somewhat offhandedly, mentioned to one of the nurses that maybe she could come stay with us at our house temporarily, as there did not seem to be much place for her with relatives. The staff of the ward jumped on that idea. Once I said it, it became fact, and I did not have the assertiveness skills to stand up to the pressure. I did not want a 4th teen around my house. I was busy and had my own three to look after. As it was, I ended up taking her home with little

155

notice. I did talk to the kids and Clark, but it was only one day before she moved in. I was not prepared, my kids were certainly not prepared, my husband was not prepared, and she was not prepared, and we all did the best we could. Her name was Phyllis. And she was 15.

There was the usual honeymoon period with Phyllis, which ended several weeks later. She was still immature and rebellious from a whole series of life events and hospitalizations, and from being 15. On one hand, she was immature, and on the other hand, she had a lot of life experience which my children didn't have, and which no young teen should have or experience. I was new enough, and naïve enough so I thought we could help, and everything would be fine. She had been and still was sexually active, and I was not sure she was not sexual, or attempting to be, with my sons or even my husband. She was smoking marijuana. (As were lots of people then, including Clark and possibly my sons.) She needed lots of extra reassurance and love, and I was already overwhelmed in time and energy. There was my job, the teens, our pets, my marriage and the housekeeping. I made a difficult decision several months later as more stress developed, that she could not stay.

I talked to her, and to the rest of the family. I went to the agency that was sponsoring her foster care. She was with us about 7 months, and went to her brother's afterwards. It was incredibly painful for me to ask her to leave, and was just as painful for her. It was a difficult time for all, but there was not enough structure, enough time, or enough "processing time" to help her, and I was concerned that my kids were being influenced in ways that I was not comfortable with. I was also concerned that with all that was going on around our house, we were not being of much help.

It was a mistake for me to take her, to not bring the kids in on the decision making ahead of time, and to think that we could help her without problems. I think there were small amounts of help. (bless her, she feels that we helped her a lot) I think that having her leave was a way of setting limits for her that she also knew needed setting, even with the pain. I did not keep in touch, after the first year or so. I believe she knew we cared. When my kids read this, I hope they will understand the whole situation better, and know that I apologize for my nonassertive poor judgment back then.

I wrote the above paragraphs in about June 2012. In October, 2012, Phyllis found us again. She had been looking for me for several years, but our paths had not crossed. We found each other within weeks after she had lost one of her sons to suicide. Such a terribly tragic and painful thing for anyone to negotiate. She was in the depths of grief, but delighted to be in touch again, as I was also. She affirmed me for her time with us, and said that I had been caring and loving toward her. I am grateful to know that. Thank you, Phyllis, for your caring, even during your grief.

She has a different first name, to celebrate being a different person, and a different last name because of marriage. She is now in a very long term relationship, and continuing to work at negotiating the grief and issues over her son's death, and some things from her past. As in many people, recent traumas bring up past traumas.

Phyllis, now named Chris, is a loving woman with much acquired wisdom, and many talents. Among them, she is often an amazing and inspired writer. She also took in foster children, 9 boys over time. It sounds like she did a wonderful job. I hope to see her again some time.

Growth Center-My First Counseling Job

As the end of my ACSW supervision approached, I could hardly wait to take the exam and find a place to work. I found what I thought was the perfect place, The Growth Center, in Allen Park. It was started by two ex-priests, and although not overtly, was a faith based counseling center. It was certainly started with a wish to make the world better and do God's work. as the men who started it were continuing their spiritual underpinnings and commitments in their secular life. I had not taken my exam yet, so had to wait to start work.

Clark – Next Chapters

Meanwhile, about this same time, our family, or rather our marriage fell apart again. I had that job waiting at the Growth Center, based on the idea that I could take my time getting started in private practice, and work up to a higher income.

At some time during my school, Clark had told me how great marijuana was for him, and how easily he could talk to others, and how good it made him feel.

He wanted to smoke together, and we did once or twice, when we were without the children. He wanted to smoke with the kids, and I was against that. They did not know I had tried it, and I would not have told them unless they had asked me. I definitely did not think it appropriate to encourage their use of substances, and especially by smoking with parents. My idea of marijuana at the time was that the long term effects were not harmful, but that the culture could be seductive and addictive.

Another activity of Clark's was going to porn movies, and he wanted me to go with him. I finally and reluctantly agreed to go, and ironically, the movie turned out to be a tender and sensitively done movie of two couples at a retreat center, such as Esalen in California. Yes, it was sexually explicit, and the two couples traded partners, but it still was a beautifully done film emotionally. There was great love and tenderness in all the encounters. He said that most of the movies were not like that. I did not suggest going again, and he did not ask.

Many years later, as I got more familiar with patterns of addiction, I recognized the co-dependence and addiction in our marriage. I was probably most shame based, and adamant about not failing in my marriage, no matter the cost, (and after all, he was never physically or verbally violent or mean, and in many ways was a satisfactory partner.) I just didn't want it to be my fault if our marriage failed. And I have no idea how much denial I used back then, and how much just plain naiveté. One cannot see what one cannot see, so I cannot even look back on that time and see in hindsight where and when I was blind. There are also many questions, even now about what was happening. Phyllis told me recently that Clark had told her that he would never have an affair because it would hurt me too much. Did he? Had he? I assumed so, and I still think so, but of course I never asked for details from him about his other "love".

Anyway, just before I started working at the Growth Center, having passed my ACSW exam, Clark came home and told me he was in love again. My first response this time was anger. I had worked really hard to get him to come back the first time, and other than the poison pen letter, I had seen no signs of problems. (And of course, back in that season of my life, I had much more sense that I could control life and solve problems.)

I was aware that our marriage was not like it used to be when new. But I assumed that was normal in most marriages, and especially ones which had run into difficulties. I knew that my life was going a different direction from his, but that seemed all right. I thought we were connected in other ways. We went for a long family camping trip out west in the summer of, I think, 1976. At that time, I was quite aware that our marriage was on the verge of destruction, even while I hoped it was not, and kept my face turned toward all the positive things. At that time, I especially wanted to protect the kids from fears that might not come true, such as separation and divorce.   While on the camping trip, we visited the house where Clark and I had started our married life, and barely noted it as we went by—as if, at least for me, it was too hard to remember right then, since it would also force me into the pain of what was missing. But at least we had fun on most of that trip.

For a while, after telling me again that he wanted someone else, he was in and out of our lives again. That became very painful, and after a short period, I stood on my strength and asked if he would go to counseling. I did not want him to leave, but neither did I want to be the therapist or seductress in our house, in order to keep him there. I did let him know that I didn't want our marriage to end, but I didn't cry and get depressed as before. Though I had strong feelings, I was less out of control than I had been before, and less frightened. He refused counseling, and eventually, around Thanksgiving, we set a time for him to leave. Pam was sick all night the night before he moved out, obviously distraught over the breakup. She was a junior, Jim a sophomore and Bob must have been in 8th grade. We had been in Trenton for several years at this point.

The Grieving Begins in Earnest

Clark seldom saw the kids after he left. His main contacts with the boys began to center around marijuana, wanting them to grow, smoke, buy and sell. I got angry and threatened to call the police if he continued to try and involve the kids. I think he was more careful after that, but because I had the burden of supporting the kids, I was not home much. Child support laws were not what they are today, and I was supporting the household. Clark brought money over occasionally, but not regularly. I kept in touch with activities at home as much as I could. I was working 4 days a week, and evenings also, and the conclusion I came to was that the best I could do was to set looser limits and hope they would follow them, appealing to them about consequences and making good decisions.

When Clark moved out, I remember moving our TV into the small bedroom downstairs, and the 4 of us sitting together, half numb, watching TV and drawing comfort from the togetherness, and closeness. It was such a difficult age for the children and a difficult time for all of us. They all needed a father or a positive male role model at that age. Some moments were worse than others, for me and for them.

I can remember getting angry when I had to attempt to show one of the boys how to tie a tie. There was a pretty constant thought in my mind "if only dad was here," or "If only Clark were around." I remember getting upset when one of the cars had trouble and there was no one to call. I knew I had to get a larger support system for us. I also realized the boys needed male role models and kept that in mind as life went on. There were times when something broke around the house, or when we needed two adults to drive kids places, or go to events.

In what I remember as one of the most personally courageous decisions I made, I decided to stay in private practice rather than to take a regular job, meaning a regular paycheck. I chose to follow what I felt was my calling, even though the income would be irregular and depend on my being good enough to get referrals. I was scared that I might not make it financially. The secure and steady income of a regular job was tempting. As I look back, it may have been the wrong decision for parenting, because it took time and energy that I could have put toward the children. Being raised as a competent stoic, I thought I could do it all. I couldn't.

Between the process of loss, and grieving, and the hard work that it took to care for the kids, the house, the cars, and myself, I used a lot of energy for things besides building relationships with the kids. And so they were left somewhat parentless.

As it turned out, within a year, I made more money than I would have working for someone else. I was able to take a week off every other month, and a month off in the summer. This meant we had some great vacations in Florida and other places.

Clark and I had talked of a possible temporary separation. But we had little contact, and neither of us seemed to initiate it. I was determined not to beg (although there were many times I felt like it). I let him know that I was still willing to try, but I was determined that it would have to be his initiative to come back. I was not going to seduce or coax, or ask him to meet my needs for comfort and care.

I was grieving not only his leaving, but the loss of dreams for the future. I especially had been thinking of life after the children were gone, and how it would be with the two of us. Because I tend to be a strong introvert, I had been quite dependent on contact with Clark for my social needs.

Bob, made an incredibly courageous decision somewhere around this time. He told Clark that his behavior was "not very father like", and that he did not want to be around that behavior (particularly the marijuana stuff). It was courageous because he was risking losing all contact with his father, at a time when his father was moving away anyway, and Bob was already grieving the loss.

My practice picked up pretty quickly, and it was a good thing. We needed cars and insurance so the kids could get themselves to the places they needed to go. By then Pam had her driver's license and could transport the other two. And then Jim got his shortly after. Those years were hectic and full of change, emotions, and confusion for all of us. As I said earlier, destruction, healing, and construction intermingled. So much happened. Many of the particulars seem to be a blur for me.

I want to leave the raw, poorly remembered emotions here, and insert a personal and less grief filled, note about that time. Around the time that Clark and I separated the second time, I had used money from my new job to buy a little Triumph Spitfire Convertible. I loved driving and riding in that car, and as soon as each child got their license, you can bet they took pride in borrowing it and showing it off.

We also had a van as a family car, and I ended up buying a third car so that the kids had two cars for their school and social activities. We were several miles from the school, and they were in swimming and other activities. However, this all meant I owned and bought insurance for 3 cars and 4 drivers. – Very expensive! (In that era, a new Datsun B210 cost me around 3,000 dollars)

A couple years later, I took an auto body repair class at a local high school—the only female in class, let alone the only adult in the class (mostly high school boys). I fixed up the Spitfire, using Bondo, metal work and all. It was rusting out from Michigan salt on winter roads. I then had it repainted in the paint booth at the school. I was very proud of that accomplishment. The van and the Spitfire were the cars I learned auto mechanics on, and ended up doing most of the car repairs, starting with putting a starter on the van. I still change my own oil on my Toyota Camry these days.

Pam was a good driver. One day she took Bob to swimming or was to pick him up. – I cannot remember which. It was very foggy and rainy out. She was gone a while, and came back in the door crying hard, saying she had been in a wreck. I quickly asked if she was hurt, and then asked where Bob was. She was crying so hard, so scared, that she couldn't answer. I asked again, and then put my arms around her until she was somewhat composed and asked again where Bob was. She either said she had dropped him off first, or had left him at a friend's house. So when she finally could tell me, I was relieved that both kids were OK. She had crossed a boulevard, and the fog was so thick, she did not see a car coming toward her at right angles and they collided. Again I was aware of how vulnerable we were with only one parent. What if something happened to me? Or to one of the kids when I would have to choose whether to be with them or work to earn our living.

First Attempts at Healing

A few months after Clark left, Lou Pambianco, my Gestalt teacher, was organizing a cruise to the Bahamas. It was both a teaching and pleasure cruise. After a lot of hesitation, I decided to go. It would be time away, an adventure, and would add to my skills as a therapist.

It was my first time on a commercial plane, and first time in Florida. Certainly my first time in the Bahamas. I figured out a double or triple layered support system for the kids. I stayed with Bruce and Desta Bailey, the former pastor of Holy Family, the night before the cruise, since they lived nearby.

The ship was a beautiful old wooden gaff rigged schooner, The William H. Albury. We had a captain (Joe) and a cook (Michelle), and we were the rest of the crew. The stress of working together, and living in tight quarters provided fodder for the interpersonal Gestalt work and the teaching during the week. For that reason, Lou named his cruises "Stress and Ecstasy". I had a great time and learned a lot. The expenses were tax deductible.

It was life changing for me, to risk new behaviour like that, and find out a little of who I was besides wife, mom, and therapist. Sailor and Gestalt student was a rich new adventure, and addition to my identity.

161

There were other attempts by all of us to get through the acute grief. I attempted to help the children do constructive things that they liked. They continued or began competitive swimming. That gave them a team to be with, and used time and energy. Jim ran cross country and the mile race for a year. Bob was taking guitar lessons, and the boys were both interested in music and playing guitar. Actually, Pam had learned guitar first. Clark had been a piano player, but we did not have a piano, and besides, at the time, guitar was "cooler". These activities helped to mediate some of the grief and stress in the kids.

Clark left in November or December, I went to the Bahamas in February, and the kids and I drove to Florida for Easter Vacation. When we went out the door to go to Florida, my legs were so shaky I could hardly walk. I was feeling the weight and uneasiness of my responsibility for the children. I was afraid I would get sick, or the car would break down. Even though Pam could drive, I was ultimately responsible for all of us. The trip went well; we had a wonderful time, and took another couple trips to Florida in the future. We swam and ate fresh shrimp, and I imagine it helped to wash away a little more grief and tension.

I mentioned our former family vacations to the Outer Banks and Ocracoke. That next summer, I took a whole month off, and we went to Ocracoke again as what I hoped still felt like a family to the kids. I wanted them to know that we could still have family fun, and we did.

On one of the first trips to Florida, Bob got his first skateboard, having planned on that for months. It started him on many years of skateboarding, and enjoyment of his body and the sport.

In my work world, I was proud of my practice. It was going well, and I only lost two clients while we were gone for that month, despite warnings from other therapists. Of course, in private practice, there is no paid vacation, so the month after a major vacation, there is little income. By then, I had saved money and we were doing OK. I was as busy as I wanted to be and was gone too many hours, both day and evening.

We hit a speed bump at home when Jim and Bob seemed to be at odds and fighting physically with each other. I came home one day in time to see one of them almost knock the other down the basement stairs. I felt frightened about either of them getting hurt, and about the extreme conflict between them, and told them we needed to find options. We talked about anger outlets, such as punching something else, or going apart and physically working out.

The two of them were very different, and in family dynamics, Jim was more stressful for me to raise. Of course, they were young males trying to prove themselves without a father around. But also, I was often more impatient with Jim and that carried over in the family dynamics. I think they will have to dissect that in their own memoirs if they choose.

I was under pressure from the schools for Jim to get better grades. He was highly intelligent but not much interested in school or grades. He may also have had what would now be called ADD. He feels he had Asperger's, which didn't exist back then by that name. He seemed somewhat depressed, and often was by himself to what I considered an excess degree. He lost many things, like his school books, winter coats, his glasses, and other important things. On camping trips, or family outings, we had to help him get his things organized, and help find, or take time to replace the lost things. My way of attempting to help him then was to encourage him to do the things he enjoyed, and also talk to him about fitting in, and doing what was expected. However, I was often frustrated and angry toward him. We also talked a lot about the consequences of his getting non-passing grades, or not doing what he was told to do to be part of a team. It all seemed to little avail. I did not know how to cope.

He was tested, and it showed how bright he was. I was also told that he had something called Minimal Brain Dysfunction. He had been in therapy a couple times, and I knew he needed male role models, and attempted to find some for him. One of his therapists filled that role for a long time, playing chess with him and talking with him. I had tried Ritalin for Jim, at the advice of his pediatrician when he was younger. It had seemed to help him tremendously, except that (before the sustained release version), when it wore off, his mood would change quickly and he would be very tearful or antagonistic. It was difficult to watch him suffer like that, and difficult to know what to do. He was later, as an adult, very angry at me for having used the Ritalin for him. At the time, I was threading my way through raising the children, with a lack of time or energy, and using whatever resources I could find. The doctor recommended the Ritalin, and it truly looked on the surface as if it was doing good things.

The boundaries I set for the kids were far too loose, but hindsight is always a hard taskmaster, allowing me to see differently what I thought was right then. I felt hopeless about entirely stopping the use of pot, alcohol and even sexuality in that season of their lives, and of the culture. I said things like: "If you are going to smoke with your friends, I want you to do it at our house. I trusted them in our home environment, more than in unknown other environments. But of course, I was not there to enforce rules. I was hoping that the swimming, and the music and other activities would keep them constructively occupied. And to some extent it did.

The 70's were a time of loose boundaries in the culture, at least the part of the culture that I was in contact with. I guess I would say in hindsight, that the up side of our lifestyle was that the children had to choose their own behaviors and consequences, right or wrong, and for the most part, long term they did well.

163

Divorce Becomes Certain

After a time of separation from Clark, I was being internally pushed toward closure or at least next steps for Clark and I. We decided to meet, and as I went to that meeting, I was torn between my longing for the love and companionship I had felt with him, and not wanting him back unless there was noticeable change in his behaviors and attitudes toward marriage, or his openness toward counseling. I was frightened to feel close to him again, and felt unable to be vulnerable. We had a hurried and superficial conversation along the lines of "Well, do you think we should get back together? No I guess not, or maybe we should". Well, maybe not." Our final "sort of decision" was no. It was not that I thought he was the only one "wrong", but that I was looking for some sign that he was willing to work with me, in partnership. However, at the same time, because I was so torn and fearful, I didn't look hard at him.

I soon went to an attorney and filed for divorce, needing to move on from uncertainty and ambivalence. I went home and told the children, and we went into another round of grief.

Incidentally, Clark never let go of attempting to continue a seductive and supposedly loving relationship with me as long as he was alive, even after he remarried. However, this always felt manipulative to me, and not heartfelt. For instance, after he was married, he wrote me a loving letter, and sent many cards that he had made. Eventually, I wrote and asked if he wanted me to visit. He had limited visiting times available, and told me no, as he needed to save them for his wife (You will understand the situation further on in this writing) The ambivalence that his overtures raised in me were unsettling and forced me to continue to reassess my own goals.

Pam and Bob were doing well in school. Pam was goal oriented and organized. At one point, she realized that her comprehension of her studies could be improved and found that the school offered a remedial course in comprehension. She took the initiative on that, and the course made a difference in her study and ease of good grades. Jim was not doing well. He continued to be oppositional about his grades, and no one could convince him to do what we all knew would be easy for him. He later told me he had decided to come as close as he could to failing, and still graduate. Bob was getting good grades, doing some extra curricular activities (swimming at this time), and finding friends.

Lou Pambianco was still having cruises, and I sent the boys on one of them. I thought it would provide both a vacation and a good male role model. They had met Lou before. The school was upset that I was considering letting Jim go because of his grades. I chose between the importance of forcing him to work on grades in the presence of no motivation, or spending time with Lou in an attempt to break the pattern. I chose the cruise. I told Jim he could not go

164

unless his grades were better, and then I backed down, hoping for a change in him after the cruise. It did not happen.

Prying Myself Away From Marriage

In November of 1977 our divorce was final. By then, both Pam and Jim were of age (18) and so I got child support for only Bob. It was $40/week. Clark, meanwhile had abandoned his car on the street, and was living in a small little lower class apartment, and generally treating himself as if he was worthless. He was still working at Voran's Funeral Home.

He and I went to Pam's graduation together, even though separated. The next year, we both went to Jim's graduation, but not together. By then we knew that our divorce was pending.

Every day I had to decide all over again not to reach out to Clark, but to spend my time taking care of business and the children, instead of getting angry, scared, or sad that Clark was not around. I had to figure out how to cope with my emotions and still see clients daily. I had to remind myself that I was not still legally attached to him, and force myself not to call him, or talk to his friends in hopes of news, or in hopes of help. I really did have to pry myself out of that marriage.

Over time, I built up a support system and my reflexes to turn toward Clark became less. A year or so later, I again had to turn away from the temptation to help and rescue him. You will hear more. My loyalty dies slowly. I often think if I do just little more, things will change. Or in that co-dependent mode, I often think I should love the person even though he does not love himself.

My mother had inherited money from my father, and her father. After getting her finances in order, and seeing whether she could afford it, she invited her children and their spouses on a two week trip to Hawaii. There would be 7 of us going. My sister and I who were both divorced my two brothers and their wives, and my mom. We were to fly out together when I suddenly realized, a couple weeks before the trip, that the departure date was Jim's graduation date. I called my mom and explained and told her that I thought it would work for me to meet them there the next day. I offered to pay any extra fees involved.

She was immediately furious at me and told me it could not be changed. My changing her plans upset her beyond reason. Her drinking was taking a toll on her personality and she had come a long ways from the person who had been accepting, intelligent, and reasonable, and involved in other's lives in helpful ways. She seemed to be left without the capacity to understand my wishing to be at my son's graduation. I called the travel agent and changed my flight, myself, and told my mother I would meet them in Hawaii the morning after they arrived.

Again, my teenagers had lots of back up during my trip, although all the close relatives would be gone. Fortunately, everything went well, both for them and for our trip. Indeed, the trip was memorable, and we all enjoyed it. I might never have gone if it had not been for her generosity. Little did I know then that someday I would live in Hawaii.

This whole season of my life was so tricky and difficult. I felt as if I was asking both the kids and myself to grow up fast. Some of that growing up involved the same issues for me and for them. It was my job to meet my own needs, help meet theirs, and guide them and love them. Also, I was attempting to grow and function well both as a professional and a person. The changes in all of us during that time were huge. I suspect that all of us felt some of what I felt, which is that I was continually walking a balance beam or a tightrope.

The children were reaching out to find their own ways of growing and healing. They turned to people and activities which would actualize their own individuality, and use their strengths. The difficult part for me was not being home to guide, parent, or even ask questions. They really were very much on their own. They did an incredibly good job of growing up with good values, and healthy pursuits, with little help from me. Their time of lost-ness was difficult for them and for me, but it was not permanent. For that I am grateful.

As time went on in the year or so after the divorce, there was a happening that was so implausible, so unexpected, and so foundation shaking for all of us, that we reeled for a long time from it. It still vibrates down through the years, surfacing in the form of questions and wondering. This was when I once more had to strengthen my resolve not to run to the rescue.

Clark's Arrest- 1978

Clark was arrested for conspiracy to commit murder, and the victim was his girlfriend's husband. If the divorce had not been shock enough for us all to absorb and integrate, this was more than enough. This person who had been an integral part of our family, the one we all had known, was now suddenly being called a murderer and sitting in the local jail under tight arrest with no bail. It was nearly incomprehensible to all of us, and because we had shared his life, we shared the shock waves and ripples of this turn of events.

He came to me a day or so before his arrest specifically to tell me this story: A group of men, workers at the funeral home and other guys, were sitting around smoking dope and talking. Clark commented that he wished he could find a way to get rid of his girlfriend's husband, as the man was abusing her and the children. The guys started inventing scenarios, various ways to accomplish the end. Two weeks later, the man was found dead changing a tire on his car outside the bowling alley. He was shot. And the scenario was one of those talked of at the party.

Clark said he had no idea who might have done this, but that he had voluntarily gone to the police because his friend and coworker Dan had been arrested for being the possible murderer. He went with the hope of clearing his name but had no idea at the time that telling the police about his remarks that evening with the guys would make him guilty of conspiracy, which would carry the same sentence as the murder. Because Clark had been there, and helped formulate the idea, he was a conspirator. By going to the police, naively, he sealed his fate.

I visited him at the local jail, talking through a glass, and watching the guards taunt him with cigarettes (which they kept in their hands since he was in handcuffs), and his glasses, which they had taken away from him leaving him very much blind. Eventually, when he went to trial, his attorney asked me to testify as a character witness. I did. It was a double trial with two juries; I suppose to save money for the county, or state. He and his friend Dan were both on trial. They were both convicted. Dan plea bargained and was released after a time in prison. Clark either was not offered that, or refused, depending on who is asked. I heard that he refused; "because he was innocent" The sentence was life, no parole.

This whole incident is not too terrible to write about 35 years later, but the emotions that the children and I went through at the time were very difficult. There was not only our private and family emotions about it, but that reflection on us by association meant that we were asked about it by others. Fortunately, most of the publicity was in Allen Park, where Clark worked, and where the murder happened, and we lived in Trenton. The two towns had separate newspapers. Therefore, the children did not get asked much in school. My practice was in Allen Park and of course I had both old and new clients ask me if I was related to him. They wondered out loud, and I wondered silently inside myself, if I could be a good therapist if I was divorced and the ex-wife of a possible murderer. I had to process a lot besides the grief of the divorce - my own questioning about how I could have chosen someone like that, whether indeed he was like that, my shame, and my sense of adequacy as a therapist.

After all, I had loved Clark, and had been married to him for 19 years. We had borne three children. I did not want to see him go to prison. My sense of loyalty was torn. I did not think he was guilty of the murder or knowing who did it. I wanted to think the best. I wanted to rescue and help him. I didn't want to see him pay for something which I did not think he had done. Nothing I knew about this man would predict to me that he was capable of this. And from that time until he died in prison, at age 54, I had to deliberately choose to take care of myself and the children, rather than put time, money, or effort into helping him.

I eventually resolved my own internal conflicts by realizing that even if he had nothing to do with the actual murder, legally, his presence in that room with the guys and his participation in the conversation constituted conspiracy, and was indeed punishable just as if he had pulled the trigger. He was considered to have helped plan it, even if unknowingly. He then may have doubly sealed his future by refusing to plea bargain.

I still do not know the real story, but here is my studied opinion. Clark had the large inheritance I had spoken of earlier. I had done what I thought was fair in the divorce, and since it was his family's money, I did not try to get any of it. I did, however, stipulate that he was to pay for the children's college. I suspect that the other man who worked at the funeral home, and who was tried, arranged to have this man shot, hoping Clark would pay him for it. After all, he had heard Clark say he wished the man were gone. It was proved at the trial that there was no large sums of money changed hands. Clark denied any agreement between them about money, or talk about the murder. He maintained that the evening's talk was just a bunch of guys sitting around "bullshitting". Thus there was no payoff, and they both went to prison because conspiracy carries the same sentence as the crime, and the crime, being first degree murder, carried a life sentence with no parole. He was there for life. Because there was no evidence of the actual murder, they were both found guilty of conspiracy. To the best of my knowledge, that is what happened. The other man plea bargained and got out of prison early.

There was a story written in the Detroit Free Press by a reporter during the trial, intrigued with the idea that employees of a funeral home could be involved in murder. He theorized that since the gun was never found, it was put in the casket with the dead man and buried. There was never any evidence or response to that story. And no proof that it was more than imagination.

Clark's money was gone. He had given it to a friend to buy an auto parts store, and the store had burned and the friend moved away—my guess would be arson for the insurance money. The children were never offered any. Clark did quit claim deed the cottage at Half Moon Lake back to the children. They kept that property a few years, and then sold it.

He may have been naïve and relatively blameless in the actual killing, but his lifestyle and the people he was running around with certainly carried its own energy. A few years after imprisonment, Clark married someone else. (There is at least one book written about women who marry lifers.) I never saw him after the first year or two in Jackson. When I did visit him, that first year, he let me know how easy drugs were to get there. He died at age 54 of a heart attack, and again I am guessing when I say he may have been using cocaine, as well as the marijuana that I know he was using.

This seems indeed, a sad ending to the life of a small town man who coped with the changes in his life in ways which brought no rewards. A sad thing for the kids to live down, and to live through. And for me? A love gone sour, a love gone. A loss of dreams and a powerful motivation to grow into the next phase of my life, and help the kids do the same - with dignity, integrity, and success.

I will never know the truth about that chapter of my life. I will never know who wrote the poison pen letter, what went on during his absences from home, or who shot the man who was shot. I will never know whether I made the right choices, or had the right picture of that time. Would I do it differently? As the person I was then, I don't know that I could have done it differently. Looking back at that particular incident and season, I think I did well. As who I am now, I can think of lots of things I would do differently. I especially wish I had been more mature, and thus less insecure after divorce and more able and willing to be a mature parent and role model to my children.

And? Onward To the Next Steps

And so, with those question marks in my background, I look back at myself. I do not consider myself blameless in the dissolution of our marriage. I certainly did the best I knew at the time, but I was guilty of thinking that my path of growth was the "right" one, and judged him to be unworthy because he was not following the same one. He did not have the self-esteem to keep a sense of self-worth against my criticism. He too judged himself unworthy of more, and chose his life accordingly. That is my shortened perception of what happened. Forgiveness is powerful. I believe I have forgiven, and believe I am forgiven.

Because of that time in my life, I believe I am capable of more firmly setting boundaries about what I will tolerate. I try to stay real and truthful about my wishes and responses in relationships. I also attempt to turn situations over to God when I find myself judgmental, confused, angry, or hungry for love. I continue to grow emotionally, and especially spiritually. I have a great reliance on the God who speaks to me about my life, and I am much happier detaching from what seems "crazy" to me, than I am judging it and trying to change it. I don't go around mad, or depressed. Not that there are not moments. I am human and I am attempting to find my way as a redeemed and sufficient human being, and servant of Christ and life. I often accomplish that, but certainly not always. Other relationships since then have shown me the issues inside my heart that have yet to be resolved. However, our divorce, and the following consequences have taught me a great deal.

Life Soon After Divorce, Dating.

I want to return to the other parts of my process after the divorce. My self-esteem and self-confidence in the area of relationships was badly bruised after our separation and divorce. It seemed that for a time, my solution was to attempt to get other men to pay attention to me so I would know that I was attractive. I had the experience from Adrian in my memory, but I seemed to need more. My introverted nature, and my wanting attention clashed. I felt like a young teen, complete with embarrassment, self-consciousness and fears of rejection. I was 41 years old, going through adolescence, and still attempting to be a mature mom to 3 adolescents.

I called a man I had met at a social work workshop, and asked him out. He was nice enough to accept, and we had a nice time,. But since he lived 50 miles away, and I was in no position to respond strongly to anyone, we never got together again. I also talked to my co-therapist, Dennis fairly often, and he was a good companion. He and his wife had divorced about a year before that, and I was still too naïve to know that Dennis was an alcoholic.

Dennis and I took our children to Toronto for New Year's. I later recalled that weekend as a time of learning how to be out in the world. Dennis was an executive at Chrysler Corporation, and traveled frequently. I had no idea of the social rules around restaurants and hotels. - How to know when to hand payment to a waitress, and when to pay at a cash register for instance. I had no idea how to check in at a motel or hotel. Our family had lived more simply and inexpensively, and I never learned those things. I was with this suave sophisticated man who taught me. I felt comfortable asking questions, and he just laughed and answered them.

In reality, I think we were both a couple of lost kids, wandering around trying to do what was right for our children and ourselves as single parents. I dated Dennis a few times in the years after that, but never often. We made better work partners than dates for each other.

I started going to singles events, although I was so painfully shy and inexperienced. I finally decided to treat these events like class sessions in a college course. It was a course on Social Behavior and Interaction, and each time I went somewhere, I considered that I was doing my homework. I watched others, tried new things, and came home and critiqued myself. By treating my forays that way, I could stay away from beating myself up for not doing well, or for being awkward. I ended up feeling like a student rather than a failure.

Over the next few years, I dated a series of men, mostly one at a time, mistaking sex for love, or for commitment. I then was disappointed when we broke up, having felt like I loved and was loved. I got lots of experience in interacting with different men, but

170

my knowledge of what comprised a good relationship, or what love or commitment was, was sorely lacking.

This cultural era was one where sexuality among single adults was open and frequent. It was shortly before the advent of AIDS. Clark was the only partner I had ever had until our divorce, and so, although one could argue the morals of the situation, I believe I learned a tremendous amount about relationships and sexuality. I grew from this period in many ways, and as I have grown older, I have looked back on this time with joy and satisfaction. My regret is that I now understand I was not very respectful of my body or my heart during that time, but I have not regretted the good and the growth that happened.

One thing I was clear about with my dates or temporary partners was that they were not my children's surrogate father and they did not have permission to set limits for the children, or enforce their own ideas. They were welcome to interact with my children, I just didn't want to confuse the kids with a series of temporary fathers, or other people's agendas for child raising.

Dancing became an outlet for me. Clark and I had not danced since college, and he was not a particularly good dancer. I loved music, rhythm, and moving my body. I especially liked the partnership feeling of dancing with someone else and creating an interactive energy that was bonding, fun, sometimes sexual, and thoroughly enjoyable. When I first started dating, I was too uptight to be a good dancer but with some practice and encouragement, I became a very good dancer, and was sought after as a partner. There were many times that I went to a singles event mainly to dance. In fact there were a few short periods that I simply used my partners for my pleasure in dancing, rather than to build friendships. At the time, it felt good, and that was enough.

Growing Through Work and Training

Meanwhile at work, my practice was full. I was also teaching classes, and doing speaking and consulting. I continually involved myself in self-awareness and growth techniques which served to help me personally, and give me more to pass on to my clients. What follows here are descriptions of some of those things, giving a roadmap of my personal journey, and the values and growth that I developed along the way.

TORI

Through the T groups and the Episcopal Training Network, I had heard of Jack Gibb, a consultant. He had written a book called *Trust, a New View of Personal and Organizational Development*. He had developed a theory called TORI, which stood for Trust, Openness, self Realization, and Interdependence. There were several groups of people through out the country who were meeting to attempt to build on and live this theory. One of those groups was in Toronto, with an offshoot in the Detroit area. I was curious and decided to attend a TORI meeting held in conjunction with the AHP (Association for Humanistic Psychology) annual meeting. This one was in Toronto.

Those terms; <u>Trust</u>, <u>Openness,</u> <u>self-Realization,</u> and <u>Interdependence</u> resonated with me and I sensed that internalized, they would help people became healthier in many ways, and deepen connections with themselves and each other.

At that first TORI I had fun, but felt uneasy. The norms and rules (although the people who were there avowed there were none) felt slippery and strange. I suspended judgment, and decided to go with it. I learned that hugs were not always sexual, and if you didn't know, you asked. I learned that it was all right to work out relationship difficulties in public, and that most of the time, the group process was trust-able, just as it had been in the T-groups.

I came back with a decision to attend the Detroit TORI, and enjoyed it for a couple years, meanwhile learning more about relationships, communities, and communication. It was also another place to meet men to date.

I started using Trust Theory in my work, quickly realizing that Trust most often meant trusting oneself. The root of self-trust is to know that one can perceive clearly, and handle effectively whatever comes up in relationships or situations. Not always easy, but practice upped the skill level, and therefore the self trust level.

I later equated the word "trust" to "faith"—trust was confidence in self or other, faith was confidence in God. Both meant that everything didn't have to be figured out at the time, or ahead of time. And while trusting God was a choice, trusting self was a matter of knowledge and skills, practiced enough to find a consistent belief in self.

TORI was a source of learning, friendship, sense of community, and support. After Jack Gibb's death, and cultural changes away from a longing for community, it slowly disappeared. Many of us who were there, still long for that sense of intentional community. It is scarce in today's culture. Few have found something to fill the hole.

Astron

Jack Gibb eventually formed an internship in Trust Theory called Astron. I joined. It was a two year commitment. We met together in 5 regional groups across the country. We met for 30 days a year in one 10-day and five 4-day meetings. As we met at colleges or retreat centers, we did a great deal of writing, interacting, and processing, and I quickly got interested in the process of collaboration. I developed many long term friends, considering moving myself and the children to Canada to be near some of them. We all felt at home in both countries in those days.

My interest in collaboration stemmed from a lack of collaborative skills and practice on my part, and a perceived lack of motivation or skills for collaboration in the rest of the world—especially between men and women. As a woman, I often felt disregarded or expected to be silent about the current opinion or idea. That did not happen much in Astron. Just as I loved that feeling of co-creating intimacy in dancing, I loved the general feeling of co-creation, or collaboration in many situations. And I didn't like unilateral decision making. Nor did I like feeling suppressed, or alone in a group. Astron evolved into a longer association of members called Omicron, and there was talk about forming a permanent live in community. However, that too eventually died out. Most of the Astron members are approaching 80 or 90 now, or are deceased. .

AHP (Association of Humanistic Psychology)

AHP formed because a group of PhD psychologists were attempting to broaden their field of knowledge and practice .They wanted to pay attention to the whole person, to humanize the clinical and academic foundations of their field. It was meant to add heart, soul and emotions to Freud, diagnosis, and treatment.

I was fascinated by the workshops at the annual meetings. I had, as I mentioned before, gone to Toronto to attend the TORI meeting in conjunction with AHP. There was a large variety of workshops including body work techniques, hypnosis, gender confusion, and comparative religion. I was fascinated with how the various techniques and knowledge could be applied to helping improve quality of life in people, and improve counseling. I attended that annual AHP conference for several years, and ended up presenting at one such conference at Princeton.

The idea of adding heart, body, and soul to psychology totally excited me.

I have always worked well with metaphor and integrating dissimilar subjects that share similar processes. Thus, exploring many facets of life which interacted within people seemed valuable to helping both myself and clients.

AHP became a path for me to continue to integrate my science background with my Social Work career. I saw the possibility to include heart, soul, and spirit in my life and my work.

There may not have been hard science to explain such qualities as agape love, collaboration, compassion, and redemption, but there surely was memory, emotions, and growth connected with the experience of such. And the boundary between body and mind is very difficult to determine. It is hard to know where chemistry or anatomy leaves off and psychology or emotionality begins. It was imperative in my mind to use all that I knew in my work, and AHP became a tool and a path to that.

I was not alone in moving into the body/mind counseling field. It was on the cusp of becoming a cultural phenomenon. It felt like a natural progression.

During this time, I discovered books on improving vision. My nearsightedness responded to exercise and visualization, and with a year's practice, I was able to leave my glasses and contact lenses behind at about age 33. I now had close to 20/20 vision.

In succeeding years, I confounded ophthalmologists who did not believe the possibility, as I showed them I could make my eyes test alternately near sighted and normal.

Eventually I was one of the presenters at an AHP conference, presenting my own experience, along with techniques, and hope for others also being able to leave their glasses behind. Back home, I also worked with individuals to help them jettison their glasses. Possibly as an outgrowth of controlling and strengthening my eye muscles, I have not had to wear reading glasses until in my mid 70's, and then only intermittently.

I continued attending those conferences, always finding new ideas and techniques for work and personal development. AHP still exists both separately and finally as part of the American Psychological Association. I have not attended for many years.

Gestalt

Gestalt training was "in the air" among therapists, but I encountered it personally at the invitation of Monica Wendling, one of my fellow social workers. She invited me to a local weekend of conference and technique on Gestalt with Lou Pambianco from California. I have mentioned Lou previously for his cruises to the Bahamas. I am still in touch with him by internet. At that first workshop with Lou, I was smitten by the technique, and by his skill. I understood the theories easily and they fit my way of processing very easily.

Lou himself had obvious mental and emotional health, and life integration. I longed to learn and practice the technique, and to have more of what Lou had. Soon Lou offered a training program once a month in Michigan, which consisted of a day of personal and individual work, and then a weekend of training. He alternated working with attendees on personal issues, and speaking about the theory and practice of Gestalt. He was a master at work

Most people know Gestalt Therapy from its most famous technique, called the "two chair technique". This was practiced and made known by Fritz Perls at the Esalen Institue.

A wide variety of issues are amenable to this technique: internal, interpersonal or relational, or matters of the heart and spirit all respond. The internal conversation regarding that issue is

174

identified, clarified and resolved by being made external. The person is speaking out loud, but more than that, they are moving between locations (between chairs) as the conflicts or sides of an issue become clear. As this process continues, the nuances of the issue become more overt and explicit. At some point, the client begins to sense the problem differently, and this new perception, and possible new options for resolution produces an "ah ha moment" (or sometimes an "oh shit" moment) where next steps become much more obvious.

I found this a very powerful tool. What starts as an "either/or" situation, can become a "both/and" situation. Sometimes the irrational or long held belief systems are seen differently and can be dropped or modified. With a successful session, there is a definite change in perception of the problem.

After a while, Gestalt became a way of life, and to this day, I often see things in terms of polarities, and then integration, bringing them into a both/and acceptance and putting them to work in my life.

Integration – Using my Growth in My Work

Other valuable tools and methods for my personal and professional growth were Transactional Analysis with the Parent/Adult/Child Ego states, and the book I'm OK, You're OK. Along with that , the Drivers and Stoppers of Tabi Kahler, Primal Therapy (Catharsis) (Janov), and of course the Developmental Chart adapted by Jo Kelsey on page 135. Bringing these things to my practice meant that my office contained things like a mattress, a tennis racket, a big pillow to hit or squeeze, and a blanket, as well as two movable chairs

In addition I sometimes used writing, singing or drawing to help others expand their view of their potential, to help them see themselves and their situations differently.

My overriding philosophy and attitude of therapy was flexibility and caring. Hopefully I lived up to that through the years though never perfectly. One of Pambianco's sayings was "There are no resistant clients, only inflexible therapists." He also taught that clients could go no deeper or further in therapy than their therapist had gone. He taught that the person of the therapist was as important as the theories, techniques, or ideas, in order to produce growth and health in the client.

I did much more than counseling during that approximately 8 years at the Growth Center. 1976-1983). I continued teaching Yoga, I taught workshops and classes at the Center, and finally, I taught at Madonna College (Now University). I consulted with groups, organizations and corporations, and I gave many speeches to groups or classes. I loved doing many different things.

This was an exciting season to be a psychotherapist. The field was growing and expanding, and counseling lost its stigma and became acceptable. In the Detroit area, the auto companies had excellent insurance which covered counseling generously, and so it was available to all who worked there.

A memory of a fun consulting day comes back: An accounting firm hired me for a conflict between the younger and older employees. The younger employees were dismayed that the strong work ethic and lack of balance in the lives of the older founders was being forced and foisted onto them. They did not want to work 7 days and evenings a week for 3 months, even if it was tax season. The older men thought the younger ones uncommitted and lazy.

I called the day long workshop "Collision, Collusion, or Collaboration." We identified the Collisions and Collusions between people, resulting from different beliefs and lack of communication, and worked toward mutual goals, understandings and respect. We then worked out some ways to set up collaborative situations and better communication. We found ways that both sides agreed that the future could be different. It was a successful day of tearing down walls, and building some bridges.

I taught with both information and experiential learning. I had learned, again from Jo Kelsey, a powerful, useful model for experiential learning. It was called the EIAG model and looked like this, except it was a circular model:

EXPERIENCE - Design and use an experience for learning
After the experience, ask:
IDENTIFY – What happened?
ANALYZE – What did we learn?
GENERALIZE – How can we use it?

(And then circle around to another designed or real life experience)

One more small work chapter was my activity with women in the Downriver Area. (Where I lived and worked) It was the season of "women's lib". I had many women in counseling who were exploring what "equality" meant in their lives. I worked closely with the local chapter of NOW (National Organization of Women) and was asked to chair the annual meeting. They had been warned that a group of aggressively militant women planned to come to the meeting and attempt to take over the meeting with their agenda, which seemed militant and destructive to most. The officers wanted an outside person who could set boundaries and mediate between factions if necessary. The meeting went well, and there was no showdown.

There were articles about me and my work in local papers around this time, and of course this brought me more clients. My clients varied greatly over those years. There were times when I had

176

several black, ethnic, lesbian, or men clients. I mention men because fewer men came to counseling, and they often wanted a male therapist. However, these men came asking specifically for me. A male therapist at the Growth Center and I often teamed up, and saw clients alternately or together for more effective therapy I felt good that the various kinds of people mentioned above trusted me to help.

I eventually was asked to teach at Madonna College, where I was thoroughly vetted and warned not to teach non-Roman Catholic views on such issues as birth control, abortion, etc. One semester I concurrently taught <u>Stress Management for Health Care Professionals</u>, and reached into my med-tech background to teach <u>Beginning Physiology</u>. I must say that the Stress Management Class was more successful. I had forgotten too much about Physiology, and didn't teach it well.

The Slide Show

Another notable and exciting time in my work was an educational slide show put together with a man I was dating,. We shared the hobby of photography and an interest in personal growth. We called show, "Journey Through Life, Return To Wholeness". It was based on that developmental chart of Jo Kelsey. It began with the idea that we are born with a certain kind of wholeness, and then through growing up with imperfect parenting (we are all imperfect), we lose some of that sense of wholeness. We then often eventually go looking in various ways to maintain or regain that sense of wholeness.

We added narration, and decided to debut this show at the singles group we attended. We were bowled over by the response. People applauded for 10 minutes, and then asked questions and talked to us for over an hour The show was later shown at churches, union groups, and in many and varied setting, including talks I gave to parents groups, and to therapy groups. It was always well received. I think that the cultural or Kairos moment existed at that season in time both for the show and for the culture.

This show was developed while I was teaching at Madonna. Madonna had a strong program in ASL (American Sign Language), and many deaf students attended because of it. All classes had a signer present. I began to wonder if the deaf students would get the emotional message of the show. They would have to depend on the signers and pictures. I spoke to my supervisor and we decided to try it in a class. It worked, and there were emotional responses among the deaf students, as well as the hearing ones. Of course that depended on the skill and heart of the signer also, but I was thrilled.

Today, we have moved beyond that moment in the culture where that particular show is so powerful. I have not shown it publicly for several years. It probably still has some value for some groups. However, I too have moved beyond that moment where it was so meaningful to me. It may be that at some point, either in the culture or in me, it will become relevant again.

It has been fun to watch my son Bob parallel my process in some ways, and even parallel some of the messages I taught, from a whole different context. This observation seems to illustrate the parallels and agreements in what may look like divergent or even disparate cultures. Bob and all my children have moved far beyond me in so many ways, moving into different cultures, and absorbing today's innovations and cultural contexts. Pam is my tech guru these days, and Jim has taught me what the human spirit can endure, learn from, and give, when the body does not cooperate.

And The Children

And speaking of the children, they were growing and moving out of our nuclear family, out of necessity and developmental age.

Pam, who had graduated just before the divorce, ended up attending Kalamazoo College. She got her Bachelor's Degree in Social Science. She was on the swim team, as she had been in high school. She co-captained her team her senior year. K College is a tough college, and also had many students there that had more financing than we did. Pam worked hard and did well, spending part of one year abroad in Madrid, Spain. Before email, Madrid seemed like the other end of the world to mom. I was pretty nervous. She ran low on money while traveling, and I think we used Western Union and sent money to the consulate for her.

She seemed to have found stability in the midst of the chaos, and whatever internal chaos she experienced she found resources to come through it functioning well, and meeting her goals of graduation and jobs. She is married to Doug Wetzel and has a daughter, Emily Karoline. She has a Master's Degree, and has worked at various positions in Insurance and banks. She currently works in Ann Arbor, and is active in many other spheres, keeping herself physically healthy and active, and well-liked and respected by many. She still loves cats, has a great sense of humor, and is sensitive to others, and to what is around her. She is seen as reliable and solid.

Jim had a difficult time moving on. He continued to get poor school grades, and was passive about studying, homework or exams. Eventually after several years of seeming to be rudderless, he joined the Air Force. There he found his niche in computer science and enjoyed his work. Within a few years was diagnosed with Multiple Sclerosis.

Jim married Kelly Sutton, and became a ready made father to Kelly's son Christopher. They had a daughter, Jennifer, together,, and are now divorced. Jim went back to college, and ended up with a very prestigious job with Oracle. He has been with them many years. He now works from a wheelchair, and is well respected in his job. In addition, he inspires people with his optimism and spunk. He is an amazing role model (does that wheelchair qualify him as a "roll" model ?) of what can be done despite loss of physical function.

Bob probably broke away from our family the most easily. It started in high school. He made some friends who attended church regularly and recruited him to do the same. He began spending more time with them. This gave him homes to go to which were unbroken, and in which there were male role models, and father models. He was attending Baptist Church, and at one point I asked him "why Baptist?" His answer was that he needed structure and a father, and he was finding both. What a wise answer for a young teen.

In 1978, at a Youth Group Ski Trip, Bob had a conversion experience, and gave his life to Christ. He has never stepped back from that moment, making it the beginning of his life work. He went to college in Texas and got a Master's in Family Therapy. He married Jackee Omdahl. Jackee and Bob have 4 children

He was a marriage and family therapist in private practice for 17 years and also did consulting, particularly in the juvenile justice field. He was then called to be a pastor by a church who wanted him because of his reputation and former church work, and interviewed nationally before choosing him.

He was at this church for 8 or 9 years, and recently left to go back into business for himself. While there, he was responsible for the oversight of several departments. His first published book, *Think Differently, Live* Differently has sold well. His second book, just published is about church leadership and called *Think Differently, Lead Differently.*

His leaving his church job was a complicated chapter in his life, encompassing much discernment and stress, both on his part and on the part of the leadership of that church. Some day, I suspect he will write of it. For now, it is too recent, and as I write this, his life is still in transition in many aspects.

It is sufficient here to say that he had to determine what his boss, God, wanted of him, and follow those orders. He is no longer shy, as he was in high school, but gregarious, fun loving, humble, and quick, with a very large view of life and humans, in spite of life's harder moments and issues. He is also a musician, and it fills his heart.

Bob has also taken a large role in parenting his children, Ian Bradley, Jillian Yvonne, Jenna Beth (Now married to Brandon Day), and Atticus Samuel (yes, named after Atticus Finch in *To Kill a Mockingbird* The children are individually beautiful people, and collectively have close bonds to each other. They are successful so far in their lives. All outstanding in what they do and are very different individuals.

Bob and his former co-workers at church have run events for hundreds and thousands of people all over the world, and have an international reputation.

I want to remark about mega-churches, since they are a cultural issue – sometimes controversial. It supposedly takes a village to raise a child, and Bob's 4 children have been raised in the village of their very large churches, first in Abilene, and now in Fort Worth. I have watched the great advantages of that, as their friends, their learning, their talents, and their spiritual development have all grown and flourished within the safe confines of that village, and are being used outside the confines in the world. It has been a remarkable learning for me watching the many facets of their development. And remarkable to see how many of those facets their church has been instrumental in providing opportunities to develop. I am, for the most part, although possibly disagreeing with part of the theology, favorably impressed with how well the mega-church seems to carry out the gospel, and instills the love of God, and the identity of being one of his children.

The House in Allen Park

After that interlude about the children, I want to go back to my life just before the children went off on their own. When the divorce was final, we still lived in that Trenton house. All the children graduated from Trenton High School. Just before Bob's graduation, I sold that house and bought a large old house in Allen Park. It was a huge old farm house, and the boys and I remodeled it thoroughly, so we could live upstairs. Pam was at college. I rented out the downstairs to some women who wanted to have a gift and antique shop. I bought a water bed for myself, and lived there comfortably, about 3 blocks from my office for the last couple years of private practice. Anyone who knows Allen Park would know that house. It is the big house on the corner of Allen and Roosevelt, across the side street from the Baskin Robbins. (What I don't chronicle here is how my son talked the employees of Baskin Robbins into free ice cream from time to time.)

In about 1982, I had a health problem and had to have a hysterectomy. I had put it off, but it was made necessary by excessive bleeding. It was scary for me, as is any surgery, but it was even scarier for the kids, and especially Bob. By then he believed that if I was not "saved" and I should die, I would not go to heaven, He cried before my surgery as he told me this, and I felt such compassion for him, understanding how frightening that was for him in his love for me, and not being able to meet him on the same belief system.

I healed quickly and easily, and life resumed as before.

180

An Unlikely Partner in Growth-A Fox and I Meet

There was one more piece of my personal growth which started during the last years of my work at the Growth Center. It was important in my development. Here is how I wrote about it a few years later.

"In about 1983, I was working in a clinic where the employees met once a month to do personal and relationship growth work as a group. We were in such a meeting, with no outside facilitator. I had been at odds for several months with one of the owners of the clinic who barely spoke to me, was dismissive in manner toward me, and obviously did not like me. We were processing, and he said to me, "You can work here, but I will NEVER be friends with you. You are sucky, needy, and sticky." I was caught unawares by his strong direct words and energy, and I started to cry.

A couple other people whom I felt closer to chimed in and said that indeed I did have those qualities, and they made it difficult to be around me sometimes, but they were my friends, and it did not affect them as strongly as it did the owner.

My mind tried to grasp what they said and to understand it, but I had no clue to the dynamics in me that would cause people to feel that way about me. And therefore, I had no way to stop whatever the behaviors were. I was caught by the unexpected and non-understood feedback. I ran out of the room crying and went into my office, not only feeling hopeless, but ashamed. I prayed for help and some answers.

I sobbed deeply for a long time, and as my sobs quieted, I had a picture/vision/feeling that seemed to come out of the blue, but in reality was an answer to my prayers. It formed like a movie before me, and at the same time as if I were in the movie. It was both something I saw, and something I felt, or became. Here is how I wrote about it at the time.

> *"I saw a tiny baby fox lying in a nest, which was soft and lovingly nurturing. It was covered over with sticks and vines with thorns on them to protect the fox. She was beautiful, and other beings were coming to admire her and touch her. But when they went to pull their hands back out, they would get caught in the sticks and the vines, and torn on the thorns, and couldn't get away."*

I went back, after lunch, to the meeting, and told the story, with trepidation and a measure of trust. And I was greeted by a chorus of "That's it. That is exactly how I experience you at times. "I want to get close to you. You are attractive and beautiful, but somehow I feel caught in the thorns and it takes work to detach."

I felt the truth of that, although I still did not intellectually understand. Indeed, my fears and protection were keeping people

181

away or stuck with me, even though I had no awareness of that in my behavior, and no conscious intention for that to happen.

As a consequence of that day, the metaphor of that fox became my teacher, therapist, helper, and message from God through the next several years. She was a constant companion to me. I suppose some might call her an angel, a spirit guide, or a medicine totem, but I involved her in my life, and growth. This was an excellent example of Gestalt work, as both the fox and I were the same person, but carried on conversations in which I found my way through some "thorny" issues.

I began, in everyday life, to be a parent to this baby fox as I would an "inner child". I asked her not to be so afraid of abandonment and not to put up so many defenses against her fears, and to live more in the open. I told her that I had been wrong to put the thorns there to protect her. She slowly changed from a nest with vines and thorns, to a room with a door, and an open nest in that room. The door could be shut, and the vines and stickers were not needed. As I did this, people's attitude toward me changed in reality. I noticed a new trust and openness in close friendships.

So, the fox stayed with me in various forms for 10 years after that. – starting as child, and at various times being companion, wisdom, vixen, goddess and playmate. My writing reflected this relationship, and reflected my own growth. The "fox child" part of my character developed and grew, and in turn I developed maturity around issues of needs and fears in my life. Here are some examples of my writing about her, used to explore and see my situation more clearly.

First baby thought.......
Inside my tangled ball of web I am—frightened, shy, bright, and wild. Tying more knots at each moment of shame or fear. Peering out, longing to get close and be touched, and not knowing how. Or afraid of what "they" may see. Scared of them.

When the longing comes, I make attempts from inside my web, being horrified when they get caught in my knots—which were only put there to protect myself - to protect me from my own reactions, projected onto others, and made reality, or from reactions of others, projected onto me.

A Prayer
Dear God, guide the little fox inside me. Protect her and keep her safe. Let her grow to love and be loved, to be clear and simple. Let her go through life expressing herself in all her passion and her vulnerability. Let her light so shine – in fear, in anger, and in passionate caring toward others. Let her not "try" to be anything. Let her simply be who she was created to be. .

Another Prayer
Dear God, I am the fox. Let me simply be. Let me be simple with myself. Let me be present with myself rather than to judge myself. Let my ugliness turn to beauty and my walls turn to bridges. Let me see myself in thy sight and through thy eyes. Amen.

And one more:
Going through life is like taking a non-path through the wilderness. It is thus because that path has never been walked before by that person or any other. Every path is unique- the path can never be the same.

The Fox Knows Best
There are some mis-beliefs that create illusions in me. She does not have those. Mine are that I'll only love when it's safe. I'll screen love to accept only part of it. I'll only see certain things as loving and get angry at the rest. And by believing these, I will do my victim act, and cry tons of tears and perpetuate my myths.

She knows better. She knows about impermanence. She lets go at the timing of the universe, knowing that there's always more. She sees everything as either expression of love or of fear. Her life is rich with courage, and with the comings and goings of life and love.

Who is Fox?
You people think that foxes are sly and shy and not very powerful. But let me tell you the rest. The fox's power is quick, intelligent, graceful and beautiful. It is wary. And the wariness makes for a balance of the loving and nurturing which is a female fox. She will fight fiercely for her kits. She is loyal to herself. Her integrity is beyond question, for she suffers even in the captivity of her own lack of integrity. Therefore, she must not be captive under any circumstances. She must be free to run, to love, and to celebrate the essence of nature. Hers is a different kind of power. She is not afraid of judgment. She dances her own dance, loves her world, and loves herself beyond compromise. She is indeed an important creation, and creator of the universe.

The She Fox puts forth her life with intelligence and wisdom, courage and wariness, playfulness, nurturance, devotion, loyalty, and a deep sense of her own fit in nature.

It is She
The intense courage of the fire of the open heart. Whatever she does, she does with her heart open. And the raging fire within shows in the passion of anger, love, or receptiveness. She is never cool and calculating, but rather hot and thoughtful. Her anger is a flaming

passion. It is that of giving and receiving love, and of stopping the flow – only to flow again.

In going through this "fox" process, I also learned a great deal about helping my clients go through their unique processes and heal the gaps in their maturity. I am grateful.

Summary of this season of my life

During this period from 1971 to 1984, I went from married to single, and from having children to having 3 individuals who were still my children, but on their own. I went from a naïve wife, to a more knowledgeable single woman. I went from being sheltered in a relationship and having continuity, to a learning packed course in relationships with others, especially men in a dating situation. I learned how to roll with the punches. I went from being employed only to the extent I wanted to be, as a med tech, to building my own business and supporting my family by necessity, as a social worker. It was a crash course in growing up.

I was lucky enough, and guided enough (by what I then did not call God, but now would), to reach out to many, human helpers, books, seminars, angels, and friends to help me along the path

My kids were ever in my heart and in my mind through all the decisions, as I attempted to do what was right for them, as well as right for me. They could not rely on me much, but hopefully I provided some grounding and some love, as well as my then instability, immaturity and lack of identity complete with stress, frustration, and not knowing nearly enough about parenting. To their credit, they have done much better than I in so many ways.

At the very end of this period of time, I heard about Richard Moss, a physician who had a conversion experience of sorts, and became a mystic and teacher. On impulse, I went to a workshop of his. It too changed my life. Although Richard didn't use these exact words, he basically taught me that who we are is contagious, and thus we influence each other. I learned from him that if one person in a room could hold an expanded state of being long enough and solidly enough, others in the room would begin to vibrate on the same frequency and soon there would be a group energy which healed by its largeness and love. I learned that there is always a larger view and action which can be found in any situation. I have ended up being at events with Richard for over 20 years now, although infrequently. He has gone through various phases of growth, none more powerful for me than those first ones. Here is what I wrote when I came back from that first workshop:

DISSIPATED STRUCTURE

(An account of a journey into expanded consciousness during a transformational workshop with Richard Moss, M.D. facilitating.)

By Karen L. Hamp-1983

Who can tell anyone ahead of time what it's like to fly? No one of course. It can only be described by oneself as a matter of record. And if someone else's soul is tuned to your record – well, that's the way the universe is –your song and their song join in harmony in that moment of a magic event.

So what is it like to go beyond oneself? It is like playing in eternity – where everything is the same, and I am the stars, and the room, and indeed, I'm even you, as you are me. When you breathe, your breath breathes me and when I breathe, my breath breaths you. And when you talk, the words come from me even as they are uniquely you.

I am a separate being through which flows the universe, and I am not separate at all. I am one with everything, and I am only one. But what of me and you? My love and yours caress and play together. My breath and yours breathe as one. My heart and yours beat to the pulse of the universe, and the "us"-ness exists in harmony with the I-ness, and you-ness.

You ask what its like? Well, that's it. The journey is uncertain. There is no destination. Only deeper into ourselves and each other, and higher into God and love.

I suppose I could say that thus far in my life, I had gone from the Superwoman who didn't express feelings and needs, and who was pretty much apart from the world, to someone who began to be an ordinary human being, vulnerable and strong, who could handle exposing my humanity, thus joining the human race in its quest for love and meaning.

OUR HOMES OF THIS CHAPTER

Wilson Street in Trenton

Allen Road-Allen Park

Clark and Jim

Clark

Comm Arts Project- fun bug

Bob with our pet raccoon and dog

Painting polka dots in Pam's
bedroom (Pam in stripes)

Pam and mom at Graduation

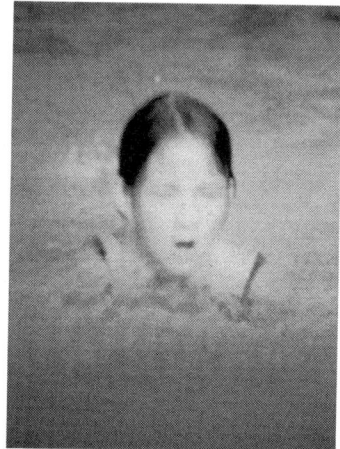
Pam in the pool

Florida-first Skateboard ever!

Sun shelter from team towels at swim meet

Ocracoke trip, kite flying, guitar playing, and lots of beach time!

Me, sis and sis-in-law

Friends-Ruth and Monica

Tree hugger

Family Christmas with AH's family – me back right

yes, its me again

My van

Friends and co-workers
Back row: Brian O'Donnell, Sue Fostey, Ruth Katz , Vic Huber
Middle Row: Jerry, John Bodary, Ruth and Carol Watson
Bottom Row: Lou Pambianco, John and Penny Ort, Gail Yauch,
And Dennis Deshaise

Me at play

Bahamas sailing-top of the mast

Penny and Karen

Teaching Yoga

Triumph Spitfire!!

HAWAII AND CAVE CREEK -- 1984-89

AGES 48-53

Somehow, that expansion, that new perception of the world, experienced at the Richard Moss workshop, combined with some powerful life events, ushered me into an equally powerful and unexpected contraction, or darkness. I then traveled through the darkest months of my life so far. I had already been through the many important changes in my life described previously. You will read more about the darkness below, as well as the journey out of it. When I wrote the piece below, I was moving on. In fact, was on my way to Hawaii. That journey, and what led up to it had come about through what seemed (and still does looking back) like a clearly divine plan.

Below, I am on my way to solitude and discovery after tumultuous and busy years. I am looking back at the tumult and recalling it. This trip to Hawaii will become a major transition, how major, I could not have guessed at the time. This writing was my last exhale of the past, before I left the life you have read about.

A Toast: To Love, Life, Letting Go

"A toast: To love, life, surrender, following ones path, and contributing to the planet." I was spending the last night before my journey with some close friends.

The last week or two had been poignant, rich, and emotion packed. I was leaving for Honolulu and would be there a month.

My children were raised, my home was sold, and I had even gotten the courage to sell my van at the last minute. I was almost certain I didn't need to own the biggest car to have friends in my life. I was letting go of the premise that people were attracted to me by what I had and did, and was hoping they would choose to be around me out of who I was. At some deep level I had been afraid that I would be alone if I didn't do or have enough.

This season of my life had started long before it become fully conscious. A year and a half before this time, I had said to the man I loved, "You know, part of me wants to take off and travel." We both laughed, knowing my penchant for wanderlust. "I want to be with you more, though," I said. He was working for an auto company, and I was looking for a new position. I wanted to change careers in a way which had both integrity and money and build a marriage with my man which included our careers, our mostly grown children, and a mind, heart, body, spirit connection which would deepen and grow. That was my dream, and it seemed possible. I thought it was also his.

Six months later I awoke from the dream to find I was living a nightmare. My man was with someone else, my best woman friend and business partner had moved to San Francisco, the clinic I worked for was closing its doors, my last child was leaving home, and I was leaving the singles group, too much in pain to see my guy with his new love.

I effectively (or rather ineffectively) lost my roles as mother, therapist, lover, and friend all within 4 months. I still had contact with a few friends, but my inner experience was that of sudden loss, despair, and aloneness. From full life to empty in a comparative heartbeat.

In the following 6 months, I slowly sank into a cauldron with no bottom and no familiarity. I tried to scream, and none came. I tried to fight, and there was no fight left. I cried and then reached a point where I said, "I've raised 3 successful children, I've had two successful careers, I've traveled, I've met all my goals, and I've lost all of my dreams. I don't want to go on (as in no reason), I can't go on (as in no life force) and I prefer to die".

I knew people cared. Those few people I was in contact with called, and came over, and were present for me in special ways .In an unfamiliar state of being for me, none of that seemed to touch me, or matter .It was as if my friends were pouring water into a pan full of holes. Or maybe something that gave the illusion of being a pan, but with no inside or outside and therefore no space to hold the water. "I" didn't exist. Somehow "I" had already died.

I heard a song by John Denver: "This is What It's Like Falling Out of Love: The future holds no promise; your life's already done".

I did realize that I had been one of the lucky people who had been in love with life for most of my 48 years. Now, I had literally fallen out of love with life. And a lot of my life had fallen away from me. Right then it seemed like a song of terminal mourning, seemingly at the end of my life.

My house was old, cold, and unfriendly that winter. It had become a tomb. There were no more teenagers, I had little to no money coming in, the heating bills were astronomical, and I lived that winter with the heat set at 55 degrees. This was the winter of cold heart, empty spirit, and aloneness. I prayed to die, and finally decided that if I didn't reach some kind of breakthrough by the first of January, a year from then, I would use the exhaust fumes of my van as a way to die.

As a measure of desperation, I began to consider going through the EST training. Although I had my possible death planned, there was a large part of me that did not really want to die. My son and many friends and co-workers had gone through EST, and I had seen positive changes. With nothing to lose, and everything to gain, I decided to trust my intuition, even while believing that if the Richard Moss workshop had not produced lasting life in me, then this probably

191

wouldn't either, I signed up for two intensive weekends of processing and being processed.

During those weekends, the trainers repeatedly said: "Follow directions, take what you get, and keep your soles (soul) in the room." I attempted to do that, and at the end of the second weekend, I had surprisingly (to me) gained back what felt like a very small window of internal light. Any window was better than all walls. I could even pray again and fervently prayed for more strength and stability. Hope seeped in.....finally.

The projector was now on and running, ready to begin the film of the rest of my life. There was one small problem however - there was no script, no plot, and certainly no finished film. The old one had seen too many reruns, it was brittle and broken, and the new one hadn't been written or even commissioned yet.

I began to use what life force I could gather, to make clear choices. Who belongs in my life now? Who do I choose to spend time around? What do I choose to do? And I listened carefully. I had no time or strength to waste.

I felt continuous loss as old activities and friends dropped away. I came across a book that spoke of "impermanence" and threw it across the room. I found a card saying: "When you have no further use for a situation in your life, it will fall away of its own accord." About the same time, I bought a T-shirt that said "Courage is the ability to let go of the familiar". I bought another shirt that said," Life is too important to be taken seriously." (Funny how a T-shirt can become a guru.)

I also began to do the normal middle class activities. I tried some new things. I looked for a job that was a step up in responsibility. I decided it was time to become a business lady, and so I bought business lady clothes, cut my hair in a business lady style, and went out to conquer the business world.

Despite interviews and lots of contacts, nothing happened. . I asked God just what he thought he was doing.

One day I surrendered once more and went back to the drawing board. I had put my house up for sale. It was tentatively sold, and my plan was that I had two months to find a job which would then let me choose my middle class singles apartment near my job.

I soon wouldn't own a house, my kids were scattered in different states, I did not yet have either a career position or a social life re-established in the Detroit area. At least I now had hope.

Meanwhile, from some friends, I was learning about friendship – being a friend and receiving friendship. I also came to understand that all this non-response to my effort seemed to be a call to "Be still and listen "When I reported that to others, some thought I was just dropping the ball, others encouraged me to listen. I decided to go with the listening.

A most amazing series of coincidences began at that point. . I felt as though the ground was moving underneath me like a moving walkway at an airport. I was being transported in surprising and serendipitous ways.

The house sold and closed. On the day of the closing, I got a letter from my friend Colin who had moved to Hawaii. He suggested I visit before he moved to Fiji in a few months. He knew of my recent struggles and quest for new life. We were not interesting in partnering with each other, but had been friends through Astron.

I agreed with myself that Hawaii was an impossibility right then. I had a life to get on with and a living to earn. "Right?" I asked myself. "Of course", I answered.

The next week, a conversation with a wise person served to change my perception. I saw my present situation through different eyes. He spoke of "being" versus "doing", and correctly deduced that I had been a doer all my life. I now had little way to "do". This was similar to my wish that people would like me for who I was rather than what I did or had.

(In my family, "doing" had been the goal. "Being" had no status or credits attached. Emotions, longing, asking for help, or just staring into space was definitely not appropriate for adults, and adulthood started at about 3 years of age. These things were considered weak, and childish, and carried a burden of shame and silence).

It felt as if I would die if I stopped "doing". I had my mother for proof. She didn't die, but her life force died after my father died, and she retired. She was now among the living dead.

My task formed again in my mind. It was to express my being in as many and powerful ways as possible. I must learn who I was, and be who I was, rather than to die because I didn't have particular and important things to do. I had many clues from TORI, Richard Moss, and other experiences and people from my past.

The letter from Colin contained the option of staying at the Buddhist Retreat Center where he lived for $10/day. Hmmm, maybe............ My resolve to keep on doing things wavered, my angels applauded. I called Hawaii to discuss possibilities with the caretaker. I found if I stayed an entire month, my room would only cost $175. I figured that I could stay there for less than $500 for the entire month, including my medical insurance, food, and other expenses. And I decided to go. I had savings.

Having made that decision, I begin to scare myself and excite myself with the possible consequences. Those consequences and the serendipity picked up speed and intensity.

At first, I almost felt as if God was checking to see if I really meant it. Suddenly, several men wanted to take me out, or start possible relationships. I was offered a job that I would have hated, but which paid well. It was difficult to say no, after a period of emptiness, and an unknown future, but new strength, and growing resolve to listen and live made it easier. It was like Jesus's temptation by Satan – I was being offered a compromised version of what I defined as success and right living.

As I said firm "no" to the inappropriate offers, the serendipity again increased. I got the last discount plane fare available out of Detroit on the date that I thought I could leave. Out of a vacuum came places to store all my furniture, and belongings, even without much effort on my part. I found the perfect home for my cat. The only effort I seemed to make was the physical effort of following through on what the universe was arranging. Friends kept me company, helped me sort, and provided the muscle power to move. Even a van and a truck belonging to friends were at my disposal.

As if I were floating down a river with the current, people responded to my decision and preparation in a spirit of validation, love, and support. I had never been given so much, or been so open to receiving. It was effortless and loving at every turn. The phrase "in the flow" took on new depth and meaning. For many days, life felt like a continuous miracle.

I was now in the eve of my departure and a friend reminded me that I would not be alone, that one is never really alone. As I got on the plane the next day, I bathed in the sense of dispelled darkness and the shining light of the present and surrounding God. This had been an amazing time.

"What is it I'm supposed to be doing, Lord?", I breathed. I had just been reading about the word at-one-ment. It seemed that much of our world was on the fulcrum of decision about at-one-ment or separation. My thoughts were that my ultimate task would have something to do with this. I was feeling at one in my heart. And once again I prayed to be open. My flight left Michigan near sunrise, and followed the newly born sun all the way to Hawaii.

The Retreat Center – Hau'u'la Hawaii

As I settled into the first day or two out in the country, on the windward side of Oahu, I noticed that I owned no keys. My storage shed in Michigan had a combination lock, I didn't own a vehicle, and the Retreat Center where I was staying was always unlocked. For the first time in my adult life, I did not have a key ring. My life was totally unlocked, freely open. Several years later, I wrote a column about the key ring as metaphor for the simplicity or complexity of one's life, and later, when doing counseling again, I often asked my clients to show me their key ring and talk about it, as a metaphor for their lives. But for now, it was time to feel my own freedom.

Thus I came keyless to the destination of this synchronous life. Our retreat center was a block or two from the ocean, and I could hear the rhythm of the tides by the sound of the waves in the distance. The mountains were in back of us. It was a welcoming and lovely setting, with simple amenities. There was a lotus pond, trees with papayas and figs, and a garden with some vegetables. The center was only used by the Lama a few times a year for retreats. The rest of the time, it was for those who came as I did, for rest, recreation, or a quiet place to stay. Surfers and meditators rubbed shoulders here.

I knew only Colin, and not very well. It took a week or two for me to see that he was attempting to use my presence with his friends and colleagues to pretend he was not gay. He invited me to parties and gatherings, ostensibly to introduce me to people, but with an attitude that said "See, I have a partner." I was tired out from the last 10 years, and had no stomach for being part of that. I stopped going to these events, simply being there at the center for myself. In fact, although I was to stay for a month, I began to think of selling my return ticket and staying until I felt like leaving. Selling a one way airline ticket was easy and possible then. The Honolulu paper had a whole classified section for that. The airlines did not ask for ID, and traveling under someone else's name was easy.

I indeed sold the ticket, and spent the next block of weeks, and even a few months in the country, not even going back to Honolulu. There were other people at the retreat center - the manager, Phred, a friend of his named Farley, a couple surfers who were hanging out, a mentally ill man from Michigan whose parents bought him a yearly ticket to Hawaii, so he would not be homeless in a Michigan winter. We were a diverse and unusual group. I was the only woman at the time.

The center was about a mile from a town so small that it consisted mainly of a small strip shopping center with a grocery store and drug store, to serve those rural residents surrounding it.

The hours of my days passed in an alternation of eating, sleeping, walking, swimming, reading and writing. Those 6 activities filled my hours, my mind, my body and my soul. The atmosphere in which they happened was a perfect incubator. The beginnings of new life formed, but so slowly at first, that I didn't notice. The old life silently dropped away. My life was a question mark which preceded me. My steps answered the question moment by moment. Only in looking back could I see who I had been that day. Tomorrow was still a question.

When I needed transportation, I relied on the busses. A month's bus ticket cost $15.00. Waiting for the bus was a meditation, being surrounded by the warm ocean breezes and sound of waves, with occasional other people fading in and out. Never crowded here in the country, I could go wherever I wanted to go. It was a rich, slow, and simple life.

I stopped processing the why and what of my life, and simply let myself be present. At any other time in my life, I would have wondered what was happening, and worried myself with thoughts of doing more, or at least worrying about not wanting to do more. I was without motivation to do the usual things. Sightseeing, shopping, meeting new people, attending classes, or getting a job didn't seem of interest. I lived simply, and simply lived—a moment at a time, or an hour or two at the most.

Because I did not try to structure my time or days, it took me months to thoroughly acclimate myself to the 6 hour time zone difference. I slept anywhere from 10 to 16 hours a day for the first couple months. I was clearly tired from the last 10 years of emotions, working, and parenting—both my children and myself. I was like a babe or a puppy or kitten. Only hunger, sleep or the sound and sight of the ocean stirred my senses at first. I interacted with others, but didn't seek them out.

I often woke at dawn or before, and walked to the beach (we were on the sunrise side of the island).There I swam, or watched the sunrise. When I came home, I ate, or took a nap. When I was ready, I went back to the beach again to swim, read, write, or nap. At the end of the afternoon, I either walked home or about a mile down the road to the store for dinner supplies. I was often in bed by 8. I sometimes cried for the losses in my life, and as an expression of letting go. I truly lived a whatever, wherever, whenever life for many months. I was living the TORI saying of "Trust the process".

This is what I penned one day at the beach. It gives a flavor of my life during that season. It is written about "She", but I am really writing about myself.

An Inside Story

She lay on the beach in that half-awake, half-asleep state which seemed so fertile. She was letting her thoughts ebb and flow through her mind and soul with free reign and range, even as the waves gently curled a few yards away.

As during many of these times the past months, the contrasts of this island she now called home seemed amazing. It was like nothing she had ever experienced in her travels on the mainland.

There was the food. It grew wild and plentiful throughout the island and was free for the taking. No person need be hungry who could walk half a mile. And yet the price of food in the market was higher than anywhere she had ever lived. Many things had to be shipped in from the mainland.

Another marked contrast in Hawaii was that of violence and peace. Everywhere she went, she saw peace, contentment, and a relaxed attitude toward, life. In fact, she read and knew that many of these people were descended from peoples who were peaceful, lived close to the earth, and had a childlike wonder toward life. And yet the Honolulu paper was filled every week with repeated stories and statistics of child abuse, fights, and accidents. She also knew that

196

some of their ancestors had been war like, throwing enemies over cliffs. Such opposite styles of being.

Even the weather here was a contrast. She had written home about experiencing the total non-assaultiveness of the mild breeze, the warm air, and the warm ocean waves. The weather surrounded the body like a soft wrap, or an invisible second skin. But of course she knew of the paradox. The weather here was non-assaultive until it wasn't, sometimes assaulting with a vengeance. There was tremendous violence in the hurricanes, tsunamis, and the giant waves of the North Shore, used for sport, but holding potential death.

Her time here had been gentle. She had been issued a gentle invitation to expansion in the energies of her body, mind and soul. She had heard from others of this same experience. It was as if there was an unfolding and awakening of dormant potential which happened often in these islands.

She had begun to read Michener's book, "Hawaii", and was pleased, but somehow not startled to find a similar concept: He said, "Here was then, as maybe now, no place known on earth that even began to compete with these islands in their capacity to encourage natural life to develop freely and radically up to its own best potential".

Her social scientist's mind worked quickly. "Of course the invitation to expansion and potential is real", she thought. "But expansion is only expansion, and can be expanded into either light or darkness. Of course there is polarization here." She continued to put together the pieces of the puzzle that she had felt and looked at ever since her first day in Hawaii.

Her mind skipped to her own journey here and the inherent polarities. A few months ago she had been a woman working in business, teaching, and seeing clients in her own practice on the mainland. She was headed toward even more complexity in her search for a new career in the business world. She had gone through a dreadful transition, losing hope and hoping to die. Never in her farthest thoughts did she think she would end up living in the country in Hawaii. She had come here for a month's vacation, sold her return ticket, and was living this simple life.

That in itself was a polarity. She had been geared toward complexity. However, behind the scenes of that complexity, the mysterious forces that some call the life force, or God, or "ones path in life" had other ideas for her and were exerting influence, nudging her toward that simplicity and the unknown. .

Some days she damned the life processes that she had gone through that taught her to tune into and listen to those forces Other days she rejoiced. Today she was simply filled with the wonderment of it all. She had ended up here through a series of incidents and co-incidents that were so powerful and so clear that she couldn't have ended up anywhere else without tremendous resistance. And never had life been so rich for her in all her 48 years. (Nor for that matter so confusing if she attempted to analyze).

She had gone through great changes in her conventional life in the months preceding her journey here. Serving others, and the world had been her focus for 30 or 40 years, and now it didn't seem to work. She had determined that this was one of those times that people sometimes pass through where one must serve oneself in order to ever again contribute to others. And so she was here serving herself and the God who so obviously brought her here.

Of course this all was very rational and logical. She hoped it was also the truth. In keeping with looking at the contrasts and polarities in life lately, the contrast to that smoothly flowing journey was her fear- the fear was that she was simply now revealing her true nature. The fear that her true nature was that of a beach bum, and her true belief system only hedonism, and that the rest of her life would be spent <u>only</u> serving herself.

The first wave of the rising tide soaked the corner of her towel, and she was brought back to the reality of the beach. The rising tide inside her was the anxiety from that idea that she may have been living out a lie, and a false idea of goodness and God-ness this past 47 years. It was disturbing to say the least.

"Who am I"? she thought. And the memories flashed on.

She had led national seminars-She had raised 3 children. She had been urged to write a book on Women and Personal Power by those women who had gained a sense of their own power in the world from her work.

She had taught Yoga, Creative photography, and Physiology. She had been an influence on a great many people. Even as a medical technologist, (her first career) she had letters and notes from patients and families who had praised her skill and her kindness in the sometimes dehumanizing experience of a hospitalization. She had done research for a pharmaceutical company. She had been a wife and mother. She and her children were friends, though she had found little time to spend with them their last years at home. She loved to ski, and dance, and swim.

And the questions came tumbling back again. "That's who I was, but who am I now? Why did I end up in Hawaii? Why do I focus on the contrasts and polarities of life? What will I do with the rest of my life And she felt privileged to have experienced her past. But how this would all fit into her future was the question that played at the uneven boundaries of her mind and soul these days.

She concluded once more that she had come too far in this journey to turn back. What she could do was to be who she was, and to see where the journey led. She must trust the process of life and of her own goodness and wholeness. She must trust the God who brought her here. She must trust that the intention of human life was to fulfill that goodness within. She had found belief in the goodness and *inherent perfection of human life. That seemed to be the one belief that had cut across cultural and religious boundaries.*

It was time to leave the beach. For just as too much sunlight burned the skin, too much insight at once was painful to the soul without the proper preparation. And her mind and soul were tired with questions.

She still didn't know who she was. She did know that as she continued to expose her body to the sunlight in Hawaii, she felt more and more healthy of body. And she did know that as she continued to fit pieces of the puzzle together in this present confusing journey of hers, her soul felt healthier. And she did know that the expansiveness of this beautiful, island seemed crucial to the process.

She could begin to feel the wholeness and the perfection of her own creation. And as she felt her own perfection, she felt and saw the perfection and wholeness of those around her. She thought of what she had taught in photography about contrast, and using contrast to make things visible. She thought to herself, "Without the contrast, I couldn't notice the wholeness and perfection. And maybe the uniqueness of Hawaii is the ability to illustrate that for me and for the world. And just maybe I won't be a beach bum forever" Her insides felt contented as she turned from the tide, faced the mountains and began to walk home.

During that first several months, as I relaxed, and let go, I went through a period of various illnesses. I got the flu, a couple colds, some intestinal upsets, and finally several urinary tract infections. I was concerned, because I was living a healthy life style, and because I had been quite healthy most of my life. I began to worry about my immune system, and after going to the health clinic and having my lab tests all be normal, I finally realized that as I let down the defenses of my heart, mind and soul, surrendering to the present moment and to God, my body followed suit. What would be more natural than that my immune system, not having to work so hard, and overcome so much stress, would also let down its defenses? After that period of frequent illness, I was as healthy as I have ever been in my life. I approached my 50th birthday with joy and equanimity, as well as peace and strength. But I get ahead of myself here.

Incidentally, when I told my mother of going to Hawaii, her response was that I could not run away from my troubles. There was never a time when this journey felt like running away. It always felt like running toward something, even if the something was unknown. Let me continue now with the rest of the journey in Hawaii.

About a year after arriving in Hawaii my first grandson was born in Texas. There was 24 hours of rejoicing before my son called again and told me that they were quite sure his son had Down's syndrome. And that he was born with a physical defect which would require immediate surgery. My heart burst with love and weeping for the little baby who would be operated on and could not be told an explanation. I knew he would be held and loved, but also knew that there was no way to help him understand what was happening. I cried for several days, even as I prayed. My son told me he would keep in touch by phone, but that I should not come, as the baby and mom were going to be fine, and Jackee's family was with them. Their reaction was heroic...Jackee was determined to pump her milk for the baby, and got up from the delivery to go to the pediatric surgeon's hospital and watch, with Bob, over their son.

I have a soft spot for animals and for children, when they are going to be hurt by other people and cannot understand....that never showed up more strongly than with Ian.

Meeting Terry – Setting the Stage for Other Adventures

Maybe 8 or 9 months into my time in Hawaii (a gestation period?), I attended a Sierra Club Meeting and met a man named Terry Ryan. He was a school teacher, now doing home repair, and asked me to go out with him. He had been in Hawaii for about a year, from San Diego and had started a home repair business. Home repair was an easier and more flexible life than attempting to get licensed and get a job as a teacher in Hawaii. His dad had been a plumber and Terry had the skills, and enough business know-how to be successful.

We eventually went out a few times, and he began to explore living at the retreat center. After several weeks of talking and getting to know each other a little better, he moved in. That started a new chapter in my time in Hawaii. I continued to swim daily, and read and write, but I also began to do home repair with Terry, doing such things as rewiring plugs and switches, laying tile, hanging drywall, and painting. Painting was my favorite. It was a physical and visual meditation, as my body danced with the paint roller, moving it across the surface - both causing, and witnessing the transformation of a room. This was a most different way for me to "work" in the world. Each moment felt more like prayer than work. l.

(I had enjoyed mechanical tasks before, when I learned to fix my cars. I had learned to love balanced days, seeing clients and then gardening, doing auto mechanics or dancing. This was a similar feeling, because the physical work itself became both prayer and passion.) Nourishing and welcome.

The Magic of Hawaii

Before I speak more of my everyday life in Hawaii, and how it progressed over time, I want to tell you of some of the experiences I had during my time there. These are experiences which transmuted "just another place on the planet" into what I now think of as the birthplace or at least the flowering of my heart, soul, and spirit. It is difficult to write in a way which conveys a large enough or extreme enough sense of what I experienced, and who I expanded into while there. Here are a few moments.

One afternoon, Terry and I were taking a long walk on a deserted beach, when a large bird glided down the beach toward us. A quarter mile away, we watched it glide closer. It was flying low, and veered toward our path, as if to discover who or what we were. As it got closer we saw that it was an albatross, a magnificent bird with a wingspan of 6-7 feet. I had only seen them soaring in the skies above the ocean, never close to land or to me. Terry was farther from the water than I, and as the bird approached it turned slightly to fly directly over my head, about 18 inches above me. I could have reached and touched it. The bird paused above my head, hovering, and turned its head to look down at me. There were no words, but a clear powerful energy passed between us. It was a communication of "being". I felt it deep within, as if there were profound "all ness" and at the same time total stillness through this connection. There was a sense of presence and communication, and time stopped. It seemed several minutes that we paused in deep connection, though it was probably only several seconds. And then it moved on.

Terry quietly said "What just happened?" I answered "I don't know, but it connected with me deeply" He said he had felt that. I knew nothing more, other than a profound sense of peace and wholeness that seemed to start with that encounter and last for many days. I add that this is not an experience that is familiar to me, or similar to others I have had. I am not the kind of person who interprets all animal behavior in human or mystical terms. It was unique. I had previous experiences of feeling connected with nature, and had tried to put myself in the place of insects or animals that I saw, but this was magnitudes different than those experiences.

Many years later, I was at home, and the TV was playing in the living room. As I walked through the room, I heard; "And the Hawaiians believe that the albatross is the god Kane, the most powerful God." And my heart sighed, let go, and smiled. Even as I write this, 27 years later, I feel the shivers and imprint of that encounter. I again feel a sense of being, and of the great power clarity, and glow of pure frequency light which filled my entire being then, lingered, and left its imprint forever.

Another experience of connection with the natural world in a very different way happened while snorkeling at Hanauma Bay. I was feeding the fish and admiring the colors, watching the shimmer of sunlight through water as I glided along. Suddenly, out of the corner of my eye I saw a school of hundreds or thousands of silver flashing fish ahead of me. They were moving in unison as schools of fish do, and I hung in the water fascinated. They were each about a foot long., and together formed a great ball of living matter, flashing this way and that as one organism. They moved toward me, and I was mesmerized when suddenly our paths joined, and I instantly found myself part of the school, twisting and turning to marvel at and join with the movement and my environment. I moved as they moved, and was moved by the force of the community. It felt like going to the center of the universe, where all was one, and I was joined and joining without effort or thought. We were simply there as parts of a whole. It was a magical moment, and then it was over, as they went on their way, and I watched them go. It was dissimilar to the experience with the albatross, in that there was no communication but a great sense of joining, becoming community. The albatross experience was a time of close connection, becoming one, and hearing from the universe, with no words. The fish experience has stayed with me as a magical moment, being allowed to share in a mysterious but, universal process of group interdependence. (Being a member of the human species is similar, but not so explicit.) The sense of this experience returns whenever I see a flock of birds wheeling through the air, or a school of minnows in the lakes of Michigan. It reminds me that I too am a part of the school of humans inhabiting our planet, and in obedience to the natural order of the world.

With the fish, my "self" melted away, and I surrendered to a larger whole. During many other moments and hours, I sat on the shore, or floated in the waters of the island, and my "self" melted to allow me to become part of the water the trees, the sand, the rocking waves, or the little crab on the beach. My boundaries seemed more permeable than ever before, and I could change my perspective in an instant. Thought stopped, and being took over. As the boundaries between me and my surroundings disappeared, I became part of the whole of nature, rather than a separate being.

Unlike those who get permeable and lose their grounding and boundaries, floating off into psychosis, or altered states, I stayed firmly connected to reality, and firmly connected to God's entire creation at the same time. Life became a constant prayer of wonderment and gratitude. I was filled with "the peace which passes all understanding. " It helped that I had no demands on my time or energy.

Here is how I described it then:

"As the waters, air and people of Hawaii, soaked my open heart, I began to be infused with the wholeness of God and nature. It affected me, and I soon found myself feeling, as if for the first time in my life, I could count on my stability, and my sense of love and being loved. I became love/nature/a spark of God and creation. I knew myself and my place in life. There was no doubt or fear"

As I sat by the ocean, or snorkeled face down, pretending I lived there in the sea, I sometimes drifted off to become part of the ocean, and occasionally I drifted off to sleep. The water rocked me, and my snorkel gave me air to breathe, even while sleeping. When I was with people, my boundaries remained more permeable but not as intensely so. So often the "I" disappeared, and there was only spirit there, working through me. It was an amazing time. I believe it was physically, spiritually, and mentally the most healthy, whole, and congruent time in my life. I can often capture this feeling, and once again become "she" for days or hours, practicing what I know is a life giving state of being. Just as often, I am a bundle of heavy or hurrying humanity, forgetting the rest of who I am. In that season of my life in Hawaii, I seem to have lived in that state of peace and expansion for months.

Another not so esoteric, but treasured time and experience during my time in Hawaii was being a volunteer docent for Sea Life Park. (the Hawaiian equivalent of Sea World.) The park was more educational than Sea World., associated with the University of Hawaii. There were dolphin shows, and whale performances using false killer whales. I was attracted to working there because of the educational focus, and the chance to interact with the animals and the visitors. The park, partnered with University of Hawaii, had great integrity at the time.

One of my "claims to fame" now, is that I was at Sea Life Park when the "wholphin" was born. This was a half whale, half dolphin, and I had the privilege of getting to observe and help record the feedings and first days of the baby. As I write this, there is a 1/4 whale, 3/4 dolphin, which performs in the shows, the offspring of the baby that I watched.

At the time, I felt some sadness that the parents had only each other in captivity, and were so bored that they "fooled around" in order to stay active and alive. (At least that was my perception.) Sex often became their recreation. They served research, but they do not belong in captivity any more than animals at the zoo, in my opinion. The upside may be that in captivity, we come to understand how intelligent and amazing they are, and have more respect for them.

There I fed the seals and sea lions during the show times so the visitors could see them eat. I cleaned up around the park, and anything else that I was asked to do. A humorous incident was the day a visitor reported the park to the Humane Society for stapling or binding a birds feet to a post. We had many sea birds that flew in for the free food and a safe place to rest, and that day, a Blue Footed Booby had come in and landed on one of the posts, sleeping with its head drooped lower than its feet. It did look strange but was in a natural sleeping position. Of course it was not tied or nailed down.

Unfortunately, when I last went to Hawaii, I wanted to go to the park, and found it turned into much more of a showplace, and much less of a natural wonder or research station for marine life. It did not feel or look the same. I did not go. The contrast with my volunteer time there was too painful.

Travel to the Other Islands

Terry and I took a series of camping trips and a kayak trip to the other islands during our time there. Molokai was the least "touristy" island, and our personal favorite. A friend had a beat up car parked at the Molokai airport, and offered to let us use it. We flew in, hopped in the car and took off to explore. One trip, we decided to go horseback riding, and came across a deserted camping site up in the hills. The flashlight, boots, tent and other equipment was left as it had been; moldy and deteriorating (it happens quickly in warm wet weather). Something had happened to the occupant.

At the same time, we had a person living at the retreat center who had gotten high on drugs and fallen off a cliff while camping on Molokai. He was badly hurt and came to the retreat center to finish healing. We thought it might be his tent, and when we got back we asked him about it. He could not verify for us the location. We brought nothing back and might not have been able to find it again. There was barely a path through jungle-like surroundings.

Another Molokai story, same trip: On the trip before, I had left one of my bathing suits hanging on a tree to dry. This time, I asked a woman who lived near there if she might have seen it. She said she wore it for a while, until it fell apart. I missed the suit, but was glad it served a good purpose.

The year before we left Hawaii, we went on a 5 day Kayak trip off the Molokai shore. There were about 10 of us using inflatable Sevlor kayaks. We were the oldest people on the trip. We had taken the precaution of asking whether it was appropriate for people over 50, and been told yes, but it turned out to be a physically difficult trip for both of us, although a highlight of our time on Molokai. We were to go from Halawa Valley, north to Kalaupapa, the leper colony where the famed Father Damien had worked with the lepers. Although leprosy (Hansen's Disease) is now curable, there were still people in the colony at Kalaupapa badly disfigured from their leprosy of years ago. They had been banished there, or gone to live with a spouse or a parent. I wonder as I write this, if there are any alive there who have had leprosy. And what has become of the colony at Kalaupapa?

This kayak trip was scary, beautiful and tiring. The leader assumed everyone's safety rather than being responsibly watchful. Terry had some trouble with sea sickness. We were in single person kayaks. Each day, we paddled along the highest sheer seaside cliffs in the world, not daring to get inside the surf line, and staying away from where the incoming waves met the outgoing or reflectance waves. Where the incoming and outgoing waves meet, there is often a kayak flipping motion in the surf.

One day, the guide was busy patching a hole in one of the kayaks, and told me to start out. Others had started a few minutes before. For probably half an hour, I was out in open ocean, and could not see any others of our group. For some reason, the isolation scared me, and I cried as I paddled, feeling like a lost and scared kid. I was in no particular danger, although open ocean always holds some risk.

At times, we paddled through lava tubes, or passed occasional small rocky beaches onshore. We camped on beaches where the wind was so strong we had to put large rocks in the tent to keep it from blowing away. Rain pelted down on us, and we wore garbage bags to keep from hypothermia, even though the rain was quite warm. The small waterfalls, trickling off the high cliffs were our drinking water. And getting to those beaches in late afternoon, and back out into the ocean in the morning was no easy task. One had to walk the kayaks in, over 8-12 inch rocks, with the open ocean surf inundating every few yards. A woman had broken her ankle on a similar trip the week before. I was grateful to be a confident and strong swimmer. Paddling in meant chancing disembarking in the big waves, while getting turned sideways and then turned over.

I had read a book called *Paddling My Own Canoe*, by Audrey Sutherland. She used that same stretch of coast for her vacations while raising her 4 children, and doing various academic jobs. Each year, she swam along that shore, towing provisions, and finally towing material to patch up a broken down shelter she had found, and made into her own. She nearly lost her life several times over the years, but remained in love with that Molokai shore. Having been there, I can understand. It is at once, formidable and magnificent.

When we got to Kalaupapa, the people from the colony, some with eaten away faces, hands and feet,(healed over for many years since the cure was discovered), helped us carry our baggage and kayaks up a hill to the colony, where we were loaded onto a plane, flying back to Oahu. We had time to tour the colony, and especially to feel the graciousness and Aloha spirit of the people who had been banished, and chosen to stay there, or stay with relatives there , the rest of their lives.

We went to Maui during whale watching season. We were able to watch the truly amazing and majestic Humpbacks and their calves. The babies are born near Hawaii every year, so it is a special treat to be there and see them. It is the humpback which sings the whale songs, extensively recorded. Their summer and fall are spent in Alaska. A lovely memory and a respect for the giant animals remain with me.

Also on Maui I was fascinated by the Banyan Tree which is a tourist attraction in Lahaina. It was planted in 1873, and now shades about 2/3 of an acre. This tree sends roots down from its branches, which then sprout new trunks, thus growing larger and larger in area. It was new to me, and reminded me of the much smaller scale bamboo forest in our California yard at age 7. We also went to the top of Haleakala, a now dormant volcano. It is best seen at sunrise, when the clouds are often below the viewer and the sun rises out of the clouds. Thus, our shadows were on the clouds below us. It was a surreal moment in time.

Each island in the Hawaiian chain has its own character, and attractions. There are many small islands, stretching for about 1500 miles, from the Big Island of Hawaii. There are 8 major islands. Hawaii, Maui, Oahu, Molokai, Lanai, Kauai, Niihau, Kahoolawe.

When we visited the Big Island (Hawaii), we were most interested in the volcanic activity. We saw houses and subdivisions swallowed by the still active volcano, Kilauea. At that particular time, the volcano was not active, although it had been active much of the time. We wanted to see the fire meeting the ocean, when the glowing lava flowed to the sea, but it was not to be. There were places with one or two homes in a proposed subdivision. It had been laid out and the streets and utilities put in, and then was swallowed by lava. Those who had built early and still lived there, lived without utilities and surrounded by hardened lava. They had to walk out to where their vehicles were.

.We went to South Point, also on the Big Island, the southernmost point in the U.S. (Key West, FL has the southernmost point in the continental U.S.) We went to a small very local fishing village, Milolii. where the wooden fishing canoes were still square at one end, and had outriggers. When we were there, there was no electricity, and no water other than rain water. Wikipedia says that the houses are now powered by solar panels.

We saw the Star of The Sea Church, a small Catholic church with scenes of Father Damien and his work with the lepers painted on the walls within. The lava was nearly to the doorway, and in fact a few years later the church was moved because the lava flow was going to cover it.

Although this had been my favorite island when my mother took us to Hawaii, I enjoyed it now, but it did not touch my heart

There are Hawaiian words for different kinds of lava, as there are in Alaska for different forms of snow. A'a' was the pointy kind which had hardened in sharp points. The name was easy to remember, because one would certainly tell a small child, "A'a" as they started to walk on it, or put their bare hands on it. The other common name was pahoe'hoe. This was smoother lava, as if a river had frozen over, and there were ripples and waves, but no sharp points.

On Kauai, we saw the beginning of the NaPali cliff trail, but decided it was too steep and slippery to be fun. We drove to Waimaia Canyon, the Grand Canyon of Hawaii. I have been several times to Kauai since then. My friends, Sonny Ching, and Reenie Christiensen live there and I have been there to housesit and cat sit for them. When I lived in Hawaii, they lived on Oahu, and Reenie was one of my social work friends. It is usual in Hawaii for the home owner to charge for the privilege of house-sitting. I have been so lucky to go there and stay and use Sonny's car while they were gone. Each time I go back to Hawaii, it renews me in spirit and heart. It is unlikely I will be going again. The thought makes me sad, even through all the gratitude for having been there.

I recently saw Terry, and he is, as I write, considering living in Hawaii. When we discussed our time there, he equally was marked by the incident with the albatross. His time in Hawaii was one of interlude, rather than profound change, but that interlude left its mark on his life, and he too has been back several times.

Of all the islands, my heart still lives out on the back side of Oahu, in the retreat center, and my time of being rather than doing. Even now, I live a balanced life in that way, and often spend what looks like empty time, but is a time of fullness or refilling. Hawaii gave me great gifts.

The Aloha Spirit

One of the most precious gifts was the concept and experience of Aloha. A matter of the heart, mixed with connectedness and sacredness, it is a way of living and relating. To the casual tourist, aloha means hello, or goodbye, or maybe "I love you". To those who are native, or have experienced more, it is a word that conveys deep meaning and connection with another, the sacred, or the heart. It is similar to the word "Nameste" in India, or "Peace of Christ be with you," in some Christian churches. It is a word which carries many meanings from kindness to a deep spiritual connection. The "ha" – (the last two letters) mean breath. To say "Aloha" to a friend is to share the breath of life.

I wish I could convey the experience to you the reader, through more than words. Sometimes I can feel that spirit of Aloha in my living, other times I lose it. Some memories of aloha here:

Riding the bus into town, I observed a mother with a crying baby, a cranky 3-year-old, and some packages. The woman across the aisle smiled and reached for the baby. The mom handed him over with relief, and paid some attention to the fussy 3-year-old. When she left the bus, another person, getting off at the same stop carried some of the packages. A third woman took the hand of the 3-year-old. None knew each other, but all knew it took a village to raise children with aloha.

Another day, Terry and I stopped to buy pineapple from one of the roadside stands. Terry asked the price, and somewhat harshly indicated the price was too high. The man handed him the pineapple without hesitation, and told him to keep it, giving as a gift, what he had previously been selling. He appeared at ease with his decision, in spite of the possibility that this stand was important to their family livelihood. If there was resentment, it did not show. The Aloha spirit puts people and relationship before money, power or success. Often roadside stands like the one mentioned are themselves an act of aloha. They are set up so that an elder or a disabled member of the family will have a job and dignity. It is a substitute for a nursing home or care home, providing family and meaning.

A final expression of Aloha was that given to me personally. I was deeply affected. When I was leaving Hawaii, I had a musician friend who was a member of a very old Hawaiian aristocracy. She was also a vocalist and entertainer, helping to maintain and revive the Hawaiian language and culture with her voice. Her name is Nalani.

Nalani knew I was leaving and invited me to her noontime singing engagement, at a local restaurant. Mostly local people came there to hear her sing old songs in the Hawaiian language. I had only heard her performing in huge crowds at outdoor festivals previously and looked forward to a more intimate setting.

Unexpectedly, after my lunch, where I enjoyed both food and music, Nalani called me up to the microphone. She announced that her friend was leaving Hawaii, and that she wanted to dedicate the next song to me. She took off the flower lei she was wearing and put it around my neck. She sang a song in Hawaiian about leaving Hawaii and always coming back one more time. She looked into my eyes and sung deep into my heart, although she had a restaurant full of people watching her. When finished, she said "aloha nui loa" (much love) and my eyes were full of tears. My heart was so filled with her love, her song, the lei around my neck, and the great generosity of her heart.

Had you been there and not familiar with the depth of heart and aloha in Hawaii, or not familiar with Nalani, you might well have thought that I had been some special friend of hers for years, or even that we were lesbian lovers. The truth was, she was very well known and well loved, had lived in Hawaii all her life, and had hundreds of admirers and many good friends. I was just a friend, and had only known her for 2 or 3 years. But the Aloha Spirit makes one feel connected in the moment, and comes from people who are raised with and steeped in it. It is not fake. I was special to her in that moment, but in her life, I was one of hundreds. That kind of treatment, so like I imagine the Christ must have been, is affirming and redemptive. That it mostly came from women to me in Hawaii, was doubly redemptive in my life, because in many ways, I was un-mothered, and the women of Hawaii mothered me with their love and aloha. For the first time in my life, as I lived in Hawaii, I felt deeply mothered.

Although I had felt very womanly after my experience at the sensitivity group in Adrian, I received the experience of being royally holy and womanly from the women of Hawaii. This was grounded in Mother Earth, and in God, with the enfolding, blanketing climate along with the womb of the ocean. My new birth there was easy. The labor pains had preceded my being there, and I was guided through the birth canal of Hawaii with no effort on my part, other than obedience and a continuous "yes" to life. Nalani's act of generosity affirmed those feelings and was her farewell gift of deep aloha that day.

Later, I could easily fit that chapter of my life into my growing Christian framework, where there is no mothering model, except God's creation, the Earth. If God is the source of life in an eternal and spiritual sense, than the Earth is source of life in a temporal and secular world, and is God's creation. Jesus walked on the Earth, and it was his only home for his body, although God was the home for his soul/heart. The Earth is the source of nourishment for our body.

It is not that I have been full of love and peace ever since Hawaii. To the contrary, my life has had ups and downs since then, just like it did before. But I always carry that seed of being the daughter of eternity, filled with Aloha, gained through the legacy of the women of Hawaii, and their spirit of Aloha. The breath of life was breathed deeply into me there. I just need to remember: This is who I am, who I was born to be, and who I am always. There are many ways to look at it. I could say that it was a religious experience, and that it was about God, (which it was), but at the time, I experienced it as you have read.

Work

I spoke of the home repair work that Terry and I were doing. It was fun for me, and as I said before, it was as if I was continually living in the moment in prayer or meditation. It involved me and the tools and materials, rather than me and the other person, as it had as a counselor. Dancing with inanimate objects is different than dancing with another person, and filled a need for me that made it equally fitting at the time.

I was curious about how people perceived and treated me as a home repair person. There are many educated people doing physical labor just for the privilege of living in Hawaii. I only volunteered my background when asked, and of the people who asked, several became good friends.

There were differences in the way we were treated by families as we worked. Some people provided water, and occasionally even food. Some made sure we knew where the bathroom was. Others insisted we take off our shoes at the door, and forbid use of the bathroom. Taking off one's shoes at the door is a common Hawaiian custom, but not appropriate for carrying heavy loads, working around nails and screws, and walking in and out often.

I am much more aware these days of the human needs, and life stories of those who serve me in my home and environment.

One of the nice perks of working for oneself in Hawaii is the lunch breaks at the beach or in the ocean. In the three years I lived in Hawaii, I suspect I either had a bathing suit on as underwear, or one in the car or in my purse, 95% of the time. And when I didn't, I often regretted it. I sometimes took the bus to town, and got off several stops early on the way home, to walk, swim and beach comb my way home. Now, after a hard day's work together, our conversation was often limited to "Which beach today?"

Meanwhile, I was beginning to have some interest in professional work. The time of pure "being" seemed to have reached fruition during my home repair season and there were times when I wanted to be doing something else. The home repair, even the painting had begun to feel like hard work. I restored the balance in my life by beginning to make some professional contacts.

I eventually found a non-profit organization called Partners In Health. This was a resource center on medical information for professionals and the public. It was sustained by membership. They asked me to do some volunteer work, and it felt like a good fit, so I began.

For the first time in my life, I used a computer, a program called D-Base. My first experiences with a computer were discouraging and maddening, and it felt like the computer was my enemy, a cantankerous being that was out to get me. 30 years later, I wonder what the world and I did without computers. I am as dependent as most, and enjoy learning more. My iPhone is nearly stuck to my hand.

After I had been volunteering for several weeks, I found out that the organization was not going to be able to remain viable and the founder had decided to close. They hired me to close it down. I had to get rid of the library, return some grants, and do whatever it took. It was a sad task, for it had been a worthwhile organization, the brain child of one woman who was deeply dismayed that it could not continue.

During this process, I made a number of contacts and friendships which would later serve me well. People had supported the organization, and were kind, interested, empathetic and collaborative, in the face of the closing. The woman who had started it had great difficulty being around during the closing. She could hire out her parting tasks, but couldn't hire out her tears.

For a few months, I then worked as a social worker for Hospice Hawaii, which was just opening its doors. I was the keynote speaker for their annual meeting that year. Since then, I have worked for several hospices, none more interesting than the multicultural experiences of death and dying which I found in Hawaii. There were cultures that did not want hospice, using instead, spell casting, or their own form of religion to either try to save their family members, or help them die. There were other cultures that were nearly dispassionate about death. It was matter of fact, and another step in life. Hawaii is a multi-lingual, multi-cultural, multi-religion place. There is much to learn from being open to differences.

I remember going to a home where the husband and father was dying. His native language had been Portuguese. He had reverted to that in his dying days, so I could not understand him, and asked his family what he was saying. He appeared to be arguing loudly with someone not in the room. They told me he was arguing with Jesus. Apparently he was asking for forgiveness, and negotiating the time of his death. I went back the next day, and he was still arguing, though with less desperation and vehemence. By that afternoon, he was peaceful and quiet, and died during the night, resolved to his salvation and the timing of his death.

I taught some courses for women at Windward Community College in Kaneohe. And I began to be asked to give talks and workshops. In Hawaii, I think I began to come into my greatest opportunities and skills, for not only using knowledge, but also reaching people and touching hearts, or minds. I received the gifts of that time and passed them on in an easy natural way. I was clear that I was still on that God journey that brought me there.

Eventually, I ended up with a full time job working for the YMCA, under contract with the US Armed Services. I was working with a team of social workers, helping service families. The Armed Services has acronyms for everything, and I worked as part of an organization called FAIRS—Family Assistance, Information, and Referral Services. We worked in "the crater", (Aliamanu), Described this way on one web site.

ALIAMANU COMMUNITY
Located within a few miles of Fort Shafter, Tripler AMC and Joint Base Pearl Harbor-Hickam, the Aliamanu Community offers homes to Junior and Senior Enlisted Soldiers and their families. Nearly 700 new homes have been constructed, including a new community center featuring a movie theatre, two multi-purpose rooms and kitchen, and a skateboard and BMX bike ramp. Adjacent to the community center is the FMWR fitness center, and Army Community Services child development center, library and swimming pool. Residents also will find an AAFES Shoppette and gas station

The amenities listed above were mostly not there when I worked there. What was true then and was not mentioned in this article was this: This community was literally built in the crater of an old extinct volcano. That meant that the land was sloped toward the bottom of the crater, and the ocean breezes never reached down there. The housing was assigned so that the lower ranks had housing at the bottom, and the higher ranks toward the top, where there was more light and coolness. Thus the families with less money, and more young children, were at the bottom. Incidentally, my office was there too. You might imagine that there were some problems. You would be right.

All branches of the service were represented here. The salaries of the lower ranks may have covered family expenses on the mainland, but they did not in Hawaii. Thus, many of our service families were on food stamps and Medicaid for the children. It was also true that many families in the lower ranks came from places in the US where they had never learned to swim, did not like water, and were frightened of the ocean. In addition, they grew up in places where there was lots of space, and few people. They hated being stationed in Hawaii, where there was too much water, too little land and space, and way too many people.

Our job was to do family counseling, put out a newsletter, and develops services for the families there. You can see from the above published description, that my team must have been successful. as there are many services that were not there when I was. The job was challenging, and fun, with both counseling and community development.

My favorite memory is of developing a successful program by rumor. There was a great deal of animosity between neighbors, as happens in many neighborhoods of mixed income and especially mixed cultures. I wanted to find something that would change the emotional climate to include less animosity and more compassion.

I had an idea that if a program was developed where neighbors were involved and helping others, it would work toward some of that compassion. However, starting a new program within the Armed Services involved layers of complications and permissions. So I started a rumor that such a program existed. I was editing the newsletter for the housing area, so I had a ready rumor spreading vehicle. True to the acronym culture of the armed services,. I named the rumored program HAND, which stood for Help A Neighbor Daily. The first article spoke of a rumor going around about a new program, HAND. I said that the program was based on each person who lived there looking around to see how they might help a neighbor, and that FAIRS was a resource if they needed one. I said that as people were hearing about the program, they began reaching out to their neighbors. I talked about theoretical cases where HAND was helpful.

As I wrote about this rumored program in succeeding newsletters, we were actually getting calls, or people dropping by to talk about how they could give their neighbor a helping HAND. Then the next issue, I used real examples of how HAND was working. Soon we had less conflict in the area and more people helping their neighbors. The goal was moving toward being met. It saved lots of time and energy to start a rumor, instead of a program, and it accomplished the same thing.

During that time of working within the military culture, I was impressed by the men and women in charge of others in the armed services. I found the degree of principles, clarity, and action exemplary. Several years later, I read that corporations were trying to hire retired military, because they had knowledge, skills and strengths that those who were not trained in the military lacked.

One article I read in a military newsletter had to do with the difference between Leadership and Management. The main point was that management was something that was done with "things" while leadership was done with people. Just that principle and way of stating it was useful to me, and I used it for many years, in talks, consulting, and even in marriage counseling, where there is often a conflict about whether one is being a leader or a manager in the marriage. - treating one's mate as a person or a "thing".

My year spent with FAIRS was a wonderful teamwork and learning experience.

Beaches

I cannot leave my Hawaiian season without talking of beaches. The beaches of Oahu were my meditation room, spa, writing room, reading place, and favorite playground, as well as a continuous classroom in marine Biology. They were often my napping place, and certainly my people watching gallery, where I learned from mostly local people. I did not live near the tourist beaches.

In fact the beaches of my entire life have been those things and more, both before and after Hawaii. Sunning on beaches and swimming in rivers, lakes and oceans has been life-giving to me with memories going back to two years old. Those first months in Hawaii, (once my skin was tan enough not to worry about) found me on the beach daily, and often for hours.

There is a false image of Hawaii that pictures all beaches crowded and smelling of suntan lotion, with surfboards out plying the waves. That image comes from the travel magazines, focused on tourism. My Hawaii has a multitude of empty beaches, which may only see people on the weekends, when the locals go there to relax. Some required a two mile walk to get to. Others were rough, and steeply un-swimmable. And then there were beaches which were just right for lounging on daily, with little or no disturbance, and little or no danger from tides, sharks, or hordes of tourists. I managed to see those crowded tourist beaches, with the predominant coconut smell, and more people than waves, but spent almost no time there.

I named my favorite beach-combing beach "Junk Beach". It was about a half mile from the retreat center near a golf course, across the fairway and a drop down a 5 foot bank. There the shore was shaped just right to catch incoming flotsam. It was also a wonderful sunrise beach. I found notes in bottles, bales of rubber, plastic bottles and floats in all languages, fishing nets, and satisfaction in my growing obsession to find the glass fishing floats from Japan that rode the current, and sometimes got knocked out of that current with a storm. It became my personal challenge to find those floats.

I found a book on glass floats on the Oregon coast. They gave formulas which proved accurate for likely times to find more floats. I then realized that the current which sometimes comes near Hawaii, also goes toward Oregon. The book said that the glass floats came in when the Portuguese Man-O-War jellyfish came ashore. This occurred because of those aforementioned storms in certain parts of the Pacific, which blew the floats out of their usual pattern. That pattern also contained the jelly fish.

Not long after that, the man-o-war were on the beaches of Oahu, and sure enough, I found a glass float or two at Junk Beach. After one or two more times of success, I was hooked. I had a secret method.

There are two main kinds of glass floats: roller floats, looking like miniature rolling pins, and glass balls with or without net wrapped around them. I came back to the mainland with 13 glass floats, ranging from 2 inches to almost a foot, and including a couple of roller floats. The biggest float, I spied glinting in the sun about ¼ mile out in the ocean, and swam out to get it. When I reached it, it was covered with Portuguese Man O War, which I was luckily not allergic to. Almost everyone stings and itches after being stung, but some people are very allergic and end up hospitalized. For the rest of us, a shake or two of meat tenderizer containing papain, takes the sting out, and I carried one in my backpack. That was more lady like and convenient than "peeing on it" which is what the Hawaiian kids learn to do.

Terry and I took our tent to Junk Beach one night. There was a particularly high tide and full moon, and I thought it likely that we would find floats. The next morning I woke up, and there were so many and such varied floats in the surf, I could not get them all. A couple broke on the rocks right in front of me just as they were getting close enough to reach. A few more were washed back out to sea before I could grab them, and some floated just beyond my reach and didn't float in. That particular beach was not swimmable, and hardly good for wading, as the lava rocks had many holes and sharp edges. It would be easy to get cut, break an ankle or get washed off the ledges in the chaotic surf. The best and safest choice was to wait on shore, or on the very edge of the water. However, that meant some floats were tantalizingly beyond reach, and beyond safe decisions. Nonetheless, I brought back 9 floats that morning. Most local people did not know or care much about the floats, and even those who did had not learned of the pattern of probability that went with the jellyfish. I still have most of those floats.

A few years ago now, I went back to Hawaii and stayed in my friends' home on Kauai, I found one float that week, noticing the man-o-war. The husband, a local Chinese- Hawaiian did not know about predicting the presence of the floats and was surprised at my find.

The beaches of the North Shore of Oahu are famous around the world for surfing and surf contests in the winter. The surfers use them with incredible grace and lots of danger. In summer, it is possible to swim there, but still dangerous. Unless one is an expert swimmer, knows the beaches well, and preferably has a surfboard or boogie board to help, it is best to stay out of that water. One summer day I stepped in the water, and within a few feet it was up to my waist. In two minutes, I got carried over ¼ mile down the beach, and could have been carried outward if the currents happened to be going that way. I was totally powerless, it was frightening, and I never went in those waters again at any time of year. The waves occasionally reach 30 and 35 feet during the winter. Waves are measured differently in different places, and you can find that information on the internet, but regardless of the measurement, the waves of the North Shore of Oahu are huge.

We had a young man living at the retreat center who was mentally ill. He practiced martial arts, was very strong, and loved to body surf – no board. One day, we picked up the paper and read that he had been helicoptered off Waimea Bay, picked out of the 30 foot waves as he was body surfing. It was a foolish thing to do, but he felt no danger. He later told us they used a bullhorn to swoop down and ask him to get out of the water, and because the road was closed by the waves, they used the helicopter. He never mentioned it to us, until we saw the paper.

Pounders beach, near us, got its name rightfully. It was a body surfing beach, pounding the body to punish mistakes. The waves there were not huge, like the North Shore, (We were on the north eastern, or windward side of the island). But they were fast. and curled well for good body surfing. The steep shore and the speed of the breaking waves meant there was a lot of snapping power for an arm, shoulder, or neck, if one got caught by the wrong part of the wave. I have a shoulder which is beginning to creak as I age as a result of an old injury at Pounders.

My reading, writing, and napping was most often done at the beach directly across from the road to the retreat center. It didn't have a name. It was invisible from the road, and I never had company unless an occasional weekend local family came there.

Some beaches have big waves because they are open to the open ocean. Others are guarded by an outer reef, leaving the inner ocean much calmer and less dangerous. My beach had such an outer reef, barely visible out toward the open ocean. Thus, there was no danger of high surf, strong currents, or large creatures near me. I snorkeled for hours finding lead fishing weights and occasional coins or jewelry. At night, one could see the headlamps of the spear fishing eel hunters there. An occasional sea turtle was around. I alternately occupied the beach and the water for hours, comfortably napping, or playing in either surrounding.

Three times I had money wash up out of the ocean at my feet. I am sure it was lost swimming, fishing, or boating. It was an ongoing problem to know where to hide car keys or money when on a beach. We hid ours in the bushes, not with our towels. Hawaii was not always paradise. There were locals who were poor, or who resented tourists and didn't hesitate to steal from cars or beaches. I tried to look as local as possible, as the bad guys and gals didn't bother locals, meaning people who lived there.

As in most cultures where the tourists have money and the local people do not, there is resentment. It is heightened by having to be polite and nice when serving those one resents. The Hawaiian word for Caucasian is "haole", and the meaning is "without breath". The word was chosen because the missionaries breathed noticeably more shallowly than the natives, and thus were labeled "without breath". When I lived there, there was a sort of what we might call "jive talk', that is, a distorted English/Hawaiian combination used among the young men, and there were often disdainful references to the haoles, even while serving them.

That last paragraph strayed from the subject of beaches, but that I put a whole section in here on beaches should tell you how important water and beaches are to me, and especially were to me in Hawaii. Having lived near the water for even that short a time in my life, I seem to be a beach snob, and aficionado. It is ironic that I have become allergic to sunshine within the past two years. Only since then do I seem to have lost my drive to find the perfect beach.

Living Arrangements

I lived in the retreat center for over a year. Our home repair business was picking up, and we were 45 minutes through traffic from any stores and supplies. I was feeling more comfortable being around people and towns, and thus willing to leave this place of my rebirth. We moved to the city.

We lived in an apartment in Honolulu for a while, rented from some friends. Later we sublet an apartment from a man who summered in Alaska, and left his freezer full of frozen salmon and other Alaskan fish for us. It was in that place that I celebrated my 50th birthday. It was a memorable Hawaiian kind of celebration.

216

The swimming pool and large deck on the 7th floor of the building was perfect for a party. There were about 30 people there. Sonny Ching, who was also a Hawaiian musician and entertainer brought his ukulele and sang and played. We had a lovely time. Sonny and Reenie brought me a ginger lei which was very special. The smell is wonderful. What a privilege to celebrate half a century of life in the midst of friends and aloha.

Because we were known and trusted, one or both of us often got asked to house sit either at houses we were working on, or for people who were traveling. Once we were in an ocean front house while the owners went back to Germany. We were invited by the couple next door to a luau. (a Hawaiian celebratory feast) They had just gotten their dogs out of quarantine, and were celebrating. When we showed up at the party, I realized that it was probable that we were the only straight people there among transsexuals, gay men, cross-dressers, and assorted confusing people. There may have been some other women there but I could not tell. Several people looked like women, but later turned out not to be. It was truly a confusing evening and a self-awareness experience for me, as I learned how I treat people differently depending on gender. Very gracious of the men to invite us, and they were gracious hosts. We enjoyed the party, learned about ourselves, and more about their world.

Another house sitting job was on a finger of land that sticks out into the ocean near Laie, Oahu. The house was up on a cliff, and I was there during the winter when the waves are bigger. There was no danger of waves coming that high, but one could feel the vibration of the house, as the waves boomed against the cliff down below.

One other house had a splash pool out by the cliff by the ocean. A splash pool is a depression up above the ocean, warmed by the sun and refilled by the splashing of the waves from below. Sitting in the warm water, and seeing the splashing water come over the side of the pool is a relaxing and glorious experience. Hedonism at its finest. While we were there, a neighbor boy with his surf board came next to the pool, timed the waves, and jumped into the ocean with his board, maybe 15 feet down the cliff, catching the outgoing surge.

Yes, of course there are people killed like that every year. The ocean is a dangerous and powerful place. It also is a beautiful and joyful place.

Looking back

You may wonder what happened to my stance of living in the present moment that developed in Hawaii. It has stayed in my body and my memory bank, although many times that part of me gets lost I have never again felt as scared, weak, or confused since I lived there. For several years, I lived out my Hawaiian, God given gifts without effort. Now I often have to call it forth, or pray. Occasionally

I fear I have lost that part of myself, but so far, she is there waiting for some aloha, from me or others.

I have a book called "Circle of Stones", by Judith Durek. Many of the pages ask in this manner: "How might your life have been different, if when you went through hard times, you had been surrounded by a circle of women, to hold you, and guide you, and love you with wisdom." For the time I lived in Hawaii, that is what happened to me. I was surrounded by a circle of women, who lived for the most part, with respect, love, spirit, kindness, generosity, holiness, and aloha. Terry was my companion in adventure, and he recognized holiness. So he was a good companion, but the women, the land, and the weather, were my source of power and love.

In my being, I clearly recognize that time as God given. I had less doubt, more knowing about God in that part of my life, than any other time. There have been times when it is difficult to discern whether something was God or me, but about going to Hawaii, and being there, it was God. no doubt. I felt led and it was easy for me to go there as I was stepping out of the darkest part of my life. There were so many "right" gifts. He sent me to where his daughters could show me that I too was a beloved daughter. He put me where his land was a womb, where elements came together with both tenderness and strength. He provided time for me to hear him, to hear myself, and the earth from which I sprang. He showed me silence and power. He gave me both comfort and strength in all that surrounded me. Hawaii became the symbol of my beloved, and the birthplace of my fullness. That place, more than any other in my life, represents the power of living with God Father/Earth Mother, as source of life, and surrender to life.

Leaving Hawaii

One day, after about 2 ½ or 3 years, I came home from the beach knowing it was time to go back to the mainland. Within the months before that, or maybe the year before that, all three of my children had gotten married. I had flown back, of course, for all the weddings: one in Colorado, one in New Mexico, and one in California.

My mother, who had been actively drinking for several years, and mostly staying in bed or on the couch had fallen, and had to have brain surgery. She was a shadow of her former powerful self, doing no community work anymore, and being difficult with all her friends. She was in denial about her situation, angry about changes or suggestions, and insisting she had many friends, although they had all died or been put off by her altered temperament.

When I went to the beach that day, the sun and the ocean felt almost abrasive. For three years, the same surroundings had been a healing sanctuary. I could hardly grasp the change. Over the next month, I tried to ignore it. I felt sad and angry. I had a small temper tantrum and cussed God out about this new turn of events. I tested the idea every which way. I listened to myself, and to God. And finally, I resigned myself to leaving Hawaii.

I talked to Terry sometime during that month, and he was as surprised as I was. He was not ready to leave, and so I resigned myself to leaving him. Our relationship was collaborative, companionable and fun, but he was not open to marriage or commitment, thus my own process needed to be more important to me than he was, as I chose to follow my promptings.

The clutch on my car went out. What a perfect metaphor for difficulty in shifting gears. My car confirmed what I already knew about myself. (No, I don't believe all car difficulties are metaphors for the owners' life, but when they are, they are!)

Terry decided to move back anyway, and so we packed up all our things and got ready to go. He was going to Oregon where he had a son and the son's mother, I was going to my daughter's in California, and get myself a vehicle and then go to Michigan.

Going to hear Nalani sing, and receiving her farewell, was one of the last things I did. I was clear that it was time to go, and I cried many tears anyway. My friends at FAIRS gave me a beautiful going away party. It was very hard to leave. I had difficulty looking at it as another death and birth. I just wanted everything to stay the way it was. I especially wanted to stay the way I was.

From this point, I traveled for an interlude on the mainland, and then you will read about my time in Arizona.

Culture Shock.

When I got to the mainland, I spent the first few days at my daughter's, totally overwhelmed by the speed of life around the Los Angeles area. About the third day I tried going toward the city to look for a car, and came home crying, not able to operate at the pace of a mainland city. My whole system needed to reset itself, at least enough to function.

I was welcome at Pam's for a while, so I decided to slow myself down to my own pace, and look in the local papers for a car rather than go back to the city. I prayed that I might find the right vehicle, and that I might know my next step. Within a few days I found a van. My son-in-law pronounced it road worthy.

I left my daughter's house, finally owning a key again. Since I had no home, I asked her if my mail could be forwarded to her, and if she would write checks for my bills. They were few, but important. I then left, homeless and free, and drove coastal Highway 1 up to Oregon. Terry joined me partway, and we spent a few days camping and enjoying the woods and ocean. He showed me the chapel at Sea Ranch with the beautiful stained glass that someone he knew had made. It is a lovely little chapel. It looks like a Hobbit house, set into nature. It feels like sacred space to enter.

After we separated once more, I went back to Pam's and from there left for Richard Moss's annual Three Mountain get together, and enjoyed the energy and the people. I then left for Michigan.

Taking Care of Mom

I drove to Michigan and took over the care of my mom. She was newly home from surgery and the hospital and was awaiting transfer to a nursing home for recovery. It was like taking care of a new born baby. She had to be dressed, fed, and diapers changed. I felt so compassionate and loving toward her, but that soon was tempered with needed limit setting. As she felt better, she got angry and nasty. Her physician had been in denial himself about her being an alcoholic, so there had been no provision for withdrawal made at the time of surgery, and she had gone into continuous seizures for a day or more until they were able to do something about it. I am sure that maximized brain damage from the fall, surgery and long term alcohol abuse.

As I took care of her, she was fighting double and triple demons—recovery from surgery, withdrawal from alcohol addiction, and not being in her home, but in a situation that was out of her control. I understood that, but probably did not understand the immensity of it. It was a tremendously difficult time for her, and for me. Compassion and anger warred in me. Her nastiness was difficult to ignore. I was torn between wanting to be there for her, and wanting to get away from her.

When she went in the nursing home, she was still confused. The unfamiliar surroundings confused her even more. There are no perfect nursing places, and there were few or no employees who knew her or had known her. I stayed with her most of the first few days, and then attempted to help her cope. Again I felt deeply compassionate.

Two things I wrote during that time, give an idea of what was happening with me. The first is a letter to a friend in Hawaii who was a Geriatric Specialist and had dealt with her own mom's aging. The second, a letter to the staff in the nursing home.

Here is the first:

```
Dear Evangeline,
    It's Christmas Day (1987) and we just put my mother in
a nursing home three days ago.
    Last year you asked me to write on how to deal with
ungrateful grouchy patients. Now I want to write something
else: How do you deal with someone whose life situation
has changed, and instead of covering up their fear with
anger, the raw fear is at the surface? For me it was
harder to deal with Mom in all her vulnerability than when
she was wearing the mask of anger and arrogance.
    She looks like a little child newly awakened into a
```

frightening and changed world as she sits with her head shaved from recent surgery, strapped into her wheel chair, adapting to her confusion, her withdrawal from alcohol addiction, and a recent move to a care home. She pleads with me that it isn't right — that she's a grown up, and she's trying to learn the right rules, and she doesn't know how. She reminds me that she has been a community leader, and that she raised five children, and that she was on the debate team in college and that she doesn't understand why people are angry at her for trying to walk, and for trying to get from bed to the bathroom on time. She can't understand about no smoking in bed. She's been doing it for years.

The truth is that mom is confused and unsteady on her feet. And she's definitely not reliable with cigarettes. We have been frightened for years that she would burn herself and the house.

For 5 years she has done it her way. Lying in bed drunk and isolated - doing nothing but chain smoking and occasionally reading. She has chased her many friends away with her insults, her arrogance, and the smokescreen, both literal and figurative.

And now she lies psychologically naked and not understanding, begging me, her daughter, to protect her, to take her home or to tell people who she is. She asks me to help her be "good". She cries and pleads, and wakes up from horrible dreams thinking that her children have been killed or that her husband is still alive. She is unable to sort out her psychic experiences from her dreams, from the reality of the voices and people around her.

Her vulnerability absolutely undoes me. Her bared soul touches mine and I long to hold her in my arms and rock her and tell her I'll keep her safe forever.

And I know I must leave her there----with people who aren't her daughter, and for whom she's just one more confused person, and with people who care, but who don't have time, or don't know her. How to do that, Evangeline, is a tough question.

I stayed with her most of the day for the first week, and I thank God I have the time and the love. I patiently tell her the rules, telling her the common reality of that particular world, and consoling her when some workers are unthinkingly insensitive, or "just following Dr.'s orders".

I stubbornly keep her out of restraints, and walk with her often so she gets stronger and so the staff can see that she walks. I protect her from what I can, and push her to do what's in her best interest. I try to see that she has as much control over her life as is safe for her. I fight with her when necessary, knowing that the more she fights out her stubborn attempts to be the person in charge with me, the less she will alienate the staff by fighting with them.

I tell her I don't want to talk about rules any more

today and I half kiddingly or rather using a joking manner call her arrogant or "lazy butt" when she covers up her vulnerability and fear with "They better wait on me, that's what they get paid for." I put signs on her wall to remind her where her children are living so she won't believe her dreams and nightmares. I continually attempt to light up the path of reality and truth in her life while at the same time helping her to fight imaginary dragons and the less than perfect system in which she finds herself living.

And always, always I love that vulnerable frightened infant in her. I protect her and teach her with my actions, my interactions, my words, and my prayers. I hug her, I rub her back, I bring her clothes, and I pray for either the return of independence or the acceptance of what's necessary.

Once again, thank you for listening, Evangeline
Love, Karen Hamp

And this one: To the nursing home staff. I was so cognizant that the people dealing with my mother only knew who she was in the present. Even though she was in her home town, she had been out of commission long enough so the young people working there had not heard of her. Of course they had to deal with her in her present condition, but knowing a little about her past I hoped might build some bridges back to some normalcy. This is what I wrote for her chart.

MARYAN BRADLEY: Things we want you to know and care about with our mother.

1. Maryan has been a community leader in Midland all her life until recently when she seems to have resigned from the world. If you lived in Midland even one year, one of her projects is affecting you or your family. This leadership has proved her competence in the past. She is still competent in many ways. Encourage her competence, not her incompetence.

2. Maryan is only 2 mo. into drying out from severe chronic alcoholism which she has not admitted. Don't encourage Happy Hour. Help her find other ways of dealing with her anxiety and depression which she now has to face directly. She is not even asking for alcohol.

3. Be aware that Maryan has isolated herself from people and stimulation for the last five years or so. She needs stimulation, but too much of it can be confusing to her, so she may need quiet time alone.

4. She has been a small eater for years. If she is eating enough to maintain her weight, let her regulate which meals and how much she wants. Hopefully you can balance this with still encouraging her eating.

5. She is sometimes hypoglycemic and then feels foggy and confused. Try orange juice with her as a first resort when she is confused. This is especially true in the morning and when she wakes up from a nap.

222

6. Remember that cigarettes are how she deals with her anxiety. She is addicted. Having dealt with addiction either in yourself, your family, or other people, you understand the panic of withdrawal or deprivation. Please inform her when she's getting low on cigarettes. (Silva Menthol Thins) She can order them from Community Drug Store and have them delivered.

7. Help her to separate her dreams and psychic phenomena from reality. Her husband and parents are dead. There is a list on the wall of her room telling where her children are.

8. Please encourage and reward her healthiness, not her illness,

Her wanting to get to the bathroom is healthy, even when it's in the middle of the night.

Her wanting to be independent and make decisions is healthy, even when it's inconvenient or annoying to you and I.

Her making contact with staff and patients is healthy — even though she sometimes does it in annoying ways like arguing or manipulating.

Thanks for treating her like you would want your own mother or father or husband or wife to be treated. We love her.

I spent Christmas with my mother that year, and Terry decided to come to Michigan for Christmas. Since my mother recognized that it was Christmas Day, I could not bear to leave her and we had Christmas the day after at AH's and Barb's.

Traveling the Country

I was living with rapidly changing circumstances and situations. I think that my brothers and sisters wanted me to stay with my mother, but I was ready for the road again. As mom became more stable, I formulated plans. I wanted to visit people that I had not seen in several years, both relatives and friends. In California, a carpenter friend had helped me build a bed in the back of the van. I also had room for a small set of lightweight shelves to hold things like camera, binoculars, office supplies, and other essential belongings. My clothes were in a large suitcase which slid under the bed.

I decided to first go see a friend in Pittsburgh who had narrowly escaped dying from a ruptured aortic aneurysm a year before. (He was driving himself to the hospital because of belly pain, and his car went over an embankment as he passed out. He was pinned upside down which acted as a tourniquet, and kept him from dying.) It brought home to me once more, the fragility of life, and the small things that happen that allow life to continue or not. And incidentally too allow friendships to continue or not.

I then came back to Michigan to reconnect with my cousins, and aunts and uncles, as well as my siblings and their children. I saw

223

many friends at some events that I attended and then I started west. I visited my children, in Texas and Colorado, an aunt and uncle in Illinois, and many other friends and relatives. When I did not have someplace to stay, I stayed in my van in motel parking lots, and occasionally used the swimming pools. It must have been because of people like me that motels started requiring key cards to get in the outside doors. Occasionally I stayed in a campground.

Many people, both friends and strangers thought I should be frightened traveling. I was cautious, observant, and careful, staying low profile in public places, especially roadside rests or truck stops. I locked my van doors once I was in, and could see out without people seeing in. It meant I made less contact with others, making it occasionally lonely, but mostly it was enjoyable time.

One night, I woke up cold in the middle of the night. I did what I usually did, when I was cold or unable to sleep. I got up and drove until I felt warm, or sleepy, and then found another place to spend the rest of the night. That night I stopped along I – 70 for a cup of hot chocolate at a truck stop. I was talking at the counter, and took the precaution of telling them that my husband was asleep out in the van. One of the men said, "Of course you have a gun, don't you?" I did not and still don't. Gun ownership and controls are a current hot issue in our culture as I write this. I feel mixed, being able to see most points of view, but choose not to be armed. I still attempt to be mindful and cautious, especially when by myself in public places, and open spaces, such as parking lots and shopping centers. I also consider myself a fair judge of people

One afternoon, coming back east from Colorado in the winter, or early spring, I was rather alone on the freeway; the weather grey and the traffic sparse. When starting out that morning, I had uncharacteristically said out loud, "God, if there is anything I can do for you today, let me know. Suddenly, the car ahead of me went off the road and rolled over, landing on its side. I carefully brought my van to a stop, discovering that I was driving on black ice and didn't know it. I got out of my car as 4 young men, probably about age 15 to 17, came crawling out of the other car. One had a cut on his head, the others were unhurt. They were from Jefferson City, Missouri and had been skiing in Colorado.

They could not tip their car back over, and I asked if they were willing to go with me. We went first to the hospital to get stitches for the one that was cut. While there, (before cell phones), the owner of the car called his father. They were to stay all night, get the car to a garage, and then come home. I suggested that I was going that way and could bring all 4 with their ski equipment and luggage the next day. The parents offered to pay for my motel, which got me out of the sub-zero weather that night. This was in Goodland Kansas.

By now, their car was at the dealer. We went and got the skis and luggage transferred to my car, and went to the motel. I noted that God had answered my prayer from that morning.

The next morning we made the trip to Missouri, arriving about 8 pm. While the boys had been friends, most of their parents had not met before, and met each other at dinner that night when we got there and they took me out to dinner. I stayed at one of the homes that night, and left the next morning. And by the way, we found out that the road back toward Colorado was closed because of ice when we left Goodland.

What are the odds that I would be the only other car on the road, and have the room for 4 extras, and all their ski's and luggage, going the right direction, and had all the time we needed to take them home. It was an obvious answer to prayer.

Back in Michigan, I found that my mother wanted to move back to her home. We helped her to move, after we made it clear that none of us was willing to stay with her, and that she had to have help. She agreed. However, she did not keep the help. One was dishonest, and one or two were not good. We knew that there are good and bad caregivers working for minimum wage for the home agencies, but she found reasons for all of them to go. We reluctantly settled for someone to come in and clean once a week. None of us lived in Midland to check on how she was doing, although we called daily, and went up there when we could. The bottom line was that she did not like someone staying there. She was willing, however, to have someone come in and clean. After a week or two, I was ready to get on the road again.

Terry and Cave Creek

I started west one more time, retracing part of my route, and seeing my children and grandchildren. It was now early 1988. Terry had ended up in a town called Cave Creek, Arizona. It was his favorite kind of place, a small unique tourist town in beautiful territory. Next door to Cave Creek was Carefree, a planned community built in the 1950's. It was an upscale town, serving upscale people. For instance, one development, Sky Ranch, had a hanger for a small plane with each condo.

I stopped to visit Terry, planning to stay a few days. He met me at the door saying he had made room in the closet for my clothes. He was clearly eager for me to stay. I felt ambivalent. I did not unpack my van. I stayed a few days and went on with my trip. While traveling, I decided to go back to Cave Creek, calling Terry and making sure it was OK.

I had some difficulty getting used to the warm air that felt, at first, so much like Hawaii, but added the harshness and dryness of the desert. It was beautiful, but very different to live there than any place I had lived. I wrote this letter to the paper after I had been there a few weeks.

Describing Cave Creek, From a Newcomer.

Editor:

I moved to Cave Creek only six weeks ago, and I want to share my experience of being here.

I have strong feelings about the earth and nature, and I was immediately attracted to the stark, simple, yet rich and majestic beauty of the Sonoran Desert.

On one hand, the giant saguaro cacti give the same sense of power, continuity and history to this area that the giant redwood trees give the forests of California.

And, on the other hand, this power is dangerous, and, like the ocean, you never turn your back on the desert. The vegetation is often physically hostile. It sticks, tears and penetrates barriers at the first careless move.

The indigenous rattlesnakes and scorpions must be reckoned with carefully and watchfully. And water, either too much or too little, is a problem.

To choose to live here takes people who are willing to recognize both the beauty and the harsh rules of the desert. It takes people with courage and the acceptance of all facets of life to feel truly alive here.

The rest die, weaken in spirit or stay awhile and then go away. It is obvious that neither you nor I ended up here by accident. We chose this place and it chose us.

Because of these things, this is a community rich in spirit. Much of its wealth is in life experience, wisdom, humbleness, respect, alive-ness and a caring for fellow human beings.

And out of this caring for each other, it is a community with heart. Carlos Castenada in his writings on Don Juan discussed the difference between following a path with heart in one's life and following one without heart. "One makes for a joyful journey; as long as you follow it, you are one with it. The other will make you curse your life. One makes you strong, the other weakens you."

The same thing is true about living in a community with heart. It strengthens one and all, and those who stay join together to become one. Our collective heart here beats strongly.

Oh, I know there are differences. I know there is conflict I read it and hear it and see it. Like any other community or family trying to live our lives, we are imperfect human beings with different perspectives, and we label each other right and wrong.

This, however, is the legacy of being human. These are the growing pains of communities, and even communities with a lot of heart and a wealth of spirit have growing pains.

As I go about the exciting, and sometime discouraging or hard task of putting my life together in a new way in a new place, it is helpful to be able to see and remember both the

226

beauty of the heart and spirit and the imperfections and the harshness of life.

So, I write this to remind me of my heart and spirit, and I write it to remind us of our collective heart and spirit, and I thank you for being a part of my journey through life.

Karen Hamp

More Choices

After a few weeks, again working with Terry doing home repair, I pondered how to make a living. Terry and I were not working as well together, and I really did not want to do home repair. One morning, in that waking up state, I had a sort of dream/idea/vision. I saw myself teaching exercise to senior women.

Sometimes, the ideas I get are just ideas, and other times they have a particular quality which feels like tuning into a larger reality, or I have sometimes described them as messages from God. When I surrender to these larger visions, and do my part, they produce good for both me and others. That is what happened when I went to Hawaii. If I turn away from them, the opportunities fade away.

This particular time, in spite of being brand new in town, and knowing almost no one, I stayed true to the vision. My default exercise of swimming was not exactly plentiful in the small desert town, and I could see myself and others benefiting from exercise, getting to know each other, and giving me a way to earn some money to live on.

Just down the road from where we lived, was the Community Center, and there were rooms rentable for such classes. As I was arranging that, I met the Yoga teacher who also taught there, and we were able to share the rent for the room. I began to teach Senior Exercise Classes and it turned into a fun, successful, joyful activity for all. I had about 20 women in my class from about age 45-75. I called it *Stretch, Strong, Relax*. Eventually, the Yoga Teacher and I began to substitute for each other. She always went to Colorado for the summer, so I took over the Yoga Classes. And when I traveled, she taught my classes.

She eventually recommended me to Weight Watchers to teach Yoga at their Spa in Scottsdale. So now I was doing Yoga about 6-8 hours/week and my exercise class twice a week.

A few weeks after increasing my number of hours of doing Yoga, I noticed that I was getting tearful more often and feeling physically and emotionally vulnerable. Paying attention, I realized my circumstances had not changed, and there was nothing to account for this in my life.

Thinking more, I realized it was possible that I needed to balance all that stretching and opening with more strengthening. My body/mind view paid off, and I theorized that all the stretching had left me "too thin skinned", stretched too thin, and the emotional

227

energy might be leaking from my leaky container. Healing that would take thickening my body, building more muscles. I began walking a couple miles a day, and lifting weights, and within a week I was feeling better. I could better contain my emotions.

The classes provided me with enough money to live on. I did not require much, and I did not have to keep using savings. I was grateful for the opportunity, and for the vision that morning, and the will to follow it.

I was just about to open a counseling office in town a few months after that. I had rented an office, when Terry decided to go to Scotland for the 25th Birthday of Findhorn, the spiritual community he had lived in for a while. He wanted me to go. The timing was awkward, because of my office, but I wanted to go, and said I would if we could go to Ireland too. He first balked and then agreed. My ancestors came from both Ireland and Scotland.

We went for two weeks, and it was a meaningful and fun trip, although cold in November. We stayed in Bed and Breakfasts, with families for the most part. For several days, we stayed at Findhorn, and although I felt a little like a stranger at someone else's class reunion, I enjoyed it and was impressed by the atmosphere and people. Here is what I wrote after I came back.

ROOTS AND WINGS

I just returned from Scotland and Ireland. Both countries are my ancestral "stomping grounds". My father's grandparents came to the U.S. from Ireland and my mother was extremely proud of being part of the MacLeans of Duart from northwest Scotland.

As I wandered the Irish farmland and narrow lanes of County Wicklow, I suddenly burst into sobs, and had the near-mystical experience of feeling my father there with me. He has been dead 18 years. I do not know, but had heard that my ancestors were from County Wicklow. I seemed to be sobbing through the longing that he and his mother before him had experienced to return to their Irish roots. And I remembered that two nights previously, when we stepped off the ferry, I had felt an urge to throw myself on the ground and kiss the Irish soil. A great healing took place as I let my sobs progress through the longing to relief. And it was as if the homecoming and the healing was happening through me, but encompassed past and future generations. It felt as if either my father brought me, or I brought he and his mother home to Irish soil.

I don't even know if I believe in experiences like this, but I am willing to let myself unfold and see what happens at these times. I do know that something in me was healed regardless of the explanation.

I remembered back to my dad singing Irish songs, and the feeling that he sang from heart and soul. His mother had died when he was 9 and there was a gentle Irish pride and longing in our family that came together on St. Patrick's Day as we all wore green, sent cards with shamrocks and at least some of us drank Irish whiskey, notably the older generations.

As we traveled in Scotland, my ancestry was more tangible and visible. Many of the people I saw looked like me, or like various relatives. I visited the castle where the present Chief of the MacLean Clan still lives. I wandered through graveyards, museums and the Battlefield of Culloden and saw the prominent evidence of past family members. I saw grave markers dating back to the 1500's with familiar family names on them - Hector, Donald, and Katherine McLean. I took pictures of the McLean Cross on the Island of Iona, and I felt the humbleness, arrogance and pride of being part of a clan described in one book as fierce fighters and gentlemen.

When I left the U.S., I had a vague idea about exploring my "roots". It is a popular idea now. I did not realize how profound, solid, and spiritually fulfilling it would be to walk on the ground of my past, and experience my foundations.

There is a sense of history and continuity in me that wasn't there before, a sense of deep rootedness in the past. The results of this are already beginning to show up in my present life. Just as the nourishment drawn through the tree roots gives birth to new life, I am sensing that my own roots are birthing a new phase of growth and blossoming in my world

It is easy to forget that we are a product of all that has gone before us, even of many generations past. It is our roots that help give us wings.

Besides that part of the experience, I enjoyed visiting the Findhorn community. I had heard of it for years, and in fact it was an assumed distant relative of mine that had been one of the three original founders. Findhorn is an intentional community of people on the North Sea, not too far from a fishing village of the same name. It was started by three people who lost their jobs, and came there to live in what we would call a trailer, and the Scots call "caravans". They arrived there in about 1963.

The founders, Peter and Eileen Caddy, and Dorothy MacLean, were prayerful and spiritual people, feeling close to the spirits or "devas" of the earth. They found they could grow huge vegetables and gardens in that part of the land, in cooperation with the land and its spirits. They attracted other people, and today, 50 years later, there are people from all over the world living at Findhorn.

Dorothy is still alive, Eileen died a few years ago, and Peter was killed in an auto accident several years before that. However, when I was there, they were all still alive.

One must have some sort of spiritual orientation to live there. No specific belief or practice system is espoused. Collaboration, kindness, a relationship to the land, being attuned to and responsive to others, and a willingness to participate and work are all required to stay there. Work is required of all, visitors and residents alike.

The community still grows vegetables for their own use, and people living there have gardens, but that is no longer the main focus. Findhorn is now not only the residents, but a worldwide network of people who carry on the hope for light, love, and aliveness in the world. There are many and varied workshops there each year with well known leaders. Over the years, the community has handled many issues, and come through with continued vitality.

It is a delightful, but not utopian place to be. There are disagreements, and processes for working through them. It would be a lesson in sustainable living with others to be there for a season of one's life. Terry had lived there several years. After we split up, he went there and lived and worked for many years again. As I write this, the community is celebrating its 50th anniversary.

My Life in Cave Creek

When we came back to Cave Creek, I officially opened my office for counseling. Between the intense mental and emotional work of counseling and the physical work of teaching Yoga and exercise, I felt balanced and busy.

I was asked to take some community responsibility, first as manager of the Cave Creek Cemetery. That gave me a laugh, having grown up around the funeral business. Cave Creek was a very small town, so everybody pitched in to help things run smoothly.

The Cave Creek cemetery is worth a visit. The town has many rugged and creative individualists, and the cemetery markers reflect that. The desert does not allow a beautiful lawn or any lawn at all in the cemetery, and the cemetery markers range from wooden crosses, and stones with names painted on them, to unique creations of stainless steel and other pieces of art. When I left, there were few if any conventional marble grave markers.

The register of grave location had been lost, and my first job was to attempt to reconstruct that. The name-marked graves were easy; the ones with no names, or no markers were more difficult. I had to make sensitive calls to people about the location of their relatives, and was glad I was trusted to do the job. Also, being part of the "wild west", there were times when a new grave would appear overnight, or over the weekend, and no one knew anything about it. .

One of the women in my exercise class became a long time and good friend of mine along with her husband. Corky and Curt Coburn were unique people and long-time Cave Creek residents. It was Corky who contributed so very much to the growth of Cave Creek long before I was there, including a library, and a renowned Christmas Pageant, with luminaria all the way down the main road of the town. Corky also served annual dinners where only food from the desert was served (rattlesnake meat, javelina, saguaro jelly and other desert delicacies). It was Corky's love of nature and her knowledge of same which made those dinners both delicious and educational. Curt died several years ago, and I have been in touch with Corky until recently when she left Cave Creek to live with one of her children. She was several years older than I and became another of my role models.

Their yearly Christmas "tree" was never a tree. They took what they found; a piece of desert flora, a saguaro skeleton, or maybe a collection of unique seed pods. These were somehow mounted and decorated with Christmas decorations. I borrowed their idea, and for many years never bought a Christmas tree, using downed branches, dead wood, or other pieces of nature to decorate. I kidded Corky for years about inviting and co-ercing people to work on community projects, and threatened to make T shirts that said "Corky made me do it." I finally made such a T shirt many years later, and sent it to Corky for Christmas.

Writing for the Paper

I had a wonderful opportunity in Cave Creek, meeting Corey Silva who worked on the local paper. I was fascinated by the process of putting out a local paper, 1988 style. We still pasted up the layout each week. Eventually, Corey became the editor of the paper, and asked me to write and do photography. The paper was named the Cave Creek Sentinel.

Corey was a gutsy, street smart, horsewoman as well as being the mother of twins, and editor of the paper. We had originally met through my community work with the cemetery and the council. She had also known I was a local counselor. We worked together, became better friends, and hatched the idea of a weekly column for the paper. For over a year, I wrote a weekly column called Balance and Choice. The title fit my life, lifestyle, and the struggles of myself and all human beings. In the planned companion to this book, will be those columns. You will note that I also kept the name for this book.

With publication of the first column, I discovered one of my insecurities. It took several weeks of publication for me to stop being self-conscious when I went outside, or downtown on the day the paper came out. I was worried about what people would think of the column. I was also worried that I could not live up to the ideals that I wrote of, and would be judged. This provided me with repeated opportunities for practicing vulnerability and overcoming shame, as well as becoming more humble and freely able to admit that I could not live up to my own ideals. Just another imperfect human!

Corey was a generous and tough friend. Not only did she urge me forward in journalism, but one day she insisted I ride her Arabian horse. I told her I was a very inexperienced rider. Bless her for not laughing at me as I bounced loosely in the saddle. The horse was great, me not so much.

Her background and life experiences made her fearless when it came to covering a news story, or doing what she thought was right. I had lunch with her one day, and on our way back, we saw a house burning. She leaped out, grabbed her camera and ducked under the barriers for pictures. One of the firemen yelled at her to "get the h...out of there". She yelled back, "OK, be right back". She got her pictures, and then came back and got in the car. She stood up to people when others backed down, whether it was a fireman, or publishing a true but unpopular article or idea in the paper. She would not play politics, nor cater to those with money. She had great integrity.

Only in a small town like Cave Creek would I have had the opportunity to do what I did with journalism. It was valuable growth in skills and confidence as well as gaining a friend. Later, as "sound bites" began to come into fashion, I could cope, thanks to Corey, and her training in journalism.

Sinking Deeper Roots into the Community

I put down deep roots in Cave Creek and became an integral part of the community. The town was going through growing pains, and the developers from out of state who wanted golf courses (locally called "Disney Desert") were pitted against those who loved the naturalness, and valued the ecology and an unspoiled environment. It is a familiar story in a small, growing, desirable town with limited resources.

I was asked to do a workshop for the Cave Creek Improvement Association, and also wrote a series of articles for the paper discussing the frictions in community building. I spoke at several meetings, and acted as a mediator for one particular conflict. I was written up in the local business news magazine. I was active and busy; a teacher, counselor, consultant, and community organizer. I loved my small town.

One summer, I coordinated the Summer Education Program for the Community Schools. I helped recruit teachers, set up classes, and do the publicity for the summer program. I enjoyed working with the education team, and was paid for the pleasure and the work.

I know it is easier to be a big fish in a smaller pond, and Cave Creek was a pretty small pond. But I was touching many of the people who lived there, and they were touching me. I had a sense of belonging to the town, much like the sense of belonging to the land and women of Hawaii. It was a lovely experience, feeling like a cog in a smoothly working series of gears -working so closely with so many, and being well known. I felt like an important part of both civic and spiritual growth there, as well as touching individuals. .

My counseling office, although a good idea when I opened it, became too difficult to sustain. It was not that business was failing. I was doing well, seeing as many people as I wanted to. It was that in such a small community, staying out of or handling dual relationships began to be wearing and wearying. A dual relationship is having both a personal and a professional relationship with a client. Counselors are warned about the folly of this. In Cave Creek, those were inevitable. Some of my clients were on committees or boards that I was on. Some were leaders of the community and were in deep trouble with cocaine, or spousal abuse, known only to me. I was occasionally responsible for appointing, or voting on someone to take some responsibility that I could not in good consciousness feel confident in, and yet I could not share any reason why, or even my misgivings. I had to choose loyalties continuously. I could not betray the privileged communication that was part of my work, and sometimes felt I was betraying the town or other people instead by keeping my work confidential.

Many times I was in a position where I had to keep secrets that had no business being kept, as these same people influenced the structure and running of the town, and affected its other citizens. . On the one hand, I was trusted to keep secrets. On the other hand, I was trusted to use my best judgment for the good of a larger group, or of the town. The internal dilemmas and a duplicitous life became not only tiring, but incompatible with my own integrity. I closed the office. I continued to work with a few clients in order to wrap up the work we were doing. I felt sad, but resolved maintaining coherence and integrity without hurting others.

Another Crossroads-Again More Choices

Terry and I went to an Astron meeting in southern Arizona one weekend. I was delighted to see my friends after a long absence. It was good to be back in the TORI /Astron atmosphere. It was Terry's first time around Astron or the people. He was sparked by the current project of some, which was finding a place for a permanent live-in community. A group had discovered a retreat center in Saugerties New York on the Hudson River. Terry had a great deal of experience in intentional communities from his Findhorn Days, and also experience in the mechanical evaluation and functioning of infrastructures. He made a trip to Saugerties, invited by the involved people.

When he came back, he had decided that if there was a community formed, he would go there to live.

I was quite devastated by this as we were getting along well, but also, because my roots in Cave Creek were so strong, and I did not want to leave. I was earning a good living with my classes and counseling, but more than that, my heart was really settled in Cave Creek.

Terry decided to move, and I decided to stay in Cave Creek.

A couple weeks later, he called and wanted me to come to NY. In my eagerness to maintain our relationship and maybe enlarge it, I said yes without asking enough questions. I consider this one of the sharpest turns away from making sure that I listened to my internal self since Hawaii. I put my hopes about having a lasting partnership with Terry, before the reality of the love, acceptance, and partnerships that I already had in Cave Creek. I ambivalently backed out of my commitments there in preparation to move. It was an error in judgment, a lack of listening to my God and my heart. It was also a case of choosing to not ask the questions, thus remaining blind to the reality awaiting me. It is one of the weaknesses in my life that although I have functioned very highly without a partner in my life, I seem to find an unresolved importance in keeping one when I have one, even if the other person is not very appropriate for the job. This is part of my ongoing growth curve. It is useless to ask "what if" about my decision back then, but useful to look back and use it to learn from.

Here is the letter to the Editor which I wrote on my leaving:

This is the only column I have ever written to fill a personal need. You see, I am leaving Cave Creek (at least for now), and I need to say good-bye.

I have deeply involved my work and my heart here. Pulling up roots is difficult though I've been here only two years. My decision has taken weeks to make. Some decisions feel solid and right. This one feels shaky. However, an opportunity appeared and I made the choice to go for it.

Is there ever a way to know the right choices? Are there any right choices, or only choices? These questions echo in my mind.

I woke up early the other morning and felt the pain of leaving. My column will continue appearing in this paper, so we will continue to touch our lives together. Let us wish each other well. And then, if I return some day, we'll be together in person again.

On Loving and Leaving Cave Creek, Arizona

I have seen the desert tortoise and the javelina.
The rattlesnake lies curled at my door.
The hummingbirds punctuate the air,
The saguaro stands tall.
The purple mountains at sunset replace the skies of day.
And my being feasts in the glory.

I "lift up mine eyes unto the hills".
And feel at one with all nature-human and otherwise.
I hear the coyotes claiming food and proclaiming life
Voices in the dark.
As the echoes fade.
I hear the stillness of a desert night at rest.

234

All desert plants live in righteous paranoia.
Spines and sparse leaves guard against drought and foe.
Not so desert people.
They are often wise and unafraid.
Sturdy and gentle.
Their spirits have lived in spaciousness.
Their hearts in generosity and surrender to softness.

I know that's true.
I know these people.
I am alive with their love and nourishment.
And I love and nourish in return.
My life moves on reluctantly now.
Pulled by a different force.

I put a bookmark in and slowly close the pages.
No one knows whether I will return.
Least of all me.
Tomorrows are always an unknown mystery.

However,
I have seen the desert tortoise and the javelina.
The rattlesnake lies curled at my door.
I "lift up mine eyes unto the hills".
And feel at one with all nature –human and otherwise.
I have seen Cave Creek and loved it.
Farewell Cave Creek.
You are ever a part of my heart.
And I am ever grateful.

I did my last exercise class, went to the dentist for a root canal, and got in my car and left for New York.

I got to Saugerties, and quickly discovered that Terry only wanted me there for my skills, not for partnership with him. I was disappointed and hurt. I mourned. I had a VISA bill to pay off, having spent money to move, and so I got a temporary job in a notebook factory. I never pictured working in a factory, but like the home repair work of Hawaii, I learned, enjoyed it, and accomplished what I needed to. I was working on an assembly station, a round rotating table with 4 people working at it. We were putting together 3 ring binders. It was a unionized company, and it took me a bit to get used to the rules – No sitting on the job, no sitting anywhere other than in the lunch room, etc. I did the same task over and over for 8 hours, with my three station mates to talk with. It was the people that made it fun, and learning how binder notebooks were made in various forms was interesting.

When I was hired, I told them I would work for 6 weeks. They said they did not hire temporary help, but hired me anyway. At the end of 6 weeks, they offered me a supervisor's job. I had my VISA paid and was leaving. The reluctance was leaving friends I had made there.

As I worked there, I noticed that this factory did an amazingly good job of recycling waste. This was in 1989, but it was also near the Hudson River where the sloop Clearwater and Pete Seeger had been socially active for years, attempting to clean up the river and enlighten people about the earth. (It was also very near where the famed "Woodstock Festival" had taken place.) I spontaneously decided to write an article for the local newspaper about the factory and its recycling. I had not asked the management for permission, nor told them I was doing it. The editor of the paper liked it, published it and totally surprised and pleased the management.

Our group of four was living in an old resort in a beautiful part of the Catskill Mountains, the site that the Astron people were contemplating buying. It was a lovely and charming setting owned by a family who had run the resort in better years. Now those resorts were out of fashion, and the family was aging and out of time and energy to maintain it. If you ever saw the movie, "Dirty Dancing", the setting was similar. A lodge, staff cabins, a home for the family, tennis courts, and other amenities for guests.

I considered staying, but the budding community did not look viable to me, and the partnership with Terry was over. One night, having been there for about 2 months, I made the decision to leave. I called my brother in Michigan and asked if I could stay with he and his wife temporarily, and got ready to leave. This was betrayal of my heart #2, although it turned out fine after some time.

My heart was calling me back to Cave Creek, but my shame interfered. I foolishly pictured people judging me, both for leaving, and for not being able to keep Terry in my life. Shame is one of life's most powerful blocks, and one of mine. I was listening to my heart, but shame would not let me follow it. Actually, those people in Cave Creek would have welcomed me back, and loved me as they did before, but I lied to myself and feared the judgment and shame.

I didn't even admit to the people in Cave Creek that I was so strongly called back. I made excuses, telling them that it felt right to go to Michigan and sort out my stored belongings, etc. All my justifications had some grain of truth, and I almost convinced my self I was doing the best thing.

However, by going back to Michigan, I traded the gifts waiting for me in Arizona, for a new start. It was true that there were gifts there also – my brother, sister, daughter, and many other relatives. But it took me several years to settle in and claim those gifts. Running away from shame, instead of toward gifts is never a good thing.

My son, in his work as a pastor/counselor, often mentions "seek first the kingdom". Indeed the kingdom had sought me in Hawaii and in Cave Creek. And when I left, I did not seek it back.

There are many other times since then, when I have used the gifts I was given, and been well in touch with, and seeking the kingdom. Life is a continuous journey, and while it may have destinations, or ideas of perfection, they are only reached moment by moment.. I moved on.

I packed the things I had in New York, and went to stay near Kalamazoo, in Plainwell Michigan with my brother, and his wife and son and life began its next chapter.

Beginning of photos from Hawaii and Cave Creek. The brilliant rainbows, deep aquamarine ocean, and the dusty green of the desert do not translate into black and white. So much of what I experienced is not seen or felt here.

Helping out at the Retreat Center

On the beach-again.

Strong, expansive and at peace

Terry

Miles of deserted beach

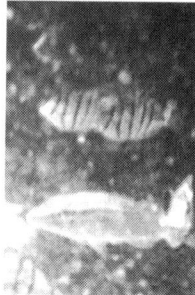
Underwater

The retreat center crew. Back row: Rob, Karen, Terry, Front:Colin, Tony,Collette, Jack.

The bay on Molokai

Glass fishing floats

The kayak trip

Looking back down the Molokai coast

On the move

My 50th Birthday

Our apartment in Honolulu

Friends- Top, Kathy and Reenie,
Bottom:Nalani, Sonny

Terry in the City

Double Rainbow over Honolulu

King Kamehameha Parade. Band
From Kamehameha High School

My Business Card

One of my co-workers at FAIRS

Jim's Wedding

Pam's wedding

Pam, Doug, Jackee, Bob, and Ian with me Cave Creek at Christmas 1985 or 86.

The saguaro cactus in the desert

My van, my home when traveling

Part of the exercise class. Me: lower left

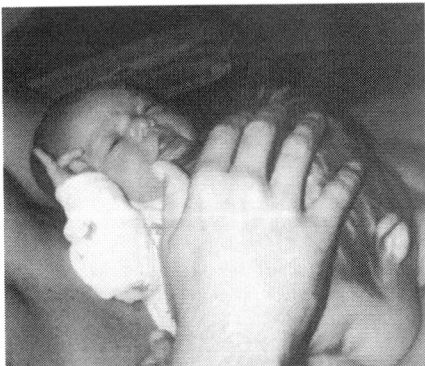

Baby Jillian is born in Texas

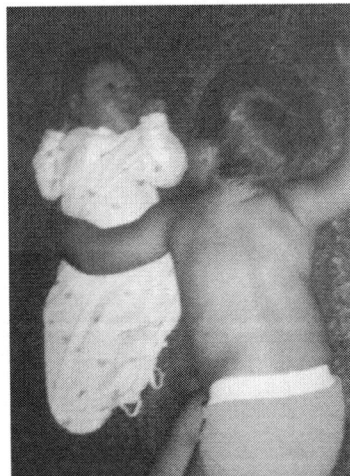

Ian and new sister Jillian

The women of the Full Moon group- me upper R

Friend Corey and her horse

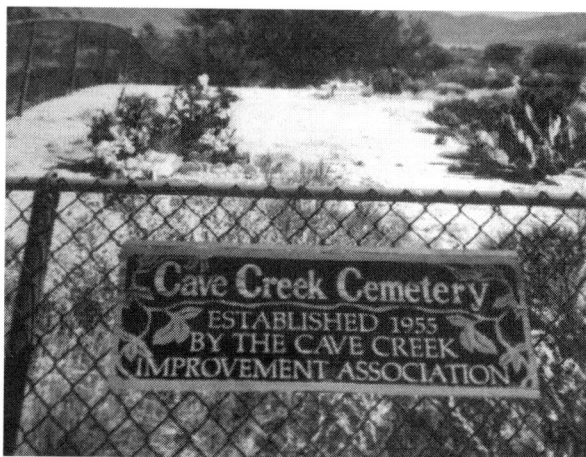

At the entrance to the Cave Creek Cemetery

MacLean Castle at Duart   Me with castle in background
Trip to Scotland and Ireland.

BACK IN MICHIGAN – 1989-2000

Ages 53-64

I was back to doing home repair, this time at my brother's home. We had agreed that I would pay rent by painting some rooms, and doing some other repairs. One fun part of doing that was that my brother, who had done much carpentry and mechanical work, learned some small tricks from me about painting. In between working there, I looked for a job, and attempted to find my way around Plainwell and Kalamazoo. I am grateful to my brother and his family for opening their home and hearts.

Finding a Job

The right job came along quickly. I would be working for Visiting Nurses of Southwest Michigan. Home visits, community resource finding, counseling, and family assessment would be my job. The goal was to maximize family care for patient recovery and functioning. It was similar to Hospice, except in this job, a family member was facing illness or recovery from surgery, rather than imminent death.

There was plenty of freedom and little supervision in this job. It fit my style of independent thinking and functioning. I had to check in at the office each morning, and then was on my own with my car as office, making one visit after another. I had a geographical territory of lakes, hills and rural territory. What better work environment could there? It was good pay, and I loved the work. The flexibility and the absence of city clamor helped me adjust to yet another beginning chapter in life following one of those speed bumps that jostle the body, re-orient the mind, and threaten the heart.

It was interesting that even rural Michigan seemed chopped up and chaotic to me when I first started working here. The natural landscape was cut into sections of small town, farmland, woods, or wetlands. The boundaries were for the most part formed by humans, both past and present, rather than those that nature put there. In Arizona and Hawaii there were large tracts of earth undisturbed for many years, which were not amenable to human remodeling. My mind and soul missed the coherence of that. I had lived so long with large stretches of undisturbed nature that my eyes and body were accustomed to it. I felt fragmented along with the land. I doubt that I could have worked in town at that point, just as I could not go to Los Angeles when I returned from Hawaii.

The transition to the job was not without other glitches. On the first day of work, I got stopped by the police before I got out of range of the office. I still had Arizona license plates on my car. I had gotten my Michigan driver's license, and changed my insurance over, but wanted to wait for my first paycheck to get the license plate.

The officer pulled me over for a burned out tail light, although I suspect the real reason was the out of state license and white vinyl top car, quite obviously not from Michigan. He asked to see my license, and asked why I still had the Arizona plates. I explained, and he commented, "I suppose you don't have any insurance either." Of course I did, and showed him the papers. I fortunately received only a notice to report to court when the tail light was fixed. The word "profiling" had not been invented yet, but I suspect I participated in a subtle form of it.

I worked at Visiting Nurses for several years, first part time, and later full time. Because I was out in the country, I took breaks to swim in the summer, and in winter I fought with the slippery snow covered roads. Some summer days found me doing my endless paper work sitting on a beach in the sun, after eating my lunch in a shady cemetery, or under a tree beside the road.

Living Arrangements and Social Life

I left my brother's home after finding an apartment. I was unaware that the complex was predominantly college students. This meant noisy parties on weekends, and an occasional parking lot fight. It also meant that when school was over for the year, I could nearly refurnish my apartment from the handy dumpster. I got everything from new furniture, to a new bicycle and some clothing that way. It became the nearest re-purposing store, and served my needs well. There was everything but a fresh food department.

Meanwhile, I was finding the beginnings of friendship and social activities. One day, in downtown Kalamazoo, a woman stopped me on the street, asking if I had a brother in town. I said yes, and was flabbergasted when she asked, "Al Bradley?" She noted that I looked exactly like him. Neither my brother nor I had realized how much alike we looked and we both got a chuckle out of that encounter.

I heard about a retreat center and intentional community north of Kalamazoo called "The Farm". I was eager to visit there, given my interest in intentional community. It had been started by some psychology professors from nearby Western Michigan University. I met several people, among them, Roger Byrd who became a lifelong friend. I was his "best person" at his wedding many years later.

Culturally, the interest in intentional communities also continued. My taste was whetted by the TORI communities, and my visit to Findhorn. Others also were looking for Utopian places to share work, play and personal growth as well as emotional and financial support. A national magazine called Communities existed, and there were directories of all the intentional communities in the country. It was tantalizing to me to think about living or visiting such places, seeking the ideal life with others.

That interest seems to have disappeared in our present culture, though some of us, including me, miss the actuality of such places, having firmly put the concept into our minds, memories and daydreams. I especially miss the dynamics of openness, communication, and face to face sharing that I took part in then. I miss a place to share deeply and be heard acceptingly. Because I have moved extensively, I seldom have many close friends around, sometimes envying those who have lived in one place for a long time. The internet keeps me in touch, but not the same kind of touch as sharing real time and real space.

Back to this transition to Kalamazoo; singles groups became another resource for my heart and body to let go, dance and meet people. Dancing again became one of my favorite ways of connecting with others and feeling close camaraderie. I was feeling more at ease.

More About Work

Meanwhile at work, my boss asked me to add the North side of Kalamazoo to my territory. This was the black and poor section of town, invisible and denied by many. I was grateful for my multicultural experience in Hawaii, leaving me open to, and curious about the "other", and although I was short on experience with the poverty and black cultures, I relied on my good intentions and my willingness to learn.

I got a crash course in both black and poverty cultures. One astounding thing was the number of grandparents and great grandparents raising small children. The parents dead, working, or lost in prison or the drug culture left the children behind for the grandparents to raise. There were many single older women, often up to age 90 raising pre-schoolers and beyond. The will and stamina were amazing, but there were some tired people there. Being 80, poor, black, female, and single was a tough job on its own. Adding child care was stressful. Nonetheless, there were some well-loved children in those homes, as well as a shortness of other resources.

Another thing I learned about was the generousity of people who had little, both toward me and toward each other. It was noticeably more present in that culture than in middle class neighborhoods or homes that I visited.

An interesting thing happened when I finally had to buy a different car. I bought a used Chevrolet Cavalier convertible. It was a lovely metallic brown with brown upholstery and top. In that North Side neighborhood, the car was culturally attractive. As I worked there, people learned who the owner was. The neighborhood, as you can guess, was one where fear was often present, and trust slow to come, but I was trusted. And as the car and I were linked in people's minds, I heard that people would say "Hey, I see that social worker was to see you today – saw her car". What happened was that even with top down and a coat, music tapes, or notebooks sitting in the seat, my car and its contents were never disturbed. I cannot say the same for downtown Kalamazoo, where I came out of a store and found someone trying to break into the car. I felt not only safe, but somewhat protected around the North Side.

It was interesting to see that when I eventually bought another car, a more ordinary looking sedan, I was no longer recognized or known there, and needed to take ordinary precautions around the neighborhood until people identified me.

Eventually, Visiting Nurses started a hospice and so I was back doing Hospice work. One of my most poignant memories was a woman whose family was inattentive, conflicted and dysfunctional. The woman simply wanted to die in peace. When I visited her, we talked deeply about her death, and about her family dysfunction, which kept people from paying attention to her when she needed it. She loved to sing, and one of her favorite songs was Que Sera Sera. (Translated, it means, Whatever Will Be, Will Be) The last time I visited, she was actively dying and I began to quietly sing that song. Her eyes cleared, she looked up at me and smiled, and took her last breath, whisperingly singing along with me. It was a spiritual, magical moment, and a peaceful death.

Hoover Street House

In 1991 I left my little apartment, buying a house in an older neighborhood. It was recommended to me as a good investment by one of the men I was dating who sold real estate.

In that neighborhood, built in the 1940's, some homes were fixed up, while others were shabby. Mine was one of the shabby ones, but fundamentally sound. It was a conveniently located neighborhood with close-by grocery stores and other conveniences.

I still had my home repair skills, strength, and motivation, and so in my spare time, I was hanging drywall, painting, and laying carpet. I hired someone to install some windows and do some electrical work as well as to install bi-fold doors which tended to drive me crazy to work on. I had a large window installed in back, and had the house aluminum sided. I had a cozy and comfortable, no longer shabby, two bedroom home, and I moved in Christmas week, forgoing most of the family celebration to heave boxes around.

I was attending People's Church, a Unitarian Church. I made friends there to camp with, potluck with, and just enjoy. The singles group was also there. I eventually became part of the fabric of that church, as I had been part of Cave Creek. I was touched when they approached me about a scholarship to the national UU Leadership conference. I told them that it was possible I might be leaving Kalamazoo, although I had no definite plans. Their answer was to send me anyway, saying that they trusted I would use the skills no matter where I moved.

I accepted their generosity. The conference was held at Beloit College in Wisconsin, a place where my great grandfather had once taught. I was touched to be there, and look up his name as a past professor. The three of us who went from our church, brought back good learning and tools to use to help build the quality of the church. They were prescient in sending me, as I did use much of what I had learned in future places and times.

I was introduced to the Synthesis Center where my friend Roger Byrd did massage. This was a center for holistic practice, founded by Ruth and Vic Eichler. Ruth was a Social Worker who also used Astrology in her work. (Her book is called "Twelve Songs of the Soul") There was a massage therapist, a Sound Therapist and several other counselors. I asked to work there, and began a practice. It was a great place to work. Our staff meetings and retreats were supportive and creative. My practice was full, and I continued to work with the body/mind as a counselor.

My Body, Myself

The combination of counseling, a social life, and physical work on the house again proved to be a nice balance. I began taking a weight lifting class at the YWCA. A few weeks later, I began feeling tired, and finally dropped out of the class. That was uncharacteristic of me, as I had great health and had felt good most of my life, other than that short period described in Hawaii.

I soon visited a doctor, continuing to feel bad, and then saw several doctors for a scary and difficult symptom that I eventually learned to call hyperacusis. This is defined as an increased sensitivity to sound, but what the medical books don't say is that the world sounds like an amplifier turned up to excruciating levels which cannot be turned down. Sudden sounds jarred my nervous system, sounding like explosions. I soon felt tension all the time from the over stimulation. At work, if I walked into a home where the TV was playing while we were trying to talk, I could hardly stand it, becoming nearly physically sick. The doctors tested me for many things, but could not find a reason or a cure. I did not yet know that people often develop hyperacusis when they start losing hearing. I suspect, in hindsight that was part of the cause and also in hindsight, unknown and unsuspected allergies definitely played a part.

The only allergies I had previously experienced were poison ivy, and a one-time case of hives from a shot of gamma globulin. I thought I might have experienced a very small bit of tree pollen allergy while in Arizona.

One week, I got very ill - so ill I barely remember it, and when I recovered, my ear was clogged. After several days, I went to an Otolaryngologist who recommended that he puncture my eardrum to

247

release the fluid behind it. I am always leery of invasive medical procedures, but I knew nothing about this, and assumed he was correct. The procedure did not work and he decided to do it a second time that same day. At one point, he said "Oh shit", and when I asked what was happening, he did not answer. Afterwards, I had a clear fluid draining from my ear for over a week, and called back to tell him. He put a patch on the eardrum, and the drainage stopped, but the ear was still plugged. In later years, it was conjectured that I had a spinal fluid leak from the puncture. It was after that when bouts of real confusion started.

I was sick off and on over the next couple years, and took antibiotics far too often for my comfort. Again, hindsight says it was probably sinus problems, from allergies, at least in part, but the symptoms were not typical. Was it because my sinuses had been so thoroughly soaked in salt water in the ocean in Hawaii? Maybe they were so cleaned out, or so sensitized or irritated that I became sensitive to pollens and other substances. I will never know. The problem was not even diagnosed as sinus or allergies.

During that winter, I discovered that when I was chilled after work, and stood over the registers in my home to get warm, I would start crying. It was not as if I thought of something sad, or felt bad. I just started crying, and within a day or two would get another infection and fever. It became very clear that something in those heating ducts was affecting me.

I got the ducts professionally cleaned, and discovered that there had apparently been a fire in the house at one time. There were ashes, and fire retardant spray throughout the ductwork. And then we discovered that the cold air duct held thousands of cigarette butts where someone had flicked them through the cold air return grates. I already knew that nicotine affected me badly. My mother's smoking made me feel quite bad. Here I was breathing someone else's smoking remains—thousands of them. Clearly the chemicals from the cigarettes must be throughout the heating system.

Even after the ducts were cleaned, I continued getting sick, and began getting confusion, forgetfulness, and disorientation. I forgot where I was going, or how to work the windshield wipers, or even how to start the car sometimes. This was intermittent, but very scary. My coordination was off although I tested just fine. I had always had a finely tuned body, and so what seemed off to me was within normal range in muscle or neurological tests. My health had been so good up until this all started that I was shocked and dismayed by the loss of well-coordinated functioning. I was especially scared by the confusion, although I was still functioning at work.

About this time, a friend, also a social worker called me and had gotten a job in Kalamazoo. She wanted to know if she could share the house, renting my extra room. I said yes and we both thought that would be fun. She was there about a year, seeing what I went through, and getting some minor symptoms herself. Neither of us came up with a good theory or cause.

I explored all areas of my life. I went to a therapist, and to some of my intentional community meetings for help with exploring spiritual and emotional issues, I went to a physician, and to a holistic physician. I was using prayer and meditation, massage and acupuncture- mostly to no avail.

At one point, I told my daughter that I was getting dementia so badly that I might need assisted living. When I did Yoga, or other exercises or movements that required positional change, I found that with the wrong movement, I felt fluid movement in the left side of my head (the side of the eardrum puncturing), and then became confused for a day or two. That also happened if I cried. My emotions became volatile for no known reason. Later I learned that allergies can affect all systems of the body, emotional and cognitive, as well as the immune system and the usual allergy symptoms.

People who knew me well, or had known me before took me seriously. That was helpful, as many doctors thought I was simply having mental or emotional problems. I learned that crying while describing my symptoms and fears to physicians, only raised suspicions of emotional instability, or mental illness. I began to dispassionately describe my symptoms instead.

I was finally convinced that allergies were involved. But allergy testing showed only grass and lake algae, with a few molds thrown in. Since my house didn't contain either grass or lake algae, I thought mold might be the culprit, but there was no visible sign of it in the house. I had a cat, but did not react to him, either in person, or according to the allergy tests.

I suspect my house may have had some sort of mold toxin in it, although, as I said, I did not find molds even when tearing apart walls to remodel. I bought HEPA filters, and good furnace filters, and had a filter on my cold air return as well. I kept my bedroom closed off from the rest of the house, and there was no heat in there. I gave away my lovely cat.

I had backed myself into living a life which seemed more and more constricted and strange to me and to others. This did not show at work, because of the flexibility and freedom I had to choose when to be around the office. I could also rest or nap during the day as I needed to.

No doctor had suggested allergies, other than the conventional allergy tests and results. I was tested for many other things - sleep apnea, venereal diseases, and neuropsych testing, complete with MRI and EEG and a large battery of psych tests. I eventually went to Mayo Clinic, but that was several years later, and it did not provide definitive answers either, although ruling out many things.

I wanted to find some way to live a normal life. And to do that, it seemed I had to find some sort of cause, or something that would help.

In the midst of the spiritual work, here is what I wrote and carried in my wallet for over 10 years: It became a companion, a template for the future, and a prayer for me.

"Whoever I am, there is a new me being born, and I need to hold her in my heart, and carry her with me everywhere. I cannot leave her home, hide her, or disown her, for she is the incarnation of yet a higher self. She is the God in me coming to the surface.

She is the one who will not be quelled, who will rage in my head until I surrender to her birth. I must make her the love of my life and the light of the world.

May I consecrate every breath to the wholeness of this new me, and the holiness of her birth. May she come in glory, in peace, and in love. Amen"

One day a group of friends was helping another friend move. I put one of his big plants in my car as well as a bunch of other stuff. We got on the road, and I became more and more confused and disoriented. I signaled the car behind me, another of the helpers, and we stopped. I took a guess that it might be the plant in my car with soil mold. (By this time I was aware of possible allergies as causative) The other person put the plant in their car, and we went on. Within a few minutes, my confusion went away.

I was going to the TORI community during this time, and we met every other week at my house for potluck and community meeting. Using TORI principles, we supported each other to talk openly of our lives. I felt supported in that group, and was able to talk about the very confusing things that were happening to me. Some people had known me before over a period of many years. They did not think I was crazy, they believed what I said, and were empathetic, and caring. It was the place I could cry, or scream, or laugh at myself, and they were there with me. This was a huge help. There was also a professional psychologist in the group whom I had known for many years, and he was the one who encouraged me to get the neuropsych evaluation. At first I resisted, thinking he thought I was having mental problems, but he later educated me to what all the tests might do.

Meanwhile, Back at Work

Meanwhile, back at work, there were things happening that I was not aware of. I had not worked in corporate situations much, and so was not experienced with corporate dynamics, or behind the scenes decisions.

After another excellent review from my boss, I left on a vacation. When I returned, my boss called me in and for two hours told me how inadequate my work was and that I was being put on notice. I was supposed to report to him every Monday so we could plan my work, and then report to him each day before work. At the end of his talk, I was left wondering how to reconcile excellent reviews with the terrible things I had just heard. I had always had good communication with my boss, which made it even more puzzling. I was scared and perplexed. And of course felt shame about the possibility of not being good enough.

In Social Work, there is always more that can be done, and so there are always ways to find fault with what is not being done, especially in information and referral services. I thought I was trusted, liked, and doing a good job. And on that day, all that seemed to have changed.

After some thought and agony, I decided that I did not want the job or the money badly enough to be treated as incompetent when I knew I was not. I just did my job as usual, not reporting to the boss each day or week. I was naïve about corporate ways, and had no idea at this point, things had changed, but it was not about me.

My boss came to me after a week or two and confronted me. I told him (with lots of pasted-on bravado) that I was doing my job, and he needed to do whatever was needed. A few weeks later, he reluctantly fired me, after pleading with me to please report to him. After he fired me, he even went to his boss and asked for time for me to terminate with my clients, and we set a date of termination together. He was clearly under orders that he disagreed with, but whatever was happening, I was following the path that seemed to have the most integrity for me.

Once past my brave speech, and up against the last day of work, I was shaky and scared. I had never been fired before, and took it personally. And when he actually walked me out the door, I had all I could do not to cry, though to his credit, he made no scene of it, and was supportive of me on the way out of the building. It looked as if we were talking over our work.

One of the clients I had been seeing was dying of Lou Gehrig's disease. She was a Christian Scientist by faith. Although the other members of the Visiting Nurses team were upset that she and her family were "in denial", only reading scripture to her and believing in healing, I felt that it kept her on an even keel, and was a lifelong faith journey for her. As I was being let go from work, this client's family sensed what was happening, although I did not mention it. They gave me a page full of written sayings and encouragement in the Christian Science manner. I still have the paper, and it is still a gift to me. I attended her funeral a few weeks after I left work, and felt it a great blessing to have known her.

Once home with no work, I began to doubt myself, and that sense of shame came to visit often. I did not want people to know I had been fired and put on a strong brave face. My body and emotions were stressed anyway from my physical struggles, and one night I woke in the middle of the night with a panic attack. I didn't know that's what it was, but I woke up gasping for breath, crying, and frightened.

A man from TORI lived with me at that time, and he helped me identify what was happening. I had never seen a panic attack before, much less had one. I had several more in the following weeks. They were always in the middle of the night, when I awoke with my belly jumping up and down uncontrollably and was finally able to draw a breath and start crying. It was alarming, and especially so because I did not know that panic attacks almost always felt alarming.

I had met a man named Mark Rycheck at TORI, and we were dating occasionally. He was going on vacation, and I asked if I could stay at his house for that week, to see if getting out of my house made any difference. I do not recall any noticeable difference, but I do recall crying most of the week, without any sense of what I was crying about. I was not feeling sad or scared, and still the tears flowed.

My friend Roger Byrd came to visit, and accompanied me to a doctor appointment. It was at that appointment that the doctor prescribed Klonopin for me, which is a benzodiazepine, related to Xanax., an anti-anxiety medicine. I didn't feel anxious, but decided to trust his judgment and try it.

I took half a pill on the way home, and about 10-15 minutes later, I said to Roger "Can we stop at McDonalds? I'm hungry" This was the first time I had been hungry in a couple of weeks. I had only eaten because I knew I needed to. I ate, I stopped crying, and it was as if everything was fine. It was like a miracle.

I took another half pill that night before bed, and that seemed to reset my whole nervous system. The physical symptoms were not gone, but the crying was. I felt much more "normal". I only occasionally took a half pill in the future and had no more panic attacks.

Meanwhile, I was without a job or income. I was also naïve about the unemployment compensation system, and ended up without any income. Later I learned that after I was fired, several people at the agency had been fired. They were all people who had been employed longer, and thus were making higher wages. I was able to stop taking it as a personal thing. They were smart enough to replace me with a lady about my age, so I could not sue for age discrimination, but she lasted less than a month, saying she could not keep up with the work.

My New Job – A Dream Come True

Within a few months, I saw an ad in the paper that was such a perfect job description for my background and passions, that I could hardly believe it. Kalamazoo Center for Medical Studies was looking for a Social Worker to be on the faculty to teach Behavior Science to the Family Practice Residents. I would be employed by Michigan State University as a faculty member. I would be teaching physicians how to interact with patients in an effective way, and even how to handle their own stress.

This position is a requirement for FP Residency programs, and I could combine my Social Work and medical/hospital experience from my medical technology days. I had always wanted to teach doctors about the human side of medicine. I could hardly wait to get my resume revised and sent. After several weeks of waiting, I was hired, and so excited about the hopes and plans for this job.

As I have noted before, new situations are not without glitches. I found I had two bosses, and it was not clear who was responsible for what. There was my office mate, a psychiatrist who was there only two days a week. And then there was the head of the residency program. What I did not yet realize was that each person expected the other to orient me, show me around, and let me know what they expected.

Since each thought the other would, I ended up totally on my own. No one gave me a tour of the building, or even showed me where the bathrooms were. I was not told anything about the schedule or the program. It took me several weeks to find out that there was a staff meeting every week, and that I was expected to be there. There were also resident conferences which I didn't find out about for a matter of months. No one ever questioned why I was not at the meetings. I suppose, each thought the other was speaking with me. Consequently, I felt and looked like I was on the outside for at least my first 6 months. I don't know what they thought. When I got employee reviews, they were only a formality, and seldom were specific issues discussed, although the reviews were positive.

An ongoing pivotal issue in that program had been that of videotaping the residents. I was told that it was my job, and was impossible because the residents were resistant. Within a few weeks I was taping, with little or no resistance from anyone. There was some self-consciousness on the part of the residents, but that was to be expected. I was able to help that by giving them a choice of whether they wanted to know they were to be taped. Taping involved a remote camera, and permission of the patient. Reviewing the tapes with the residents was somewhat difficult because of their busy schedules. I reviewed all tapes, and those that had teaching moments in them, were the first to be reviewed with the residents and faculty. It became an ordinary and useful part of the program. I mentally gave myself kudos.

I loved the idea of the job, although the reality was somewhat flawed. Besides the confusion about my tasks and schedules, I was the only woman, and the only non-physician on the faculty. At that time, medicine was still a traditionally male dominated field, and though we had a few women residents, it was a lonely position in some ways. We eventually got a woman physician as part of the faculty, and that restored some balance. There were subtle ways of exclusion, given that both faculty and male residents formed an old or young guys club almost without question. Also, in most Family Practice Residency Programs, the Behavior Scientist was low person on the totem pole, and though there were no overt signs of this, there were more subtle ones. Just being a non-physician meant some differences which were not at all personal.

My boss (the psychiatrist), took me to my first meeting of the Behavior Science Association of Michigan. This was a nationwide organization of all the Behavior Science Faculty, with our chapter being all those from Michigan. It was a fertile and fun organization, meeting once a month, for presentations and discussion. It was a nourishing mix of camaraderie, support, and learning, lots of laughter and fun. We shared ideas for our jobs, and commiserated about the commonalities of the position that made it difficult. I looked forward to it.

I also especially enjoyed participating in a national and even international on-line list-serve for faculty and physicians in Family Medicine. I often write more easily than I talk, and it was a privilege to think through issues with such a fun and intelligent group.

I gave several presentations at the weekly resident's meeting, and got good feedback and enjoyed doing it.

Western Michigan University was nearby, and I received permission to take on a social work intern. That would provide a positive for the clinic, the university and the reputation of the Family Practice Residency program. It turned out to be probably not a good placement, as there was not enough for her to do or learn. She was used extensively to help patients and so got some good practice, but it was difficult to use her for the program itself.

While working there, I decided to go to Mayo Clinic for those mysterious symptoms that continued to plague me. One recent symptom came as I walked with friends at noon hour. I was wearing comfortable shoes, but when I had walked, I would get huge blood blisters on the bottom of my forefoot.

Mark went with me to Mayo. We went without an appointment, and were there a week. I was seen within two days, and the rest of the time was testing and appointments I was highly impressed with their thoroughness and organization, as well as the caring attitude. The results of my tests were inconclusive. That was disappointing, but I felt it had been a worthwhile time, as so many things were discussed, theorized and ruled out. There were some suggestions for symptom relief also.

I was involved in a Weight Watchers group at work, and continued to eat well and exercise at Mayo. The week was freezing cold and windy in Rochester, with wind chill about 10 below, but we bundled up and went for walks, and enjoyed finding our way around. I would not want to spend every winter there!

After 4 years on the job at KCMS, I left my "dream job". I was then 60, and eligible for Social Security under Clark's account. I had sold my house, and gotten an apartment out in Mattawan, a few miles from town. I loved being back out in the country, and was hoping that the country and a fairly new building to live in might help any symptoms that were caused by allergies. Getting out of work and driving into the country felt like a daily vacation. After work, I walked or biked, picking elderberries or grapes in season. I hoped to travel and maybe do another road trip across the country.

In fact, I did do an 8000 mile road trip, similar to the ones I had done when crossing the country after coming back from Hawaii. I had a small station wagon, put a mattress in the back, fixed up curtains, and for the fun of it, challenged myself to go without paying for a place to stay for the whole trip. Here is what I wrote on my return:

Ten years after moving back to Michigan, two months before my 63rd. Birthday, and 6 months before the millennium start, I set out for a month of vacation.

I took my tent, put a bed in my station wagon, took a stove, a few (very few) clothes, and proceeded to drive 8000 miles through 16 states and visit 8 different households of friends and family. That meant that on the days I drove, I was driving at least 500 miles.

I have already mentioned that this was, in some unconscious sense, a scavenger hunt for jig-saw puzzle pieces. The conscious sense of it was a process of flow and exploration mixed with times of celebration, some unease, and much sense of belonging. There were many periods of rest.

I wondered out loud about the results of this journey as I sat comfortably in a friend's house in Arizona. We talked of life and travels. I realized how much I was taking for granted the sense of being at home.

I prayed with my son and felt closer to him, closer to God and closer to myself. Closer felt good.....in all dimensions. We celebrated.

I visited two towns where I attended first grade back when my dad was in the armed services, and I was a so called, "army brat". The kinesthetic sense of climbing the hill to the school, or finding the crack in the rocks where my brother and I used to play was a delight, and I felt the carefree 6 year old spirit inside my considerably older body. This was also the trip of that incident of remembering my dog almost drowning and my dad saving him.

My car collided with a beautiful male pheasant just taking off into flight. I cried. At another point, I saw an obviously lost and scraggly little dog walking down the middle of the country road. Four miles later I turned the car around, determined to pick him up and keep him, though having little idea of how to work that out in a very full car with a week yet on the road. He wasn't there. I mourned for him and for me.

I played and talked with my other son and his family. My son's health is deteriorating, and it was very difficult to see, and to imagine what it might be like living inside his body and his life. I mourned

I watched sunsets over the Pacific, blizzards in the mountains, and rain in the rain forests of the Olympic peninsula. I picked California poppies and creosote bush, sage and other unknown flowers to surround myself with beauty and aroma.

I listened to books on tape, took pictures of fullness and emptiness, and recorded the sounds of the birds in the desert and the waves on the beach. I recorded in my mind the sounds of my grandchildren laughing and playing. And felt their bodies next to mine as we hugged or played.

I met people in person that I had only known in cyber-space, and they became three dimensional friends with movements and voices.

I knit my life together, people and place wise, covering sites, sights, and people that I had known some time during my life

The trip was wonderful. Each day I picked up the kaleidoscope of my life and looked though it and saw a marvelous pattern.

When I got back to Michigan, I finished up the several months at my job, and then retired.

As preface to the next part, I want to explain: By this time, I had known Mark several years- probably 4 or 5. We had a rocky history. We alternated seeing each other for periods of time and breaking up.....again. We both dated others. His history of chronic and ongoing clinical depression and the medicines he took, and then tried to stop made him erratic and moody. It was definitely not love at first sight, and the relationship remained unstable. What happened next was unexpected and I was again faced with familiar choices, balancing past present and future, and choosing which fork to take. But let me not get too far ahead.

Nova Scotia and then Oklahoma.

In one of our off times, Mark decided to move to Oklahoma where he had raised his family. His house in Michigan sold more quickly than expected, and as I was about to set off on yet another road trip to Nova Scotia. I asked him if he wanted to travel with me. Two people often travel more inexpensively than one, as well as the added gift of companionship along the way. We were not dating at the time, but since he was in a fairly stable period, it seemed do-able.

256

He agreed to go if we could go to Prince Edward Island where his ancestors had been to explore family history. I was agreeable. We took off on a fun and lovely month long trip to Nova Scotia and PEI . We sort of fell in love on that trip to the surprise of both of us. And we have been together ever since, albeit with the normal (for us) instability, sometimes severe.

I must say, that I remember that trip as the coldest camping trip I have ever been on. It was the middle of October, and nearly all parks and campgrounds were closed for the season. We found other places to camp, including an attempt in the middle of a blizzard in the Prince Edward Island National Park. The storm was the result of the tail end of Hurricane Irene (1999).

Actually, the wind and snow were blowing so hard that we could not keep the tent up. There was an open picnic shelter, and we moved the tent in there, but it simply blew down, skittering across the ground in the snow. We left, not knowing where to stay, and I remember saying "Well, worst possible case, we will sleep in the car tonight, sitting up". We drove, and came across some closed tourist cabins with a phone number. We called, and the woman was motherly and empathetic. "Oh you poor dears". She came over and we ended up in a cozy heated cabin. The next morning, we woke up to the snow all melted and sunshine outside. It was surreal after the night before.

We stayed in more unconventional places too. We were both young enough to feel more rugged and resilient. We stayed in closed and deserted camp grounds with permission of the authorities. We also stayed in a few people's yards – with permission. In one place, there was a miniature light house which called attention to a store with a home attached. The people first said they did not know of any place we could stay, but suddenly said there was a little room up in the light house. Although they did not ask for any money, they gladly accepted our $10, and we had a shelter for the night in a round, roughly finished room.

Another very cold night, we were in a park which had a few enclosed picnic shelters with tables inside. The inside reminded me of the camp dining rooms I had experienced in my camp days We fixed our dinner inside with our camp stove, and with the cold and wind, decided to put our sleeping bags on the picnic tables for the night. We were just getting to sleep when there were car lights outside. I looked out and saw someone with a flashlight come and look in our car and in the windows, and then drive away. We assumed it was a local patrol, or police who saw our license plate from the US and took pity on us in the cold, leaving us alone to sleep more warmly. We were thankful for the kindness.

One night, cozy and warm in our tent, morning broke and Mark picked up his water bottle to take some morning medication. The water crackled and froze solid in his hand, having been super cooled in the tent overnight. Yes, it was that cold!

Probably the strangest place we slept was in Maine. We asked about campgrounds and there were none nearby. The man we asked was actually building a campground on his property and had the bathroom building constructed, and the plumbing roughed in. He first said he could not accommodate us, as there were no facilities, but then offered to let us sleep in the roughed in building. He brought a piece of plywood to put our sleeping bags on, and set up an infrared light in the room. We piled on all our blankets and slept warmly between two would-be toilet stalls. Remembering this trip, you might guess rightly, that I remember it for its interest, its beauty and the cold!

We got smarter during the last part of the trip, and started staying more often in hostels. We were also in a part of the country where there were more of them.

One, near Wentworth Nova Scotia, was run by a young man with a beautiful and most unusual dog named Spirit. Spirit appeared to be maybe a cross between a Great Dane and a Lab. He was probably the most "human" dog I have ever met, but without forsaking his "dog-ness". He listened when people spoke, and seemed to understand and respond to much of what was said. His owner spoke to him in sentences, and Spirit responded by going and doing whatever was asked. He knew where his limits were inside the hostel. The owner told us he would not come in our room, and indeed, he sat outside the door, even when invited in – wanting to interact, but not crossing the threshold. He was well mannered and playful, and seemed to inhabit the universe with seriousness, intelligence, joy and centeredness, full in spirit – true to his name.

"A Place To Stay Inn", was the name of a hostel at Souris PEI. I remember little about the hostel itself. What I remember was going to the nearby library the next morning to check email, and learning that one of my best women friends, Pat Chalmers, had died suddenly the night before. It was not entirely unexpected, as she had severe brittle diabetes which had affected many of her organs including her heart. But I burst into tears in the library, and went over and shared my grief with one of the employees. Pat was only about 55 years old. The librarian was most empathetic. When I left the library, I saw a large church next door. The door was open, and I went in, sat in the pews, and cried and prayed. (Later I brought Mark back to see the paintings on the ceiling of that church. I had never seen a painting of the Sacred Heart before, and he was able to tell me what it was. It was a lovely old church. I do not even know the denomination. Anglican?

I went back to the hostel, still tearful. The woman who ran the hostel sat me down and brought me tea, "white with cream". She patted me on the back and told me to cry as long as I wanted. She

checked on me every few minutes, bringing me more tea as needed..
She insisted that I rest until I was cried out, in spite of us being there past check out time. It was a nourishing experience, akin to having a mom or an old friend there with me in my grief. I was touched.

Several weeks later, on our way back to Michigan, we went to Toronto, Ontario to attend a memorial service for Pat with the remains of the Toronto TORI community. She had been very active, and a favorite in the community. It was a fitting memorial for one who had been so alive and given so much. A year later, I visited her longtime partner in California, and was honored to have him ask me to clean out her closets and help him get rid of her things. He gave me some of her earrings, and a shirt of hers which I loved. In a way, it was a closure for both of us.

Just a few months before her death, Pat had spent a week with me in Hawaii. That time was nourishing for us both. Her diabetes gave her some trouble when she first arrived to join me there, and we thought she might have to go to the hospital. However, she felt better in a day or two, and we started out to see Kauai. It soon became clear that Pat was too unsteady to make it fun for either of us. She was too likely to fall, and got very tired. I, with hesitation, suggested a wheel chair. I told her we could use the chair to get her from place to place and save her energy for seeing the things she wanted to.

Although resistant at first, she saw the rationale of the plan and agreed. What a good decision that was! We were both able to do more, see more things, and get around better without worry. We even got her to the beach and got her legs in the surf. She was thrilled!

The place we were staying, (taking care of the house and the cats for my friends), was not near the road, and had a narrow and stony path to the door. Both Pat and I were concerned about her being able to get there without falling. At the beginning of the week, it was almost impossible for her, and we planned about 20 minutes to get from the door to the car, with plenty of rests and stops along the path. The wheelchair would not work in the rough ground. By the end of the week, she was so much stronger, she felt like a miracle had happened. She called me after she got home and was beaming about how much stronger she had become.

I was so grateful, those months later after her death that I had that time with her, and that she had that time in Hawaii.

Continuing the saga of the Nova Scotia trip: One day I looked at the map and said, "See this place way out here on the end of this peninsula? Let's see if we can go stay there." We were delighted to find that there was a hostel there, and we made reservations for Brier Island, on the end of Digby Neck. This part of Nova Scotia is known for its extreme tides. It was not the place on the map that said "Highest Tides", but we were assured that the tides there were about 25 feet. I was looking forward to seeing another out of the way and unusual place.

As we were on our way, we passed a rocky beach. I have difficulty passing beaches with stones on them without stopping to find the prettiest ones, so we decided to stop, and then realized the tide was receding at a visible rate. We found that we could hardly keep up with the receding water as we walked. It emptied the bay ahead of us at a fast pace. Neither of us had ever seen anything like this.

Had we been more educated, or from some other place in the world, we might have been worried about a tsunami. A tsunami is preceded by receding water which goes out further than the usual tide, and then comes in inundating the land. Luckily, nature was for us rather than against us this time. It was not a tsunami, but rather one of the famous tides of the Bay of Fundy. The tides there vary as much as 53 feet depending on the area of the bay. They are the largest tides in the world. In this shallow bay, they simply receded out quickly. Other places, they were said to recede down sharp cliffs and make rivers run backwards. We continued walking, and soon could not see the water in front of us, nor could we see what had been shore in back of us. We stood there on a giant gravel field which stretched forever. It was a unique experience. Some of the stones we found have been polished and sit in our memory bowl of polished stones in our living room.

We continued on to Brier Island on a schedule. There were two ferries to catch, timed so one could get from one to the other. They only ran twice a day. When we got there, we found the hostel, and were delighted to learn that it was billed as Nova Scotia's foremost eco-tourism destination. Brier Island is known for its birds, and for its relatively undisturbed natural setting. We were not avid birders, though both of us were interested, but we loved the unspoiled and simple lifestyle set into such a lovely natural setting.

We had planned to stay just one night, but ended up staying three or four. It was a charming, restful place. The young man in charge of the hostel surprised us with a dinner invitation from his parents, who lived a mile or so away.

They were approximately our age, and had been military people, used to making friends easily and on the spur of the moment. We enjoyed both the food and the company. They probably had few visitors from off the island and especially ones their age. We seldom saw people our age camping, especially that time of year, when few people were camping anyway. It was a mutually enjoyable time with this couple.

In addition, they acted as consultants on seeing the island, telling us where to go and what to see. The next day, we followed their advice, driving out to one of the lighthouses, and then enjoyed wandering the island and taking pictures.

From our window, we could see several boats at dock. Those famous tides displayed in front of us twice a day. When the tides were in, the boats were even with the docks. When the tide went out, they were about 20 feet below the docks sitting on the bottom of the bay. There were ladders to get up and down if people needed to do so. It was quite amazing. I suppose if one lived there, it might be more ordinary feeling, but we were like little kids, seeing it for the first time.

Leaving Brier Island, we headed for the south shore of Nova Scotia and Peggy's Cove. That is probably the most famous destination in Nova Scotia. We also visited a small town called Prospect, next to Peggy's Cove, and I was smitten. I wanted to be sure and go back there some time again. It has not happened and probably won't. I seem to collect places I want to go back to, but never get there. I continue to be grateful for all the places I have seen even once!

We were lucky enough to be at Peggy's Cove during full moon, and our pictures of the lighthouse, with the moon shining over it, could not be more picturesque. There are huge rocks on shore, worn by the waves. There is a wall showing figures of many people, carved from stone in town. I forgot to write down notes on the purpose or the artist, but the visual memory is tucked away.

Halifax, the capital of Nova Scotia, was a brief visit for us. We tend to stay away from cities. We then spent more time in Lunenburg, the home of many shipbuilding companies, and the docking place of the ship, Bluenose. The Bluenose has been an important symbol of Nova Scotia. It was, when first built, a fishing and then a racing boat. The original was built in 1921, eventually sank, and a replica was built in 1963.

We then drove around Cape Breton, which is a largish peninsula on the end of Nova Scotia. It is rural, with a perimeter road, similar to Highway 1 in California, but much more rural, and less dramatic. The fall colors were spectacular, and the population sparse compared to other parts of Nova Scotia.

I want to say more about PEI, and Mark's ancestor research. You heard about the snow storm, but probably Mark would say that the height of seeing PEI for him was researching his family. He had a cousin who had started the research, so he went to the town records, and then to the churches where his family on his mother's side was indicated to have been. He found some records and some gravestones. We stopped in a home where some Murphy's lived (one of his mother's family names) and they indicated remembering someone talk about his mother, and possibly corresponding with her. We spent an hour with them, conversing and graciously eating cookies and drinking tea. We then circled part of the island, and

261

debated about stopping in the Anne of Green Gables Center, which is well known. Neither of us had read the book, and so we did not stop.

It was a good trip. There was much we missed and much we saw. The hostels are an economical and fun way to stay, or were then.

What you cannot see in the pictures are the colors of Nova Scotia. There is even a common paint here in the USA called Nova Scotia Blue. The boats, houses and other buildings are lovely shades of turquoise, deep bright blue, green, yellow, and red. That alone makes it a lovely place to visit. It never seems gaudy, but always bright, solid and alive.

When we returned to Michigan, Mark started packing to go to Oklahoma. Our bond was stronger but I was reluctant to go with him because of the rocky history, and my contented life in Michigan. I assisted him with sorting and packing and then decided to go see my grandkids in Texas for Thanksgiving. I was still considering moving with him, knowing that Oklahoma would put me closer to my kids in Colorado and Texas, but would take me away from Pam and her family here in Michigan as well as other family.

Mark left for Oklahoma close to the time I left for Texas. I got to Texas, and within a few days, my daughter in law's younger brother died suddenly and totally unexpectedly in New Mexico. It was such a shock for her and her family. I stayed around long enough to help them pack up the children, and then to clean up after they left, and decided to go to Oklahoma for Thanksgiving. It was a different Thanksgiving than I had visualized with my grandkids, but seemed like the next best option. I called, and Mark had no plans, so I drove to Bartlesville Oklahoma to meet him.

Mark was staying with a longtime friend, who also welcomed me into her home. We had nowhere to go for the holiday, so decided to help at the American Legion where there was a dinner for the homeless and poor. I then left for Michigan, having decided to move with him. I was going home to pack.

I look back now on that decision and think maybe it was another mistake - wanting to put relationship before the rest of my life, but we have now been together 14 years, and have known each other almost 20. It has not been an easy time, but we have learned and grown. I have been forced to strengthen boundaries and maintain connection by my decision to stay together. We have also had lots of fun together. There were many shorter camping trips together while in Michigan, and many walks along the shores of the Great Lakes. This is one of those times that a look back makes me philosophical; saying that while it might have been a poor decision, life is good anyway. I am fortunate that I seldom spend time and energy beating on myself for my past errors or weaknesses. I move onward.

I took my time packing up my things, and storing the rest of them at my daughter's house. Meanwhile, Mark rented a small house in town in Bartlesville, and when I got there, he was already moved in and I moved in with him. The year was 2000.

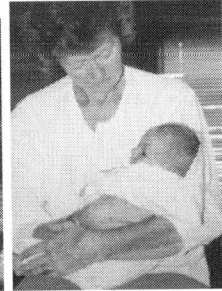

The before and after pictures of my home in Kalamazoo. ...   ..A visit to Calif. –Emily

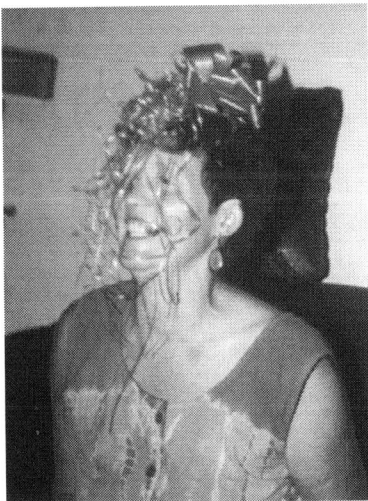

Silly on my 60th Birthday

TORI Community, Kalamazoo

Synthesis Center – me second from left

Roger Byrd and I – I am "best Person" in his wedding and we are getting ready.

Fun in the Michigan winter snow

Summer pose

Pat Chalmers and I

Pat in Hawaii with me.

Mark and I when we first met

Making friends with a statue –
In Kansas for Mark's son's wedding.

Bridge from New Brunswick to Prince
Edward Island to begin our Nova Scotia Trip.

Trying to keep warm in NS

Peggys Cove-full moon

Boathouse at low tide

The huge rocks around Peggy's Cove vicinity in Nova Scotia

Brier Island –Mark doing
Tai Chi way over on the left.

Packing my car and trailer for OK

OKLAHOMA-2001-2006

Age 65-70

It was an unfamiliar Oklahoma that I landed in, even though I had lived there many years before. It was a different area, a different culture, a different time, and of course a very different me. Bartlesville itself had a very familiar feel. There was that Midland and Kalamazoo feel of a company town, a highly educated and mobile population, an invisible poor, and some division between the company people and the rest of the people in town. There was also a constant coming and going of people transferring in and out of the town from various branches of the company, to stay a week or a while. There was the common attitude of paternalism from the company toward the town, which worked for good, but had its downsides.

Mark had worked for Phillips, which gave him some "in" with the company people, and he knew many retirees who had stayed in town. He also knew many people from his old church. I knew no one in town but him.

We were trying out our "new and improved" relationship, born on the Nova Scotia trip and largely untested, I suppose it would be nice to say we lived happily ever after, but that would not be true. We had and have our growing pains. We had a rocky start in Oklahoma. What I will say is that I nearly came back to Michigan. However, you will see that my time in Oklahoma was very satisfactory in so many ways.

We began attending that liberal Catholic Church, where Mark had raised his family. I had never attended a Catholic Church regularly, and probably would not have attended most Roman Catholic churches. The same priest, Fr. Bill Skeehan, had been there for 22 years. He was a man who had entered the priesthood after a career as a graphic designer, and was a product of the Vatican II time in the culture. There was no question that I was welcome, at the communion table, and in the church. As I had done at People's Church, I was able to find a niche, some leadership tasks, and some friends. I was delighted with the acceptance and the chance to serve, and grateful to those who gave it. They had known Mark when his family was intact, and their church was generally anti-divorce, so I had not been sure how they would respond to us.

I want to branch off here, and speak briefly of my spiritual history.

I refer to myself as a non-denominational Christian. I can comfortably and with integrity call myself Christian, but many other practices, principles and prayer forms have appealed to me through the years. I have been attracted to much in Buddhism. And the

Islam or Muslim practice of an automatic call to prayer 5 times a day is something I could easily embrace. I like the idea of being reminded to turn to God at given times, and have set up my own system of daily reminders at various times in my life. But I suspect that a universal community call to prayer might produce a powerful experience of a dedicated sacred unity and faith.

Whatever or whoever brings me closer to God, or furthers my following in the action footsteps of Jesus, and deeper into myself, resulting in love, peace, freedom, relationship, and awareness I attempt to incorporate as part of my "church". I am turned off by the wasted time and energy of comparing denominations and labeling them right or wrong, better or worse.

As you previously read, my grandmother read me bible stories on her lap, complete with color illustrations. Jesus became my role model and hero. Grandma's shine-in-the-dark bookmarks then helped me to see that Jesus wanted to be inside me, and I should open the door to him. The picture on them was of Him knocking on a doorway to a person's heart. As I grew up, I was attracted to people and places that seemed to give off the flavor/aura/likeness of Jesus. Since God was his father, God became my father too. He protected, held me, listened to my prayers, and gave me a child's faith. Of course sometimes I prayed to my dog, Timmy and cried in his fur, and that helped too.

As I grew up, and then older, I found celebration, ritual, prayer, support, love and a broad understanding of life and God in many ways and places. Although we attended church seldom in my childhood, I have, for periods of time, as an adult, attended Presbyterian (remember the Sunday School, parking meter incident?), Methodist, Unitarian, Unity, Episcopal, Non-denominational, and Catholic churches. I also have turned to nature for holiness. You have read about the time our family spent at Holy Family Episcopal Church, one of my attempts to have my children in a place where they could feel what it was like to follow Jesus example. I now attend a United Church of Christ. I understand that because we humans run our churches, and then get confused about whether we are in charge or He is. All churches will have flaws. So do all corporations, families, and non-profit organizations. However, I look for places and people, who care, are inclusive, have a sense of soul and spirit, do good works, and continue to turn to God for next steps. I want places that accept me, can teach me more, and change my life, and have values compatible with those of Christ, but do not insist on a certain code of belief or action. I want places where I am seen, valued, and can contribute. A few churches in my life have been influential-the Methodist Church of my high school days, where teens were valued, and the minister made me think about how to live my life, the small Episcopal Church where we took the children, and hoped that they experienced age appropriate developmental tasks within a community which attempted to practice Christian values. There was People's Church, where Christ was prominently mentioned and loved, and where people seemed to live his values quite fully. Besides that, I found the vehicle for the growth of my faith and love in the various activities and communities that I have mentioned before, especially the Episcopal Training Network, and the Association for Humanistic Psych, and TORI.

And now there was St. James in Bartlesville, I suspect Jesus would have felt at home. The order of service was unfamiliar to me, but meaningful. Over time, I saw the Catholic value for preferential treatment of the poor inspired Jesus-like action in ways I had not experienced in other churches. (My only argument was that "poor" must be defined as more than economic) I admired and respected the charities sponsored by St. James, a church which gave one half its income to the poor. Although Catholics know little of the Bible they know a lot about feeding the poor, tending the sick, and taking care of those who need it

There were unfamiliar ways there. Some took me a while to figure out. One was the well-known Catholic guilt. It was not that I had no regrets about my life, or actions, but those regrets did not threaten my status in the Kingdom or the church as sometimes happens in Catholicism. My life was without powerful judgments causing separation.

A surprising apparent belief system came to light one day when I was running a women's workshop, and asked the women to name something they liked about themselves. There was complete and unbroken silence, as if I had broken a well-known and unwritten rule. I realized that this was generally true among Catholic women. They would not speak well of themselves.

Another characteristic was a covert agreement to deny anything conflicting with church teachings. For instance: If a church couple had a bad marriage, and the church said divorce was bad, no one gave credence or notice to the bad marriage or the pain it caused. Both the couple and their friends acted as if everything was fine, even if asked directly. A woman in our parish committed suicide, and since that was punishable by God, according to beliefs, no one spoke of it. Someone asked how she died, and no one answered. These kinds of behaviors were foreign to me, and difficult to get used to. I am much more direct. I was startlingly direct in the eyes of those people.

Father Bill Skeehan was a faithful and caring priest. I suspect Jesus would have liked him, and given him a job. Actually, I guess they were on speaking terms and he had been given a job. ☺ Fr. Bill was unafraid to stand up to the hierarchical institutional church or the local bishop. Unfortunately, just as he was moving toward retirement, the hierarchy of the church was gearing up for regressive change. Fr. Bill saw no need for change within his parish, and especially regressive change. He had built a parish of faith, good works, and guidance from the beatitudes. He began to have difficulty with depression and alcoholism as he tried to adjust to being older and his church (the hierarchical church) began to betray him, and the values he taught and lived. It was a painful time, for Fr. Bill and for St. James.

During this period, I naively suggested a women's retreat, not knowing that in Catholic-ese, retreat meant to gather and have a priest or nun come to speak.

By then, I was assimilated and trusted enough to be listened to, as I described my meaning of retreat. I described the women coming together at a retreat center, putting on workshops, having fun, members as speakers, some prayer or meditation time, and sharing food and fellowship. I framed it as renewal of spirit and a joining together in the company of the Trinity, who would show up wherever two or more were gathered in His name.

They loved the vision, and acted on it. We used the Girl Scout Camp, shared a potluck breakfast and lunch, shared favorite mugs and possessions. We heard from our 90 year old wise woman. There was prayer time and time in nature. We had almost 50 women from age 30 to 85. It was a warm, loving and sharing day, repeated for two more years, until Father Bill was forced to retire and a new priest was brought in.

I put this next part in because I was part of that church, and the happenings went against my own values so thoroughly that I got involved in the fray. You will read more about how I was affected, as well as my church and my friends who had been raised Catholic.

For the last few years, history is being rewritten within the Roman Catholic Church. Between the time of writing and editing this, history may be taking another drastic turn. Breaking all protocol, Pope Benedict resigned and a Jesuit who took the name of Pope Francis took over. He appears to be ready to undo some regressive change, and especially some of the scandal which has surrounded the church and the hierarchy in the last few years. It is too early to tell.

Under Benedict, Vatican II was/is being reinterpreted, and put forth as something very different than the way it was lived back in the 1960's-1980's. This is the clearest example I have seen in my life of rewriting and reinterpreting history, and makes me suspicious of all the history I have ever read.

I saw, in Catholics of the 70's, a new freedom and sense of life - A spiritual framework and guidelines which had become less dogmatic and more user-friendly. Roman Catholicism, and thus the world, became more inclusive and less insular. The changes served life and increased aliveness. That aliveness existed in Fr. Skeehans church in Bartlesville.

269

When Father Bill retired and the new priest came, a dramatic story ensued. He brought chaos with him to St. James as well as animosity, confusion and drastic change. He was a hard hearted messenger for that regressive change. Step by step, he dismantled what had been St. James. He brought in statues, cloths, and other accoutrements, symbols of doctrine and history, (after judging publicly that we were a bad parish for not having all we needed to be faithful or to worship). He told us they were gifts from him and we were expected to be grateful. It was difficult to tell if he knew what he was doing, or was just that kind of person. He was an ex-boxer, and ex-policeman, with karate for recreation. He brought a night stick to his first sermon and brandished it around telling us how he had hunted down homosexuals, and criminals. His immediate and long term effect was devastating for individuals and the church community. I was aghast at the power of the clergy given by this RC parish, and accepted out of centuries of tradition and hierarchical reign. My previous church experience was of a more equal distribution of power between clergy and congregants. I helped the parish where I could, but was fighting an unfamiliar battle. The below, is what I eventually wrote and had published in the National Catholic Reporter (a liberal Catholic voice) to express my, and our, dismay. Their topic of the month was: Excuses:

EXCUSES::
Our Parish did things with love and social justice. What wasn't done, we found a way. We didn't make excuses
The excuses started on our new priest's first Sunday. He preached a loud and proud sermon about himself. We excused it, thinking he was new and insecure.
He followed this for months with multiple judgments on our building, attitude, actions, words and former priest. His excuse? "He was the CEO" and "following the bishop's orders".
One day he scolded that the least anger in the room might ruin the Eucharist for all. He said he was "enforcing the rules"
He changed our chapel chairs from a circle to rows, using Vatican II as his excuse. He couldn't join us to share peace during Mass, and "turn his back on Jesus". (Imagine our surprise—we thought Jesus was among us, as well as on the altar.
Eighty people met in protest. We gave him signed and written results. He promised to meet with us and didn't—he excused himself.
Then we excused ourselves, from Mass, meetings, collections, and events. Ill parishioners even excused themselves from dying until they knew he would not be there.
After a while, we returned to our work. He still tears down what we had, damages form, function, community, and what our former priest had accomplished.
We continue to do Christ's work with no excuses.

All over the country the hierarchical church was instituting these changes. - More distance between the priest and the congregation, forced retirement, or curtailment and silencing of the few older Vatican II educated priests, as well as influential scholars, doctrinists, and theologians who did not keep to the new party line.

It did not affect me at my core, as I was not instilled with Catholicism from birth, and did not feel compelled to follow the decisions of the hierarchy. But it deeply affected me, a human being with friends in the fray. This whole part of my experience was a deep lesson in organizational dynamics, and the clash between good and evil. I hope for an equitable solution within Roman Catholicism. For me, the time I spent at St. James helped me to respect and come to love some things about Roman Catholicism as practiced there. I am, along with "real Catholics", hopeful about the new Pope.

Within the present RC church, the issues of women clergy, the sex abuse scandals, abortion, finances, and corrupt power continue to seethe, with the hierarchy being dragged painfully to the table, by a people who see the light.

This whole chapter in my supposedly spiritual life emphasized to me how far away from Jesus' example a church, a person, or a denomination can get. The question in churches should not be how shall we do it, and which way is right, but rather, who are we? Once we human beings really understand our identity, and our relationship with God and Christ, the path becomes clear. What we do to live out that identity evolves with integrity and love, through that identity and relationship.

That is where my journey has taken me so far. Ask me again next year, or next decade. I am closer to the end of my life than the beginning. I continue to pray to keep on a right path, not to be seduced, but to be led, to listen, to follow, and to contain the strength to carry on through faith and hope.

Swimming Once More

Having finished my accounting of my foray into Catholic schisms, I now take you back to the rest of my life in Oklahoma. I needed something to do with my days, and asked Mark to find out if I, as his partner, was eligible to join the Phillips Recreation Center. I was longing for a place to swim. He asked, and I joined, and once more jumped in a pool.

My default exercise is always swimming – has been all my life. Bartlesville had been an enthusiastic and well supported swimming town in the past, with facilities to prove it. The Phillips pool was a convertible 25 yard/25 meter pool, with a wonderful filtering system, good chemical dispersal, and great upkeep. Also in Bartlesville, was an older diving pool built specifically for Olympic practice back in the 40's, and a 50 yard outdoor pool like the one I had grown up with in Midland. The latter two were aging, and now have been refurbished and are once again nice facilities.

I swam daily, deciding to learn to swim a mile a day. I was then 66, and my workout had always been ½ mile.

The first couple days of increased effort required an afternoon nap. A German woman, older than I, was inspirational. She swam 2-3 miles every day. I kept at it, and soon swam my first continuous mile. That day called for a long nap and a feeling of total triumph.

Soon, I was swimming a mile a day, 6 days a week, and doing flip turns learned from watching my competitive children as I sat at their swim meets years before. I decided to join the National Masters Swim Organization, with the idea of competing. I joined, but never competed. Carrying the membership card reinforced my identity as a swimmer, yet I found my enthusiasm lagging to practice longer and harder with a team and a coach. It remained my fun, my meditation, and was incidentally good for body and mind...competing would have meant imposing hard work on me, and I think it is never good when a passion becomes hard work, or forced.

We bought a home, and began remodeling (you will hear more later), so I soon was working at home more and swimming less. But I had met my goal, and could swim a mile whenever I wanted to. I was and am very proud of that accomplishment at that age.

Winter happens in Oklahoma too. It is different than Michigan, and often hardy pansies bloom in the snow. Ice storms are frequent, and snow doesn't often last. The wind that comes whipping down the plains in summer blows snow and bitter cold air around in winter. Our first winter brought a storm with 16 inches of snow, staying on the ground more than a week. Oklahoma towns have sparse equipment to handle snow like that.

Like all northerners in a southern state, we got a chance to show off and teach our winter driving skills. We spent the day of the blizzard driving cars out of snow banks. People had trouble with the counter-intuitive instructions, and asked us to do it. My chance to be a heroine for a day – part of me loved the hard work in adverse weather, and having the ability to help others. On the other hand, my car was parked on the street, and that night, was hit by someone who couldn't negotiate the corner, and didn't even leave a note. Ugh.

After the community service, and the walk shoveling, Mark got out his cross country skis and skied all over town for the next few days. There were a couple other northerners who joined in.

That House (The Ranch)

We found a house. Actually, I found it and fell in love with the location. It turned out to be a pretty naïve love affair. It sat on an acre of prairie, right next to a wild horse preserve. I have never been one to pay a lot of attention to the practicality or condition of the places I buy, and a couple of builders from town asked if we were sure we wanted to buy that place. We both fell in love with the view and the setting, and settled for what we thought was a good inspection before we bought. We were only 4 miles from town. The view was indeed to die for. Occasionally while we lived there, strangers stopped to look. The 300 degree view and the wild horse bands next door added beauty and interest. We could see both sunrise and sunset, and as our eyes took in the views, our souls were fed.

The horse preserve was set up to hold wild horses from Nevada, brought there by the US government to relieve overcrowding and lack of food for them in their native land. It was a controversial program, with the government paying ranchers to keep these horses. However, we enjoyed watching and learning as the horses came and went from our fence line. They had been gelded, and separated from the females, and then penned in, albeit with hundreds of acres to roam. They were still wild, but in far from wild circumstances.

Six months of the year our upper deck became our bedroom, an air-mattresses our bed. We watched meteor showers, eclipses, and occasional low flying planes, as well as the sunrises from our outdoor bedroom. Best of all, the mosquitoes didn't seem to fly that high. Only occasionally did we hear the buzz or feel a bite. The skies were dark, and noise infrequent. When we moved, there was a large bright mercury light on a tall pole at the entrance to our drive. We paid extra to the electric company (who owned it) to install a switch so we could turn it off and darken the skies. They got more money for less electricity used, and we got dark skies most of the time, and a light to mark the driveway for visiting friends.

It sounds like a dream house on paper. The view, country, setting, horses, and outdoor bedroom were indeed a dream come true, but the house itself was more of a nightmare. We discovered the truth that the builders already knew as we tried to function over time. The time began within a week after we moved in.

You have seen houses on stilts near beaches, in order to let the wind and water flow underneath unimpeded. Whoever built this house chose that design. The next owner saw no use for that, and decided to fill in the bottom and have a two story home. He had big ideas and small skills. He attempted to use the stilts as studs to hang drywall and siding on. However, he butted the siding and drywall against the stilts, nailing top and bottom instead, and leaving cracks to expand and contract with temperature, moisture, and the efforts of critters. Those cracks were the doorways through which came rain, snow, scorpions, and all sorts of insects and lizards. Did you know scorpions fluoresce under ultraviolet light? We bought a light in self-defense, hunting for scorpions in the house, rather than waiting for unexpected bites. What we really had was an open first story, with attempts to fill in the openings with those panels. There was the usual plumbing, carpeting and wiring, but what we didn't realize was that the owners we purchased it from had just finished cosmetic work, making it look new and sturdy, and had also hidden the things that could not possibly work.

It was bad enough living with involuntary air conditioning, no insulation, and self-opening and closing cracks in the wall, but with the first torrential rain the library flooded, and water started to run onto the living room carpet. On closer inspection, we found that the cement slab under the house, stuck out farther than the walls. This gave the rain a platform to fall on, and run under the walls .Even as a young camper I learned not to let the plastic stick out from under the tent, and here we had a whole house with the slab sticking out from under the walls.

We spent our first month jumping from one crisis to another attempting to keep warm, dry and free of critters. Fortunately there were no tornadoes during that time, as we had no place to go for safety, either indoors or out. We were clearly naïve and star struck but had counted on our inspector to warn us. We now suspected that the owner paid off the inspector and we later became sure of that, as we found one code violation after another. We discovered a lot of what our friends the builders were trying to tell us as they questioned our purchase.

The second year we were there, one of those ice storms left us without electricity for four days. Our propane heaters worked. (The heat for the house was two propane fireplaces, one upstairs, and one down. They worked well and made a good atmosphere.) But during this storm, we had no hot water and no blower on the heaters and of course no lights. We were isolated, as we could not get down the ice covered hill to get to town. Finally the 4th day, we managed the trip down hill, where the lower elevation had melted the ice. We were finally able to take a shower at the fitness center. Boy did that feel good!

We have often agreed since then, that the advantages of living there were worth "camping out" for 4 years. But it surely was a project to keep warm and dry, and make it a "home".

My first project was to buy a couple cases of indoor outdoor paint-able caulk, and caulk cracks everywhere, even inside the light switches and plug plates. My second was to take off the rough sawn cedar baseboards, which we found hid the water stains around the downstairs lower drywall, and turn the boards into shutters for the outside of the house. It made a huge and lovely difference in the looks of the outside.

Our labor paid off. Our creative solutions and hard work quieted things from crisis mode to project mode. One more piece of remediation was to re-grade the yard so the water flowed away from rather than toward the house. Even that turned out to be a shocker for both the workers and us. They immediately broke their rented Bobcat on a 4 foot boulder just below the surface. And they continued to find one huge boulder after another as they valiantly struggled to grade the yard. We gave them the boulders as part of the payment. They could sell them for landscaping. We finally had no more wet floors.

The propane pipe needed to be moved during re-grading, and we discovered that instead of the 18 inches it was required to be buried, it was 2 inches under the surface. We saved several thousand dollars, as a friend, a young man from the propane company, agreed to look the other way as he helped us move the pipe out of harm's way, and move it back into its 2 inch trench without reporting it.

I am not finished. That same deluge that first flooded the house took a quarter of the shingles off the roof. We discovered they had been stapled on with short staples, were the wrong kind of roofing and the tabs had not been removed from the sticky strip that bound them together. We spent many hours putting the shingles back on more solidly, and when we sold the house, the buyer would not buy without the correct roofing, so we paid to reroof. Ahhhh another lesson hard learned.

The biggest adventure on the roof was the day they burned the prairie. Each year, the Hughes Ranch (the wild horse ranch next door) did a controlled burn starting at our fence and going away from us. They expertly had done this for years. They waited until the temperature, and especially the wind velocity and direction were right, and then we got a call telling us "today is the day." One day they called as we were up nailing shingles back on the roof.

We looked down as they rode their horses or jeep along the fence, using a blowtorch to start the fire. The fire quickly moved across the prairie in the stiff wind, and the heat created its own increasing draft and wind. Suddenly, I had to lie down on the roof, in order not to be blown off. It was a dramatic demonstration of how forest fires spread themselves by their own draft. Late that night, down in the valley where there was usual darkness, rows of fire licked themselves onward, until they crept up out of the valley, tiring themselves out next to the highway.

Two cats came with the house, and we quickly discovered that they were both pregnant. We noticed that the neighborhood was filled with matching feral cats - all long haired and gray. Obviously this clan had been around a few years. Ours were the tip of the iceberg. We had to get organized around this issue along with all the above ones. Fortunately, I like cats, unfortunately Mark didn't. (He is now a full convert). Within a month after moving in, we had 13 kittens. One of the mothers was negligent, and the other took over, nursing all 13 most of the time. I had never known that mother cats shared litters. Both moms got neutered as soon as the kittens were gone. We put an ad in our church bulletin headlined "Holy Cats!".

We then tackled the neighborhood ferals. We got a live trap, and found a vet to neuter ferals for a reasonable price. We determined to neuter a few, and do away with the rest, reasoning that the sheer numbers were out of balance with the bird and critter population. I felt ambivalent but made the decision, considering it to be the best course. We still have one of the cats as I write this. She is now 14 years old.

I viewed that horse ranch daily, and was itching to hike there. One day, I called them up to ask permission. I knew they were a long time, well known, well connected family in town, but knew nothing else. John Hughes response was to say "Drive over here, and we will give you a tour." He followed that with directions to the house. We got a wonderful tour of the land they had grown up on, complete with family stories and memories. There was the river, the caves, the horses and the cattle. They owned or leased many square miles. They gave us permission to freely roam their land, and we spent many hours doing just that. We were asked not to talk about it to others, as they often had unwanted hunters or visitors on their land without permission. We found horse skulls, unusual sandstone formations, and remnants of both Indians and the oil industry. Once again, when I left work, I had a place in the country to come home to. We were grateful for the friendship and generosity of the Hughes family. We learned as I was writing this, that John had died. I imagine his son Robert is still there working the ranch.

On the way home from work, we dealt with 39 Hill, the one that got icy in winter. We never knew how it got its name, but it was a steep, narrow, and treacherous quarter mile of road, just before the turn to our house coming from town. On one side was a cliff, on the other a deep ditch and washed out gulley. No guardrails. In late afternoon, the sun was directly in one's eyes. Twice I was nearly forced off the road by a car coming the other way. I always thought of it as a test of courage. Most Oklahomans just thought it was an Oklahoma country road. No big deal.

Our ranch adventures, after the walls and floors were secure, included bees and chickens. The bees were Mark's idea and the chickens mine.

I had always wanted chickens. A temporary pen out of (what else?) chicken wire kept our 8 babies in bounds. At first the cats thought they were dinner, but as cats are willing to do, they soon learned they were family members and not only left them alone, but helped protect them. In the daytime, they roamed the yard freely (both cats and chickens), and at night we tucked the chicks in a covered cardboard box for safety. Miraculously, they all survived.

Meanwhile, we built a chicken house out of pallets and spare lumber. The slits in the pallets let the air circulate to cool the birds, and with the right choice of pallets, kept the critters out. All told, including the plastic panels for the roof, we may have spent 100 dollars. When winter came, cardboard and feed sacks lined the inside, keeping out the bitter cold wind and snow. Occasionally, a

276

long extension cord was used to put a light bulb in there for warmth. A heated pan of water outdoors, used by chickens, cats, birds, and an occasional sleepy raccoon or possum completed living arrangements.

When grown, our chickens did what came naturally and roosted in the trees. Chickens quite easily fly if their wings are not clipped. One night we heard horrible squawks and chicken screams, and sat up on our air mattress to see an owl circling our formerly sleeping chickens in the top of a 7 foot oak tree. It was about 2 AM. Mark became an instant hero, dressing, (I suppose including his Superman cape) getting the ladder and bringing the chicks down one at a time. You see, if you grab a chicken by the feet, they will hang down like they are dead. Easier to carry down a ladder that way. After that, we shooed them into the chicken house at night behind a shut door. No more owls. We had saved our egg supply.

Coyotes eyed our chickens too. That was my inadvertent chance to be Wonder Woman. One day I heard lots of squawking. I ran outside and rounded the corner just in time for a young coyote to round the corner from the other direction. We were both surprised! His reflexes stopped him still for a moment, just long enough to receive the product of my reflexes as I kicked him in the side yelling "Get the F... out of here". He did, and I did, and the chickens were safe. I got bragging rights. After all, how many people....................?

The interest in bees came through some friends, who invited Mark to the local club of beekeepers. Mark bought two hives of bees and we sat back and waited for honey. Like most things, it turned out not to be that easy. We bragged that we owned a Bee Ranch with" 10,000 head of bees" But we kept quite still when our first year's honey turned out to be not sweet, but bitter. The consensus was that the bees may have feasted only on our oak trees, and it tasted horrible. We also had to learn about keeping bees warm in winter, cool in summer, and free of mites. We wondered what they ever did as wild bees. We hope that the descendants of those bees may find it a little easier to survive today's woes because we treated them well, and kept them healthy.

Our next fun idea was to get a demonstration hive. The bees would be in a transparent hive inside our house where they could be seen. They entered through a tube, through the wall. It was fun watching until, after several months, they were attacked by a colony of aggressive bees, and wiped out. We didn't replace them.

Mark was out of town one day. I went out to get eggs, and noticed that the bees were swarming. I called the local bee guru, and he and his wife came out and helped get the queen back into the hive, and the others followed. And then I fed them supper.(The couple, not the bees).

Nine-Eleven

We were living there on 9/11/2001, the day the twin towers fell. Like most, I remember where I was when I heard. I had left the house about 8 that morning to see a client, and then do some errands. My dear friend Helen was having cataract surgery. I stopped to see how she was about 11 AM, and everyone in her living room was ashen. Helen took a look at my smile and said, "You have not heard, have you?" I had not and immediately looked over at their TV. I was probably one of the last to know. That day and the next, Mark and I moved our TV into the bedroom, watching over and over, along with all the other stunned people in the country, crying and wondering what this meant. I kept saying "Our country will never be the same".

A couple nights later, with the air ban still in place (all planes were grounded), we were on our deck ready for bed when two planes flew over. This was probably around 11pm. They were going somewhere between south and southwest. The next day I called the FAA, and the Air Force base nearby, reported our observations, and tried to find out something. There were no answers. Our imagination came up with many possibilities. As I was writing this, I researched both Google and Snopes.com in an attempt to see what was known about flights for those times. There were indeed flights given permission to fly by the FAA. The only ones mentioned were emergency medical flights, such as organs for transplants, and by one story, a patient was flown to where there was snake venom.

Snopes did mention that within the week after the air spaces were reopened, there were several charter flights of Saudi Nationals, including relatives of the Bin Ladens flown from the US to Saudi. They added that these flights were inspected carefully, and the people checked carefully for connections to 9/11.

Here is what I wrote the day after 9/11:

৯——৶

Sept 12,2001
Yesterday marks the day that our country and all of humanity died a bit.

The gravestone for yesterday reads; "Here lies the birth of fear, the death of trust, and if God wills it, and humanity intends it, the birth of the hope of the human race

We thought that Y2K might be the end of the world as we know it. We were wrong! That came 21 months later when hate stole wings and used them in the service of fear and revenge. That day came yesterday, September 11, 2001, and it changed the world.

I woke up this morning and looked out on the prairie at the stars in a clear sky. Nothing there had changed. The peace and continuity were there. God was there. Love was still the fabric of the universe. Nothing looked changed to the naked eye.

But my eye was naked no longer. It had been filled with the knowledge of good and evil and had covered itself with shame, with whatever it could find, forgetting that it had been safe in its nakedness for so long.

How many have been wronged by the government that represents me? How many blacks? Women? Gays? How many children in Africa by a greedy pharmaceutical company who oversteps the boundaries of love and caring?

How many angels, or Palestinians, or generic human beings for that matter can dance on the head of a pin without the pin falling, the dance ending in chaos, or the will to dance going away?

How many thousands died in this one violent plan of which we had so many forewarnings? The questions become meaningless in the face of no answers.

The answers must be in the basics.....Love thy neighbor as thyself. Do unto others as you would have others do unto you. Put God first, Keep the main thing the main thing, and admit that we are powerless.....human.....inadequate.

I am neither knowledgeable enough or can stretch far enough to know what I would do if I ran the country.

But I can pray for those who do, that they can throw out the false separation between church and state, mind and spirit. That we as a country can live by the laws of spirit and love, as well as those of our legal system.

That we might act as compassionate and inclusive mediators to the Middle East.... listening to all....and pray for God's peace there. And encourage love and justice. And that we take the mote from our own eye and make our country a living example of love and justice..............For those "tired and poor", underserved and underfed, and all beings who live in our towns, our neighborhoods, our country.

And when its too big to comprehend, as it is for me today, I ask God's help to start with me, to push me to love my neighbor, listen with compassion, do what I can, write my officials, and pray.

Nothing has changed out there in the stars, but it has changed in the world and I pray that it has changed in me.

I pray for love and courage and for us all that we can draw from the unchanging stars and the unchanging God, and whatever else is larger than us and unchanging, to change our world ...before there is no choice.

↾—↽

I, as you can see, was like most: deeply affected by 9/11. Several months later, the next spring, I would write this piece below, discussing the process of what our country went through in the days and first months after 9/11, as well as the possible outcomes.

"More people attended Ash Wednesday services in 2002 than in the memory of the present clergy. People everywhere are re-evaluating their priorities, making changes, refusing to wait any longer to live their lives in a more satisfying way, or with more integrity, or for some, with more dishonesty, or excitement. Many people at once seem to be facing future with determination, courage, decisions, and even more violence, than has been seen in a long time.

This plethora of conflicting and polarized reactions is occurring, seemingly in a wave of energy, having a life of its own, and catalyzed on September 11th, 2001. And though the direction and the outcome of these reactions cannot be sorted out neatly, or measured exactly, there seems more movement of energy within the human systems of the planet Earth than for a long time. Process is on the move, personally, locally and globally.

Major corporations go bankrupt, or are exposed as having a grave lack of conscience, or dubious practices in the way they run their business. Atrocities escalate around the world. Heroes fall into disrespect, and yesterday's Gods become today's enemies. No sooner is there a moment of peace in the world, or a hopeful development, than violence breaks out in new places with new intensity. Desecration and de-sanctification of hundreds of human bodies are discovered. The people in charge, local funeral directors, who were known as "good neighbors", had a life and a crematorium in deathly disrepair.(A recent news story tells of this and the local shock that followed as local servants were exposed as working against their neighbors, instead of for them.)

Life could be called chaotic. In our work, country and government, words and actions don't match. Denial is rampant, scapegoating is politically correct, and spirituality becomes a tool of the government. Everything that we know about how to live is being violated. Our energy prices lower, and thus we use more and more of a resource that is known to be scarcer and scarcer. We wage war to bring peace, and demonize our neighbors as an Axis of Evil, and as "terrorists", and extremists, while we run The School of The Americas, turning out educated people who learn to do exactly the things we accuse the "terrorists" of......kill and destroy in the name of the nation and the causes they support.

Our military now has permission to become political, and plant false news in the world media as a weapon of war. We politicize the corporate chaos, and attempt to spiritualize government ala "faith based initiatives", done in the name of Christ, or Allah, and paid for by the government. Poor people of faith are getting poorer in the name of financing the country... The boundaries which people have counted on for a sense of belonging, trust, knowledge, and security have all become blurred into each other like a giant kaleidoscope which perpetually turns until no one knows any sense of order, and cannot track any particular system or path.

Those individuals that I am in touch with lately exhibit either a poignant and strong hunger and determination to move toward fulfillment, or a more hopeless confusion, fear, or withdrawal as they are caught up in the cultural, global, emotional, spiritual soup that is today's life.

In the days following September 11, people experienced a sense of order, unity, meaning, purpose, community, compassion, and love for their country that had not appeared in our culture since World War II, and before that, maybe during the American Revolution when our entire country was united against Great Britain.

That kind of unity is addictive, and contagious. Humans seem hardwired to like being part of a team. With the right focus, it is also healing.

However, there are two points I want to bring forth. First is that when that unity goes away, it is often replaced by cultural chaos, lost ness, lack of purpose, and hunger for something to replace it.

The same thing happens after falling out of love, or going to a retreat, or a revival, or convention, and becoming part of a strong unified community and then going out again, sans those connections. The resulting emptiness is a powerful force, driving people to seek more of what nourished them. This is strong enough to label a non-sexual way of "being in heat."

The second point is that in this country, it will be noticed that we have nearly always had to have an enemy to feel this unity and community. There may have been two short exceptions. In the 60's, Flower Power reigned in some parts of the country, and its participants, mostly young, were labeled "children", and dismissed or maced. It happened again for a very short time right after September 11th, but quickly divided into those who wanted peace and those who wanted war -those who turned toward deity, and those who created demons.

When the enemy, or the movement, or the cause dissipates, or becomes diluted, or unclear as in recent days, the unity disappears, the hunger fills its space, and people set out to find more.

It is up to each of us to notice our hunger, to be aware of past fulfillments and losses, and our present driving forces. It is important to know what we are dedicated, consecrated, and committed to, and in what direction we intend to move. It is important to understand how we react and move as individuals, as a family, an organization, or a country. Some attend Ash Wednesday service, hoping to find it "there". Others change their lives, reaching for what they have postponed too long, moving past barriers to fulfillment, determined to no longer tolerate the emptiness, or the barriers.

Others feel hopeless and go out for a drink or get high. They may steal from others; neglect their crematoriums, their jobs, homes, and fellow humans. The fearful get creative in non-ethical pursuits and take pride in the creativity, leaving ethics behind.

281

The cry for chaos grows as does the cry for order and the dissonance makes for craziness, and forced choices in polarities.

Surely, in mysterious ways, in all systems, chaos eventually begets order, just as order begets chaos. And in these chaotic days, we can only live as if our future and that of the world depended upon our decisions, intentions, and actions. And we can pray for clarity, charity, courage and strength.

The waves of chaos have washed up debris, since the unity went away. It is everyone's job to take care of the debris as they can, and hold the hope that, like the ocean, when storms wash mountains of trash onto the beach, the oceans are left cleaner, and order comes again. Then hunger and emptiness are assuaged. It is everyone's job to create order and unity within and among.

Each of us can move toward our ideals. And when we hit a barrier or a fear, we can choose to turn toward whatever greater order we can summon in our souls, and trust that the cosmos is unfolding as it should.

And though unity and advancing one's beliefs are ideals of both terrorists and pacifists, we can hope for commonality instead of estrangement. We can intend to work for goodness, and Godness rather than to fight for "our" victory. We can look toward collaboration rather than conflagration. We can hope that humanity, and we, are hardwired, deep in our primitive circuits to live in peace.

&—&

Our culture has settled on "never forget" for this event. What people intend to remember is different for each person. I intend to remember my nakedness and my deep need to be inclusive, to reach out, and to feel love even in the face of "not love".

Now I want to go back to the stories from our Oklahoma ranch, which went on in spite of 9/11, and in spite of, or sometimes because of the difference it made in me and in the world. .

One ranch experience worth mentioning is that of seeing the majestic billowing clouds and storms build and move across the prairie. It occasionally was frightening, since we had no tornado shelter, but mostly it was awe inspiring. I learned a great deal about watching clouds for rotational movement, and other defining characteristics. I also learned gratitude for the awe and beauty. I got some fabulous photos of sunrise or sunsets. We were lucky there were no tornadoes during our prairie years.

One year, it was our yard overflowing with wild prairie flowers which produced the prize for awe and beauty. We had tired of mowing an acre, and especially with a temperamental mower. We decided to let the lawn grow and have natural prairie, leaving a cleared space around the house for fire prevention. A few weeks later we were blessed with a huge field of Black Eyed Susan, and many other flowers – a riot of wild color and waving blossoms! Had we tried to grow such a beautiful display we could not. We had strangers and friends ask for advice, and had to refer them to Mother Nature.

Mother Nature produced a rattlesnake adventure one day. Mark's young grandchildren were visiting. Either they or one of us saw a snake sticking out from under a board on the back porch. I assume he was attempting to stay cool. It was a typical Oklahoma hot summer day. We could see it was a rattler, although we had not seen one in our yard before. This one was sizable.

Mark and I conferred on what to do. Neither of us wanted to kill it. We told the boys to get out of harm's way, up on the deck while we changed into jeans and boots. Mark then took the shovel handle and put it under the coil that we could see. As he lifted and pried, more of the snake appeared. It was annoyed to be exposed, but not aggressive or rattling. It simply wanted back into its cool covered spot.

After two or three more tries, the snake was out in the open. I could almost hear him saying "Now what"? And we were saying the same. I said to Mark, "I wonder how he would react to a rain storm?" We got the already hooked up hose, and began squirting water into the air, letting it fall on the snake. I swear I heard, "Rain? I'm getting out of here". And he did. He began to slither toward our back fence. Luckily the hose was long, and the mother of all rainstorms followed the snake out to the property line. We never saw him again, but did get a picture to prove it.

Work

The ranch adventures combined with my swimming and my work to create a good life. I was working for Samaritan Counseling Center. I had met the supervisor soon after we moved, and wanted to work there, but did not have my Oklahoma License yet. . I studied some, but because I had always done well on exams, and had been a social worker for a long time, I did not study enough. I passed the exam by only three points. I had been away from textbooks and theory for a long time. The exam was full of textbook questions, rather than those best answered by long experience. I had good integrative ways of working, but had let go of much specific knowledge about theories and their specifics. I was grateful to pass, and soon got over the blow to my ego.

The next hurdle was the many credits of Continuing Education, due only three months down the road. I attended a flurry of workshops, applied some credits from Michigan and made the deadline. Now I was free to renew my newly earned license, draw a breath of relief and begin my work as an Oklahoma licensed social worker.

Samaritan Counseling is a national organization, and encourages its counselors to be faith based as well as having excellent skills and credentials in counseling. It felt very good to be able to include and integrate the spiritual dimension, as I had longed to do in other places. I could address so much more of my client's lives and use much more of myself in my work. People's beliefs, and the values they base their lives on are very important, and for some, those spiritual values carry more weight than the ethical, societal or parental values, or the psychological dynamics. In fact, at the very heart of identity for many is ones identity in relationship to God, or Christ. If that is true, then to work with people in helping their lives, is to include, or even start with this identity and those relationships.

After a while, I also accepted a part time position with Green Country Hospice. I had worked in Hospice in Kalamazoo and Hawaii, and have that history of a multi-faceted relationship with death, from growing up in a funeral home, to working in hospitals in two different careers, to working in other hospices. Death has permeated my life and work. This hospice team was excellent, and the head nurse was especially good in pain control and holistic means of sustaining quality of life. This work was a nice balance to my work at Samaritan.

Several of us from Samaritan attended a supervision group in Tulsa. We staffed cases, and talked about various issues as therapists. I was inspired at the time to write a poem about the integration of self as human being, spiritual being and counselor. I called it: *THE SECULAR SPIRITUAL CIRCULAR SPHERICAL COUNSELOR (The paradox of being a human, being holy, and being a counselor, and keeping it all straight).* That is a long name for a poem, but the process of living it was long and ongoing also.

At age 69, I began to feel some changes in my body. They seemed sudden and disquieting. I was hoisting myself to the roof from the ladder, as I had done countless times, and it felt difficult for the first time ever. Never before had I experienced feeling weak, or older unless temporarily ill. I was running, swimming that mile a day, and had never felt a loss of strength or balance in any situations. I had gotten some plantar fasciitis in my feet, and other than that, felt as I had when 30 or 40. This incident surprised and alarmed me. I am writing this only 9 years later, and have lost a great deal of once easy ability in that 9 years. It continues to be a difficult adjustment for me. I now understand that younger people, (even me at age 65) have no way to understand what it is like to age. I could not have conceived of the changes that began and continued in me even with good food, exercise, rest, and preventive measures.

The plantar fasciitis started in the season I was swimming so much. I believe there is a connection. The foot and ankle are held extended while swimming, a motion which tightens the plantar fascia. Over time, with no opposing exercise, or stretching, it is easy to see where there might be shortening of the fascia and the resulting irritation when walking It is just my theory. I still swim, and have more trouble walking right afterward. I now try to counter-stretch, and to walk during the swimming season, but this does not take away the years that I didn't. And of course, the aging process continues, but so do my efforts toward health and whole person strength.

Shortly after we moved to the ranch, before the bees and chickens, Mark and I decided to go to Alaska for another one of those extended trips. We went there about as naively as we had gone to Nova Scotia. We were fortunate that weather and fate smiled on us for 6 weeks of wonderful time. We covered probably 5000-7000 miles by driving, and another thousand or more by ferry. We had a small station wagon, and a small tent..

Mark had not seen the Canadian Rockies, nor had I since my kids were young. We saw Banff and Jasper, and took a tour of the Athabasca Glacier. We went to Liard Hot Springs on the recommendation of a Canadian friend. We camped in campgrounds, and non-campgrounds, and drove the ever changing and under repair Alaska Highway. The highway is mostly bedded in permafrost, which constantly heaves and changes, taking the road with it.

We saw presentations on the building of the highway, and on the Northern Lights. We visited a newly opened Indian museum. (The Tlingit Heritage Center). We saw Lake Louise and the turquoise blue of the glacier flour lakes along the way. There were magnificent peaks, and stone filled river beds a half mile wide. There were stretches of highway with no other cars for 50 miles, and nothing but trees, lakes and sky to be seen. It was magnificent!

I was stretched and changed by being in the experience of WILDERNESS!! It is similar to the experience of aging in that one cannot know it until they experience it. I thought I had been in wilderness - in the middle of woods with no sounds of civilization, up on mountains where no towns can be seen, or in a lake with no access for boats, and no roads. This was another order of magnitude. Traveling 50 or 100 miles or more without signs of civilization, other than the road, or looking out of our tent at night and seeing no lights as far as we could see gave me an expansive experience that I carry with me still. I encourage you to read "Coming Into the Country" by John McPhee. I thought of the first pioneers in any place, and what it must be like to push through wilderness, risking whatever conditions are ahead.

With the understanding of how much space there was with no humans nearby, I got more concerned about things like car trouble, or medical emergencies. I realized just how vulnerable we were, and how naively we had started out. Living in Alaska is not like living in the lower 48, unless one lives in a city. For instance, we camped one night in a campground behind a small store and restaurant. Next to us was a man who told us the following story: *"See that RV over there?? The driver is here, recovering from a concussion and nasty cut on his head. Two days ago, my wife and I were driving our RV and came across them half off the road. We stopped to see if they needed help. Their TV, mounted above the driver's seat, had come loose in a pothole bounce, and fallen on his head. He managed to stop the RV and then passed out. His wife couldn't drive it. Until we came along, an hour later, they had no help. My wife drove our RV, and I drove their rig here. We got some bandages and I guess he will be all right, but he will be here a bit"* I asked about doctors and he said there were none for about 100 miles. No hospital for farther than that.

Another late afternoon, as rain pelted our car, we passed a lone bicyclist. He was loaded for camping. We had not seen a car for many miles, and the pouring rain had been going on for hours. It was about 60 degrees F. He doggedly pedaled on down the two lane, head down, as we passed him. Had he fallen, or had mechanical trouble, he might have been on his own for many hours. We thought of how far we were from car parts, extra gasoline, or an extra tarp. Even a candy bar or a proper bathroom was not within easy reach, and those were the easy things to do without. There wasn't a McDonalds or Wal-Mart within a day's driving distance. I am not even sure there are any there at all. Just trees, lakes, and that lonesome road.

We thought we were smart to have gotten a real wheel and tire for a spare, rather than a donut spare. We now realized how small that was. It was some insurance, but our car had 160,000 miles on it, and there were few small cars in Alaska. People either drove SUV's, or Suburu Outbacks, with all-wheel drive. Luckily, we had little car trouble on this trip, and some of it was our fault. The emergency brake got left on, and the brakes subsequently needed replacement. At least they were working, and we were advised to drive to White Horse, another hundred miles, where the parts and labor would be available within a day or so for a much more reasonable price.

We saw lots of wildlife. The Grizzly bears, or what they called Brown Bears, topped the list for me, or maybe were second to the ravens. One day, we almost hit a baby black bear who ran in front of our car. I wrote in our diary that I could almost hear the momma bear growling at him: "I told you to look both ways before you crossed that road". In fact, we did not see the momma.

We learned that baby bears were turned away by their moms at about two years old to make room for other cubs. One day we watched a pair of twin Brown Bears foraging along the road. They looked uncertain, and we thought maybe they were newly on their own. We saw no one feeding bears, and the signs said not to. It establishes a dangerous precedent and the bears become dangerous looking for handouts. We also saw a lynx, mountain goats, eagles, moose, elk, and those totally fascinating ravens, having an almost

286

human range of sounds. It was my first experience with ravens, and I was captivated by their sounds. Crows and ravens are among the smartest of the birds.

We saw the Aleyeska Pipeline (Commonly known as the Alaska Pipeline), with no signs of leakage or spill. We saw a 60 mile cleared strip of land which forms the border between the Yukon and Alaska, and is also the 142nd parallel. Kluane Lake was one of my favorite places, and the reflection pictures I took there remain some of my favorite photos of the trip, and of all time.

One disappointment in going in the summer is that one does not see Northern Lights. Daylight remains for most of the night. The upside of that is that the dark does not descend before you are ready for it. During our Nova Scotia trip in November, we were often caught by early darkness at 5 pm. In Alaska, we took a picture at midnight just because we could. We thought so much light would interfere with our sleep. It did not, and we found we did not require as much sleep. The Alaskans validated that, saying they slept much longer in the dark winter – maybe 10 hours, but awoke in 5 or 6 refreshed in the season of eternal light.

We had planned to take a ferry to Sitka, an island on the inland waterway, and the former Russian Capital of Alaska, to see our friends from Hawaii, Phred and Auriella. As we lived our day by day adventure, we discovered we were running short of time due to the long distances and interesting scenery and activities. Our decision was to put our car on the ferry, and go all the way from Haines Alaska to Seattle. We would still be stopping in Sitka to see our friends. It was 2002, and people were still curtailing vacations as a result of the aftershocks of 9/11. Although the Alaskan Ferries ordinarily require reservations, the light traffic that year gave us the advantage of a last minute decision.

We got on the Alaska Marine Highway (the ferry system), our car riding on one of the car decks below. There is access to cars only during certain hours. There are state rooms available, although we opted to sleep on deck chairs in our sleeping bags. Some people put their tents up on deck. There were infrared lights above us producing enough heat to make the cold nights easy. There is food available, and a naturalist who advises passengers of icebergs, bears, whales or dolphins. We stopped at several places such as Prince Rupert Island, and Ketchikan. We took our car off at Sitka, our scheduled stop, and drove to the home of our friends who own the Bed and Breakfast. The ferry came to Sitka twice a week, Tuesday and Friday. We had a three day visit.

On Sitka, Phred, now just plain Fred, was head of maintenance at a local college which has since closed. There we walked a trail, along which were antique totem poles from now deserted villages, brought there for historical interest and preservation by the college. This was also the place of the ravens. I spent an hour in the woods enthralled and in a trance of delight listening to, and attempting to interact with the ravens. It felt magical.

Sitka has lots of Russian architecture. We explored the town by foot and car, visiting and catching up with our friends in between. On Thursday night, we took our friends to dinner, and reluctantly left the next morning on the Friday ferry to continue down the coast. We also got to talk with their son, Kila Orion, who I had last seen when he was about 2 years old.

We spent a day and a half on Vancouver Island with some old TORI friends, and explored the island, continuing on to Seattle. Our trip had been the trip of a lifetime.

I still hope to take that ferry trip again. I would go in spring or fall, the better to see Northern Lights. A good look at northern lights is on my bucket list.

We also made many other trips while we lived in Oklahoma. We went to California to a Richard Moss Workshop, visited Michigan several times, once for my 50th high school reunion, and went to the East Coast, and camped at Ocracoke. I wanted to show it to Mark. We did lots of camping and traveling. Nearer places were the Grand Canyon, and many parts of Oklahoma, as well as visiting his son and grandkids in Kansas.

Fast forward now, through a few more years of Oklahoma, I began to think of the future. Ranch living was a lot of work, and some isolation. I had no family nearby.

Mark has much strength, and like everyone, he changes over time. At the time, it was not one of his strengths to keep things up, or keep them orderly. He has improved, thanks partly to my nagging, but that is not a part of my behavior that I like to reinforce. I could see that I could not continue to carry the load of the undone tasks, and things that needed updating, doing or fixing. I worried that as those effects of older age accumulated, our lives would become disheveled. Adding to this was that periodic chronic depression which Mark had struggled with all his life. During those times, he was not available for relationship, nor helping with the things that needed doing.

The final straw came not from Mark, but with the announced plans to build an Indian Casino just down the road. We pictured lots of traffic on 39 Hill, lights on all night, spoiling our stargazing and silent nights. There would be probable drinking with all its consequences. The casino would take away the very reasons we loved being there.

I realized that I did not want to grow older living out in Oklahoma alone, or with Mark, in a situation with no family, and a partner who was satisfactory but unable to partner in many ways. I needed to be where I felt safer.

I knew that part of the reason Mark moved back to Oklahoma was to be nearer his grandchildren, but we had seen them seldom, and he was not reaching out toward them. And so I made a decision that I knew might break up our relationship. It was the same one I had made with Terry when I knew that it was time to leave Hawaii. I told Mark I was ready to go back to Michigan, and I wanted to move. My daughter was there, and my brother and sister, and many cousins and nephews and nieces. We were almost 70. And I was facing "older".

My mother at 70 was actively drinking and making a mess of her life. I did not know how to do better, but I knew I had to. I do not drink, and I stay socially connected. I was determined to keep her good qualities and not move toward her kind of failures. That meant I would have to find what I did want to move toward. It felt like uncharted territory.

I had Helen Dunne as a role model. When I met Helen, she was 86 years old. She was an amazing woman with an amazing background. Gutsy, sassy, level headed, a perfectionist, wise, smart, clear thinking, greatly admired and loved, and a person who drew people in and kept them close. Now that's the kind of role model I needed! Helen and I became very close friends.

One thing I open-mouthedly admired about her was her realism in the face of aging. Her husband was nearly deaf, and they found their way through that. He then got dementia, and she, who had seemed quite dependent on his capabilities made the decision alone to sell their house, sell their furniture and move into an apartment. It was amazing to watch. She sold furniture that she had hand finished and painted 40 years before, and was able to watch it go out the door. She sold precious art works which her artist friends had given her. Even her own art was given and sold. Within a month, the house sold and the move was made.

Just a year after that, her husband got worse, and she subtly made the decision to put him into an assisted living place about ½ block from the apartment complex. She went every day to see him. By then, she had been feted at her 90th birthday party. At that party, she always said she would probably die soon, but now she felt as if she would live to 102. (As of this writing, Helen just had her 100th birthday party - 2013)

She then moved into a smaller, less expensive apartment. This 90 year old woman, who had been an avid tennis player and swimmer, as well as supporting herself with her art when she was single, had carried out two difficult moves and all the life decisions that went with them within a year. After that, I asked her one day if she wanted to swim again (she had not for many years). I loaned her a suit, and she got in the apartment complex pool and started swimming lengths.

I have, in my house, a large art piece hanging on the wall, a collaboration of Helen and I. The background is a collage of my photos of clouds taken in Oklahoma. Against that background, is the very fine scissor work of Helen, depicting life on earth. It was her idea, and was her gracious way of collaborating lovingly with a good friend who was not an artist (me). The signature, instead of being written, is a very small picture down in the corner, of Helen and I with our heads together.

I always hope to see her one more time. We saw her this fall when we went on a long trip (2013). This was a few weeks before her 100th party. She has been a huge gift to my life.

Mark was willing to leave Oklahoma, and we stayed together. We sold our house for our buying price, but got out in pleasure what we lost in money. We think we got the better end of the deal. We have the memories, the photos, and the feeling of living there. We packed up our things, and headed to Michigan, leaving behind those gorgeous views, that upper deck bedroom, and the people who had supported and accepted us. We took our two cats with us.

I wish someone had made a movie of our trip back. The U-Haul, Mark driving, was in the lead, pulling an auto dolly with Mark's car on it. We had hired professionals to pack the U-Haul, and it was filled from front to back, and bottom to top. They put in the bicycles last, and one held the bike while the other closed the door. It was that close. Behind the U-Haul I drove my car, with lots of precious breakable things, and two cat cages, each holding one vociferous and miserable cat.

These were the days of poor cell phone coverage and limited minutes. We bought walkie-talkies to communicate. Every time we tried to use them the batteries wore down.

Picture two rank amateurs at the art of towing, getting the U-Haul and trailer stuck in a space too small to turn around. We asked for help, and the man who helped skidded the trailer, leaving tire marks on the pavement, and us hoping the trailer would still pull all right. Add in the stress of two cats who didn't want to be in any car.

We never guessed that our cats would yowl for 2 and ½ days. I thought they would settle down but it never happened. I tried petting them, putting them together, covering the cages, and screaming at them. Nope! The only relief was at night in the motel, after we sneaked them in and opened the cages. I suppose it was their only relief also. To this day they have never learned to trust a running car.

We arrived frazzled and safely, and my daughter and her husband escorted us to the apartment that they had found for us. And then they totally unpacked our U-Haul and we were in our apartment in Whitmore Lake, Michigan. It was 2006.

Our notorious ranch house

Hanging out with one of our chickens

Faux "American Gothic"

Prairie Horse Preserve

Ice on Birdfeeder

Me the ranch carpenter

Mark and grandkids

Helen and I at the retreat

Rattlesnake

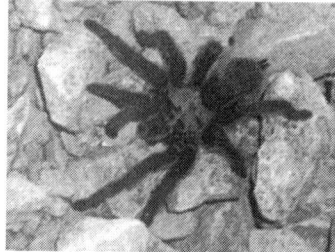

Tarantula- (2 " gravel)

Bee swarm

Possum after cat food

Cleaned up for town

Burning the prairie

Helen and Joe

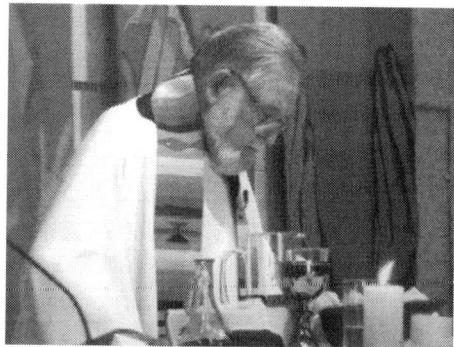

Fr. Bill Skeehan

Women B'ville friends – Vickie
Eastman and Fran Stallings

In Calif. At Moss Workshop

Alaska

(Trying to give you a flavor of our trip to Alaska is similar to attempting Hawaii or the Sonoran Desert of Cave Creek. It does not translate into black and white very well)

Mark and I with Fred in Sitka

Amazing beauty

At the Athabasca Glacier

Reflections

Whew, we made it

Tent on old gravel road end.

Multi- purpose business

BACK IN MICHIGAN- 2006-2014

Age 70-78

These last 6 or 8 years were the hardest to write about. It is often more difficult to write about recent happenings than those which have had a chance to be analyzed, softened and integrated, but besides that, there has been a large difference in what I thought and visioned that this time would be like, and what it actually was and is. I thought I was coming back to Michigan to continue being the person who worked part time, swam, and found friends and belonging, with the result of receiving and contributing to life. I thought my days of forming and reforming my character were over with, and maybe they are, but it seems too soon to tell right now. In addition, I knew I would have time with my daughter and her husband, and with other relatives scattered across the state.

I am not working, I have been going through yet another confusing and unfocused time of my life, and all sorts of unexpected happenings have occurred. Adapting to aging on many fronts is one of the happenings – much more prominent than I imagined. I do get to see my daughter.

Many of the choices I have been faced with seemed, on the one hand choice-less, and on the other hand, impossible to weigh. Many times, any option I chose would have had difficult consequences. The choices seem to be getting harder as I am growing older. I think you will understand more as you read.

The beginnings of this time were outstanding! The day after we moved into the Whitmore Lake apartment, we went to Plainwell where my daughter in law from Texas, in collaboration with my Michigan relatives, had arranged a 70th Birthday party for me. There were 30 people or more covering three generations. My siblings, their children and grandchildren, two of my children and their children, and a couple of wonderful first cousins gathered for a celebratory day. I had a wonderful time at what is one of the nicest birthdays, and nicest gifts (the party itself) I have ever received. We have lots of pictures. My siblings gave me money for my new computer, which started a tradition of special gifts for the 70th birthday. Becky turned 70 this year, and we paid for her already accomplished trip to Disney in Florida. I wonder if I will live to see Charlie turn 70 in 2023? I am the matriarch now other than for my mother's sister, turning 90 in Illinois.

I have been back in Michigan 8 years at this point. What I know for sure is that these years, (for the most part, has not had the color, aliveness, solidity, or energy of the rest of my life. I feel less like life is an adventure, and more like I am walking uphill carefully, or wading with difficulty, into my future.

Adventure and careful walking are not mutually exclusive, but it is sometimes hard to see both concurrently. Looking back, I can see that I have done quite a lot. I have contributed my time and energy to the church we attend and to God's Kingdom, I have been on the board of our condo association, nudged a few activities into being, and contributed occasionally to others. I have swum, kayaked, and vacationed. I have made friends, learned new electronics, and have relatively good health and enough money if I am careful. We have gone on several short or long trips. The most recent was a long trip out west in a rented car that Mark initiated as sort of a "bucket trip" for himself. At the time, he was experiencing some difficult times.

But besides the things I have done and experienced, noted above, I have also experienced loneliness, disappointment, exhaustion, depression, lack of passion, and a wandering sort of searching. I have no close friends. I thought I had a handle on my life processes. I have considered myself quite stable as a human being ever since Hawaii. I thought I was listening to what was important for me, and in my life, and was making good choices.

I relate the circumstances here of the last years, not to whine or find sympathy, but to give you an idea of what my life has been and who I have been recently, and how I have learned to continue a journey with heart. I am certain that, given my past track record, this time is birthing something valuable – inside me, and in relationship, if not in huge projects in the outside world. If there has been any time that creating balance, and making conscious choices has been important for me, it is now - in the season of my writing this.

Here is my accounting of these years: I hinted before that I came back to Michigan expecting life to be similar to what it had been I assumed that we would travel and find our way to a similar life in a new setting. I was looking forward to having family around, at least within the state. What happened instead has been mostly unrelated to my assumptions.

We moved to that Whitmore Lake apartment, and decided to take a year to look for a home to buy. However, during that year, my son, Jim decided to divorce his wife, and move to Ann Arbor, about 15 miles from us. He asked for my help.

At that time he could transfer himself from bed to wheelchair and back. He wanted to live in an apartment.

Ordinarily, as a Social Worker, I know the resources of the surrounding area, but because we were new here, and I had not been working, I was not of much help in the resource department, and it took research on both our parts to find what he needed. Mark and I made several 100 mile round trips to where Jim lived, helping him pack and get ready to move. We also made several unexpected trips to respond to urgent situations. He was stuck on the toilet and his wife was not there. He could not get to his chair. He had fallen

295

and no one was there to help. He had no one close by. It was shocking to me, not having seen him in a couple years, how much help he now needed. I was filled with a mom's grief, and desire to love and help.

We (he and I with our research) found an apartment in Ann Arbor, and some agencies that would help with his care. Although Mark and I did not do the actual moving of furniture and belongings, we helped unpack, and I agreed to do his grocery shopping once a week, and help with other things. Within a short time, it was apparent that he had less leeway financially, and needed more help than he had planned on.

It was good that he was close by. But his physical ability was decreasing faster than he thought it was, and my physical ability was decreasing faster than I thought it was. He thought he had adequate help, and I thought I would be adequate fill-in when he needed it. Instead, we were often in a bind. Help didn't show, he couldn't transfer, etc. Several times a week, we got a call, and made that 30 mile round trip, attempting to provide stability and help for him, so he could continue working and maintain his health. One of those times, there alone, I had to call 911 when he slid to the floor as I tried to get him on his bed.

Increasingly, his hygiene was poor from lack of care, and his apartment became messy, and added my allergy problems to every visit to him. I found I could not handle him physically, especially after he gained some weight. He and I have a long history of conflictual relationship, and often his decisions and demands seemed to me to be unhealthy for him, or didn't make sense to me.

He attempted to save money by firing the agencies and hiring private help, and got into some dangerous and deteriorating situations. He seemed not to recognize that his health was at risk (in my opinion of course.) He had a caregiver that turned out to be mentally ill and threatened him. We had to get the locks changed, and see that the man did not come in again. Meanwhile, I was getting physically ill from being around the apartment as it deteriorated, and my allergies piled up.

Things were smoothing a little, when he told me he had met a woman over the internet, and wanted to move to New York state to live with her. She came to visit, and I met her and was heartsick. I got a very bad and scary impression of the way she seemed to perceive Jim and the way she treated his body. He decided to go anyway, and a year after that, Mark and I made a trip, and enlisted my brother and his wife with their pickup truck, to go get Jim. He was being emotionally and physically abused and was ill with kidney trouble. That trip and the hardship on all, including Jim and my brother were my wakeup call not to rescue, and to remember to care about myself.

There were two more moves after that, each about a year apart. All involved work and emotional stress on my part. We were all further stressed by the ongoing difficulty of my relationship with Jim. However, I did not attempt to help as much, or get as weary as I had before.

Meanwhile, about the time of the move to New York, Mark was diagnosed with prostate cancer. He had a prostatectomy with a difficult surgery, nearly coding on the table, being over narcotized, and hemorrhaging. He ended up in intensive care, coming home in 5 days rather than the usual 2. The upside was that there were no positive margins and we were told he should now be cancer free. However, when his PSA was tested a few months later, it was nearly as high as before the surgery. That was a shock as we had expected a zero.

After extensive testing, it is assumed that he has micrometastases. He was put on hormone blocker, and the effects of that, plus the stress of the surgery, plus the devastating news that he still had cancer brought his old enemy, clinical depression, rushing back with a vengeance He spent more than a year nearly inert and refusing help.

I still had hopes of friends and part time work, although by now, the idea of part time work in a community loaded with Social Workers was fading some. My difficult job turned out to be companion and caregiver to a man who spent about 18 hours in bed, and was nearly non-functional. I felt consistently torn between doing things by myself and trying to involve Mark in life.

Fortunately, before the surgery, we had found a place to buy. A couple, old TORI friends, lived in an over-55 community, and we found it suitable and a good buy. Best of all for me, it had a beach where I could swim. From the beginning, I attended the monthly co-op meetings, and agreed to run for the board and had been elected. That gave me a way to know what was happening, and to meet some people. I was also taking some responsibility at church on the long term planning committee.

It turned out that I fit the board and committee work in between helping Jim, and caring for Mark. It was both my respite and more stress. I was pretty much alone, not having time to socialize, and not knowing people much. I didn't share much of what was happening either, other than with my family.

(Incidentally, you should know that between my desperation and insistence, and his lack of energy to resist, we finally found some wonderful help for Mark's long term depression. He deals with depression less than I have ever seen him and we are both elated about it.)

Mark was then diagnosed with chronic anemia which did not respond to the usual iron, and was determined not to be from the surgery. We were afraid it was the cancer, but it turned out to be still another life changer. He was proven to be gluten sensitive, and his intestines were irritated by gluten and could not absorb B vitamins and other nutrients. This caused his anemia.

What it meant for me was learning to cook all over again. After many years of cooking for a family, I could, with little effort, prepare nutritious and good meals. Now they were poison to Mark.

We did what we needed to do, but frustration was served with our dinner more often than not. Only 5 years later, it is simple (although more costly) to cook and eat gluten-free. It has become culturally indigenous to give up gluten, and there are whole shelves of gluten-free flours and products in regular stores. When I started, there was none of that. It felt like another large adjustment to life as we knew it.

Five years after we moved to Michigan, Jim was finally at the end of his moving frenzy and in Colorado. Mark was beginning to recover from his gluten damage, and depression. And I was able to manage the cooking. I knew that I needed to be doing healthy things, around healthy people. I began to think again about work and play. But there was more.

While I was active in church, the church itself went through a severe pastoral crisis and people focused on the Long Term Planning Committee for hope and help. I was the co-chair. There was incredible stress before our pastor resigned by mutual decision with the church council.

On the condo board, expectations and norms for seniors were changing. Thus helping govern a senior living site in the 1970's was not like governing one in 2009. We even had to revise the by-laws, and those who wanted change were polarized against those who didn't. The board was expected to make everyone happy. Conflict reigned, and I finally resigned after 5 years of service.

We were both attending exercise classes after Mark felt better, but our relationship, never easily supportive, left me feeling vulnerable and longing for love and support. I suppose that my work and other activities had kept me buoyed up and satisfied in our years together, and now there was mostly just the two of us – both stressed. It was not enough for me.

Suddenly, in 2012 it seemed it was my body's turn to misbehave. I had been swimming winter and summer. I began to be allergic to chloramines, the breakdown product of chlorine in pools. I tried the salt generated chlorine pools, and even they caused hives, so I was no longer free to swim in pools, or be in hot tubs. At least there would be summer swimming.

Then I got allergic to sunshine. It happened suddenly, 2 days after a colonoscopy (although there is no apparent connection). Something in my body seems as if it irreparably changed. Solar urticaria, or hives from sun, is difficult to treat. I now swim early in the morning or toward evening in long sleeves and tights. And I sometimes have to take antihistamines as well. Otherwise, hives on all exposed skin turn into a severe intestinal bout and add up to no fun, and probably could be serious.

In the last 3 years, I have also had to have a bladder suspension, and a kidney stone surgery, with one large kidney stone yet to go. All take their toll, even though they are not serious surgeries. I have felt angry from time to time that this stuff didn't happen when I was 50, or 60 or even 70. Recovery from anything seems harder when older.

My coping in the past depended on swimming, sunshine, exercise, work, friends, and joy. My life has been transformed, and I am still in the process. As people in our co-op are fond of saying, "It beats the alternative", (meaning death), and that is certainly true, but I hardly recognize myself or my life.

I am guessing you now understand some of what I said in the beginning, about ending up with some instability and burnout.

I want to write about the beginnings of the upward slope also, now that you have read several pages of downward slope.

Winter does not seem as much fun when I cannot ski, or move around as easily, or even go to a pool and swim, and so partial winters in Florida have been a good thing.

We went to Florida for 2 years before I was sun-sensitive. My brother and his wife, and my sister, my other brother and Mark and I rented a condo for the winter months. We went for 2 months the first year, and a month the second. We may go this next year also, as the warmth feels wonderful, and I can use antihistamines and sun block to somewhat mediate the sun reaction. (by the way, I am also allergic to nearly all American sunblocks other than zinc oxide, and am trying out the European ones.)

I have an extensive shell collection from Florida excursions, but the rare Junonia shell, occasionally found on Sanibel, eluded us all. After I finish this project, I may work on a way to display those shells.

I am also putting together a companion to this book – the products of my life. Some of the specific things I have written, had written about me, or flyers from workshops, as well as letters of thanks. It lends meat to the stories and history in this book.

As I was finishing up this book, I heard a song from my high school days (Blue Tango). It occurred to me that while I had mentioned roller skating in high school, and dancing as a single person, and classical music in grade school, as well as singing in the car when we traveled as a child, I had not talked much about the part of music in my life. The rhythm and melodies of music have been part of my growth and development, as well as touching my heart.

Dancing with my boyfriend Chuck in high school transported me, because similar to the skating rink, he was a partner who brought grace, rhythm and partnership to dance. Thus the big band music and the organ music of the rinks are built into my history. I loved waltzing, and polkas, and mentioned going to the wedding receptions. As memories of songs came back, I realized that three of my all time high school favorites had started with the word "Blue:" Blue Tango, Blue Moon, and the Blue Skirt Waltz.

Every weekend back then, I tuned into the Bay City radio station to listen to the Polkas and other Polish music. At night, my radio was turned to WCKY, Cincinnati, where I listened to country music.

Later, when my children were young, I took accordion lessons, and learned to play some of those polkas and waltzes. The accordion stood out straight on top of my very pregnant body during one season.

In Hawaii, I tuned into the Hawaiian radio station, went to many performances, and gatherings, and loved the old Hawaiian music. I have an extensive collection of it from the period I lived there. It is the rhythm, simplicity and heart that call me. .

I am often moved and encouraged to move by percussion, or any music with a strong beat. Rhythm and melody influence me more than words. I have never been a musician other than my short stint with the accordion, but music has accompanied the life and development of my heart, body and soul.

Recently it is songs such as; *River in Judea, Somos El Barcos* by Pete Seeger, *Halleluja,* and *Forever Young,* also the version by Pete Seger that have touched me. I was a folk music fan in the 60s and 70s and have continued to enjoy Folk concerts. At home, I often can be found with my Hawaiian music still playing in the background.

The various genre which have impacted me throughout my life are part of my life, my cells, my chemistry, and my heart and soul. I connect with others, the past, and God more easily when there is an easy flow of music available and heard in my life.

I am pleased that I am able to continue to grow and learn with technology. My computer and iPhone give me great pleasure and use. I started the list serve for our church to further communication, and I am active on Facebook and Twitter. With no paying job or regular work, I have to be careful that I don't get addicted to that iPhone. It is my main camera now, and my GPS, as well as my connection with friends around the country.

My realization that I was depressed and burned out, happened quite suddenly, and I began to change course and do something different. The long term planning committee was long disbanded, and I left the board. I was essentially alone in a crowd no matter where I went. I am an introvert, and more so when low energy, so I withdrew from lots of people, activities and things. However, I did start this project and it has been a valuable look back and integration of my life.

I have continued to swim and exercise, when not interrupted by physical ills or treatment. I taught a senior exercise class for a year, and was happy to see that I was still an effective teacher. People's lives and bodies changed through my class. Two years ago, as I was realizing that I must build my energy stores back up; I took horseback riding and tap dancing. Those were great fun!

I am having difficulty finding ways and places to form closer connections and then hang out with them. In Florida, everyone is an import, and reaches out to make friends readily. At least that is true where we go. In our complex here in South Lyon and the rest of this area, people grew up around Detroit, worked in the auto industry, and have friends from way back, and family nearby. We had planned on Ann Arbor for stimulation, but do not get there frequently, and parking is scarce. Freeway driving in cities is harder than it used to be.

My faith is strong, and I regularly pray, and try to live my life connected to God's agenda, or marching orders, or when that fails, I curl up in his lap and let myself be loved. I do that by hanging out in nature, by finding His love inside me and passing it on, and with music, reading, writing, or random acts of kindness.

However, I still find myself lonelier and more tired than I would like. I assume I will continue to make decisions that help me recover over this next year. Both Mark and I are in counseling, together and separately. Now that is unexpected for me, although welcome. It is definitely making things better for the two of us, separately and together. I would not have learned how to set firmer boundaries, choose my actions more carefully, or speak with such pragmatism had I not gone through the depression and counseling this last couple years. It has honed and strengthened those skills.

Part of my motivation this past year or two was knowing that my mother did not know how to live "old age", and also meeting people who do, such as Helen from Oklahoma, and some of the people living here at the co-op. I must not let go of the being I have become. I have experienced closeness and an open heart, as well as faith, hope, and love. Those have been great gifts, and there is no reason to lose those as one ages. There is no reason for me to lose them as I age.

My body, that one of the long ago tomboy, sensuous sexual woman, dancer, lover, wrestler and swimmer, is losing muscle, strength, and what it takes to feel young and active. Active often happens now in my mind, memories, and heart. I am fortunate to have reasonably good health, although, nothing physical feels certain or reliable anymore. It is a daily question mark preceding me

My need for and use of psychological boundaries is changing. I don't have as much use for some of the old ones: those that protected me from predatory people, and too much contact with others. I used to have to use those a lot.

I don't attract predatory or dependent people much now, and I am not working with people constantly and having to rest up from human contact. I have more use for boundaries to protect my emotional and physical energy while I reach for human contact. I am sometimes overlooked, or my abilities minimized, both because I am somewhat withdrawn and low energy, and because of stereotypes of aging in the culture.

The last time I was at the ocean, I had to get out on hands and knees through the waves, which threatened to knock me down. I was perfectly content to do so, and was enjoying myself, when a young man came running over, worried that I was drowning and needed help. I was grateful that he cared, but sad that he saw only my weakness, and not my capability. I had just swum a good distance in ocean waves. Indeed, the process of aging may be the ultimate in higher education.

Inside of this woman growing old is still a little child, an uncertain teen, a sexy woman, a competent professional, and a passionate swimmer. Sometimes the little child hopes to jump on a trampoline or roller skate again. I have to explain to her that the body of this woman cannot do these things, but that we can have fun some other way, and we are not giving up our identity in our own mind. Then I take her hand and we go back out on the lookout for adventure, love, companionship, humor, and God.

I can feel the tiredness and depression getting less, and my heart and passions and joy in life re-growing. I continue to become more of who I am, especially in relationship with my fellow human beings. I recently wrote the following piece, and excerpt here from it:

Leaning In (excerpt)

...........*My partner too has some beginning dementia. I notice that as his ability to remember and find his way to familiar places declines, his ability and wish to connect with people grows. He is closer to me than ever, he is reaching out to others and to God in new and more connected ways.*

Both men are leaning into the human connection, as their intellect becomes less useful. As they drift away from education, organization and the ability to master numbers, time and distance, they lean toward a shared life with others. As they lessen in ability to take care of business, they grow in a seemingly innate longing to take care of their heart and soul. Though names are being forgotten, connection is being pursued.

It is an important and valuable observation for me. I am 78, and I, like the wife above, have been a strong and capable woman, and can go it alone if necessary. But I must learn to lean in, away from alone-ness, toward connection; away from mandatory strength and toward mandatory vulnerability, away from well-honed statements, and toward mystery and questions.

I cannot approach my end on earth as my mother did. She tried to keep the façade, the past life, until there was none, and then she crashed and burned into an angry shell. Occasionally her wish to love came through, but much more often her wish FOR love came through in twisted anger and lashing out. She died, mostly unconnected and disliked.

I want to lean in and connect and I will continue to learn, lean, and love.

.

AFTERWORD

Some things are under our control and some beyond it. Check out climate control- a current debate and issue. Each generation has had to adapt to many things. My grandparents had to adapt to automobiles and electricity, my parents to airplanes and television, and my generation to electronics and a world that has become both more collaborative and connected, and more distant from each other. It is hard to know the neighbors, let alone those who influence us in other countries. We know the events but not the people. Few in our country even live near family anymore.

Here is one way our world has changed in my generation. I asked a 20-something young man a few months ago if he wanted my map of Michigan. He was visiting and about to go exploring. I thought the map might give him a broader picture of the territory than his iPhone maps. He declined, admitting that he had never used a paper map, and did not know how they worked. He uses his GPS and his phone to get where he wants to go.

I wonder about the future, his and others. How will young people now see the bigger picture? And is there any way to connect the pictures to humanity? Is history dead, getting lost as it is unrecorded in books, but only occupies the electronic spaces fading away to make room for the next event, tweet, message, or drama. Who will bother to know their neighbors, or to notice that separate or different does not always mean enemy? Where will all the people, displaced by war, weather, and earth changes go? Will they have a "home"? What will the children learn and how, as they are isolated against "strangers", and the forests, mountains, and waters of the earth? I hope there is a way for me to see through the ages after I die.

More personal down to home questions occupy me lately as well. Should I buy another car? Mine is getting old, and I am not sure how much longer I will be driving. Should I do anything about those silent kidney stones, or will I outlive them, staying alive while they stay dormant.

I have moved from infant dependence, to a lone, isolated, individualistic child and young adult, to a compulsively independent person who arrogantly didn't need anyone, to learning about and practicing inter-dependence and collaboration. As you know, I recently lost my way again and am in the process of finding and being found. I can see that I am moving toward some necessary dependence, as my abilities lessen in some ways. It really does take a village, not only to raise a child, but to get through a lifetime. Our nation was founded on independence, and most espouse that value for their personal life, but humans, at their best are tribal, and interdependent. My quest these days is partially for a tribe. My life has been nomadic and has provided me many gifts and strengths, but it is time for me to stay in one place, while the rest of the nomads move on.

I may not have many years left. One of my greatest fears would be to die alone or estranged, my love for others unlived and unused and me uncomforted in my grief of leaving. I hope to reach inward and outward and find that woman from the past, and inhabit her again, and at the same time, realistically realize that she is 78, and running out of reserves and time. It is time to live more consciously. It is more important than ever to create balance in my life, and to choose wisely every day.

As I picked pictures for recent years, I noted that they proved what I wrote. I have no pictures other than with family or Mark or by myself for the last few years.

In Pittsburgh   In the water   In a fashion show   Having fun

Me and my kids

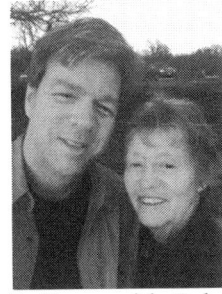

Mother's Day, 3 Generations
Me, Pam, Emily

In Colorado with James

In Texas with Bob

And Grandkids – Some of them

Ian

Jenna

Emily's graduation

And Otherwise

Mark and Karen at Bryce
Canyon

Sibs when there were still 5

Me in Texas
Looking younger
than I feel

L to R: Me, A.H, Kate, Charlie, Barb and Dirk

The youngest and the oldest

ACKNOWLEDGMENTS

So many people have been instrumental in sharing their lives and gifts with me, helping me to become who I am today. As I think through my life, I attempt here to name or acknowledge those who I especially remember as contributing their gifts, love, knowledge, skills, or life force to me. Some do that by giving in specific ways—teaching, showing, confronting, listening, etc, and others just by being who they are. I have many of both to thank.

First in chronology were my parents and grandparents and all those who came before, leading them to become who they were. I am especially thankful to my grandparents for helping me feel valuable, validated, and loved. My parents' greatest gifts were freedom to create my life without much interference, and a relatively stable family. Intelligence, leadership and community involvement came from my mom. Humor, curiosity, and acceptance of diversity from my dad. Also a nose for spontaneous adventure. The instillation of strong values, practicality and a good business sense from both of them. Faith and belief in a higher power, specifically for me God and Jesus came from 3 of my 4 grandparents. That gift, fortunately for me, came as part of everyday life, and not from force, rules, fear or the organized church. My early life could not have been richer in caring and validation.

School teachers, especially the ones I mention in the text—Evelyn Ritchie, Barbara. Smith, Agnes Gaughan, Harold Tweedie, Stan Kuick, and Jessie Duncan, among others. In each of their presence I became a little more, than I might have been otherwise.

Then there is the whole neighborhood gang, and those people in high school that gave me a sense of belonging, continuity and fun.

In college, my generous and fun loving roommate, Sally Shively became a friend and a teacher of sophistication and fun to me. She helped a small town girl become more acclimated to a large university, and nixed my need to be arrogant.

I must acknowledge my ex-husband, Clark Hamp. From him I learned resourcefulness and a greater affinity for music. He used tree branches to make a bench in the campsite, and he played the piano with his heart as well as his fingers. I later learned resilience as my world was jolted by our broken marriage and events that followed. His most obvious contribution to my life was that of fathering our three children.

Then there were the people of my changing years as I changed marital status, career, and outlook on life. There were many. Among them are, in no particular order, Joan Cullinan, Ruth Kellogg, Brian O'Donnell, Lou Pambianco, Josephine Kelsey, Richard Han, Phil and

Elaine Alexander, Bruce Bailey, Jack Gibb, Don Barley, Dawn Audrey Adams, Pat Chalmers, Vic Huber, Bob Hawkes, Les Beach, Gail Yauch, John and Penny Ort, Richard Moss, the people of the TORI community, the Episcopal Leadership and Development Community and the Pathwork Community. My fellow Social Work Students helped me to belong, and the instructors accepted my unconventional approach to school and writing papers, and liked me anyway.

From my time in Hawaii: I went there a haole (Caucasian) and left a native Hawaiian. I am especially grateful to Fred Knowles, Nalani Olds Napolean Reinhardt, Reenie Christensen, and Sonny Ching. Also the many women of Hawaii who showed me how to mother and be mothered on a whole different level. There were companions who worked with me at Partners in Health, and Hospice Hawaii. And those people in power who gave a new Hawaiian a chance to teach, speak, and learn all over Oahu. I also enjoyed working with the crew from FAIRS. My boss Larry was inspirational and the rest of the team joyful and caring. Although I don't remember her name, I especially have prayed for my secretary from there all these years that she found life in a life giving way.

I spent 5 years of my life with Terry Ryan in Hawaii and Arizona. From him I learned the skills and confidence to work in home repair, and decide whether to charge people "time and material" or "by the job" for work. . Terry introduced me to Findhorn and intentional communities, and we visited Scotland and Ireland together. We were adventurers who lived carefree lives in paradise and made life work well. I look back with laughter and caring.

The people of Cave Creek Arizona embraced me in the midst of the desert, and allowed me to make a difference in their lives, as they did the same for me. Especially I acknowledge Curt and Corky Cockburn for hospitality, and superb role modeling in many parts of life, as well as uncommonly generous hearts. Corey Silva, I will never forget for the opportunities she provided, and the tough love she dished out to all. So many others, Tom Sonandres, Nancy Tsuchiya, Evelyn whose last name does not come to me, and the members of our exercise and yoga groups.

Back in Michigan, I must acknowledge Roger Byrd and all the people of the Michigan TORI who met at my house every other week for dinner and community. It was my place of vulnerability, safety, community and expression. From Dick Brown I learned what it was to have love and practicality at two separate ends of reality without a way to bring them together. It was during this time that Jeannine Floyd joined Roger Byrd and became a loving example of survival, and equanimity in the face of disease. She became another of my sheros.

I will always be grateful to my brother, Al and his family , for taking me into his home. His home gave me shelter and bedrock from which to start over one more time.

I became part of another tribe or community at the Synthesis Center. It was the above-mentioned Roger Byrd who got me there to work, and the staff became a quasi-family. At another place of work, the Family L listserve was an online community where I found an internet home among professionals, and grew in confidence and knowledge from the exchanges. Names are missing for both Family-L and the members of Michigan Behavior Science Association, my colleagues in sanity and fun during our meetings.

There were people I met online before I ever met them in person. Tom Warren, still one of my special "forever friends", must be acknowledged for keeping me on the internet all night, having fun, and together creating heat and steam online. Later, when we met in person several times, he and his new wife were delightful hosts for a friendship that crosses a continent and carries many memories of friends and fun.

A few years later in Oklahoma, Fr. Bill Skeehan, a beautiful, liberal priest, made St. James a welcoming place for all, including non-Catholic me. Helen Dunne became my best friend, even though she was 86 years old to my 65. And then there was Kay Martin, Susan Murphy (one of my sheros for her action in helping the underserved), Cliff Sousa, and the many women who welcomed me even though they were Catholic and had been friends with Mark's ex-wife for many years. I am grateful for being integrated and accepted into that community. I am proud of having worked with the Cornerstone Hospice teammates; I was inspired by and admired Jodie, one of the most open and excellent hospice nurses ever. My fellow therapists at Samaritan Center became yet another team to which I proudly belonged.

Just before my 60th birthday, I met Mark Rycheck in Kalamazoo. For 15 years now I have been living with him. He is my partner, my challenge, and my companion in adventure and growth. We have, together and separately, been struggling with aging, various health issues, and each other for those 15 years. The joy interspersed in the struggles has been lovely. Like Terry, Mark is an adventurer, willing to go at life not only with answers, but questions and openness, seeking for those answers. We have, most likely, slept over 100 nights in a tent together from Nova Scotia to Alaska, and lots of places in between We have co-discovered people and places that delighted us. For many years we were involved in a quest for the continent's best cinnamon roll. I am grateful to Mark for the opportunity to not only adventure, but to provide the circumstances where I have continually pushed myself to grow in strength, resilience, patience, and keeping track of the small gratitude occasions when the big ones eluded me. I also learned clearer communication, and firmer boundaries. All these serve me well in the rest of my life. Our partnership would not be what it is, nor would I be what I am without Mark and our shared history.

I believe that aging is the hardest task yet in my life, as abilities and gifts go dormant, and I must rely on parts of myself that are largely underdeveloped. I especially want to thank my daughter for being understanding and kind with me, during this process, and during this time in my life. I was not around for so many important parts of her life. And my son Bob for spending time with me this past year in the midst of his sometimes chaotic and always very busy life. He also carves out time in person and on the phone with me and encourages my relationship with my grandkids. His life is an example to me in many ways. My son Jim has gone past our differences to welcome me and love me when I have traveled his way. We understand that we love each other, but we don't always understand how to get past the differences. I appreciate his willingness to choose love. All my children are amazing human beings and I watch and learn from them now, as they once did from me. Our foster daughter for a season, Phyllis Chris Crubaugh has validated us for her time in our home, and continues to face her past and future with struggle, determination, and a growing wholeness. Thanks for telling me we made a difference, Chris.

I also want to thank a recent acquaintance, Daniela Wittmann, the best therapist I have ever met. My only regret is that I think we would be good friends if I were not her client, and thus I miss out on a possible delightful friendship.

There are a multitude of recently met, but dearly appreciated people in southeast Michigan that have my gratitude. Cheryl Cunningham is a savvy, multi-faceted woman who thinks and feels deeply. Her authenticity, responsiveness and caring friendship have nurtured me well over many lunches and talks, and our co-created ideas reside in my brain for a long time. In addition, she helped hold our small church together as a consultant through a difficult season. Her husband John Cunningham is a man of depth, faith, fun, and caring. Separately and together they contribute a great deal to our lives, and to the world.

I thank Paulette Brodbeck and Dana Howe for genuine friendship. Also Paul Van Den Branden and his wife Lee. Paul served on the co-op board with me, and he and Lee have offered gracious hospitality a number of times. I am always struck by their genuine caring for me and others. They were good parents to their children, and are good parents to those of us younger here at Centennial Farms (Paul is 90).

Judith and Don Skiff were old TORI friends, now living nearby, helping me feel less a stranger in this part of Michigan. (A special tribute to Don further on). Greg Liptow and his wife Marilyn—huge hearts and builders of community. Greg's big heart brings larger than life caring greetings at unexpected moments, and many hidden good deeds and acts of caring. He is a multi-talented man who hides those talents too well. Marilyn is my welcome lunch partner, upbeat, fun, and serving others with her every act.

I must acknowledge my students in the senior exercise class, taught when I was 77. That they saw my resurrected teaching knowledge and skills, and benefited and let me know it, gave me a huge boost.

Webster Church, my present place of worship and care, and the ever-changing friendships there support me daily. Especially there have been the women of the now defunct women's group, a valuable resource when I was new. Several couples join us in a small weekly group, which nurtures and connects. I am grateful for the quality and consistency of the interaction. Judy Bemis is a social Worker who personifies a transition to artist as a way to age. Lynn Booth is another of my sheros for her determination to make the world better no matter the obstacles (which have been formidable for her recently). And the camaraderie of Judy Bemis and Donna Champine, fellow mental health workers, along with Donna's husband Jerry, who volunteers in a mental health setting, gives me people who understand a common language and calling. It is comforting and comfortable, reminding me of who I have been.

My siblings good naturedly put up with my repeated attempts to gather family, family pictures, and family info together and probably wondered what I was doing when I was a wandering absentee, with only short visits. I have asked for facts and memories from them during this process of gathering my life together. And I continue to hunger for and enjoy them on our Florida trips, and other family occasions.

Becky is always ready with a word of praise for my photos and words on Facebook. She knows there will be trouble if she isn't. She is the extrovert to my introvert, and I am often wishful of being more like her in ways. We have an unspoken loyalty even when we don't quite understand each other.

AH, (Al) has become, of sorts, the wisdom brother, even though I am the oldest child. My very young playmate now has grown into principles of living, creative ideas and determined actions which have all been gifts to me. He is an amazing man who knows what it is to fall hard, get back up and recover. I have seen him go from anger to love, getting to giving, and loner to family man. I admire and love him.

I owe a debt of gratitude to my special-needs brother, Deke. He could only be who he was, and that was enough to gift me with the opportunity to love, follow his lead, and contribute to his life the best I knew how. My life grew immensely from my repeated attempts to do that. Because we went there as a family, he was also the focus which drew us together.

Charlie admonished me (with his quiet and definitely humorous smile), to let everyone know that he was the real star of this book and of my life, because when he was born and I met him, it changed my life! Indeed it did. And when we got to finally know each other more almost 60 years later, he changed my life even more. I would definitely not be who I was, nor would the book be what it is without my constantly keeping in mind that he is the better writer, and will be reading this. And that I have years of experience in life on him. We are cut from very similar cloth in some ways. I am the oldest and most somber and serious, he the youngest and life gets humorous and lighter around him, even when he is working through the unexpected speed bumps and difficulties in life. He is an alchemist, turning the speed bumps to waves of poetry and song which have the ability to sink into both my funny bone and my heart. He is a dreamer, a writer, a motorcyclist. He is an ex 9-5 person who has a much larger and deeper view of the world, human beings, and human nature than that job would let him have. We share many characteristics and I connect with him both as my littlest brother, and as a growing friend. We could easily be partners in adventure, or find ways to get into trouble, or to contribute to others, if I were not so far away and our ages not so far apart. He is 17 years younger, and I can't keep up with him, on land or in water. He is the best youngest brother I could imagine or ask for.

As for acknowledging the process by which this book came about, I want to mention my cousin Tom Bradley who is a genius at family history, dates, and responding to questions. Thank you, Tom, for your always-present help when asked, and for the many facts about our family that I would not have known if it weren't for you.

There were those who read parts of it and encouraged me: Susan Hansen, Nancy Putney Abernathy, Don Skiff, and Mark.

Many people, on hearing about my attempts here, have genuinely said they can't wait to read it, although I always add the caveat that my life isn't very exciting or extraordinary.

I have reserved one of the biggest chunks of gratitude and acknowledgment for Don Skiff. He is a longtime friend and TORI person, who happens to be another of those people who hide his talents under his exterior qualities of caring and quietness. I could name his many talents, but I want to acknowledge these - his technical expertise in Microsoft Word, and in the process of publishing a book. This book might be only a Word Document without Don. He has spent a hundred hours or more formatting my work, patiently correcting my documents from my lack of knowledge and skill, turning old articles into Word Documents, and advising me on next steps. He patiently answered my questions, taught me, and sat with me as an interested, patient, and involved person, even in the midst of his own struggles and agendas. He helped design the cover to this book and put it together with his software. He is one of the finest writers I know. His recent books have evolved into fiction which comes directly from his synthesis, analysis, and deep thinking about ideas, life, and the human condition, using his knowledge, life experience, many interests and a lifetime of voracious reading. I encourage you, no, strongly encourage you to go to his website (donskiff.com), or blog (wetland-wetland.blogspot.com). Then buy his books and prepare for a satisfying read.

Don has been generous, patient, non-judgmental, and easy to work with. I don't even have words for how grateful I am that he was there for me, that he was willing and skillful, and that in the midst of his own life, he took on part of mine. Thank you, dear friend. And to his wife, Judith, thanks for putting up with me in your home bent over the computer for many hours.

To my children for teaching me from the time of your births, even as I taught you, and led you. You have surpassed me in so many ways, and now often lead me. We all did the best we could, and I am so proud of you!!!

To the hundreds, and probably thousands, who have touched my life throughout 78 years, and whom I have not acknowledged directly, I share my gratitude for belonging to this human species, walking this walk with me and touching each other in some form along the way.

34127327R10176

Made in the USA
Charleston, SC
29 September 2014